Risk Budgeting
A NEW APPROACH TO INVESTING

Risk Budgeting
A NEW APPROACH TO INVESTING

Edited by Leslie Rahl

Published by Risk Books, a division of the Risk Waters Group.

Haymarket House
28–29 Haymarket
London SW1Y 4RX
Tel: +44 (0)20 7484 9700
Fax: +44 (0)20 7484 9758
E-mail: books@risk.co.uk
Sites: http://www.riskbooks.com

Every effort has been made to secure the permission of individual copyright
holders for inclusion.

© Risk Waters Group Ltd, 2000

ISBN 1 899 332 94 4

British Library Cataloguing in Publication Data
A catalogue record for this book is available from the British Library

Risk Books Commissioning Editor: Emma Elvy
Desk Editor: Martin Llewellyn

Typeset by Marie Doherty

Printed and bound in Great Britain by Bookcraft (Bath) Ltd, Somerset.

Contents

PART III: PRACTITIONERS' THOUGHTS: CASE STUDIES IN RISK BUDGETING

Authors

Jerome Abernathy is managing partner of Stonebrook Structured Products, LLC, an alternative investment firm based in New York. In this capacity Dr Abernathy is responsible for introducing hedge fund products such as the volatility hedge programme, the Stonebrook foreign exchange programme and the Stonebrook enhanced trend following programme. Previous to starting Stonebrook, Dr Abernathy was director of research at Moore Capital Management, a hedge fund in New York. As director of research he was responsible for developing and supervising Moore Capital's research and technology efforts as well as trading IMS Global I, an offshore derivatives fund. Prior to Moore, Dr Abernathy was a vice president at Merrill Lynch, Pierce, Fenner & Smith Inc, a registered securities broker-dealer and FCM in New York, where he managed the Analytical Trading Group within Capital Markets. In this position Jerome was responsible for trading the firm's proprietary capital pursuant to quantitative techniques. Dr Abernathy began his career as a trader/researcher in the Derivative Trading Group at Morgan Stanley & Co, where he developed and traded quantitative strategies in the derivative and currency markets. Dr Abernathy holds a BS in electrical engineering from Howard University in Washington DC and both a SM and PhD in electrical engineering and computer science from the Massachusetts Institute of Technology.

Gabriel Bousbib is currently managing director, Strategic Marketing and Business Development at Reuters Financial. He is responsible for expanding Reuters' presence in the investment management community through internal product developments, partnerships, joint-ventures and acquisitions. Mr Bousbib is also responsible for the strategic marketing activities of Reuters' Application and Enterprise Solutions product line, which includes trading systems, order management applications and infrastructure products. Gabriel was previously senior vice president and chief operating officer of the Risk Management Division at Reuters America Holdings. He had overall operational responsibility for Reuters' order management and risk management activities in the Americas, including sales and marketing, technical and application support, as well as development and financial engineering. Prior to joining Reuters, he was a managing director and principal of the CBM Group, a management consulting firm specialising in financial services and risk management and he is also the founder of MYCA Inc, a software company developing risk management systems for derivative dealers. Gabriel previously worked for Merrill Lynch Capital Markets as a risk manager in the derivative area. He holds a MBA from Columbia University Graduate School of Business and is a graduate of the Ecole Polytechnique in Paris.

Christopher L. Culp is director of risk management services at CP Risk Management LLC in Chicago and is also adjunct associate professor of Finance at the University of Chicago. At CPRM he is the practice director for consulting on matters of financial risk management control, risk-adjusted capital allocation and asset/liability management. He was previously president of Risk Management Consulting Services, Inc, prior to which he served as a senior examiner in the Supervision & Regulation Department of the Federal Reserve Bank of Chicago, as research economist at GT Management (Asia) Ltd and as currency options trading strategist at TradeLink LLC. He has published widely in the areas of derivatives, risk management and financial regulation and is a managing editor of *Derivatives Quarterly*. Dr Culp is also senior fellow in financial regulation with the Competitive Enterprise Institute in Washington DC. He holds a PhD in finance from the Graduate School of Business of the University of Chicago and a BA in economics from The Johns Hopkins University.

Leo de Bever is the senior vice president of Research & Economics at the Ontario Teachers' Pension Plan Board, which administers the retirement plan for many Ontario teachers. His department is responsible for the Fund's asset mix research, risk management, tactical asset allocation and for the economic backdrop to its investment strategy. They also manage the Fund's real return bond portfolio. The group recently implemented a quantitative risk measurement system, which is now used to allocate active management risk. Leo began his career at the Bank of Canada in Ottawa and then moved to the Toronto office of an economic consulting firm owned by Chase Bank. From there he moved into asset management, first at Crown Life and then at Nomura Securities. He joined the OTPPB in 1995. He is past president of the Canadian Association for Business Economics and current editor of the *Canadian Business Economics Journal*. He received his PhD in economics from the University of Wisconsin.

Michael de Marco is senior vice president and a member of Putnam Institutional Management's Strategic Relationship Team – a dedicated service and relationship management group for Putnam's largest, most sophisticated institutional clients. He is also a member of Putnam's Profit Sharing Retirement Plan Advisory Committee, the Association for Investment Management and Research, the Boston Security Analysts Society, the Chicago Quantitative Alliance and the International Association of

Financial Engineers. Before joining Putnam, Michael was at the GTE-Investment Management Corporation and began his careers at Citicorp as an international equity portfolio manager. He has also spent some time in Argentina and Puerto Rico with the Citibank-International Banking Group. He gained his BS from Carnegie-Mellon University and his MS from the Massachusetts Institute of Technology.

Amy B. Hirsch is CEO of Paradigm Consulting Services, LLC, a registered investment advisor that provides quantitative portfolio analysis and continuous risk management to institutional investors with alternative investment portfolios. Throughout her 20 years of experience in this field, Ms Hirsch has worked in numerous capacities, primarily focused on hedge funds, futures and commodity pools, interbank currencies and derivatives. During half of her twelve year tenure at Merrill Lynch & Co, she was vice president, ML Futures Investment Partners, Inc, where she created and ran the trading group for MLFIP, Inc, a commodity pool operator. She was then senior vice president of Smith Barney, Harris Upham, & Co, responsible for the Managed Futures Group. She spent two years with Link Strategic Investors and was a founding partner of Paradigm LDC in 1994. Ms Hirsch speaks frequently on the subject of alternative investments and has chaired numerous industry conferences. She is a member of the NYMEX Institutional Money Management Advisory Committee. Ms Hirsch received her BA, cum laude, in economics from Fordham University.

Wayne Kozun is a director in the Research & Economics area at the Ontario Teachers' Pension Plan Board where he manages a quantitative currency portfolio. His other duties include risk management, strategic and tactical asset allocation, quantitative investment strategies and currency exposure management. Prior to joining the OTPPB, Wayne worked in the Treasurer's Department of Imperial Oil Limited, the Canadian subsidiary of Exxon. Before this he worked in an electrical engineering capacity for Northern Telecom. Wayne holds a MBA from the Ivey School of Business at the University of Western Ontario and a Bachelor's degree in electrical engineering from the University of Western Ontario. He obtained his CFA designation in 1996 and is a member of the Association for Investment Management and Research and the Toronto Society of Financial Analysts.

Robert Litterman is the director of Quantitative Resources at Goldman Sachs & Co. Robert is the co-developer, along with the late Fischer Black, of the Black–Litterman Global Asset Allocation Model, a key tool in the Investment Management Division's asset allocation process. Prior to moving to the Investment Management Division, Robert was the head of the Firmwide Risk department since becoming a partner in 1994. Preceding his time in the OT&F Division, he spent eight years in the Fixed Income

Division's research department where he was co-director, with Fischer Black, of the research and model development group. They wrote two papers, "Asset Allocation: Combining Investor Views with Market Equilibrium", (1990) and "Global Asset Allocation With Equities, Bonds, and Currencies", (1991). He also wrote *Managing Market Exposure* (1996), with Kurt Winkelmann and was the sole author for *Hot Spots and Hedges* (1996). Both he and Mr Winkelmann also published *Estimating Covariance Matrices* (1998). Additionally, in 1998 The Firmwide Risk department of Goldman Sachs, under Robert's leadership and in collaboration with SBC Warburg Dillon Read, he co-authored the book, *The Practice of Risk Management*. Before joining Goldman Sachs in 1986, he was an assistant vice president in the Research Department of the Federal Reserve Bank of Minneapolis and an assistant professor in the Economics Department at the Massachusetts Institute of Technology. He received his BS from Stanford University and a PhD in economics from the University of Minnesota.

Jacques Longerstaey came to Goldman Sachs as a vice president in from JP Morgan. He subsequently joined the GSAM Risk Management group and then became co-head of the group with Jacob Rosengarten and later, a managing director. At JP Morgan, Jacques was responsible for helping to develop *RiskMetrics*. Jacques was also responsible for risk management advisory for Europe, the Middle East and Africa and in that capacity, worked with many clients to help implement risk management technology and processes. Jacques also held positions running JPM's Bond Index group and covering the Benelux countries from an economics/fixed income strategy perspectives. Jacques holds a degree in economics from the University of Louvain.

Michelle McCarthy is a managing director in the Deutsche Bank group; she heads Deutsche Bank's RiskOffice risk measurement service bureau (formerly known as RAROC 2020), which serves institutional investors. She came to Deutsche Bank through its merger with Bankers Trust. She has held a variety of positions since joining Bankers Trust in 1986, including risk product manager for IQ Financial Systems, head of risk management for the asset management division, head of European risk management for the bank's internal risk management group and marketing and trading interest rate, equity and currency derivatives. Michelle holds a Master's degree from Harvard University and a Bachelor's degree from the University of Washington.

Ron Mensink is the quantitative analytics director at the State of Wisconsin Investment Board, where he guides analytical activities relating to asset allocation, performance measurement, and risk measurement. He gained his MBA in finance from the University of Wisconsin and is a Chartered Financial Analyst.

Andrea M. P. Neves is a vice president at CP Risk Management, LLC based in Chicago. Andrea specialises in financial risk measurement, volatility analysis and managerial risk consulting. Prior to joining CPRM, she was senior technical consultant at Risk Management Consulting Services, Inc. Her previous experience includes work at a derivatives litigation support firm and research for the Center for the Study of Futures and Options Markets. Andrea has co-authored several publications on risk management topics such as VAR and asset management. She is also one of several instructors for the Risk Management course in the Executive Education Program of the University of Chicago Graduate School of Business. In addition to her degrees in physics and economics, Andrea is currently pursuing a MBA from the University of Chicago with a concentration in analytical finance.

Joseph G. Nicholas is founder and chairman of the HFR Group of Companies. During the past fourteen years, Mr Nicholas has contributed to a broad range of landmark industry developments, including: the HFR Database, the industry's only daily transparent hedge fund database, the industry's first and only strategy-pure daily hedge fund indices, the first multiple strategy mutual fund and the industry's only position-level tactical manger allocation and system. Mr Nicholas' publications include *Market Neutral Investing* (Bloomberg Press, 2000), *Investing in Hedge Funds* (Bloomberg Press, 1999), "Structuring a Hedge Fund Investment Portfolio" and *Hedge Funds* (Irwin, 1995). He also wrote the Chicago Mercantile Exchange's booklet *Exchange-traded Derivatives in a Professionally Managed Portfolio*, "Managed Futures for Institutional Investors – How to Structure the Investment", *Managed Futures Today* (1992) and "What's Happening to Performance?" in the *FIA Review* (July/August 1992). Joseph is a frequent lecturer on topics relating to alternative investments. He received his Bachelor's degree in science in commerce from DePaul University and the degree of Juris Doctor from the Northwestern University School of Law.

Todd E. Petzel is president and chief investment officer of Commonfund Asset Management Company, Inc. Prior to joining Commonfund, he was the executive vice president for Business Development of the Chicago Mercantile Exchange. He began his career by joining the Coffee, Sugar and Cocoa Exchange in New York as chief economist and then became vice president at the Financial Research for the Chicago Mercantile Exchange. While in Chicago, he also taught finance classes at the Graduate School of Business, The University of Chicago. Dr Petzel is the author of the book, *Financial Futures and Options: A Guide to Markets, Applications and Strategies* and numerous articles and reviews. He serves as referee for a number of journals devoted to economics and finance and as editor of *Derivatives Quarterly*. Todd holds AB, AM and PhD degrees from the University of Chicago. Subsequently, he taught at Macalester College and Stanford University.

Leslie Rahl is president of Capital Market Risk Advisors, Inc, a risk management consulting firm. Prior to founding her consulting firm in 1991, Leslie spent 19 years at Citibank, nine of which were as head of Citibank's Derivatives Group in North America. Ms Rahl was named among the "Top 50 Women in Finance" by *Euromoney* in 1997 and was profiled in both the fifth and 10th anniversary issues of *Risk* magazine. She has been published numerous times. She was a director of the International Swaps and Derivatives Association (ISDA) for five years and is currently a member of the Board of the International Association of Financial Engineers and the Fischer Black Memorial Foundation and a member of the Board of Advisors for the financial engineering programme at the Sloan School. Ms Rahl received her undergraduate degree in computer science from the Massachusetts Institute of Technology and her MBA from the Sloan School of Management.

Stephen Rees is director of Quantitative Research at Baring Asset Management in London. His investment career spans 13 years and has been devoted to the development, implementation and marketing of quantitative techniques. He began his career at BZW Investment Management (now Barclays Global Investors) where he developed one of the first systematic stock selection products for the UK equity market. He also worked at Quorum, the quant boutique, and, prior to Barings was head of Quantitative Research at Rothschild Asset Managament. He is a frequent speaker at quantitative investment and risk management conferences. Stephen holds a first class honours degree in physics from Imperial College in London and a PhD in mathematical physics from Cambridge University.

Jacob Rosengarten is a managing director and is the co-head of the Risk Management group for the Asset Management Division. Prior to this he was employed by the Commodities Corporation (acquired by Goldman Sachs in 1997), where he had worked since 1983. At Commodities Corporation, he was the director of accounting, assistant controller and controller and before that he was the director of risk analysis and quantitative analysis. In this capacity he directed a group responsible for measuring risk associated with individual positions, managers and portfolios of managers who trade a variety of products including futures, derivatives, equities and emerging markets. Prior to his tenure at Commodities Corporation, he worked as an auditor for Arthur Young & Co. He holds a

BA in economics from Brandeis University and a MBA in accounting from the University of Chicago. He is also a Certified Public Accountant.

Myron Scholes is a partner in Oak Hill Capital Management and is also the Frank E. Buck Professor of Finance Emeritus, at the Stanford University Graduate School of Business. He is co-originator of the Black–Scholes options pricing model, which is the basis of the pricing and risk-management technology that is used to value and to manage the risk of financial instruments around the world. For this work, he was awarded the Nobel Memorial Prize in Economic Sciences in 1997. He was the Frank E. Buck Professor of Finance at the Stanford University Graduate School of Business and a senior research fellow at the Hoover Institution where he served as the Edward Eagle Brown Professor of Finance in the Graduate School of Business and also an assistant and associate professor of finance at the Massachusetts Institute of Technology's Sloan School of Management. Professor Scholes has consulted widely with many financial institutions, corporations and exchanges and continues to lecture for many organisations around the world. Prior to Oak Hill, he was a principal and limited partner at Long-Term Capital Management and a managing director at Salomon Brothers, a member of Salomon's risk management committee. As co-head of its Fixed Income Derivatives Sales and Trading Department, he was instrumental in building Salomon Swapco, its derivatives intermediation subsidiary. He received his PhD from the University of Chicago. Professor Scholes also has honourary doctorate degrees from the University of Paris, McMaster University and Louvain University.

Andrew B. Weisman is the chief investment officer for The Nikko Securities Co. International, Inc, where he is responsible for asset allocation and management, portfolio analysis, quantitative risk management, product development and proprietary trading. He has developed several risk management products, analytical tools and trading methodologies used by Nikko and other money management firms, including the Call Option Linked Trust (COLT) developed for Cargill Financial Services. He joined Nikko having been the senior vice president and manager of Yamaichi International Structured Products group. Previously he was the head of the Bankers Trust's Automated Currency Trading Unit, director of Currency Fund Management for Credit du Nord and US and Senior Asset manager for Commodities Corporation. Andrew is a graduate of Columbia College where he gained his BA in Philosophy/Economics. He attended the Columbia University School of International and Public Affairs and earned his Master's in International Affairs. He gained a doctoral fellowship to Columbia University's Graduate School of Business and completed all of the course work and comprehensive examinations toward a PhD.

Kurt Winkelmann joined Goldman Sachs in 1993 and is vice president and head of institutional client research and strategy. This group focuses on strategic issues that are of interest to institutional clients. Prior to joining Goldman Sachs, Kurt spent five years in London at the Fixed Income Research Group as Head of Global Fixed Income Portfolio Strategy. Kurt has written and co-authored several papers, "Managing Market Exposure", (1996) and "Estimating Covariance Matrices", (1998) and "Using the Black-Litterman Model: Three Years of Practical Experience", (1998). He has also worked in the investment technology industry and as an economist for First Bank Systems. He received his BA from Macalester and his PhD in economics from the University of Minnesota.

Barbara Zvan is a director with the Research & Economics Department at the Ontario Teachers' Pension Plan Board. The department's primary responsibilities include long-term asset mix, short-term tactical asset allocation and risk measurement as well as introducing alternative investments to the pension fund. Barbara's particular area of responsibility relates to asset liability studies, used to set the strategic asset mix and to investigate how different surplus policies affect the risk of the fund. Prior to the Ontario Teachers' Board, Barbara worked in a quantitative research group at a major Canadian bank. Barbara is a fellow of the Society of Actuaries and with the Canadian Institute of Actuaries. She attained her Master's in mathematics from the University of Waterloo.

Acknowledgements

Any proceeds that I receive as editor of this volume have been pledged to the Fischer Black Memorial Foundation (FBMF). Without the seminal work of the late Fischer Black and his colleague, Myron Scholes, none of the advancements outlined in this volume would have been possible. I would also like to note that without the training and passion for intellectual excellence that Fischer Black, Myron Scholes and myself (as well as several of the other contributors) received from the Sloan School at the Massachusetts Institute of Technology, the still evolving world of risk management and financial engineering would not have developed as far as it has.

Leslie Rahl

Introduction

Leslie Rahl

Capital Market Risk Advisors, Inc.

I am honoured to have been asked to edit this book, as it is the most significant single source of information to date on the exciting and emerging practice of risk budgeting. As you will see, even to the leading-edge players who have contributed to this book, the art and science of risk budgeting is still evolving.

It is important to note that despite the fact that there is an ever-growing group of "converts", there are still many risk budgeting sceptics. Criticisms of the approach include:

- ❑ "I can't spend risk-adjusted returns"?
- ❑ "There are so many assumptions required, I am more comfortable with relying on simple givens such as 'my equity portfolio will always earn 5+% per annum'".
- ❑ "Risk doesn't really matter, all that really matters is whether or not my managers outperform their benchmark".
- ❑ "Measuring risk is so imprecise, why bother"?

While these arguments are not totally without merit, they are really no different from the types of arguments that we risk pioneers have encountered at each stage of development and evolution.

Asset allocation is *familiar*. Risk budgeting requires a new way of thinking and thus poses new challenges.

This book is designed to provide a comprehensive assessment of the leading-edge thinking on the subject of risk budgeting and risk management for institutional investors and plan sponsors as of summer 2000. I fully expect that many of the concepts put forth here will advance exponentially over the next few years, but I am also convinced that this compendium will provide an important basis for that evolution.

In the first chapter, I offer a historical perspective on risk and a general overview of investment risk management.

In Chapter 2, Myron Scholes, the esteemed 1998 Nobel Prize winner and veteran of Salomon Brothers' derivatives business and LTCM, offers his thoughts on risk and crisis management.

Kurt Winkelmann shows how well-established principles of portfolio theory can be applied to risk management at the total fund level in Chapter 3.

In Chapter 4, Andrew Weisman and Jerome Abernathy, present a simple method for more realistically defining the performance characteristics of hedge funds known as Generic Model Decomposition (GMD).

Chris Culp, Ron Mensink and Andrea Neves present their thoughts in Chapter 5 on applying value-at-risk (VAR) to asset managers. They describe the importance of VAR as a tool that allows asset managers to better ascertain whether the risks they *are* taking are those *they want and need to be* taking or *think they are.*

Chapter 6 by Michelle McCarthy separates risk budgeting and VAR measurement from classic investment risk practices. Such practices include asset allocation and classic investment risk measures, such as standard deviation. This chapter also shows the unique and valuable insight these new techniques add to the investment process.

Bob Litterman, Jaques Longerstaey, Jacob Rosengarten and Kurt Winkelmann discuss the role of portfolio managers in Chapter 7. These managers take risk on behalf of their clients and name the appropriate range for risk taking as the "green zone". This is agreed upon as the suitable term in the context of a portfolio management assignment.

In Chapter 8, Amy Hirsch offers her observations on and experience with "risk obsession" and in Chapter 9, Joseph Nicholas, Founder and Chairman of the Hedge Fund Research group of companies, provides insight into market-neutral hedge fund risks.

In Chapter 10, Gabriel Bousbib shares his insights about deploying and using technology for the delivery of time-critical risk information to various participants in the investment management community.

Chapter 11 by Leo de Bever, Wayne Kozun and Barbara Zvan provides an insight into the use of risk budgeting at Ontario Teachers' Pension Plan (Teachers) where VAR has standardised and simplified the measurement and comparison of risk across asset classes.

In Chapter 12, Michael de Marco shares his perspective that adopting risk budgeting would be a valuable exercise for any investment fund sponsor. Many of the most crucial assumptions are so deeply embedded in the organisation's investment philosophy that trustees and investment staff no longer consider questioning them.

And finally, in Chapter 13, Stephen Rees argues that the traditional buy-side risk management – tracking error – should be put to the sword and replaced by value-at-risk.

Part I

Overview

Risk Budgeting: The Next Step of the Risk Management Journey
A Veteran's Perspective

Leslie Rahl

Capital Market Risk Advisors, Inc.

Risk management is a journey, not a destination. It is *not* a one-time exercise to implement best practice tools, but rather a lifetime's odyssey. As I look back at the risk management tools used when I first became involved in derivatives and risk 20 years ago, I laugh. Phrases such as, "all mortgages have a 10-year average life" and, "there is a constant volatility", have not stood the test of time, but were considered important advancements at their inception. One must agree that in the years to come, we will look back at our primitive approaches to risk budgeting with the same amusement. The graph in Figure 1 illustrates the evolution of risk measurement.

DRIVERS OF THE RISK REVOLUTION

So, what are the drivers behind this risk revolution? Improvements in technology is the most significant factor followed by increased fiduciary awareness that has led to the interest and ability to ask more questions (eg, by trustees, plan sponsors, supervisors, directors and regulators). In addition, the now-famous surprises have led to the need to update guidelines and definitions and an increased demand for fund transparency.

Investors have begun to focus on risk dollars spent to achieve return. The increasing trend to focus on reward *and* risk at the instrument, manager and overall portfolio level has resulted in a need to ensure that compensation and fees encourage the type of risk-taking that the primary fiduciary desires. The universe of risks that need to be addressed is enormous. Perhaps the most important thing on the galaxy of risks chart in Figure 2 is the "(partial listing)" footnote. Valuation difficulty became a significant problem during periods of market dislocation (eg, the US interest

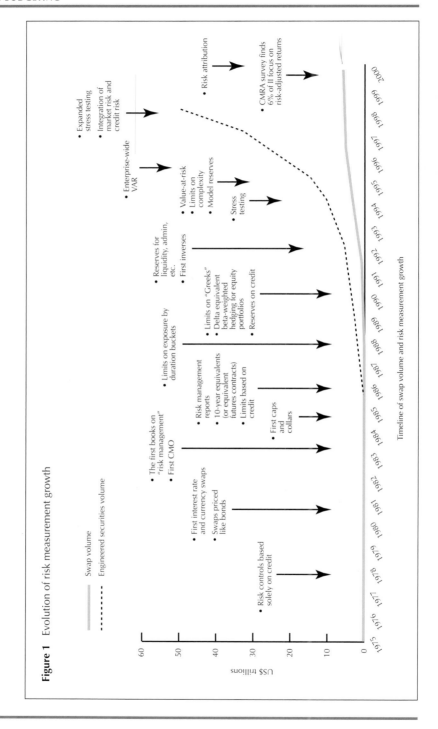

Figure 1 Evolution of risk measurement growth

Timeline of swap volume and risk measurement growth

Figure 2 Galaxy of risks

• Accounting risk	• Daylight risk	• Liquidity risk	• Regulatory risk
• Bankruptcy risk	• Equity risk	• Market risk	• Reinvestment risk
• Basis risk	• Extrapolation risk	• Maverick risk	• Rollover risk
• Call risk	• Fiduciary risk	• Modelling risk	• Spread risk
• Capital risk	• Hedging risk	• Netting risk	• Suitability risk
• Collateral risk	• Horizon risk	• Optional risk	• Systemic risk
• Commodity risk	• Iceberg risk	• Personnel risk	• Systems risk
• Concentration risk	• Interest-rate risk	• Phantom risk	• Tax risk
• Contract risk	• Interpolation risk	• Political risk	• Technology risk
• Credit risk	• Knowledge risk	• Prepayment risk	• Time lag risk
• Currency risk	• Legal risk	• Publicity risk	• Volatility risk
• Curve construction risk	• Limit risk	• Raw data risk	• Yield curve risk

(Partial listing)

rate hikes, the Mexican peso devaluation, the Russian/LTCM Crisis). Unidimensional quantitative measures failed to control or identify many loss situations. Changes in margin requirements coupled with volatility in the market during the Fall of 1998 caught many securities without adequate liquidity.

One of the important lessons learned from 1998's Long Term Capital Management (LTCM) crisis was the significance of "iceberg risk". We learned that even though the visible tip of an iceberg is large, what lies beneath the surface can be many times larger and may also take on unpredictable shapes. In essence, the more that is revealed, the more questions are asked. This analogy applies well to the process of risk management. For instance, the following tactics represent just the tip of the iceberg with respect to what needs to be done to update the risk management process.

❏ "All mortgages have an average life of 12 years" was a breakthrough concept adopted by the risk world.
❏ Credit risk was measured as a percentage of notional principal based solely on maturity, independent of the credit quality of the counterparty.
❏ Interest rate caps were priced at a constant volatility, independent of maturity and strike.
❏ Volatility of swaptions was calculated as the volatility of caps minus 3%.
❏ The Thai baht was a low-volatility currency and long-dated options on it were priced as if it would remain a low-volatility currency.
❏ Restricting investments to "AAA and less than two years in maturity" was a common and reasonably effective risk management tool.
❏ Limits on notional principal, independent of maturity, were commonplace.
❏ "Market-neutral" was believed to be the same as "neutral to the market".

Whether you share my history and memory or not, I am sure that you will agree that the pace of advancement in risk techniques has accelerated, and I believe will continue to do so. Risk budgeting is a crucial, evolutionary step in this process.

RISK MANAGEMENT FOR INSTITUTIONAL INVESTORS

When we take more risk, are we in fact getting more return? How should we set limits to guard against maximum loss amounts? These are some of the fundamental questions risk managers must contemplate. Capital Market Risk Advisors (CMRA) surveyed institutional investors in December 1997, and revealed that less than 6% of respondents focused on risk-adjusted returns and 40% of respondents planned to move to risk-adjusted measures by December 1998. Progress has accelerated in the new Millennium, but we still have a long way to go.

Institutional investors have a different set of needs from banks and broker/dealers. Therefore, they need to also consider the following risk development issues:

❏ Longer time horizons;
   – Holding period;
   – Evaluation;
❏ Multiple asset classes;
❏ Multiple portfolio managers/firms;
❏ Distinct fiduciary responsibilities; and
❏ Historical focus on performance versus risk-adjusted performance.

Since institutional investors typically have longer time horizons, the liquidity of their positions will be lower. The investment horizon of the investor as well as the liquidity characteristics of a fund need to be included in the risk quantification process. Portfolios with long investment horizons and/or low liquidity need different risk measures than those that have shorter horizons and are very liquid. Figure 3 illustrates how the choice of time horizon depends upon the objectives of the portfolio and liquidity of its positions.

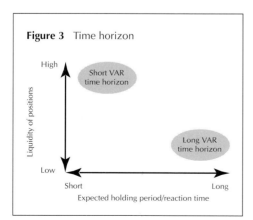

Figure 3 Time horizon

High — Liquidity of positions — Low

Short VAR time horizon

Long VAR time horizon

Short — Long

Expected holding period/reaction time

ASSET ALLOCATION VERSUS RISK ALLOCATION

Historically, institutional investors have used asset allocation as the core process by which they determine their investment strategy. The asset allocation process classically starts with the choice of asset classes and follows the direction of the flowchart in Figure 4.

Figure 4   The asset allocation process

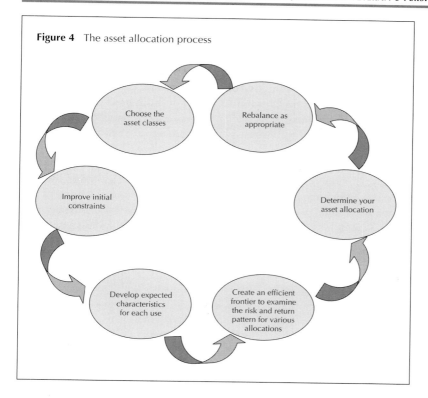

Allocating investment dollars is an important tool but it ignores the need to efficiently allocate risk appetite and to reflect the changing dynamics of risk. Asset allocation emphasises return, out-performance and P&L flows. Risk budget monitoring adds another dimension, it is also a function of volatility and correlation as well as a function of dollars. Constant assets in a risk budgeting framework can result in widely fluctuating risk.

RISK BUDGETING

One must remember that risk budgeting is *not* an optimisation exercise. The conventional optimisation approach uses a mean-variance model, which optimally allocates investments between different assets by considering the trade-off between risk and return. Users generally find that the supposed "optimum" is extremely sensitive to the return forecast – the input with the least certainty. Varying the return forecasts results in wide swings in the supposedly optimal portfolio, until its variance constraint is confronted. Exposures created by long/short positions with passive assumptions on risk can create significant risk with no expected return. Obviously, the practice of investing no net capital while taking on huge risks, usually results in no intrinsic reward.

RISK-ADJUSTED PERFORMANCE

There has been active debate on the definition of "risk-adjusted performance". In March 1995, the Securities and Exchange Commission (SEC) solicited comment from the financial community on methods to improve mutual fund risk disclosure. An overwhelming 3,700 comments and letters were submitted in response, and were mostly from individual investors. While there was general agreement on the necessity for more information on risk, there was little consensus on a suitable measure of risk and risk-adjusted performance.

All else being equal, an investor that maximises risk-adjusted performance will perform better than one who does not. Whether the investment objectives are aggressive or conservative, it is critical to recognise that risk is not a fixed characteristic of a portfolio; it can be altered to match investor preferences. Investors should separate decisions regarding the amount of risk to incur from the type of portfolio held, in the same way that the swap market has allowed them to separate decisions involving the credit they choose to hold from the currency in which they hold the position.

While risk budgeting and risk-adjusted return management need not necessarily go hand-in-hand, they usually do. Risk budgeting enables a plan sponsor to evaluate the portfolio contribution to various exposures to risk. This framework for analysing a broad range of critical decisions is an approach that sponsors must start to take. The first step is to determine current risk exposures. Once a plan sponsor has developed the ability to measure the risk of each of its managers and strategies, using the risk measure as the denominator of the risk-adjusted return equation is a simple and powerful next step. The ultimate accomplishment in the process is to have risk as the basis of "strategic risk management".

VALUE-AT-RISK (VAR)

Now let us focus on VAR itself. As the following chapters will show, VAR has become an important component of risk management and measurement and is the underpinning of most approaches to "risk budgeting". Since the 1990s, enterprise-wide VAR has been embraced by practitioners and regulators, as well as academics, and has been considered a vital component of current risk management best practices. It is defined as the maximum loss a portfolio can incur over a specified time period, with a specified probability. However, what VAR is *not* is probably even more important than what it is. Table 1 outlines its characteristics.

There are many different ways to calculate VAR and each method will yield a different result. The various methods are summarised in Table 2.

What do the shapes in Figure 5 have in common? They all have an area of 12, but they have very different profiles. This is a good visual representation of how the same portfolio can have drastically different VAR values.

Table 1 The characteristics of VAR

What VAR is	What VAR is not
• VAR is the maximum loss a portfolio can incur over a specified time period, with a specified probability	• VAR is NOT the worst case scenario
• VAR is a vital component of current "best" practices in risk measurement	• VAR does NOT measure losses under any particular market conditions
• VAR is embraced by practitioners, regulators and academics	• VAR does NOT address cumulative losses
• VAR is valuable as a probabilistic measure of potential losses	• VAR – by itself – is NOT sufficient for risk measurement

Table 2 VAR methods

Methodology	Variance/covariance. Historical simulation. Monte Carlo
Horizon	One day to multiple years
Confidence level	84%, 95%, 97.5%, 99%, etc.
Data look-back period	One month to 14 years

Figure 5 Not all VAR results are the same

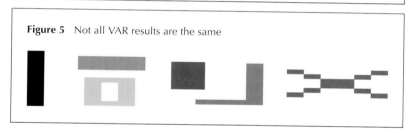

The effective use of risk budgeting requires a sophisticated understanding that not all VAR calculations are the same. It is important that all portfolios being budgeted using a risk amount adopt a consistent methodology for measuring risk.

During the Asian meltdown in 1997, for instance, the VAR of a sample portfolio calculated using historical simulations versus equally weighted variance/co-variance versus exponentially weighted variance/co-variance varied considerably. Figure 6 shows the performance of a fund using three different types of portfolio daily VAR. As we can see, VAR varies even with simple portfolios.

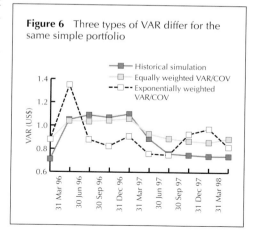

Figure 6 Three types of VAR differ for the same simple portfolio

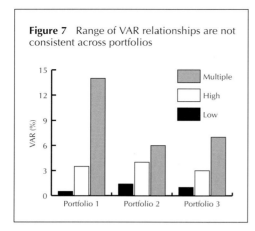

Figure 7 Range of VAR relationships are not consistent across portfolios

Another example would be to apply the same three VAR approaches to three separate portfolios. This is illustrated in Figure 7. Although the second and third portfolio confirm that the portfolio risk will look quite different depending on the risk calculation methodology chosen, the relationships are not consistent and/or extrapolate across portfolios.

Many funds (for instance, even the sophisticated, quantitatively adept funds such as LTCM) were caught short in autumn 1998. VAR alone does not capture many spread risks. The flight to quality that impacted credit spreads and even widened the spread between the 29-year and 30-year treasury, and the instability of "euro convergence", are among the examples of the missing risks in a basic VAR equation. A key to effective risk management is to include the results of stress tests as a component of the risk to be budgeted and allocated.

TRACKING VAR OVER TIME

Analysing the VAR reports for a fund *over time* can provide valuable insights. Comparing the *ex ante* risk for an individual fund with its target provides the investment manager with an assessment of whether the risks taken are in line with expectations. Significant deviations would need to be discussed. It can also be useful to analyse a stray portfolio over time that pushed a manager's guidelines to the limit. Figure 8 illustrates how the effects of various factors can influence a portfolio. By trending VAR sensitivities, investors are permitted to proactively diagnose "style drift" and avoid surprise shifts in risks/returns. Risk diversification has evolved through several approaches to VAR.

VAR attribution reports also highlight the extent of diversification within a fund and whether there are any concentrated positions or exposures that should be discussed with the hedge fund manager. Such risk analysis needs to take into account many factors.

❏ *Absolute VAR* – This is expressed as a percentage of market value and allows for comparison across funds.
❏ *Marginal VAR* – This is the difference between overall portfolio VAR and VAR excluding specific accounts, risk factors or positions. Marginal VAR measures the risk differential.
❏ *Relative VAR* – This tracks portfolio risk *relative* to its benchmark.

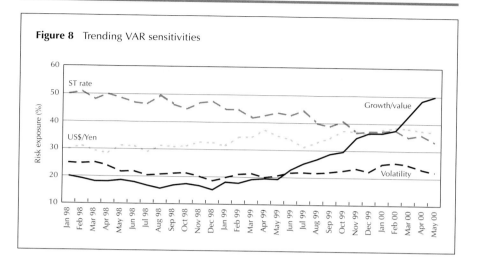

Figure 8 Trending VAR sensitivities

STRESS TESTING

There has been at least one major market that has moved by more than 10 standard deviations every year for the past 10 years. Unexpected financial shocks include the 1987 Stock Market crash, the 1990 Nikkei crash, the 1990 High Yield tumble, the 1992 European currency crisis, the 1994 US interest rate hike, the 1994-95 Mexican peso crisis, the 1995 Latin American crisis, the 1997 Asian crisis, the 1998 Russian/LTCM crisis, and the 1999 Brazil crisis (see Figure 9). While most institutions address exposure at a move of two or three standard deviations, markets regularly move more than this amount.

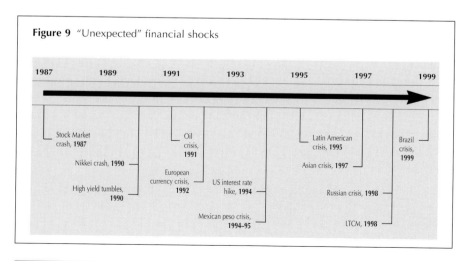

Figure 9 "Unexpected" financial shocks

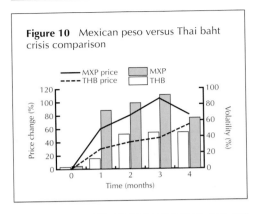

Figure 10 Mexican peso versus Thai baht crisis comparison

Table 3 Shape of the distribution curve for the Thai baht: January 1993 to May 1997

	Thai baht	Normal
≤ 1 st dev	83.9%	63.4%
> 1 st dev	8.9%	31.7%
> 2 st dev	3.8%	4.6%
> 3 st dev	1.5%	0.3%
> 4 st dev	1.0%	0.0%
> 5 st dev	0.7%	0.0%
> 6 st dev	0.3%	0.0%
Kurtosis	2.1×10^{-6}	0.0%

There are various approaches to stress testing. It can be based on historical events, generalised scenarios or institution-specific scenarios. Stress testing based on historical events is a valuable tool when used to predict the damages of the next impending crisis.

For instance, the Mexican peso crisis in 1994 could serve as a proxy for the Thai baht crisis in 1997 (see Figure 10). The Thai baht move was only half the severity of the Mexican peso crisis, but a simple stress test could have quantified the devastating impact. Suppose the Hong Kong dollar devalues. Will it behave in a similar fashion to the Thai baht or the Mexican peso? No one knows for sure, but both scenarios could be useful stress tests to refer to.

Another complexity to consider when assigning risk to many asset classes, including emerging markets, is that the standard assumption of normal distribution may not be representative. Table 3 gives the distribution of the Thai baht during the period from January 1993 to May 1997. It shows that the normal assumptions differ drastically from the actual distribution, even before the crisis.

Similarly, stress testing results can be interpreted in various ways. They can involve an evaluation of tail events, progressively severe market moves or extreme standard deviation scenarios. As the risk profiles in Figure 11 illustrate, the empirical return distribution can be very different from the theoretical return distribution in times of crisis. Kurtosis is a measure of how fat probability distribution tails are. The Thai baht shows a greater value for kurtosis than the normal distribution curve meaning that dramatic market moves occur with greater frequency than predicted by the normal distribution.

Clearly, the results of stress testing are as important to the risk equation as VAR. The underlying questions that stress testing attempts to answer include:

❏ Which variables, given a small move, cause a large move in price?

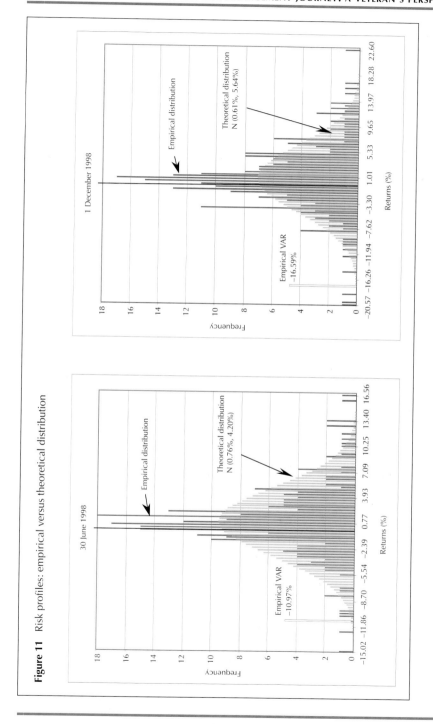

Figure 11 Risk profiles: empirical versus theoretical distribution

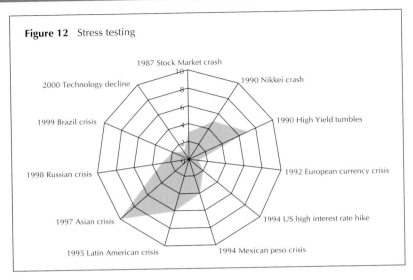

Figure 12 Stress testing

❑ Which variables that are important to your portfolio have a high likelihood of change?

❑ Which variables or exposures are assumed to offset each other, and by how much?

❑ How wide is the variance of results produced by other commonly used approaches? How is this different from yours?

❑ What is your approach's acceptance in the market place? Do the majority of your peers use a similar approach?

A visualisation approach to stress testing might be used to compare a manager to his or her peer group by stress test decile. Figure 12 shows an example of this.

While risk budgeting is an innovative and important concept, risk needs to be more broadly defined than VAR and/or traditional risk measures. Stress test results and sensitivities need to be integrated into the denominator of the risk-adjusted reward equation. Stress testing results need to include not only sensitivities to market moves but also to the *assumptions* underlying the strategies; VAR, and mark-to-market 20/20 hindsight is a wonderful but unavailable perspective in many cases. However, it would be irresponsible in this new Millennium not to consider the impact of liquidity premium, on-the-run versus off-the-run spread-differential credit spread sensitivity, haircut sensitivity and sensitivity to correlation, etc, in a robust approach to risk management and, therefore, as a component of the *risk* definition that is *budgeted*.

While it is common knowledge that during times of crisis all correlations move to +1 or –1, this knowledge is not always integrated into risk management or risk budgeting. The CMRA post-LTCM crisis survey in 1998, for example, found that before the crisis only 9% of respondents stress tested correlation. Integrating a credit risk and potential future exposure concept into risk budgeting is key to success. Risk budgeting needs to take a *broad* view on how to recognise the risk one is budgeting.

LEVERAGE
Fund managers control risk by closely monitoring individual positions and ensuring that their portfolio has diversified exposures. Portfolios with many managers tend to focus on the *leverage* (or position sizes) employed by fund managers as an important measure of the fund's risk. However, the use of leverage has its limitations. For instance, a manager may have 200% notional gross positions, but most of these positions may exist only to offset or neutralise unwanted exposures and thus explicitly *reduce* risk. As another example, an equal amount of leverage in two different investment strategies (eg, fixed-income arbitrage versus equity market-neutral) could result in significantly different risk levels.

LIQUIDITY RISK
Liquidity and the lack thereof is probably the one risk that has traditionally received the least focus and yet has inflicted the greatest damage. Understanding the liquidity of a portfolio is a critical component of effective risk management.

One of the lessons learned from the Russian/LTCM crisis is that valuing positions at mid-market when positions are large and liquidity is poor can be very misleading. When CMRA conducted a survey of the top banks and dealers, post-crisis, we found that only 64% marked positions at the bid when they were long and at the offer when they were short. The survey also revealed that only 25% of banks and dealers made adjustments for large/illiquid positions prior to the crisis. Prime brokers and their clients learned the hard way that the consequences of the haircut setting process caused major problems for both sides. While only 42% of respondents indicated that they explicitly shared their haircut methodology with their clients before the crisis, 75% indicated that they did so post-crisis. This raises the questions: how many funds consider their sensitivity to haircut changes as part of their risk management and measurement process? And, how many plan sponsors request information on how their managers who lend or borrow securities manage this sensitivity risk?

The LTCM debacle was a clear example of the need to understand the liquidity demands of the fund. It is also a clear example of how the lack of a crisis plan exacerbated the problem. Figure 13 shows the widening of the bid-ask spread and the correlation convergence that the Russian/LTCM crisis triggered. Experience has demonstrated that a crisis can dramatically dry up liquidity. While it is a natural human reflex, liquidating the most liquid instruments in a portfolio to meet margin demands can be, and was

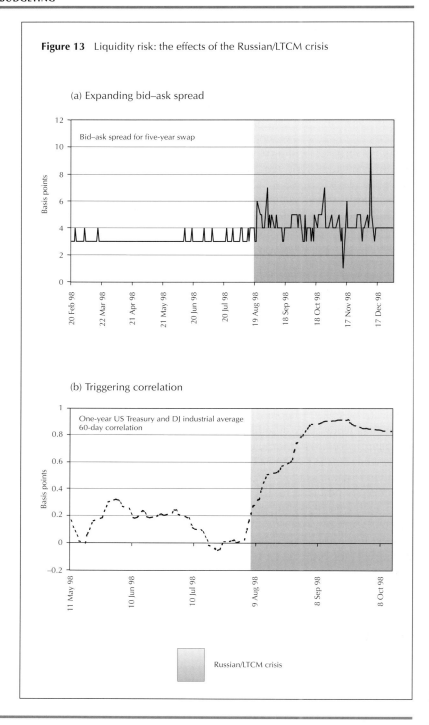

Figure 13 Liquidity risk: the effects of the Russian/LTCM crisis

(a) Expanding bid–ask spread

Bid–ask spread for five-year swap

(b) Triggering correlation

One-year US Treasury and DJ industrial average
60-day correlation

Russian/LTCM crisis

in many cases, a death knell. The remaining portfolio is skewed to illiquid instruments and, therefore, even less able to meet the liquidity demands of a fast-moving market than the original portfolio.

During periods of market stress, bid/offer spreads tend to widen – further exacerbating the liquidity risk and cost. Additionally, market crises tend to send historical correlation out the window. All instruments move to a correlation of +1 or –1. While on some level we all know about this correlation truism, it is rarely factored into the risk equation. Strategies such as convergence trades, basis trades, etc, are most vulnerable to this correlation phenomenon. It is critical for such funds' needs to include a measure of this crisis effect.

BENCHMARKING

Adding to the complexity of measuring and monitoring risk for institutional investors is the dimension of *benchmark relativity*. While banks and broker dealers have traditionally measured both risk and return on an absolute basis, the institutional investment community has traditionally viewed performance in relation to a benchmark. A survey of hedge fund risk management practices in early 2000 by CMRA revealed that although 57% of the respondents calculated VAR on an absolute basis, only 9% calculate VAR relative to a benchmark. Furthermore, only an additional 4% plan to calculate benchmark relative to VAR. Figure 14 illustrates the split.

In the brave new world of risk-adjusted returns and risk budgeting, however, there is still a need to relate to a benchmark. The question then becomes: Why did the manager perform relative to the benchmark and how did the risk of the actual

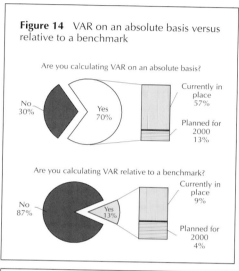

Figure 14   VAR on an absolute basis versus relative to a benchmark

Are you calculating VAR on an absolute basis?

No 30%
Yes 70%
Currently in place 57%
Planned for 2000 13%

Are you calculating VAR relative to a benchmark?

No 87%
Yes 13%
Currently in place 9%
Planned for 2000 4%

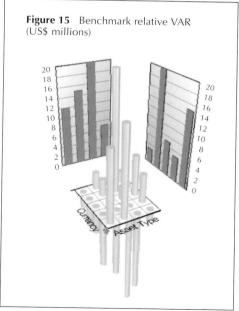

Figure 15   Benchmark relative VAR (US$ millions)

portfolio compare to the risk of the benchmark portfolio? Ideally, a manager would be able to produce a three-dimensional graph illustrating the benchmark relative VAR (for example, see Figure 15). This approach has made the selection of an appropriate benchmark increasingly important.

If two managers with the same style and the same benchmark each have a performance of 50 bp over the benchmark, who is doing the better job? Who would you want to reward more highly? Who would you want to allocate more funds to? It is easy to say "to the fund manager who took less risk to achieve the same reward", but how do you measure the risk taken?

Let us extend the hypothetical example above and postulate the following scenario:

	Manager 1	Manager 2
Style	Same	Same
Benchmark	Same	Same
Performance	Benchmark +50	Benchmark +50
VAR *(calculated in a consistent way)*	US$12 million	US$12 million

It would appear at first glance that the risks and rewards of both managers are equal. But if I were to tell you that:

❏ One manager had 90% of his exposure in one instrument, while the other had no more than 10% in any one instrument?
❏ One manager was invested solely in highly liquid instruments with readily transparent price discovery and the other was heavily invested in highly structured, less liquid instruments, with opaque price discovery?
❏ One manager had a 10-year track record and the other a one-year track record?
❏ One manager was heavily invested in BBB instruments while the other held only AA or better paper, or that both managers used OTC instruments but that one only dealt with AA or better counterparties while the other dealt with any investment grade counterparty?
❏ One manager had structures with a maximum maturity of three years and the other had structures with a maximum maturity of 15 years?
❏ One manager had a disciplined robust internal risk management policy and practice and the other did not?

Obviously, the seemingly similar portfolios postulated above could in fact have very different risk characteristics.

EFFECTIVE COMMUNICATION OF RISK ON A COMPARATIVE BASIS

Effective communication of risk on a comparative basis involves many steps. First of all, it is extremely important to select measures that are *actionable*, *comparable* and *can be aggregated*. There should be the ability to comparably measure VAR, stress test results and other risk measures, and to comparatively benchmark the funds' relative to a *risk profile*. Specifically, there should be the ability to measure risk in total and by independent risk factors ($/yen, ST Rates, etc.), measure risk relative to peers of similar strategies and funds in general, and track a fund's *risk profile over time*.

Risk visualisation enhances our ability to digest the *comparative risk* profiles across "similar" portfolios. The ability to compare and contrast the risks of managers with similar styles is a key benefit of risk profiling. Risk visualisation can ease investors' increasing desire to "get under the skin" of funds, effectively communicate risk to non-academic parties, support the aggregation of risks across portfolios, reward diversification of risk, and protect proprietary strategies of the funds.

Plan sponsors need to be able to aggregate the risk portfolios of individual managers in order to evaluate the risk profile of their aggregate portfolios. This is especially crucial as the diversifying effects of alternative investments are increasingly sought. Without the ability to measure, aggregate and visualise the risk of each portfolio individually and to assess the diversification value of the aggregate, the reality of the alternative promise is hard to measure. This is especially true of a fund of funds. While this is an important and growing segment, without proper risk tools it is almost impossible to determine whether the mix of managers diversifies risk or doubles-up on certain risk components. Figure 16 shows an example of the correlation benefit of combining two portfolios. The risk maps in Figure 17 show the risk profile of two managers.

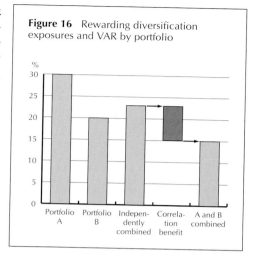

Figure 16 Rewarding diversification exposures and VAR by portfolio

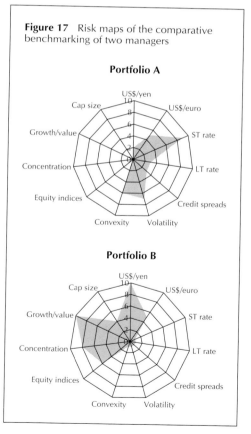

Figure 17 Risk maps of the comparative benchmarking of two managers

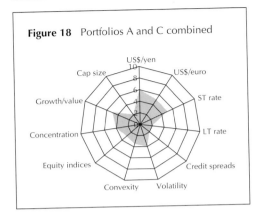

Figure 18 Portfolios A and C combined

Figure 18 shows the risk profile of the combined portfolios. As you can see, the combination of portfolios A and B produces a distinctly different risk profile from that of each portfolio standing alone.

Investors' need for information will sometimes be in direct conflict with managers (especially hedge funds) because of the need to protect their proprietary strategies. The use of a third-party intermediary to transform position-level data into aggregate risk information is gaining in popularity. Firms (such as ourselves) are increasingly being asked to provide this kind of risk transparency service.

CHALLENGES OF IMPLEMENTING EFFECTIVE RISK MANAGEMENT

The challenges of implementing effective risk management (which includes the ability to quantify, report and monitor risk properly) are plentiful but well worth overcoming. One of the major hurdles is convincing investment managers to "buy in". Other obstacles include creating an infrastructure that allows the aggregation of positions and risk across a plan, applying appropriate netting of exposures, implementing rules that do not extinguish returns, and providing discipline while retaining an innovative edge. Adapting to "risk-adjusted" economics takes time.

Risks are often hard to spot. Areas to beware of include cross hedging, basis risk, concentrated sources of return and risk, complexity and illiquidity.

It is also important to keep in mind that some asset classes are more difficult to manage than others. Asset classes that have historically suffered during times of crisis include CMOs for their non-linear structures and dependence on prepayment modelling assumptions, high yield bonds for their gapping credit spreads, and emerging markets for their lack of history and incomplete yield curves. Also included are real estate, private equity and alternative asset classes due to insufficient data for accurate modelling.

The lessons learned during the crisis in the autumn of 1998 have significantly changed many of the practices and procedures in place at major banks and prime brokers. Plan sponsors and money managers are also beginning to integrate these changes into their risk thinking.

ENTERPRISE-WIDE RISK MANAGEMENT

It is crucial that the risk measurement and management approaches selected provide regular feedback to the organisation. Quantitative

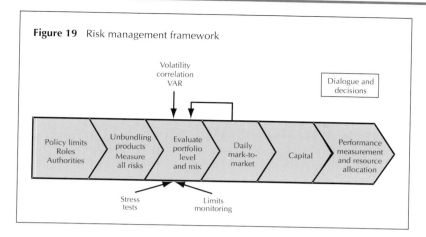

Figure 19 Risk management framework

measures such as VAR can be extremely valuable tools when used in conjunction with wisdom and good judgment. Risk management is nothing new. Figure 19 illustrates how a risk management framework operates.

Unfortunately, in this example the dialogue and decisions box is completely unconnected to the quantitative and qualitative measurement process. It is only when dialogue and decision making are connected to the risk management process output that the full benefit of the effort is realised. Integrating all aspects of risk management budgeting requires a self-assessment of "risk governance style".

While there is no right or wrong answer as to where an organisation should be on the scale illustrated in Figure 20, understanding the risk "culture" of your organisation is key to successful risk management. It is not uncommon for different members of a senior management team to have different assessments of where the fund currently sits on this scale, as well as where they would like it to be. Clarifying how an organisation chooses to risk govern itself is an important first step in developing effective risk management.

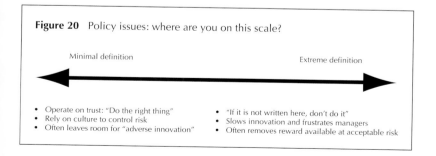

Figure 20 Policy issues: where are you on this scale?

Table 4 Samples of "old" risk controls that failed

AAA and less than two-year maturity
Low interest rate risk
Low currency risk
High liquidity
No commodities
Hedging is allowed
Speculation is not allowed
Highly correlated

There is no substitute for qualitative judgments in investing decisions. The goal of risk management is to provide risk insight. Often quantitative reports provide *data* but not *information*. This needs to change if risk management is going to be effective.

In all too many firms, the true power of risk management is lost as the process is isolated from the dialogue and decision-making process. Table 4 gives examples of some static "old" risk controls that changed as a result of this. Integrating the risk budgeting and risk management process into an ongoing dialogue and discussion-making process is the key to success. To achieve this, however, a common risk language is required.

THE "ART" OF RISK BUDGETING – THE QUALITATIVE COMPONENTS

While many of the chapters in this book delve into the use and calculation of VAR, which has become a standard measure of risk, I would like to address some of the non-quantitative issues that need to be addressed when implementing risk budgeting or any other concept of risk-adjusted returns.

Risk budgeting alone – or any single approach for that matter – is not the answer. An organisation needs a disciplined approach to risk, one that includes the quantitative aspect but does not rely exclusively on it.

Figure 21 outlines the range of actions that are required for a robust risk management programme.

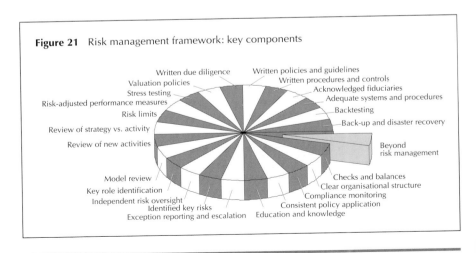

Figure 21 Risk management framework: key components

Written due diligence
Valuation policies
Stress testing
Risk-adjusted performance measures
Risk limits
Review of strategy vs. activity
Review of new activities
Model review
Key role identification
Independent risk oversight
Identified key risks
Exception reporting and escalation

Written policies and guidelines
Written procedures and controls
Acknowledged fiduciaries
Adequate systems and procedures
Backtesting
Back-up and disaster recovery
Beyond risk management
Checks and balances
Clear organisational structure
Compliance monitoring
Consistent policy application
Education and knowledge

It is important to note here that while the quantitative components are important, they only represent one-third of the key components of a robust risk management pro-gramme. Figure 22 identifies those quantitative components from Figure 21.

It is also important to remember that there will always be that small wedge that cannot be controlled, just minimised. This wedge is beyond risk management and cov-ers such events as clever new forms of fraud, paradigm changes in mar-kets, "new" market moves and surprise regulatory or other infrastructure changes or the "act of God" equivalent. These factors should be as small as possible.

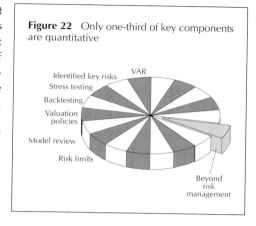

Figure 22 Only one-third of key components are quantitative

Identified key risks
VAR
Stress testing
Backtesting
Valuation policies
Model review
Risk limits
Beyond risk management

The technology debacle of 2000 is an example of why a simplistic defini-tion of risk is not adequate. A risk budgeting approach, for instance, focus-ing exclusively on VAR would not have adequately measured the risk of a NASDAQ-heavy portfolio (see Figure 23).

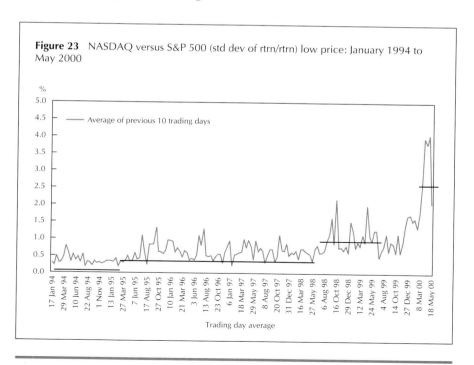

Figure 23 NASDAQ versus S&P 500 (std dev of rtrn/rtrn) low price: January 1994 to May 2000

Average of previous 10 trading days

Trading day average

THOUGHTS FOR THE NEW MILLENNIUM

As we enter the new Millennium, both issuers and investors are confronted with an expanding choice of risk/performance measurements (for a partial list, refer to Table 5).

While each has its advantages and disadvantages, no one measure tells the whole story. As we have seen, quantitative methods used to measure and manage risk include VAR and stress testing, and these have evolved significantly in recent years. The result has been that risk management has progressed tremendously over the past three decades. In the 1990s, quantitative risk measures such as VAR were embraced by the finance community. However, the measurement of risk is not enough. Sound risk management practices must include discussion and preparation for the "unexpected" (or not so, as the case may be) shocks. Given that every year for the past 10 years there has been at least one significant market move, the next crisis may not be too far away. As a community, we should be making new mistakes, not reproducing those already made by others. The following are points that we should all contemplate and remember:

❑ Risk in itself is not bad. However, what is bad is risk that is mispriced, mismanaged, misunderstood or unintended.
❑ *Both* senior managers and quants play a vital role in risk management.
❑ Mathematics and models are necessary but not wholly sufficient to control risk.
❑ Always ask yourself "what if I'm wrong?".
❑ While pricing is often based on the *most* likely events, risk management must also address the *least* likely events.

Table 5   CMRA's galaxy of risk/performance measures

• Absolute return	• Long/short leverage
• Appraisal ratio	• Residual standard derivative of returns
• Benchmark-relative VAR	• Risk of ruin
• Beta of returns	• Semi-variance
• Borrowing leverage	• Sharpe ratio
• Cashflow-adjusted equity market index	• Shortfall probability
• Cash-on-cash returns	• Sortino ratio
• Downside deviation	• Standard deviation
• Downsizing risk	• Target deviation shortfall probability
• Drawdown risk	• Time-weighted rate of return
• Individual standard division of returns	• Tracking error
• Information ratio	• Treynor's measure
• Jensen's measure	• Value-at-risk
• Liquidity-adjusted VAR	• Vintage year's comparison

(partial list)

❑ Risk is real, increasing and of concern to investors – it needs to be proactively managed and prudently disclosed.
❑ Risk can best be quantified and communicated on a *comparative* basis:
  – comparably measuring VAR;
  – comparative benchmarking;
  – tracking over time; and
  – consistently comparing across standard independent risk factors.

The final word on risk budgeting should probably go to the philosopher of our industry, Peter Bernstein,[1] who put it most eloquently that: "You cannot manage outcomes, you can only manage risk".

---

1   A financial historian and head of an investment advisory firm, Bernstein has been in the investment world since the 1950s. He helped launch the *Journal of Portfolio Management* and is the author of *Capital Ideas* and *Against the Gods*.

2

Crisis and Risk Management*

Myron Scholes

Oak Hill Capital Management

The reputation of financial risk modelling – and options pricing in particular – has been badly damaged by a series of market crises. But critics have misunderstood the changing relationship between credit risk and market liquidity.

During the early part of 2000, risk again surfaced as an investor concern, particularly in the high-technology sector of the economy. I have been specifically interested in the risk and return of alternative investments because they lie at the heart of financial intermediation, whether at insurance companies or hedge funds.

From theory, alternative investments require a premium return because they are less liquid than market investments. This liquidity premium varies over time as a function of preferences, leverage technology, the developments in financial technology and changes in institutional arrangements. The dynamics of the liquidity premium depend on institutional reactions to financial crises.

During 1997–98, financial crises have shifted around the world, from Southeast Asia, through Latin and South America, then Russia and back again to South America. Financial crisis has also infected Europe and the United States, especially during August–October 1998.

The increase in volatility (particularly in the equity markets) and the flight to liquidity around the world resulted in the firm I was associated with, Long-Term Capital Management (LTCM), experiencing an extraordinary reduction in its capital base. This culminated in a form of negotiated bankruptcy.

---

*This chapter is an edited version of a presentation delivered by Professor Scholes to Risk's fifth annual European Derivatives and Risk Management Conference Congress in Paris on 12 April 2000. It was first published in *Risk* 13(5), (2000), pp. 50–3.

After LTCM, the press and others began criticising financial modelling, and, in particular, the value of option pricing models. In truth, mathematical models and option pricing models played only a minor role, if any, in LTCM's failure. At LTCM, models were used to hedge local risks. In 1998, LTCM had large positions, concentrated in less liquid assets. As a result of the financial crisis, LTCM was also forced to switch from being a large supplier to a large demander of liquidity at a cost that eliminated its capital.

Although the Russian default, the LTCM bankruptcy and the financial difficulties of other financial service firms are the most visible manifestations of the crisis of late summer and autumn of 1998, there is still much greater volatility and lack of liquidity in many debt-related and equity-related financial markets. For example, during summer 1999, three to five-year long-dated volatility on the S&P 500 index was quoted in the 25–30% range – average volatility levels on the S&P index that have not been seen before. To be consistent with market expectations, the realised quarterly volatility on an annualised basis on the S&P 500 would have to average 30% over the next five years, and even higher levels, starting one year from now since the current quoted one-year volatility is less than 30%. Even today, three to five-year volatility is quoted over 25%. In my view, this is extremely unlikely even given the evolving nature of the stocks that make up the index.

To put this in perspective, the quarterly realised volatility on the S&P 500 has averaged well below 15% over the past 10 years, and has never averaged more than 25% in any five-year period. These high volatility quotes are not restricted to the United States. In fact, in Europe three to five-year volatility was quoted as high as 40% in 1999 and quotes are still in the mid-30s.

Credit spreads and mortgage spreads have also widened dramatically. Although early in 1999, spreads narrowed somewhat, during summer 1999 they widened to even higher levels than those of August–September 1998. In fact, recently, the credit spreads have widened dramatically to the point where it is difficult to secure below investment-grade financing in the market. For these spreads to be default premiums, the market must expect large numbers of defaults, and defaults with little chance of recovery. I believe these outcomes are highly unlikely. Moreover, during August 1999, the 10-year on-the-run swap spread was as high as 112 basis points (bp) over treasuries, more than 15bp greater than at the height of the September 1998 crisis. These spread levels are extraordinary in that swap spreads were generally in the high 20s to the low 30s from 1992 to mid-1998, and never reached this level even in 1990, when banks including Citicorp and Bank of America experienced extreme difficulties.

It is hard to believe that these spread levels are attributable only to expectations of defaults in the credit market. Take the off-the-run swap spread as an example. The Libor rate is set for a time-frame, say three months, by averaging the quoted borrowing rates on a truncated set of the then 16 top-rated banks in the world, and does not depend on the survival of any particular bank. That is, if a bank were to become risky because its own prospects had diminished, it would be excluded from the computation of the next Libor index. Thus, for swap spreads to be entirely credit spreads, the market must perceive that the entire worldwide banking sector is to experience difficult times. What is even more amazing is that this perception would have to be true, not for this coming year, but for nine years starting one year from now. At the time of writing, one-year Libor is quoted at only 25–35bp over general-collateral-reverse repurchase agreements (reverse repo). That is, to borrow treasury bonds to sell to someone else in the market and to return similar bonds to the lender, the bond borrower would receive about 30bp below Libor. Thus, for the swap spread to be a credit spread, Libor must increase dramatically relative to repo rates, on average, during the nine years starting one year from now.

If these spreads are not entirely credit related, it is my belief that they must be liquidity spreads. At different times the market demands more liquidity and will pay for it. During the past couple of years, the number of liquidity providers diminished. Many financial institutions that previously devoted part of their capital to earning returns by supplying liquidity to the market withdrew from doing so or would only commit capital at much higher expected premiums.

To provide liquidity, an investor must have a longer horizon than the average market participant. Interestingly, because the liquidity premium is generally small relative to the expected return on alternative investments, liquidity providers are generally leveraged investors that must hedge other factor exposures. For them, risk management, particularly during a crisis when both credit risk and liquidity risk premiums balloon, is crucial.

INFORMATION SHORTAGE
Understanding risk management technology provides insights into the dynamics of liquidity premiums in asset returns. The risk management practice at large financial institutions, such as Citicorp or Merrill Lynch, affects the supply of liquidity and therefore the required liquidity premium. As liquidity premiums change, credit spreads and other spreads increase in the debt and equity markets around the world.

For a financial institution, a conventional balance sheet does not provide adequate information to insiders, or to outsiders such as investors or creditors, as to the risk of the entity. Balance-sheet leverage is a reduced-form static measure of risk; it provides no forecast of the firm's profit and loss as economic factors unfold in the economy. A risk management system is an exposure-accounting system and a control system. An exposure-accounting system is a dynamic system that gives managers an opportunity to assess the effects of changes in economic factors such as interest rate movements, yield curve shifts and reshaping, currency and commodity price moves, stock price movements, etc, on the economic profit and loss of the entity. It determines the firm's need for capital to support its positions.

During the past five years, value-at-risk (VAR) has become an accepted standard in the financial industry and forms the basis for determining a bank's regulatory capital for market risk. Many financial entities use it as a dynamic risk measure and it is often disclosed to investors. This approach to exposure accounting assumes that the future movements in risk factors are similar to past movements. That is, the variances and correlation matrix among factor exposures affecting profit and loss do not change over time. They are assumed to be stationary and normally distributed. The VAR measure is a probabilistic measure of loss potential measured over a specified holding period and to a specified level of statistical confidence. For example, the VAR might be calculated to be US$100 million for a two-week period with 99% probability. This implies that there is about a 1% chance that a loss greater than US$100 million would be sustained in the next two weeks.

Correlation patterns and variances, however, are not stationary, especially when market prices move dramatically. Factors that might exhibit low levels of correlation or association most of the time, appear to be highly correlated in volatile times. When the value of nearly all asset classes are moving in step, diversification is not helpful in reducing risk. The actual realised correlation patterns appear to be close to one. In these times, the volatility of profit and losses will be far greater than VAR would predict. In addition, liquidity and risk premiums change dramatically, resulting in far greater measured underlying asset volatility.

In periods of extreme market stress, as with global markets in 1987, in Japan in 1990 and so on, many statistically uncorrelated activities using historical data exhibited high degrees of association. For example, in 1998 the spreads over treasuries widened on US AAA bonds, AAA commercial mortgage pools, credit instruments, country risks and swap contracts. Moreover, volatilities on stock and bonds increased to levels not seen for decades. For example, on 21 August 1998, one week after Russia defaulted on its debt, swap spreads, the difference between the yield on 10-year swaps and government bonds, shot up from 60bp to 80bp in one day. This 20bp change was a 10 standard deviation move in the swap spread. After this date the volatility of the swap spread increased from eight-tenths of a basis point a day to 8bp a day and remained high throughout 1999.

STING IN THE TAIL

To protect against extreme shocks such as these, many financial entities impose stress-loss limits on their portfolios. These stress limits attempt to protect against extreme shocks in individual risk factors, as well as groups of risk factors. Their intent is to capture more extreme moves, the so-called "tail exposures". These stress limits might preclude the entity from concentrating in any one strategy or project, or from maintaining a position even though additional or continued investment had expected positive present value when using conventional present-value analysis to decide its worth.

Before the financial crisis in August 1998, most financial institutions were well within the guidelines for capital adequacy specified by the Bank for International Settlements (BIS) on standard measures such as VAR, leverage, or tier I or tier II capital. Then in August, investors rushed to more liquid securities increasing the demand and price of liquidity around the world. Investors liquidated large portfolios of assets in Asia and Latin and South America by selling into a market with high transaction costs. Many leveraged investors were forced to liquidate holdings to cover margin requirements.

Maybe part of the blame for the flight to liquidity lies with the International Monetary Fund (IMF). Investors believed that the IMF had given implicit guarantees to protect their investments against country-specific risks in the underdeveloped and less-developed regions of the world. But, when Russia defaulted on its debt obligations, market participants realised the implicit guarantees were no longer in place. Similarly, there may be a belief in the United States today that the Federal Reserve Bank provides a support to the markets in times of crisis by providing liquidity. This has led to the theory that investors should buy, or do buy, assets in a crisis. This, however, is not a sustaining policy, for if prices are inflated because of this implicit support, the policy will fail; the bubble will burst.

In an unfolding crisis, most market participants respond by liquidating their most liquid investments first to reduce exposures and to reduce balance sheet leverage. Transaction costs including spreads tend to be smaller in these markets. Since it is not possible to know the extent of the unfolding crisis, holding and not selling the less liquid instruments is similar to buying an option to hold a position. More liquid markets tend to be large and can handle large trading volumes fairly quickly. After the liquidation, however, the remaining portfolio is most likely unhedged and more illiquid. Without new inflows of liquidity, the portfolio becomes even more costly to unwind and manage. This leads to increased volatility in spread markets.

There has been little modelling of the stress-loss liquidity component of risk management and its implication for the price of liquidity. Although researchers are starting to adapt theory to studies of extreme moves in prices and their frequency of occurrence, these measures are reactive, claiming to provide a sufficient cushion of capital in the event of a stress shock. Financial institutions use stress-loss limits and capital cushions to mitigate crisis risk. They have moved from a static risk measure – leverage

– to a dynamic risk measure – VAR – with a static overlay – a stress-loss cushion – to provide an extra capital reserve in the event of a stress loss.

Any static risk measure, however, is not time-consistent. In a dynamic world, a dynamic policy is required to describe what actions to take as the cushion deteriorates or after it has been breached. What does the risk manager recommend as prices deteriorate further in the market? Obviously, risk reduction is not what a firm is interested in achieving. The important firm policy is profit maximisation. Thus, the firm must decide when to get back into the market and provide the liquidity that the market is willing to pay so highly for. Although stress-loss constraints appear to protect against the extreme market moves, they offer no dynamic answers once the cushion is breached.

It is commonly known that, as the adjustment gap between the stop-loss (the firm demands liquidity by selling positions into an illiquid market) and the price at which the firm re-acquires the position (again provides liquidity to the market) becomes small enough, the strategy is equivalent to replicating an option in the Black–Scholes world. Thus, a dynamic stop-loss policy values an option. This is currently not taken into account in stress-loss technology.

In this light, we can see that a put option provides the equivalent of a dynamic liquidity cushion. A put-protected position self-liquidates as money is lost and markets become more illiquid. We know that a long call option position is equivalent to a dynamic asset position plus borrowing. As the market price of the underlying asset falls, the put becomes increasingly in-the-money: its value moves inversely with, and more in line with, the price of the underlying asset. The cost of this protection is the value of liquidity. In reality, put options replace the role of the static stress cushion.

Conceptually, to value risk or to price reserves for its position, an entity must value the options it is not buying to protect itself in the event that it has an increased demand for liquidity. Since the stress limit is not priced, this tends to create the wrong capital allocation incentives within financial entities. If an entity buys options, it protects itself in a crisis and against negative jumps in asset values. Therefore, it must allocate capital to protect its tail exposures. Traders might argue that the cost of this protection is too great or not available. This might be true, or institutional arrangements have not yet been developed to provide this tail protection. More likely, the various risk desks would prefer that this cost not be explicitly priced into their trading books. This would reduce measured short-term profits and bring the measured profits closer to economic profits in non-crisis situations. This would tend to smooth profit participation and therefore the compensation of the participants of the business, who generally prefer to be paid larger amounts in non-crisis situations.

If, however, the entity establishes its own reserves, it must increase its reserves as position values fall or volatility increases, thereby forcing a dynamic adjustment to its reserves. The cushion (so to speak) must be dynamic. The entity, however, by dynamically hedging on its own account, cannot protect itself entirely. Gaps or jumps (unless of specific forms) cannot be hedged by employing internal dynamic adjustments. Providing for dynamic adjustments, however, is superior to the static risk cushions currently in place. Many financial products have two-way markets. Financial entities enter into contracts with customers and with other institutions and they tend to be long and short contracts with customers and other dealers. Because its exposures tend to net, the net risk position is quite low. This activity is called a matched book or agency business. The gross number of positions, however, becomes quite large. In addition, to reduce credit risk, many dealers and sophisticated entities post collateral to each other on price moves in the amount of the payment that would have to be made to a counterpart on a forced liquidation.

For many of its proprietary products, however, financial entities need to hedge risks by using the bond or equity markets. In a market crisis, the greatest losses most likely occur in this hedged-book business. In August 1998, those who were receiving in swaps and hedging by shorting government issues or selling long-dated equity options, and hedging by buying equity futures, suffered the greatest loss as spreads widened dramatically. The hedged books suffered loss because of changes in the economic fundamentals and because of an unanticipated jump in the demand for liquidity.

Again, in summer 1999 and spring 2000, as corporations and others issued bonds or hedged an anticipated increase in interest rates, the demand for liquidity increased with a decrease in institutional supply, as these institutions also demanded liquidity. Stress-loss cushions were violated and many financial entities reduced the size of their hedged-book positions at significant liquidation costs. Because the stress-loss cushions are static, entities have an ill-defined policy on when to supply liquidity and in what amounts. Banks and financial institutions are not the natural suppliers of liquidity and add to the volatility in financial crises.

In applying statistical risk models to analyse the hedged-book activities of financial institutions, changes in institutional arrangements must be factored into the models. United States interest rate swap spreads recently reached all time highs, with the 10-year on-the-run swap spread closing over 130bp (the off-the-run at 100bp).

Treasury bonds have long been used as hedging instruments. For example, dealers would hedge their inventory of corporate bonds by shorting treasury issues. After the crisis of 1998, dealers have moved to use swaps as hedging instruments. Although swaps have much lower credit risk and are closer to treasuries in risk, these institutional changes have resulted in a much higher degree of association of interest rate swap spreads with credit products in the market.

The United States is running a surplus and is expected to do so for the foreseeable future. Mr Summers and his cohorts would like to use the surplus to retire part of the federal debt. The Treasury has been repurchasing long-term treasuries. Traders and hedge-fund managers worry that a short position in treasury bonds cannot be maintained until maturity of the swap contract. As the supply of treasury bonds decreases, the market will become more vulnerable to short squeezes, and this will widen the repo-Libor spread. As perceived risks increase, investors rush to more liquid treasury issuers. Investors demand liquidity. Moreover, in this day and age, crises are more likely to be linked globally as correlations among instruments around the world approach one. These factors, coupled with the feared diminishing supply of treasuries, have led bond dealers to accelerate their movement away from treasuries to swaps to hedge their hedged-book business. Moreover, hedge fund capital is not as available as it used to be and that which still exists is more reluctant to receive in swaps and short treasuries to earn the carry on the trade.

Fannie Mae and Freddie Mac, maybe the world's two largest hedge funds, in an attempt to seize an opportunity to be the liquidity provider, now mimic the issuing schedules of the federal government to provide the hedging instruments to the market. Since their bonds are backed by a line of credit from the United States government, they have profited well by issuing at Libor −20 and buying mortgages to earn the spread. The Treasury, however, does not appear to favour the agencies inserting themselves as the supplier of hedging vehicles.

What does this mean for the future? As financial institutions rely on government paper to hedge their risks and to supply financial products and debt paper of various risks to the market, and do so on a leveraged basis, a new way to hedge risks is needed. In Europe, governments regularly tap markets to increase the supply of treasuries if short squeezes develop.

In Hong Kong and in countries running surpluses, institutional arrangements allow for government debt issues to be fungible. This reduces the possibility of short squeezes. The supply of bonds is effectively increased by allowing substitutions of adjacent issues with price adjustments. These changes may be necessary in the United States, as the demand for both new debt issues and financial products continues to grow. Moreover, new forms of capital providers will come into existence. I see a future where holders of longer-term capital can provide contingent capital to the capital markets as the price of liquidity increases. Currently, insurance companies, pension funds and other long-term holders of assets provide liquidity to the market by buying off-the-run and less liquid instruments. They tend to make longer-run decisions based on capital flows. There are insufficient dynamics in current institutional arrangements to smooth out the price of liquidity. But, forms of contingent capital will develop to affect the provision of liquidity and reduce the magnitude of spread increases in financial crisis.

CONCLUSION

Over the past few years, regulators have encouraged financial entities to use portfolio theory to produce dynamic measures of risk. VAR, the product of portfolio theory, is used for short-run, day-to-day profit and loss-risk exposures. Now is the time to encourage the BIS and other regulatory bodies to support studies on stress-test and concentration methodologies. Planning for crises is more important than VAR analysis. And such new methodologies are the correct response to recent crises in the financial industry.

The financial industry will become more creative in supplying or finding a source of supply of "liquidity" options and contingent capital to supply liquidity in times of stress. As the reinsurance market has developed for excess loss, similar markets could develop and add value in financial markets. This becomes an important role for alternative investments. The financial industry's use of the stop-loss technology produces volatility in liquidity premiums in many financial instruments. It does take time however, to develop new products and to educate potential new entrants into the market to replace them. More dynamic cushions will reduce the fluctuations in the price of liquidity and markets will become less prone to a financial crisis. The marketplace will find alternative providers and ways to supply liquidity.

From time to time, it is argued that financial quantitative modelling has failed because, even with the increase in measurement techniques, their use has not precluded financial crises or financial failures. Financial crises are prevalent throughout time and across countries. Although this might seem somewhat discouraging and a slam against financial modelling, it is not. This is so because better risk measurement models reduce costs and, as a result, financial firms develop new products and activities that make their constituents better off. Most likely, these new developments increase risk levels once again. As costs fall, economics predicts that agents move to the envelope.

Part II

Understanding Risk Budgeting

3

Risk Budgeting: Managing Active Risk at the Total Fund Level*†

Kurt Winkelmann

Goldman Sachs Investment Management

The main goal of this chapter is to show how institutional investors can utilise standard risk and portfolio management tools to systematically manage risk at the total fund level. In so doing, institutional investors may make better informed decisions regarding the composition of their portfolio. Specifically, we will review issues inherent in managing a multi-manager portfolio where the inclusion of many asset classes and many managers within each asset class make this exercise particularly applicable. To facilitate discussion, we use four examples to illustrate the four main steps in the analysis. Initially, we review the risk analysis of a strategic benchmark as an important first step in looking at total fund risk. This topic is important for two reasons:

❑ Most of the total risk in a multi-asset fund is likely to be due to the asset allocation decisions.
❑ Most funds have the choice of implementing their asset allocation through a purely passive manager roster.

Next, we address total active risk, and show how we can aggregate risks for individual managers, in the form of directional bias and tracking error, to find total fund risk characteristics. We also show how total fund tracking error can be decomposed for investment policy purposes. Additionally, we

*This chapter is reprinted with the permission of Goldman, Sachs & Co. It reflects the comments and suggestions of numerous GSAM professionals who work closely with these issues, including Robert Litterman, Tom Healey, Jacob Rosengarten, Alec Stais, Stan Kogelman, Thomas Dobler and Tracy McHale Stuart.
†This chapter contains simulations. Simulated results do not reflect actual trading and have certain inherent limitations. Please see appendix for further disclosures.

discuss how we can apply a Bayesian procedure (similar to the Black–Litterman global asset allocation model) to the process of manager selection. In particular, we demonstrate how one can combine market-wide information on managers with an investor's particular views on these managers to determine important characteristics such as the total fund information ratio, the total fund tracking error, and the allocation of risk by asset class and by manager. Finally, we show how one can apply this framework to decisions such as the use of global tactical asset allocation, rebalancing an existing manager roster and the use of portable alpha strategies. In this chapter, we discuss techniques that are relatively straightforward applications of risk management and asset allocation methodologies used throughout modern finance. We do not address issues that relate to asset classes where data collection is imperfect (eg, Private Equity). We will address these in future research reports.

Three key trends have recently emerged in institutional asset management. First, most institutional investors rely on asset allocation analyses to establish strategic benchmarks. Second, many managers (both passively and actively oriented) use the tools and terminology of quantitative analysis in the execution of their investment strategies. Finally, many institutional investors are exploring the application of the risk management technology that is used in many large banking operations. These three trends are unified by their reliance on the basic principles of portfolio theory.

This chapter shows how these principles apply to the problem of managing active risk at the total fund level. This problem can be naturally decomposed into two pieces, namely, the *measurement* of the active risk from an existing manager roster and the *development* of an optimal manager roster. In particular, the second step shows how the principles of portfolio theory can be used to establish an *active risk budget* (or an allocation of active risk) to individual asset classes and/or individual managers. More specifically, the idea that risk should be taken up to the point where the ratio of the incremental impact on performance to the incremental impact on portfolio (or fund) risk is the same for all asset classes (or managers), can be applied to find an optimal risk budget. *This phase of the analysis provides a framework for considering such practical decisions as the number of managers or the allocation to passive managers.*

Decomposing the problem in this way is especially useful because most funds have an existing manager roster (ie, a manager roster consistent with the optimal allocation of active risk) which provides a useful insight into those changes that are likely to have the most significant impact on the risk-adjusted performance of the total fund. Importantly, the analysis in this chapter relies on tools and techniques that are broadly familiar to institutional investors. The main contribution of this chapter is to show how these techniques can be practically applied to systematically manage risk at the total fund level. In so doing, institutional investors will be better able to make informed decisions regarding the composition of their portfolios.

This chapter is organised as follows. In the next section, the risk characteristics of a hypothetical strategic benchmark are analysed. The following section explores the active risk of a hypothetical active manager roster using a familiar risk decomposition methodology. The fourth section shows how standard portfolio optimisation techniques can be used to find a manger roster, while the fifth section discusses applications of the framework to global tactical asset allocation (GTAA), active portfolio restructuring and "portable alpha". Concluding comments are in the final section.

RISK CHARACTERISTICS OF A STRATEGIC BENCHMARK

There is a well-established procedure that many institutional investors use to establish their strategic benchmarks. This process usually begins by finding a target portfolio return, set with reference to the characteristics (actuarial or otherwise) of the liability stream.[1] After the target return has been set, practitioners usually select a set of asset classes that are relevant for their investment problem, and determine the long run risk and return characteristics of these asset classes.[2] At this point, an optimiser is generally used to develop an efficient frontier that shows the return maximising portfolios at various risk levels. From this efficient frontier, a portfolio is selected that best meets the overall risk and return characteristics of the liability stream. Finally the strategic asset allocation is translated into exposures to underlying indices (eg, the US Equity exposure for the strategic asset allocation is translated into exposure to indices such as the S&P 500 and the Russell 2000). The exposures to the underlying indices constitute the strategic benchmark.

Setting a strategic benchmark

In principle, the investor has the option of passively investing in the underlying indices. *Consequently, the risk (and return) characteristics of the strategic benchmark (ie, the purely passive alternative) are central to understanding and managing the risk (and return) characteristics at the total fund level.* For example, investors concerned about periods of negative returns in the capital markets may want to identify and structure a hedge. Alternatively, investors may want to know whether their portfolios are accurately reflecting their long-term strategic views. Solutions to questions such as these are predicated on an understanding of the basic risk (and return) characteristics of the strategic benchmark.

In this chapter, it is assumed that the process of finding a strategic benchmark has been completed. For illustrative purposes, it will be assumed that the result of the optimisation exercise has produced the strategic benchmark shown in Figure 1.[3] For comparison, Figure 1 also shows the weights for a global capitalisation weighted portfolio. The global

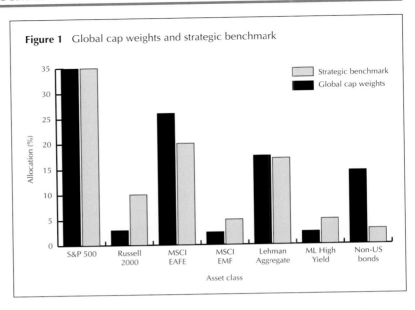

Figure 1 Global cap weights and strategic benchmark

capitalisation weighted portfolio serves as a useful reference point for portfolio analysis for two reasons: first, it is easy to observe and second, principles of basic portfolio theory suggest that each investor's portfolio should be a combination of cash and the global capitalisation weighted portfolio (Sharpe, Alexander and Bailey, 1995).

As illustrated in Figure 1, the strategic benchmark allocations are overweight equity in general, and US equity in particular. In the global capitalisation weighted portfolio, the US equity market is roughly 38% of the total equity weight. By contrast, in the strategic benchmark portfolio, US equities account for approximately 45% of the total equity exposure, with a bias towards small cap stocks (again relative to what is observed in the global capitalisation weighted portfolio). Furthermore, the strategic benchmark has a modest home bias (ie, tilt toward domestic equity) in its overall equity allocation.

Summary risk characteristics

Three questions can be asked about the strategic benchmark. First, in the aggregate, how do the risk and performance characteristics of the strategic benchmark compare with those of the global capitalisation weighted portfolio? Second, what are the principal sources of risk in the strategic benchmark? Finally, what are the implied views of the strategic benchmark and how do they compare with the returns associated with the global capitalisation weighted portfolio?

Table 1 shows the excess return (return over US cash rates), the volatility of excess return and the Sharpe ratio for the strategic benchmark and the

Table 1 Risk and return characteristics

	Strategic benchmark	GCW portfolio
Estimated expected excess return (%)*	4.10	3.95
Volatility (%)	9.20	8.55
Sharpe ratio	0.43	0.46

*There is no assurance that the strategy will achieve the estimated expected returns set forth above. Like any statistic characterised by uncertainty of outcomes, mathematical estimation methods are used in its derivation. Accordingly, there can be material variability associated with the estimation of expected return. In particular, expected return describes the average of a distribution of returns – it does not describe the variability or uncertainty embedded in the distribution of returns. Accordingly, these estimated expected returns are objectives, may not be achieved and are not guaranteed. These estimated expected returns do not represent actual trading, and future rates of return may vary significantly from those presented herein. Future returns are not guaranteed and a loss of principal may occur.

global capitalisation weighted portfolio. The volatility calculations were made with a covariance matrix representing the long-term (or strategic) volatility and correlation of each of the underlying asset classes (see Litterman and Winkelmann, 1998, for more detail on covariance matrix estimation). Portfolio returns for the strategic benchmark and the global capitalisation weighted portfolio were calculated using equilibrium returns for each asset class. These returns are illustrated in Figure 2.[4]

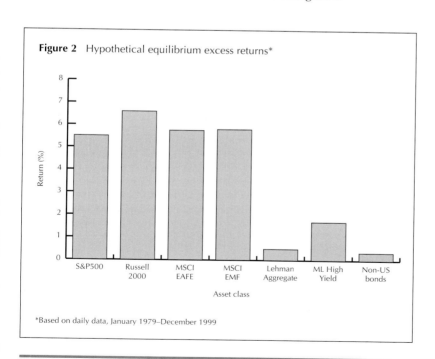

Figure 2 Hypothetical equilibrium excess returns*

*Based on daily data, January 1979–December 1999

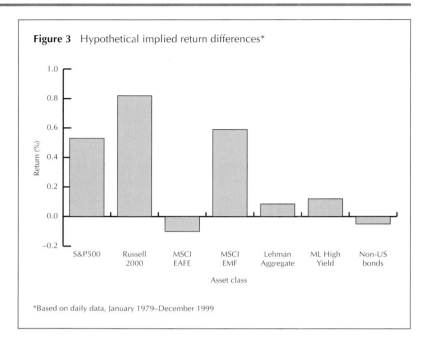

Figure 3 Hypothetical implied return differences*

*Based on daily data, January 1979–December 1999

We can see that the global capitalisation weighted portfolio is less volatile than the strategic benchmark, due in part to the higher exposure to fixed income. In addition, the strategic benchmark has a lower Sharpe ratio than the global capitalisation weighted portfolio, due to the lower level of diversification of equity risk.

Of course, the fact that the strategic benchmark has a lower Sharpe ratio than the global capitalisation weighted portfolio, on the basis of the equilibrium returns, is not surprising. The strategic benchmark has a tilt away from international stocks and towards US equity in general and US small cap in particular (shown in Figure 1). Thus, the issues are what views on expected returns are implied by the strategic benchmark and how these views compare with the equilibrium returns.

This question can be answered by appealing to an implied views analysis, shown in Figure 3. This exhibit shows the difference between the implied returns on the strategic benchmark and the equilibrium returns. The implied returns on the benchmark, in turn, reflect those returns that would make the strategic benchmark an optimal portfolio at the 9.2% volatility level. (More detail on implied views analysis is available in Litterman, 1996.)

In Figure 3, the implied equity returns on the strategic benchmark (relative to the global equilibrium returns) are generally bullish, which is consistent with the higher allocation to equity (again relative to the global capitalisation weighted portfolio). Furthermore, the implied return difference shows that the strategic benchmark is reflecting a more bullish view on US equity in general and small cap in particular than what is embedded in the global capitalisation weights. In the international markets, the strategic benchmark is expressing a relatively bullish view on emerging markets, and a relatively bearish view on developed markets.

How could this analysis be applied at the fund level? Two obvious applications are as a check on the actual strategic views and as a guide to potential restructuring. For example, suppose that the actual strategic asset allocation away from emerging markets and into US and international equity, the implied strategic views will more closely resemble the actual strategic views.

Identifying principal sources of risk

The final question that must be addressed about the strategic benchmark is its allocation of risk. Reiterating a point made earlier, this analysis is important because the strategic benchmark can be viewed as the purely passive alternative. Figure 4 shows a risk decomposition of the hypothetical strategic benchmark (shown in Figure 1) by asset class.[5] As is evident from the exhibit and consistent with the allocations shown in Figure 1, the strategic benchmark is taking the bulk of its risk in US equities. More specifically, 63.7% of the volatility of the strategic benchmark can be attributed to US equities. Figure 4 also shows that the second largest source of risk in this strategic benchmark is the allocation to developed International

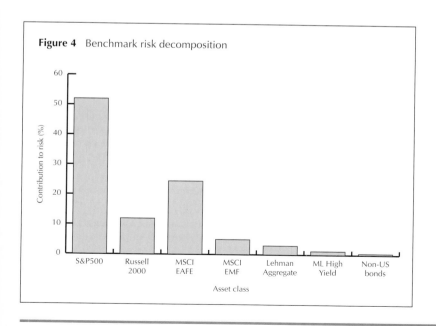

Figure 4 Benchmark risk decomposition

Equity: the exposure to MSCI EAFE accounts for approximately 25% of the volatility of the strategic benchmark. How would a fund apply this type of analysis?

Suppose that the fund were concerned about a general depreciation in global capital markets. Because of the potential impact on surplus of negative asset returns, the fund decides to pursue a short-term hedging strategy. An obvious strategy is to hedge the entire strategic benchmark by, for example, purchasing a basket put. However, this strategy has the disadvantage of being potentially expensive to the fund, due to the pricing on less liquid components of the portfolio (eg, emerging markets equity) and the general lack of correlation-based options products.

An alternative solution is to use a risk decomposition such as in Figure 4 and purchase puts only on the largest sources of risk. For example, US large cap and MSCI EAFE account for almost 80% of the portfolio volatility. These are two of the largest and most liquid sectors of the capital markets. Consequently, the cost of options strategies in these sectors can be anticipated to be lower relative to other sectors such as Emerging Markets Equity.

So far our analysis has focused on risk analysis of the strategic benchmark. As discussed above, this emphasis stems from the perception that the bulk of any investor's risk can be attributed to the strategic asset allocation decision. However, most institutional investors take active risk relative to their strategic benchmarks. The next section discusses how the same tools (implied views and risk decomposition), can be used to analyse the active risk at the total fund level.

ACTIVE RISK DECOMPOSITION

Many institutional investors have manager rosters that blend a number of portfolio management styles. The most obvious example is the trend towards blending passive and active managers. Active managers, of course, are added because of their presumed ability to outperform their benchmark. In adding value at the total fund level, active managers will consider decisions regarding the asset allocation, directional biases, security selection, sector rotation and other potential sources of value. Each of these decisions is likely to cause the actual total portfolio to deviate from its strategic benchmark.

Given the probable deviation of the actual portfolio from the strategic benchmark, it is useful to ask risk-based questions at the total fund level. For instance, we may want to calculate the total fund tracking error. Additionally, we may want to know how the total fund tracking error and the volatility of the strategic benchmark combine to produce total fund volatility. We may also want to know the sources of total fund tracking error: for instance, how much of the total fund tracking error can be attributed to the asset allocation decisions, directional biases and other

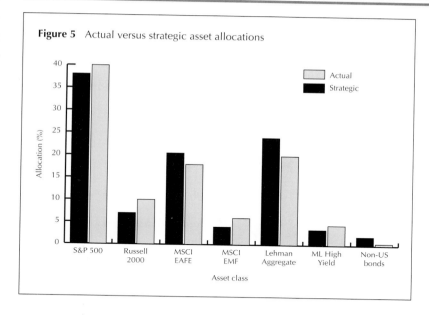

Figure 5 Actual versus strategic asset allocations

components of the active manager roster. Finally, we may want to know how each of these risk calculations performs in periods of financial stress.

These issues can be explored by continuing the example of the preceding section. Figure 5 provides an illustrative actual portfolio mix and compares it with the strategic benchmark. It is evident that the actual portfolio is overweight US equities in general and small cap in particular, underweight developed international equity, overweight emerging market equity, modestly underweight US investment grade fixed income and modestly overweight high yield. How do we calculate to total fund tracking error?

The total fund tracking error depends on any asset allocation mismatch (at the asset class level) and the tracking error for each asset class. The tracking error for each asset class, in turn, depends on the tracking error taken by each of the active managers. Thus, to compute the total fund tracking error we must first use information on the directional bias (see Litterman and Winkelmann, 1996) and tracking error for each manager to arrive at an asset class tracking error.[6]

Calculating tracking error within an asset class

Table 2 illustrates how to compute the tracking error within an asset class. The example uses a hypothetical roster of US large cap managers, each of which is measured relative to the S&P 500 index. Information on the tracking error, beta and weight of each manager is shown in the table. From these data, we can compute the tracking error and beta of all the US large cap managers.

Table 2 Hypothetical US large cap manager roster assumptions

Manager	Beta	Tracking error (bp)	Weight (%)
1	1.10	400	15
2	1.30	700	10
3	1.25	500	20
4	1.00	5	40
5	0.97	200	15
Total large cap	1.09	178	100

Table 3 Hypothetical tracking error by asset class assumptions

	Tracking error (bp)
S&P 500	178
Russell 2000	378
MSCI EAFE	298
MSCI EMF	654
Lehman aggregate	125
ML High Yield	374
Non-US bonds	129

It is important to keep in mind that the asset class tracking error depends on the correlation of excess returns between managers within the asset class.[7] For example, as the correlation of excess returns between two managers increases, the portfolio is taking on more exposure to the same underlying source of active risk. Consequently, the tracking error for the asset class also increases, since the sources of active risk in the asset class are becoming less diversified. Thus, one practical implication of our analysis is that investors should look for investment management styles that are complementary (ie, a correlation of excess returns close to zero) rather than substitutes. By doing so, the total fund tracking error can be reduced and the sources of active risk better diversified.

To compute the total fund risk characteristics, we need the risk characteristics for all of the asset classes. Continuing the example, Table 3 provides the hypothetical tracking error for all of the asset classes in the preceding exhibits. In Table 3, the asset class with the highest tracking error is emerging markets equity, followed by US small cap.[8]

Finding total fund active risk

Just as an assumption about the correlation of excess returns across managers *within an asset class* was required to determine the tracking error of an asset class, so, too, is an assumption required about the correlation of excess returns *across asset classes*. This assumption can be interpreted as measuring the degree to which active managers across asset classes are exposed to the same active risk factors. For example, a high correlation of excess returns between US investment grade fixed income managers and US large cap equity managers would indicate that active managers in both asset classes were using the same risk factors to take active positions. In this situation, active managers in both asset classes would be anticipated to outperform (or underperform) their benchmarks at roughly the same time.

Table 4 shows the aggregate risk characteristics for the example, under the assumption that excess returns are uncorrelated across asset classes. As the table shows, total fund tracking error is 223 basis points, with a beta of 1.09 and a total portfolio volatility of 10.25%.

Figure 6 illustrates how sensitive the total fund tracking error is to the assumption about the correlation of excess returns across asset classes. The impact of changes in the correlation assumption on tracking error is simulated for two portfolios. The first set of simulations uses the actual asset allocation differences (ie, those of Figure 5) while the second set of simulations shows the impact of the residual correlation assumption if the actual asset allocation equals the strategic benchmark weights. In this example, when asset class excess returns are perfectly correlated and the actual asset allocation is used, the total fund tracking error increases to 314 basis points. By contract, when asset class returns are perfectly correlated and there is no asset allocation mismatch, the total fund tracking error is only 250 basis points. This sensitivity analysis is important, as it provides a sense as to the potential ranges for predicted tracking error. These ranges can in turn be used to set overall fund policy.

Table 4 Total fund summary risk characteristics: model results	
Simulated total fund tracking error (bp)	223
Benchmark volatility (%)	9.20
Portfolio volatility (%)	10.25
Portfolio beta	1.09
Please refer to Tables 2 and 3 for assumptions.	

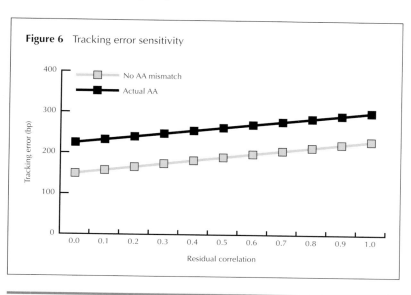

Figure 6 Tracking error sensitivity

The impact of "stressful" market environments

For example, suppose that markets are characterised by a "normal" period and a "stressful" period. Furthermore, suppose that in the normal period the correlation of excess returns across asset classes is close to zero, while in the stressful period, the correlation is closer to one. Using the figures in Figure 6 and the asset allocation mismatch of Figure 5, the total fund tracking error would be approximately 223 basis points in the normal market environment, while in the stressful period, the total fund tracking error would be predicted to be around 314 basis points. By contrast, the predicted total fund tracking error ranges from 135 basis points to 250 basis points if there is no asset allocation mismatch.

Suppose that the total fund policy is structured to tolerate no more than 220 basis points of predicted tracking error (set, for example, by the Investment Committee) – under normal circumstances – the fund would be close to the target range. However, when stressful environments occur, the predicted tracking error would violate the total fund policy. Among the policy choices available at the total fund level are the following: reduce the targeted tracking error to better represent the "normal" and "stressful" environments; explicitly characterise the tracking error target as corresponding to the "normal" environment, and reduce the magnitude of the asset allocation mismatch.

Identifying the sources of total fund tracking error

The total fund tracking error is an interesting figure in and of itself, as it provides information about the risk of deviating from a purely passive strategy. However, from the perspective of portfolio structuring, additional information is required. In particular, we would like to be able to identify the sources of the total fund tracking error.

Figure 7 decomposes the total fund tracking error at the asset class level under the assumption that the correlation of excess returns across asset classes is zero. At this level, it is evident that the bulk of the active risk is being taken in US equity: approximately 73% of the total fund tracking error can be attributed to US equity (36% large cap and 37% small cap). By contrast, only 1% of the total fund tracking error is attributable to US investment grade fixed income and non-dollar fixed income contributes nothing to total fund tracking error. Does this mismatch provide a re-balancing opportunity?

Suppose we assume that US fixed income has a positive active return. Under this assumption, the fund could possibly better diversify its total fund tracking error by re-balancing active risk away from US large cap and into US fixed income. Looked at differently, the fact that US fixed income is contributing negligibly to total fund active risk is consistent with an implied view that US fixed income cannot add value over what is embedded in the benchmark. Thus, the policy choices are either: re-balance or switch to passive managers in US fixed income.

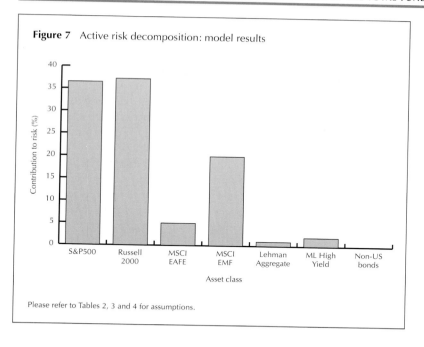

Figure 7 Active risk decomposition: model results

Please refer to Tables 2, 3 and 4 for assumptions.

Decomposing risk at the policy level

In addition to decomposing risk at the asset class level, we can also decompose risk at the total policy level, as illustrated in Figure 8 (and maintaining the assumption that the correlation of excess returns across asset allocation policy, beta (or directional) policy and residual policy (reflecting the impact of security selection, sector tilts, yield curve trades, etc).

In this example, 38% of the total fund tracking error is attributed to the asset allocation policy, while 38% is attributed to beta policy and 24% to residual policy. What are the actual portfolio management implications of these figures?

The beta and residual policies are reflections of the underlying portfolio management styles of the active managers. By contrast, the risk attributable to asset allocation policy is a reflection of policies at the total fund level, and is a direct result of the asset allocation mismatch shown in Figure 5. These mismatches can be intentional, ie, the result of a conscious decision to overweight or

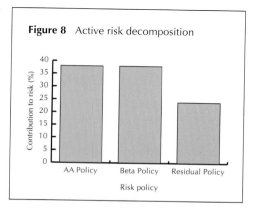

Figure 8 Active risk decomposition

underweight a particular asset class or otherwise (eg, infrequent re-balancing of the actual portfolio). *Irrespective of the source, however, it is the one decision that can be easily managed at the total fund level.* For instance, in our example the total fund tracking error decreases to 135 basis points when the asset allocation mismatch is eliminated.

How might the asset allocation mismatch be managed? Suppose that the mismatch is a result of infrequent re-balancing combined with periods of substantial returns in one or two asset classes. One obvious solution is to re-balance the portfolio back to the benchmark weights more frequently. However, this process by necessity increases transactions costs. An obvious alternative is to use a futures overlay programme to re-balance the portfolio on a more frequent basis.

Attributing risk at the individual manager level

The final important issue is to determine how much of the total fund tracking error is attributable to each manager. Table 5 provides an illustration, using our hypothetical manager roster. With the exception of two US equity managers, most of the active risk is distributed fairly evenly across the managers: one US large cap manager is contributing almost 13% of the active risk, while one US small cap manager is contributing around 19% of the total fund tracking error.

Table 5 Contribution of specific managers to total active risk

Manager	Asset class weight (%)	Benchmark	Risk contribution (%)
1	15	S&P 500	5.50
2	10	S&P 500	7.20
3	20	S&P 500	12.70
4	40	S&P 500	7.50
5	15	S&P 500	2.00
1	15	Russell 2000	4.03
2	20	Russell 2000	8.80
3	50	Russell 2000	18.60
4	15	Russell 2000	4.54
1	20	EAFE	1.06
2	50	EAFE	2.65
3	30	EAFE	3.40
1	50	EMF	10.20
2	50	EMF	9.20
1	30	Lehman Aggregate	0.24
2	30	Lehman Aggregate	0.24
3	40	Lehman Aggregate	0.24
1	50	WGBI × US	−0.12
2	50	WGBI × US	−0.12
1	40	ML High Yield	0.98
2	60	ML High Yield	1.30

The active risk can also be attributed to policies at the individual manager level. In the case of the small cap manager, the 19% contribution is attributed as follows: 10.3% is due to asset allocation policy (both the allocation to small cap and the allocation to the particular manager); 6.9% is attributed to beta policy and only 1.4% is attributed to residual policy. One policy implication could be to reduce the allocation to this particular manager or reduce the overweight position in US small cap in general.

By contrast, the US large cap manager's contribution to total fund active risk is decomposed as follows: 1.8% from asset allocation policy; 8.9% from beta policy and 1.9% from residual policy. These figures indicate that the most important contribution to risk from this manager will be their ability to decide when to be long or short exposure to the market.

It is important to bear in mind though, that the one decision that can be easily managed at the total fund level is the asset allocation mismatch. As discussed above, total fund tracking error can be reduced to 135 basis points simply by eliminating the mismatch between the actual asset allocation and the strategic benchmark. In addition to its importance in the definition of the strategic benchmark, asset allocation also seems to be important to the total fund active risk.

The examples have shown how risk can be measured and monitored at the total fund level. These examples have relied on hypothetical data and assumptions regarding the correlation of excess returns across managers and across asset classes. It is fair to conclude that to fully implement this approach at the fund level imposes additional requirements for data collection. For example, the correlation of excess returns across managers within an asset class could be corroborated through either commercially available products or the collection of daily returns. The same sources can, in principle, be used to corroborate the correlation of excess returns across asset classes.

FINDING AN ACTIVE MANAGER ROSTER

The preceding sections focused on measuring and monitoring the active risk at the total fund level. Our discussion was cast in terms of illustrative examples, when an underlying hypothetical manager roster was assumed. However, we can turn the problem around and ask how we determine a manager roster from first principles. The framework suggested here can also be used to find solutions to such questions as:

❑ In which asset class should active risk be taken?
❑ How many managers should be chosen? and
❑ What percentage of the assets should be actively versus passively managed?

Each of these issues is addressed below. It is a truism to state that active deviations from the strategic benchmark are taken in anticipation of

A BASIC OPTIMISATION PRINCIPLE

Our basic optimisation principle is that the information ratio is optimised when the ratio of the marginal impact on performance to the marginal impact on active risk is the same for all assets, assuming no constraints. Of course, the marginal impact on total active performance for any asset is just the asset's return. Consequently, the optimality condition can be restated as saying that the ratio of the asset return to the marginal contribution to active risk should be the same for all assets. One convenient way to restate this condition is that the relative returns on any two assets should equal the ratio of the marginal contributions to risk.

Figure A plots these two ratios in a two asset portfolio. The ratios are plotted as a function of the allocation to the first asset. As the graph illustrates, the expected return on the first assets is two times the expected return on the second asset. This ratio does not vary with the allocation to the first asset.

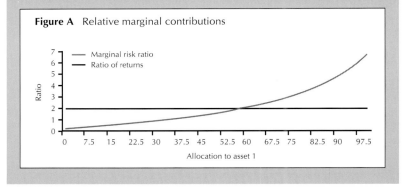

Figure A Relative marginal contributions

outperforming the strategic benchmark. However, it is also true (as illustrated previously) that active deviations from the strategic benchmark lead to active risk. Consequently, a useful way to think about the level of total fund tracking error is in terms of the information ratio, ie, the ratio of active performance to active risk.

Suppose that the objective is to maximise the information ratio at the total fund level. Active managers will be added only if their expected outperformance (or alpha) is positive, and adding an active manager (or making a larger allocation away from passive into an existing active manager) will increase the expected out-performance at the total fund level. However, the impact of additional active managers on the total fund

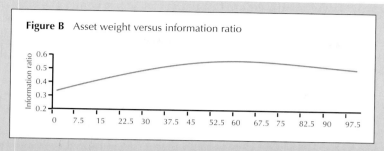

Figure B Asset weight versus information ratio

The graph also shows the ratio of the marginal contributions to risk. For small allocations to the first asset, the marginal impact on total portfolio risk of the first asset is dominated by the marginal impact of the second asset. Consequently, and as illustrated in Figure B, the total fund information ratio increases by switching from the second asset to the first.

However, for allocations beyond the optimal allocation, the marginal impact on active risk of the first asset relative to the second asset dominates any potential return enhancement. As a result, the information ratio begins to decline.

tracking error (or total fund active risk) is not as straightforward. As it turns out (and as illustrated in the previous section), the impact of increasing the allocation to an active manager depends on the manager's tracking error relative to their benchmark, the correlation between the excess return of the manager and all other managers and the relative allocations to managers. Thus, the impact on total fund information ratio of increasing exposure to an active manager is uncertain. However, a general principle can be followed: the total fund information ratio is maximised when the ratio of the marginal impact on total fund expected out-performance (net of fees) to the marginal impact on total fund tracking error is the same for all active managers. Indeed, this principle is merely an extension of the one used to determine an optimal asset allocation.

Of course, applying this principle to an entire universe of managers would be cumbersome, would run into many constraints and could lead to a non-intuitive manager roster. Consequently, it is worthwhile to impose a loose structure on our problem. The structure explored here works as follows: first, we will consider optimal active risk allocations to asset classes, under the constraint that the actual and strategic asset allocations are the same. The output from this step is an allocation of active risk at the asset class level. Second, we will consider optimal manager structure within an asset class. The output from this step is the number of managers and the split between active and passive managers. Finally, we will consider the implications of relaxing the constraints on the asset allocation.

Active risk allocation at the asset class level

Our first step is to find an optimal allocation of active risk at the asset class level. The principle just outlined for selecting an entire manager roster can also be used at the asset class level. In this case, active risk is taken in asset classes up to the point where the ratio of the marginal impact on total fund excess return (over the benchmark) to total fund tracking error is the same for all asset classes.

The general principle can be easily restated as follows. Looking at the performance part of the ratio, the marginal contribution to performance for any asset (or asset class or manager) is merely the return on the asset (or asset class alpha). Hence, the asset class contribution to total active performance is just the portfolio weight multiplied by the asset return (or asset class alpha). Turning our attention to the risk part of the ratio, by multiplying the marginal contribution to risk by the asset weight and then dividing by the overall risk level, we get the asset class marginal contribution to risk in percentage terms. Thus, the general principle can be restated as saying we want to take active risk up to the point where the ratio of the contribution to total active performance to the marginal contribution to active risk in percentage terms is the same for all asset classes.[9]

To implement this principle, we must now describe projected out-performance, projected tracking error and the projected correlation between excess returns at the asset class level. Fortunately, median excess returns and tracking errors can be described by using readily available data. For illustrative purposes, we will assume that the correlation between excess returns at the asset class level is zero.

Table 6 illustrates the type of information on median managers that could potentially be used. The table shows (hypothetical) median tracking errors and information ratios (net of fees) for all of the asset classes used in the preceding sections. The table also shows a (hypothetical) targeted information ratio for each asset class.

Table 6 Active manager information by asset class

Asset class	Hypothetical median manager information ratio	Hypothetical median manager tracking error (bp)	Hypothetical targeted information ratio
US large cap	0.04	525	0.17
US small cap	0.47	825	0.63
International equity	0.42	750	0.54
Emerging markets	0.38	900	0.56
US fixed income	0.37	100	0.59
US high yield	0.36	400	0.51
Non-dollar bonds	0.26	350	0.55

In this table, the excess return (net of fees) and corresponding information ratio of the median US large cap manager are close to zero. Thus, one might be tempted to structure a purely passive portfolio in US large cap. However, doing so means that we are ignoring the evidence that some managers have done better (at least historically) than the median manager.

Alternatively, a portfolio could be structured that made use of only the information on the targeted managers. Following this approach, though, ignores the information that half the managers will do no better than median performance. Ideally, we would make use of all available information to arrive at our total active risk in US large cap.

One possible resolution to our problem is to apply a Bayesian optimisation environment similar to that described in the Black–Litterman Global Asset Allocation Model (Black and Litterman, 1991). The Black–Litterman model provides an intuitive way to calculate expected returns at the asset class level from market-determined expected returns and an investor's own views. For instance, the expected return on US large cap stocks is a function of the market equilibrium and an investor's view of the US stock market (and potentially other views). As less weight is put on the investor's views, the expected returns more closely resemble the market equilibrium returns. This approach is by now a standard part of the tool kit for finding strategic asset allocations.

The same tools can be applied to our problem by reinterpreting the market equilibrium and the investor views in the context of active manager excess returns. Suppose, for instance, that the median manager excess return and tracking error take the role played by the market equilibrium return and volatility in the strategic asset allocation. These data are readily available to all investors and consequently represent market-wide information. The median manager information ratios play the same role for the active management problem as the market equilibrium returns do for the strategic asset allocation problem; they represent a neutral reference point.

Similarly, suppose that there is a specific manager roster about which investors have a particularly favourable view. In this setting, the targeted information ratio for this specific manager roster plays the same role as an investor's views on asset returns does for the strategic asset allocation. Now we can find the active expected return by assigning weights to each component. Looking again at US large cap, when more weight is assigned to the "equilibrium", the active excess return is close to zero and consequently little (if any) active risk is taken in US large cap.

Table 7 illustrates these points by showing the median return, the hypothetical targeted return (representing the manager roster about which we are assumed to have more specific information) and the expected active return for each of the asset classes of Table 6. The data in Table 7 assume that the tracking error is the same for the median active manager and the hypothetical manager roster. (Relaxing this assumption does not

Table 7 Hypothetical mean excess returns by asset class*

Asset class	Median manager hypothetical excess return (bp)	Targeted return (bp)	Blended hypothetical excess return (bp)
US large cap	21	90	30
US small cap	388	520	450
International equity	315	405	350
Emerging markets	342	504	465
US fixed income	37	59	49
US high yield	144	204	174
Non-dollar bonds	91	193	137

The hypothetical mean excess returns are based on the Black–Litterman model adjusted to reflect our subjective expectation that the returns of an asset class in excess of the risk-free rate will be higher or lower than they have been historically. These adjustments and the ensuing hypothetical rates of return as well as the volatilities and correlations are used solely to apportion investments to each asset class, and they are shown here solely to illustrate that process. They are not actual historical returns. They also are not, and should not be viewed as, predictions or projections of future returns of those classes of assets or any investments, including any fund or separate account managed by GSAM, GS & Co., or any other brokerage account. Future returns may be different from historical returns or from these hypothetical returns.

qualitatively change the procedure.) Now our task is to find the total fund risk and return characteristics.

Table 8 shows an optimal allocation of risk for the expected active return figures of Table 7 and the strategic benchmark allocations of Figure 1. The output from such an optimisation exercise includes the contribution to active risk in percentage terms, the contribution to total expected active performance and the tracking error within each asset class. *Thus, the process of determining an optimal risk budget also sets the tracking error within each asset class.*

For example, the contribution to total active performance to US fixed income is 12 basis points and the contribution to total tracking error is 10%. The combined tracking error for all US fixed income managers that achieves these figures and *is consistent with the rest of the active risk allocations* is 100 basis points.

Table 8 Asset class risk and performance characteristics

Asset class	Contribution to total active risk (%)	Contribution to Active performance	Asset class targeted tracking error
US large cap	5	7	40
US small cap	20	25	400
International equity	40	55	200
Emerging markets	14	20	600
US fixed income	12	15	100
US high yield	7	8	400
Non-dollar bonds	2	3	125

Selecting specific managers

The tracking error figures shown in Table 8 serve as targets for the aggregation of the manger roster within each asset class. However, there are multiple combinations of managers that can achieve the tracking error target. For instance, in Table 8 the optimal tracking error in US large cap is 40 basis points, with an expected contribution to active return (net of fees) of seven basis points. These risk/return characteristics can potentially be met with one manager with identical portfolio characteristics, or a combination of managers with less volatile and more volatile performance. (In the limit, the risk/return characteristics for US large cap can be met with a passive manager and one active manager with higher overall tracking error.) What choices need to be made in selecting managers?

The first issue to confront is the size of the manager universe. Implicitly, the size of the universe has already been reduced to those managers for which the investor has specific information. The universe can be further reduced by looking for managers with uncorrelated excess returns, we are able to diversify the active risk across individual managers. An additional benefit of this process is the potential to reduce management fees.

After reducing the size of the universe, the second issue is to develop allocations to each active manager. An optimal allocation to managers can be found by applying the general principle outlined above: allocations to managers should be made up to the point where the marginal contribution to expected out-performance (net of fees) is equal to the marginal contribution to asset class tracking error.

The final issue that must be confronted is to adjust the total asset class tracking error from the optimal manager selection to the tracking error selected in the asset class optimisation. This is the step that solves the active/passive split. For example, suppose that the optimal allocation to specific active managers leads to a US large cap tracking error of 75 basis points. However, the result of the asset class optimisation produced a tracking error of 40 basis points for US large cap. This target can be achieved by reducing the allocation to the portfolio of active managers and increasing the proportion that is passively managed (under the assumption that the correlation between manager excess returns and the strategic asset allocation is zero).

This section has developed a general approach to establishing an initial manager roster. The framework relies on commonly used asset allocation techniques. In particular, the framework uses a Bayesian approach similar to the Black–Litterman model to determine the active return in each asset class as a function of market-wide information (represented by the characteristics of the median manager) and investor-specific information. By applying the condition that risk is taken up to the point where the ratio of the marginal contribution to performance to the marginal contribution to risk is the same across all asset classes (or active managers) we arrive at an optimal manager structure. The next section applies this methodology to the following problems: adding a GTAA mandate; restructuring an existing portfolio and so-called "portable alpha".

APPLICATIONS

The optimisation framework outlined in the preceding section was predicated on the assumptions that an initial manager roster was being developed, and that the portfolio's asset allocation equalled that of the strategic benchmark. This section explores the implications of relaxing both of these assumptions. In particular, this section discusses how the framework of the previous section can be applied to the evaluation of global tactical asset allocation, the re-balancing of an existing manager roster and the use of portable alpha strategies.

Global tactical asset allocation

Relaxing the constraint that the portfolio and strategic benchmark have the same asset allocation provides an opportunity to take advantage of tactical asset allocation products. Global tactical asset allocation (GTAA) products take advantage of potential opportunities from trading across asset classes. To fully exploit these products, we believe the active risk attributable to asset allocation from all other products should be close to zero. That is, the active risk decomposition (as discussed in the third section of this chapter) of the remaining managers should have close to no risk attributable to asset allocation. If this is not the case, then before a GTAA programme is implemented, the asset allocation risk from the other managers should be neutralised, either through portfolio re-balancing or through a futures overlay programme.

The issue now becomes one of deciding how much active risk should be taken in GTAA. This question can be easily answered by appealing to the earlier principle: that is, allocations to GTAA are made up until the point where the ratio of the marginal impact (net of fees) on total fund performance to total fund tracking error is equal to the same ratio for all other products. When the ratio for GTAA exceeds that of the remaining products, the total fund information ratio can be improved by adding GTAA exposure.

Re-balancing an existing active manager roster

The discussion in the preceding section was based on the assumption that an initial active manager roster was being developed. However, most investors already have manager rosters. Furthermore, there are transactions costs (both explicit and implicit) of re-balancing the manager roster. Thus, even if an investor wanted to re-balance the entire manager roster, it would not necessarily be prudent to do so. How can our framework be applied?

A natural question would be to ask which changes in the active manager roster are likely to have the most significant impact on the total fund information ratio. To answer this question, the investor would begin by identifying an optimal manager roster, using the techniques discussed in the preceding section. Next, the investor would compare the active risk and return of the optimal manager roster with those of the existing manager roster. Finally, the investor would identify those changes in the manager roster (both allocations to existing managers and the introduction of new managers) that move the total fund information ratio closest to the optimal information ratio. Usually, a small number of changes to the manager roster lead to a substantial improvement in the risk-adjusted performance.

Evaluation of portable alpha strategies

A portable alpha strategy is one where the active performance relative to one benchmark is superimposed on another benchmark. For example, the active return for a US fixed income manager would be superimposed on the benchmark return of the S&P 500. In this example, the fixed income active performance is "ported" to the S&P 500 benchmark. To port the active return from one benchmark and gain exposure to the other benchmark. The reason for this is that the manager is naturally long the asset class where they are expecting to gain the active return. In our example, the US fixed income manager is naturally long exposure to a US fixed income index (eg, the Lehman Brothers Aggregate Bond Index).

One obvious way to transfer the active return from one index to another is through the use of total return swaps.[10] In our example, the manager is naturally long US fixed income (the exposure that must be hedged) and would like to be long the S&P 500. Thus, the manager would enter into a swap where they agreed to pay the return on the S&P 500. Consequently, the active return versus the Lehman Brothers Aggregate Bond Index has been transferred to the S&P 500.

The existence of portable alpha strategies and implementation vehicles such as total return swaps provides another means of enhancing the total fund information ratio. For example, suppose that the strategic benchmark has 28% allocated to US fixed income and 35% allocated to US large cap. Suppose furthermore that the expected information ratios are higher on US fixed income than on US large cap. Including the constraint that the actual and strategic asset allocations must be the same means that the active manager roster will never have more than 28% allocated to US fixed income nor less than 35% allocated to US large cap. Thus, the constraint imposes the real cost of not being able to take full advantage of the extra information available through the US fixed income managers.

Now, suppose that the constraint is relaxed and that the optimal manager roster is overweight in US fixed income by 3% and underweight by the same amount in US large cap. In other words, the actual allocation to US fixed income is 31% and the actual allocation to US large cap is 32%. For discussion purposes, suppose that the reallocation of active risk adds an extra five basis points to the *total* active performance. This structure has the advantage of gaining exposure to the active return in US fixed income, yet also has the disadvantage of exposing the total fund to potentially unintended asset allocation risk.

The natural solution to this problem is to transfer the alpha from the incremental 3% back to the S&P 500. Using our example, a total return swap for 3% of the portfolio value would be used to transfer the alpha from US fixed income back to the S&P 500. Of course, we would need to weigh the cost of the swap against the incremental active return. For illustrative purposes, suppose that the net cost of the swap to the *overall* portfolio is one basis point. As a result, the net return at the fund level of shifting active risk away from US large cap and into US fixed income is around four basis points. From a risk perspective the asset allocation component has been neutralised, yet the higher active return available (in our example) from US fixed income has been more fully exploited.

CONCLUSION

This chapter has explored ways in which standard risk and portfolio management tools apply to the problems of managing a multi-manager portfolio. This exercise should be of particular importance to funds with many asset classes and many managers within each asset class. The chapter initially discussed the risk analysis of a strategic benchmark. This topic is important for two reasons. First, most of the total risk in a multi-asset fund is likely to be due to the asset allocation decisions. Second, most funds have the choice of implementing their asset allocation through a purely passive manager roster. Thus, understanding the risk of the strategic benchmark provides an important first step in looking at total fund risk.

After discussing risk in the context of the strategic benchmark, the chapter next addressed the issue of total active risk. In this context, the chapter showed how risks (in the form of directional bias and tracking error) for individual managers can be aggregated to find total fund risk characteristics. The chapter further demonstrated how total fund tracking error can be conveniently decomposed for investment policy purposes.

In addition to discussing total fund risk analysis, the chapter has discussed how a Bayesian methodology (in the spirit of the Black–Litterman model) can be applied to the manager selection problem. In particular, the paper showed how market-wide information on managers can be combined with an investor's particular views on managers to determine important characteristics such as the total fund information ratio, the total fund tracking error and the allocation of risk by asset class and by manager.

Finally, the chapter showed how the framework can be applied to decisions such as the use of global tactical asset allocation, re-balancing an existing manager roster and the use of portable alpha strategies.

The techniques discussed in this chapter are relatively straightforward applications of risk management and asset allocation methodologies used throughout modern finance. The research issues left open here relate to asset classes where data collection is imperfect (eg, private equity).

1   The strategic benchmark can also be viewed as that portfolio of assets that best hedges the liability stream. Interpreted as a strict hedge, the strategic benchmark is that portfolio that minimises the volatility of the surplus (ie, the volatility of the difference between the return on the assets and the "return" on the liabilities).

2   The determination of long run return and risk characteristics for each asset class is a central component to finding a strategic asset allocation. To assess long run returns, many practitioners use historical average returns. These returns, however, are dependent on the choice of time period. Many practitioners are now finding their long run expected returns as a blend of a market equilibrium return and a predicted return (driven by models or fundamental views). (See Black and Litterman, 1991.)

3   A survey in *Pensions and Investments* (January 25, 1998) assessed the asset allocation of Corporate Defined Benefit assets as follows: US equity – 46.7%; US fixed income – 27.2%; international equity – 14.2%; international fixed income – 1.7%; cash – 2.1%; private equity – 2.8%; real estate – 3.3%; other – 2.0%.

4   The equilibrium returns can be interpreted as those returns that would make the global capitalisation weighted portfolio optimal. (See Black and Litterman, 1991, for a description of the calculation of equilibrium returns.) To calculate the equilibrium returns, an asset pricing model must be calibrated by the selection of a risk aversion parameter. In Figure 2, the risk aversion parameter was chosen so that the equity premium (return over cash) on the S&P 500 is 5.5%.

5   Since the calculation of volatility is non-linear, the risk decomposition is a local approximation. Litterman (1996) has a deeper discussion of the decomposition of risk.

6   Underlying the analysis is the following model. Denote the return (over cash) of manager m in asset class i for period t as R_t^{mi}. Similarly, denote the return (over cash) of the asset class i benchmark as R_t^{ib}. Let b^{mi} be manager m's beta with respect to benchmark i and let e_t^{mi} be the residual term. Manager m's returns can be represented as $R_t^{mi} = b*R_t^{ib} + e_t^{mi}$. Now, decompose e_t^{mi} as $e_t^{mi} = u_t^i + u_t^{mi}$ where u_t^i is a residual term that is common across the asset class and u_t^{mi} is idiosyncratic to any manager m within the asset class. Finally, assume that u_t^i is orthogonal to u_t^{mi}. This structure gives us the flexibility to both aggregate the tracking error in the way described and decompose the risk into the policy decisions described later in the main text.

7   The correlation of excess returns within an asset class essentially captures the extent to which two managers are substitutes. The more highly correlated the excess returns of two managers, the more they are acting as substitutes.

8   For the purposes of Tables 2 and 3, the correlation of excess returns across managers within an asset class is assumed to be 0.25.

9   In an unconstrained world, the optimal portfolio weights must satisfy the following condition: $[R_i / \bullet \{X_j * cov(R_i, R_j)\}] = [R_k / \bullet \{X_j * cov(R_k, R_j)\}]$, for all pairs of i and k, where X_i and R_i are the holding and return of asset i. Multiply the numerator and denominator of the left-hand side by X_i. The quantity $X_i R_i$ is the total contribution of asset i to portfolio performance, which can be denoted TCP_i. The optimality condition now says that $TCP_i / X_i * \bullet \{X_j * cov(R_i, R_j)\}] = [TCP_k / X_k * \bullet \{X_j * cov(R_k, R_j)\}]$. Now, multiply both sides by the portfolio variance. Rearranging slightly, the optimality condition is now: $TCP_i / pct_i = TCP_k / pct_k$, where pct_i is the marginal contribution to portfolio volatility in percentage terms from asset i.

10 Total return swaps are not the only vehicle for implementing portable alpha strategies. In addition, futures can be used (where they exist). The choice between futures and swaps depends on transaction costs and basis risks, to name two.

ADDITIONAL NOTES
Simulated, modelled or hypothetical results

Simulated performance results have certain inherent limitations. Such results are hypothetical and do not represent actual trading, and thus may not reflect material economic and market factors, such as liquidity constraints, that may have had an impact on the Adviser's actual decision-making. Simulated results are also achieved through the retroactive application of a model designed with the benefit of hindsight. The results shown reflect the reinvestment of dividends and other earnings, but do not reflect advisory fees, transaction costs and other expenses a client would have paid, which reduce return. No representation is made that a client will achieve results similar to those shown.

The following table provides a simplified example of the effect of management fees on portfolio returns. For example, assume a portfolio has a steady investment return, gross of fees, of 0.5% per month and total management fees of 0.05% per month of the market value of the portfolio on the last day of the month. Management fees are deducted from the market value of the portfolio on that day. There are no cashflows during the period. The table shows that, assuming that other factors such as investment return and fees remain constant, the difference increases due to the compounding effect over time. Of course, the magnitude of the difference between gross-of-fee and net-of-fee returns will depend on a variety of factors, and the example is purposely simplified.

Period	Gross return (%)	Net return (%)	Differential (%)
1 year	6.17	5.54	0.63
2 years	12.72	11.38	1.34
10 years	81.94	71.39	10.55

The hypothetical mean returns are based on the Black–Litterman model adjusted to reflect our subjective expectation that the returns of an asset class in excess of the risk-free rate will be higher or lower than they have been historically. These adjustments and the ensuing hypothetical rates of return as well as the volatilities and correlations are used solely to apportion investments to each asset class, and they are shown here solely to illustrate that process. They are not actual historical returns. They also are not, and should not be viewed as, predictions or projections of future returns of those classes of assets or any investments, including any fund or separate account managed by GSAM, GS & Co., or any other brokerage account. Future returns may be different from historical returns or from these hypothetical returns.

The portfolio risk management process includes an effort to monitor and manage risk, but should not be confused with and does not imply low risk.

BIBLIOGRAPHY

Black, F., and R. Litterman, 1991, "Global Asset Allocation with Equities, Bonds and Currencies", Goldman, Sachs & Co, Fixed Income Research.

Litterman, R., and K. Winkelmann, 1998, "Estimating Covariance Matrices", Goldman, Sachs & Co, Risk Management Series.

Litterman, R., and K. Winkelmann, 1996, "Managing Market Exposure", Goldman, Sachs & Co, Risk Management Series.

Litterman R., 1996, "Hot Spots and Hedges", Goldman, Sachs & Co, Risk Management Series.

Sharpe, W., G. Alexander and J. Bailey, 1995, Investments, Fifth Edition (Englewood Cliffs: Prentice Hall).

4

The Dangers of Historical Hedge Fund Data

Andrew B. Weisman and Jerome D. Abernathy*

Nikko Securities International and Stonebrook Structured Products LLC

Risk budgeting provides an excellent framework for combining the competing interests of mean-variance efficiency and the precise liability constraints faced by an institutional investor. Such a framework is not, however, directly applicable to certain classes of investments, most notably hedge funds. The risk budgeting process typically requires the development of statistically derived characterisations of targeted investments. If statistically derived descriptions are inaccurate or systematically biased in some respect, then the optimisation process will tend to "error maximise" and produce undesirable portfolio allocations. Hedge funds are highly susceptible to mischaracterisation. The typical shortness of hedge fund track records, in conjunction with the lack of stationarity of returns and the inaccuracy of performance data, presents a substantial challenge to portfolio managers who wish to include such investments in their portfolios. This chapter presents a simple method for more conservatively describing the performance characteristics of hedge funds known as Generic Model Decomposition (GMD). Additionally, this chapter presents two sample decompositions and discusses two potentially troublesome performance measurement bias issues that become evident through the use of GMD.

Risk budgeting provides institutional investors with a rational and reasonably objective framework for formulating and justifying asset allocation decisions. This methodology allows an investor to formulate decisions in the context of modern portfolio theory, the capital asset pricing model and institution-specific liability considerations. Additionally, it provides a valuable optimisation criteria with respect to both asset-class and active-risk allocation. The risk budgeting framework is not, however,

*The authors would like to thank Mark Anson, Masao Matsuda, Timothy Birney and Richard Michaud for their thoughtful comments. The authors remain responsible for any errors.

directly applicable to all classes of investments. So-called "alternative" investments, particularly hedge funds, require additional consideration.

Institutional investors, in an effort to achieve ever-greater degrees of mean variance efficiency, have been making strategic allocations to alternative investment vehicles. While the bulk of this investment has been directed at venture capital, in the past few years there has been an increasing interest in hedge funds. In order to accommodate hedge funds into an institutional asset management framework, investors have been forced to deal with a number of very thorny issues. Most notably, hedge funds are referred to as "alternative" investments precisely because they tend to employ hybrid strategies with unique approaches to trade selection and money management, and because they were usually created to take advantage of relaxed indexation. Almost by definition, therefore, they are difficult to incorporate into a traditional investment program due to the lack of appropriate benchmarks. Consequently, there is a lack of properly developed measures of risk, return and correlation. Despite this concern, hedge fund portfolio managers ("fund of funds" managers) and consultants make extensive use of historical data for the purposes of manager selection and portfolio construction. Sadly, the use of historical hedge fund data in association with conventional portfolio optimisation techniques frequently results in portfolios that, in practice, maximise risk and illiquidity.

QUANTIFYING HEDGE FUND RETURNS

Most methods of quantitative analysis assume that managers' distributions of returns and correlation coefficients versus those of other managers are stationary. This is reasonably true in respect of correlation coefficients, but never true for distributions of returns. While historical returns can be useful for characterising risk and return, this is usually true only when data of adequate length and accuracy are available to permit a measure of a manager's performance through a broad range of market conditions. Unfortunately, the length and accuracy of historical track records of hedge fund managers is rarely sufficient.

Since the vast majority of hedge fund track records do not fully characterise a manager's behaviour, it is necessary to make use of alternative methods for evaluating a manager's returns. Described below is a simple but effective method for characterising hedge fund returns referred to as "Generic Model Decomposition" (GMD). This method is less dependent on the length and accuracy of historical returns and yet is capable of providing substantial insight into a manager's behaviour over a broad range of market conditions.

GMD consists of a non-parametric factor analysis of a manager's returns. GMD models can be used to estimate a manager's behaviour in market conditions not exhibited during the manager's historical track record. It can also extract insights into the sources of return.

HEDGE FUND STYLE ANALYSIS

The past decade has witnessed a substantial increase in the number, asset size and importance of hedge funds. Correspondingly, there has been an attempt to analyse these new investment vehicles by extending or modifying the factor analysis that was successfully employed by Sharpe (1992) to analyse the performance of mutual funds. Examples of this research include Schneeweis and Spurgin (1998), Liang (1999) and Fung and Hsieh (1997).

Fung and Hsieh extended Sharpe's factor analysis to include factors that captured stylistic differences of alternative managers. They identify five hedge fund-style categories (distressed, global macro, systems, opportunistic and value) that are shown to explain somewhat more of hedge fund return variation than Sharpe's original factors. The primary result of Fung and Hsieh's research, however, was to categorise hedge fund styles, without using factor analysis, to identify the specific factors that explain hedge fund returns. When Fung and Hsieh used the same factors as Sharpe to explain hedge fund returns, they found that 48% of the hedge funds had R^2 below 25% compared to half of mutual funds having an R^2 above 75%. Even when the new factors are included in Sharpe's original set, Fung and Hsieh found that they could produce reasonably high R^2 for no more than 40% of the hedge funds they studied.

Schneeweis and Spurgin (1998) modeled hedge fund returns using four factors:

- ❑ the natural return of an asset class;
- ❑ the ability to go long and short;
- ❑ intra-month volatility; and
- ❑ temporary price trends.

They used this common set of factors to explain the returns of hedge funds, mutual funds and commodity trading advisors. This research was performed to draw very general conclusions about the factors that determine hedge fund performance. However, they note in their paper, as did Fung and Hsieh, that the heterogeneous nature of hedge fund styles may require detailed examination of individual hedge funds to render an understanding of their specific return generating processes possible.

This chapter departs quite substantially from prior research in terms of the methodology used for identifying and analysing the return – generating processes of individual hedge funds. Additionally, a conscious effort is made to incorporate the authors' professional experience in both managing hedge funds and analysing hedge funds managed by others. This experience is partially relied on to select candidate factors likely to explain the returns for individual hedge funds. The authors believe that qualitative information can substantially enhance the quantitative process of modelling manager returns.

GMD: A METHOD FOR CHARACTERISING THE RETURNS OF ALTERNATIVE INVESTMENTS

In brief, GMD constructs non-parametric factor models of managers' returns using factors (and/or proxies of factors, herein referred to solely as factors) that explain the unique characteristics of specific hedge fund strategies. Additionally, GMD relies upon a review of an individual manager's trading methodologies and historical records (as part of the due diligence process) to select candidate factors that best explain manager performance. This represents a significant departure from previous factor-analytical techniques, as there is no attempt to draw broad conclusions about hedge funds in general. Rather, models are developed for individual managers in recognition of the uniqueness of many hedge fund strategies and managers.

GMD is conducted in two steps. The first step is to identify a universe of candidate factors that are related to the manager's sources of risk and return. This is done as part of a qualitative due diligence study. The second step is to perform an optimisation to weight the factors to best "fit" our model to the manager's returns.

We can define the GMD returns model as:

$$\hat{r}(t) = \sum_{i=1}^{n} a_i(t)s_i(t)$$

Where $\hat{r}(t)$ is the estimate for the manager's actual returns, $r(t)$. The task is to select the universe of candidate factors, $\{s_i(t)\}$ and weights $\{a_i(t)\}$ that results in an $\hat{r}(t)$ that best replicates $r(t)$ in the sense that:

$$\min_{S,A} C(r(t),\hat{r}(t))$$

where one minimises C, a cost (objective) function that represents the goodness of fit over time between manager's returns $r(t)$ and the returns of the associated GMD model $\hat{r}(t)$.

To pick the universe of candidate factors, a qualitative due-diligence analysis of the manager's portfolio and trading strategy is required. The candidate factors consist of various time series such as equity and bond indices, their associated option contracts, and returns resulting from simplistic dynamic trading techniques. As shown later in two examples, we employ option-contract time series (as suggested by Fung and Hsieh, 1997, and Glosten, 1994) to serve as a proxy for dynamic trading strategies and to represent the option-like behaviour of certain securities held by hedge funds.

The objective function used to derive a GMD was designed to allow for the definition of the most important characteristics of a manager's returns.

To accomplish this, a non-parametric, non-linear objective function is used that attempts to match large winning and losing months, as opposed to just fitting in a mean-square sense.

Assume:

x_i = The selected manager's net asset value (NAV) for period i.

y_i = The generic investment strategy's NAV for period i. It assumes a common starting date and equity amount as the selected manager.

n = Number of periods in the performance history.

d_i = The difference between the ranks assigned to $\%x_i$ (selected manager's percentage return for period i) and $\%y_i$ (generic investment strategy's percentage return for period i) for a given set of paired data $\{(\%x_i, \%y_i); i = 1, 2, \ldots n\}$

$$C = \text{Objective Function} = \frac{\left[\sum_{i=1}^{n}(x_i - y_i)^2\right]^{1/2}}{\left[1 - \left[\frac{6 \cdot \sum_{i=1}^{n} d_i^2}{n(n^2 - 1)}\right]\right]}$$

The numerator of the equation represents the root mean squared error of the differences in the equity curves.[1] By ensuring that the two performance series have similar absolute rates of return, the derived GMD investment strategy will be forced to reflect an appropriate degree of leverage.

The denominator is a non-parametric measure of correlation known as Spearman's Rank Correlation. This correlation statistic tends to force the factor weights, $\{a_i\}$, in the GMD to appropriately describe the sources of return inherent in the manager's strategy by aligning the various inflection points in the two equity curves. Additionally, the use of a non-parametric measure of association makes the resulting factor weights less likely to be negatively affected by non-Gaussian or inaccurate data. As will be demonstrated below, these can be very significant issues when using conventional style analysis.

By minimising the above objective function, a specific factor weighting is derived that will estimate, as closely as possible, the manager's reported returns. The factor weightings, which include leverage, represent allocations to the underlying factors that best characterise a manager's return series.

We must acknowledge that the generic model derived in this manner is subject to criticism. Simply put, there is an "identification" issue; we can never be certain that the derived factor weights in any sense fully describe the manager's behaviour. This is essentially a "guerrilla statistic" designed to be used in an environment of highly imperfect information. Unfortunately, given the constraints associated with accuracy and transparency in the hedge fund world, it may not be appropriate to attempt to extract too "optimal" a result or to ascribe too much significance to specific return factor estimates.

Presented below are two simplified sample GMD studies. The data employed in the two examples cover the period from the inception of trading for each manager up to August of 1998. With the exception of the final month, this time span was a reasonably trouble-free period in the history of hedge fund investing. By selecting a highly favourable period we can demonstrate the value of GMD with respect to the evaluation of out-of-sample risk. Much of the "reported" volatility in the hedge fund world occurred directly following the analysed period.

SAMPLE GENERIC DECOMPOSITIONS

Convertible bonds: manager A

The performance record presented in Figure 1 is for an undisclosed, convertible arbitrage manager: Manager A. Manager A experienced one volatile period in late 1993 through to the end of 1994. In general, however, Manager A reported very little volatility. Manager A's annualised standard deviation of return is 4.83% while the Sharpe ratio is 1.97. The maximum

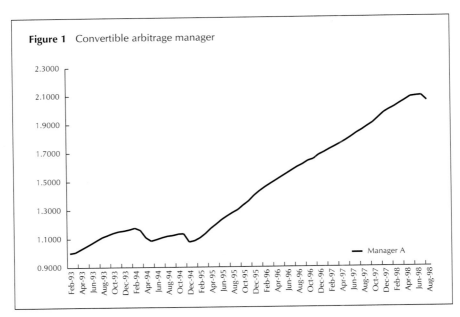

Figure 1 Convertible arbitrage manager

Table 1 Convertible arbitrage manager

Manager A

Decomposition weights	US$/1000	PCT
At-the-money 10-Year-Note Call Premium (% of assets)	−14.16	−1.42%
At-the-money 10-Year-Note Put Premium (% of assets)	−7.7	−0.77%
Out-of-the-money 10-Year-Note Call Premium (% of assets)	−0.31	−0.03%
Out-of-the-money 10-Year-Note Put Premium (% of assets)	−0.17	−0.02%
At-the-money S&P Call Premium (% of assets)	0.1	0.01%
At-the-money S&P Put Premium (% of assets)	−15.23	−1.52%
Lehman Brothers Corporate Bond Index	1466.6	146.66%
Assets borrowed	466.6	46.66%
Option premium borrowed	37.46	3.75%
Statistical profile comparison		
Generic model decomposition		
Annualised rate of return	8.30%	
Annualised standard deviation	9.43%	
Sharpe ratio	0.88	
Manager		
Annualised rate of return	9.50%	
Annualised standard deviation	4.83%	
Sharpe ratio	1.97	
Manager actual exposure		
Net S&P exposure (% of assets)	26.00%	
Net bond exposure (% of assets)	121.00%	

monthly loss of capital was 5.07%, while the maximum peak-to-trough loss of capital was 8.43%.

Manager A owns a portfolio of convertible bonds and attempts to lock in excess returns by shorting equities against the convertible security's embedded equity call options. A short equity position is not a perfect hedge for a convertible security. The value of convertible securities can be dramatically impacted by volatility in the fixed income markets and liquidity effects.

The most likely components of risk and return are the corporate bond market, the degree of leverage, and the structure of the manager's derivative exposure in both the fixed income and equity markets.

Table 1 presents the results of the optimisation using the GMD objective function. The output provides a formula for replicating the manager's returns by making allocations to the securities that represent the major sources of risk and return for the manager. The first element in the formula is at-the-money 10-Year-Note Call Premium, which equals −1.42%. This represents the allocation to at-the-money exchange-traded US 10-Year-Note call options expressed in percent-of-equity terms. The other option premium variables are presented in a similar manner. The Lehman Brother Corporate Bond Index allocation is equal to 146.66% of total available equity. Assets Borrowed represents the amount that must be borrowed in order to fund the levered allocation to the Corporate Bond Index. Option Premium Borrowed, which equals 3.75%, represents the total value of the premium received on a monthly basis. This is netted against the required borrowing associated with the levered allocation to the Bond Index. The three entries below GMD present summary statistics for the generic allocation strategy, ie, annualised rate of return minus the risk-free rate, standard deviation of return and Sharpe ratio. Similarly, the three entries below "manager" represent the same information relative to the analysed manager. Finally, Net S&P Exposure and Net Bond Exposure represent the net equity and fixed income exposures that are calculated by determining the notional futures equivalent of the options exposure, and then (in the case of the fixed income exposure) netting this against the allocation to the Bond Index. These summary statistics indicate that the manager's investment strategy has historically been roughly equivalent to a 26% long S&P position, plus a 121%, levered, long Lehman Corporate Bond Index exposure.

Figure 2 presents the equity curves for Manager A and its GMD equivalent. From Table 1, we see that Manager A does not use excessive leverage; approximately one and a half times. However, they are negatively affected by increases in volatility in the fixed-income markets because they are effectively writing options (shorting volatility) to generate returns. His short fixed-income-volatility exposure is illustrated by his negative

Figure 2   Convertible arbitrage manager

allocation to at-the-money and out-of-the-money fixed income options. Furthermore, Manager A is negatively affected by declines in both the stock and bond market. From Figure 2, we note by inspection that the generic strategy is somewhat more volatile than Manager A, and tends to lead chronologically both in recognising losses and profits. This could well be an indication that Manager A is under-reporting the periodic changes in value of their portfolio and subsequently smoothing reported monthly returns.

By performing a "best fit" analysis of the distributions of monthly returns for both Manager A and its associated GMD, we can compare the distribution of monthly returns for Manager A versus the associated GMD investment. By performing a best fit analysis of the GMD over a substantially longer period of time than the manager's performance history, we are able to obtain a clearer picture of the volatility potential of the manager than is provided by their brief performance history. The derived distribution of returns indicates that there is a 10% chance of observing a loss of 0.57% or more in any month. By contrast, the derived distribution of returns from the GMD indicates that there is a 10% chance of observing a loss of 2.55% or more in any month. The GMD provides a more conservative estimate of Manager A's monthly loss potential. In both the actual and GMDs, the distributions show positive means and modes, but negative skews.

Table 2 presents the results of a series of Monte Carlo simulations that make use of the derived distributions of monthly returns and estimates of serial correlation. This analysis is performed in order to gain an understanding of the distribution of annual rates of return, maximum monthly losses of capital and maximum peak-to-trough losses of capital. The GMD once again provides a more conservative measure of risk. Manager A's reported returns indicate only a 5% chance of observing a year-end loss of 12.73% or greater. The generic model shows a potential loss of 36.4%. The GMD also indicates a 5% chance of seeing a peak-to-trough loss of capital in excess of 47.74%, while Manager A's reported returns distribution indicates only a 5% chance of observing a peak-to-trough loss of capital greater than 12.72%.

The generic model for Manager A depicts an investment manager who is fairly conservatively levered. There is a relatively small probability of having a major loss in any given year. The major sources of risk are downturns in the equity and corporate bond markets, and increases in volatility in the fixed income markets. Additionally, Manager A probably underestimates the volatility of his portfolio. By calculating the ratios of the standard deviations of return for the GMD versus actual performance histories, we discover that the manager may be reporting as little as 50% of his actual monthly volatility.

Finally, it is worth considering whether these insights could have been gleaned through the use of conventional style analysis. While this issue is

Table 2 Distribution of monthly returns

	Annual rate of return		Maximum draw down		Maximum peak-to-trough draw down	
	Actual	**Generic**	**Actual**	**Generic**	**Actual**	**Generic**
Minimum =	−52.56%	−68.21%	−6.70%	−6.18%	0.00%	0.00%
Maximum =	166.14%	106.75%	8.07%	9.80%	52.56%	78.49%
Mean =	15.53%	17.99%	−1.07%	−0.97%	1.76%	18.94%
Std Deviation =	19.14%	34.05%	1.38%	2.63%	5.07%	14.92%
Variance =	3.66%	11.60%	0.02%	0.07%	0.26%	2.23%
Skewness =	0.76	0.10	0.16	0.55	3.86	0.74
Kurtosis =	5.47	2.34	4.34	2.93	20.63	3.12
Mode =	11.44%	14.63%	−2.64%	−5.14%	0.00%	0.00%
5% Perc =	−12.73%	−36.40%	−3.26%	−4.76%	0.00%	0.00%
10% Perc =	−6.60%	−26.80%	−2.72%	−4.20%	0.00%	0.00%
15% Perc =	−2.48%	−19.55%	−2.40%	−3.75%	0.00%	1.53%
20% Perc =	0.67%	−13.32%	−2.12%	−3.35%	0.00%	4.59%
25% Perc =	3.34%	−7.70%	−1.91%	−2.98%	0.00%	6.99%
30% Perc =	5.74%	−2.46%	−1.72%	−2.61%	0.00%	9.34%
35% Perc =	7.91%	2.63%	−1.54%	−2.29%	0.00%	11.30%
40% Perc =	10.01%	7.43%	−1.38%	−1.96%	0.00%	13.26%
45% Perc =	12.05%	12.25%	−1.23%	−1.62%	0.00%	15.09%
50% Perc =	14.12%	17.02%	−1.08%	−1.27%	0.00%	17.04%
55% Perc =	16.19%	21.92%	−0.94%	−0.90%	0.00%	18.86%
60% Perc	18.34%	26.87%	−0.78%	−0.55%	0.00%	20.78%
65% Perc =	20.66%	31.92%	−0.61%	−0.17%	0.00%	22.96%
70% Perc =	23.19%	37.26%	−0.44%	0.25%	0.00%	25.21%
75% Perc =	25.92%	42.95%	−0.24%	0.70%	0.00%	27.89%
80% Perc =	29.14%	49.14%	−0.02%	1.26%	0.00%	30.95%
85% Perc =	33.28%	56.14%	0.24%	1.90%	2.48%	34.84%
90% Perc =	38.77%	64.37%	0.61%	2.68%	6.59%	39.97%
95% Perc =	48.35%	75.49%	1.18%	3.86%	12.72%	47.74%

not conclusively examined here, it is worth noting that a preliminary examination of the data reveals a substantial degree of serial correlation of the manager's monthly returns. The one-period lagged correlation is 0.55 with a standard error of 0.09. This yields an extraordinarily high t-statistic of approximately 6. With such a high degree of serial correlation, the resulting factor estimates may be unbiased, but their statistical significance will most likely be indeterminate.

Mortgage-backed securities: Manager B

The second GMD analysis is performed on Manager B (a mortgage-backed securities manager), presented in Figure 3. From Figure 3 we see that Manager B did not have a single losing month and therefore, when measured in terms of month-end performance, has a maximum peak-to-trough

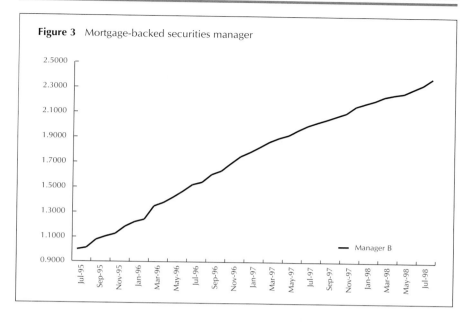

Figure 3 Mortgage-backed securities manager

loss of capital of 0%. The annualised standard deviation of return is 5.62%, while the Sharpe ratio is 4.99.

Manager B invests in mortgage-backed securities on a levered basis and may invest in a variety of mortgage derivative products. Consequently, Manager B is apt to be adversely affected by increases in fixed-income volatility. The most likely components of risk and return will be the performance of the underlying asset class (the Lehman Brothers Mortgage-Backed Securities Index), the degree of leverage and the structure of the manager's fixed-income options exposure. Table 3 provides the parameter values for the derived GMD of Manager B, while Figure 4 presents the equity curves for Manager B and his Generic equivalent.

From Table 3 we see that the generic strategy employs greater than eight times leverage in order to match manager B's performance. The generic strategy attempts to mimic the low volatility of Manager B through the short sale of fixed-income options. The relationship between short-selling options and volatility is dealt with more fully in the attached appendix. In general, the GMD parameter values indicate that Manager B is highly susceptible to both a decline in the mortgage-backed securities market and an increase in volatility in the fixed income markets.[2]

As noted above, by deriving a GMD, one is able to examine the probable performance of a manager during periods outside the manager's actual history. This capability is particularly useful when analysing managers with short histories. While Manager B's actual performance record starts in 1995, we have examined the performance of the GMD for the period

Table 3 Mortgage-backed securities manager

Manager B

Decomposition weights	US$/1000	PCT
At-the-money 10-Year-Note Call Premium (% of assets)	−29.85	−2.99%
At-the-money 10-Year-Note Put Premium (% of assets)	−35.07	−3.51%
Out-of-the-money 10-Year-Note Call Premium (% of assets)	−27.32	−2.73%
Out-of-the-money 10-Year-Note Put Premium (% of assets)	−7.63	−0.76%
Lehman Brothers Mortgage Back Securities Index	8201.62	820.16%
Assets borrowed	7201.62	720.16%
Option premium borrowed	99.87	9.99%
Statistical profile comparison		
Generic model decomposition		
Annualised rate of return	17.74%	
Annualised standard deviation	29.53%	
Sharpe ratio	0.60	
Manager		
Annualised rate of return	28.03%	
Annualised standard deviation	5.62%	
Sharpe ratio	4.99	
Manager actual exposure		
Net bond exposure (% of assets)	724.00%	

Figure 4 Mortgage-backed securities manager

starting in January of 1992 to the end of August 1998. This analysis provides the opportunity for estimating the manager's performance over a period such as 1994, which was a particularly difficult period for mortgage-backed securities managers. The two fitted distributions present starkly different images of the performance of Manager B. The distribution of monthly returns for Manager B appears lower bounded above 0%. The returns also appear to be highly positively skewed. In sharp contrast, the distribution of returns for the GMD depicts a non-trivial probability of having monthly drawdowns in excess of 10%. Furthermore, the returns are negatively skewed. In both the GMD and actual histories, the modes and means of the distributions are positive.

Table 4 presents the results of a series of Monte Carlo simulations using distributions of monthly returns and estimates of serial correlation in order

Table 4 Distribution of monthly returns

	Annual rate of return		Maximum draw down		Maximum peak-to-trough draw down	
	Actual	Generic	Actual	Generic	Actual	Generic
Minimum =	3.31%	−99.91%	−22.05%	−39.97%	0.00%	0.31%
Maximum =	2222.14%	11284.01%	−0.21%	60.82%	0.00%	99.91%
Mean =	35.09%	98.35%	−2.31%	−1.61%	0.00%	46.83%
Std Deviation =	42.11%	306.38%	1.51%	8.63%	0.00%	25.49%
Variance =	17.73%	938.71%	0.02%	0.75%	0.00%	6.50%
Skewness =	19.49	11.53	(2.71)	0.17	–	(0.01)
Kurtosis =	814.36	275.13	17.32	4.44	–	1.97
Mode =	18.98%	−38.53%	−1.53%	−8.78%	0.00%	46.05%
5% Perc =	10.24%	−78.46%	−5.10%	−15.44%	0.00%	5.65%
10% Perc=	12.49%	−65.63%	−4.06%	−12.11%	0.00%	11.05%
15% Perc =	14.29%	−54.21%	−3.51%	−9.75%	0.00%	16.16%
20% Perc =	15.96%	−43.60%	−3.12%	−8.18%	0.00%	21.17%
25% Perc =	17.57%	−33.43%	−2.83%	−6.86%	0.00%	25.89%
30% Perc =	19.13%	−22.71%	−2.58%	−5.68%	0.00%	30.46%
35% Perc =	20.73%	−11.66%	−2.39%	−4.57%	0.00%	34.87%
40% Perc =	22.39%	−0.61%	−2.21%	−3.59%	0.00%	39.12%
45% Perc =	24.20%	11.57%	−2.07%	−2.60%	0.00%	43.26%
50% Perc =	26.13%	24.99%	−1.93%	−1.66%	0.00%	47.25%
55% Perc =	28.31%	39.44%	−1.80%	−0.73%	0.00%	51.28%
60% Perc =	30.64%	56.03%	−1.67%	0.20%	0.00%	55.33%
65% Perc =	33.36%	75.52%	−1.56%	1.16%	0.00%	59.39%
70% Perc =	36.56%	98.38%	−1.45%	2.25%	0.00%	63.40%
75% Perc =	40.53%	127.26%	−1.34%	3.50%	0.00%	67.46%
80% Perc =	45.59%	165.37%	−1.23%	4.87%	0.00%	71.67%
85% Perc =	52.44%	216.92%	−1.11%	6.51%	0.00%	76.23%
90% Perc =	62.83%	301.55%	−0.97%	8.80%	0.00%	81.28%
95% Perc =	84.31%	485.65%	−0.81%	12.62%	0.00%	87.46%

Table 5 Analysis of variance

Source	DF	Sum of squares	Mean square	F value	Pr > F
Model	6	100.26724	16.71121	0.89	0.5095
Error	46	862.86171	18.75786		
Corrected Total	52	963.12895			

Variable	Parameter estimate	Standard error	Type II SS	F value	Pr > F
Intercept	−18.07965	9.52221	67.62188	3.60	0.0639
tycall	0.00822	0.02744	1.68481	0.09	0.7658
typut	0.02036	0.02071	18.13687	0.97	0.3306
otmtycall	−0.00186	0.00968	0.69454	0.04	0.8483
otmtyput	−0.00165	0.00577	1.52838	0.08	0.7766
mlibor	40.97034	20.41950	75.51485	4.03	0.0507
lmbsi	1.58152	1.72594	15.75003	0.84	0.3643

Bounds on condition number: 16.383, 234.09

The above model is the best 6-variable model found.
No further improvement in R-Square is possible.

to gain an understanding of the potential annual rates of return, maximum monthly losses of capital, and maximum peak-to-trough losses of capital. Once again we see some very sharp contrasts between the actual performance history and the GMD history. With respect to the distribution of Manager B's reported rates of return, the data indicate that there is only a 5% chance of seeing a yearly rate of return of less than 10%, and virtually no chance of ever seeing a negative return in any month or year. By contrast, the GMD indicates that there is a 5% chance of losing almost 80% of one's capital, a greater than 50% chance of having a losing month, and 5% chance of losing in excess of 15% in any given month.

It is worth pausing once again to consider the feasibility of conventional style analysis. Table 5 presents the results of a regression that makes use of the same factors included in the GMD model.

Perhaps the most important results presented in Table 5 are the F-statistics presented for the four fixed-income options factors. The F-statistics indicate that none of the fixed-income option's factors are statistically significant. This would imply that fixed-income volatility should play no real role in determining the manager's performance – a condition we know to be untrue. Additionally, the most significant return factor is identified as a monthly libor return series. Given that the monthly libor return series is essentially a positive constant, and that the manager reported a profit every month, the strong degree of association is likely to be merely a statistical artefact.

The above example highlights the dramatic range of interpretation that can occur when characterising a performance history from two different analytical perspectives. A direct, traditional examination of Manager B's performance history depicts a high rate of return and virtually no risk, whereas the GMD analysis reveals substantial leverage, large short sales of volatility and a penchant for underestimating the periodic changes in value of the portfolio. By calculating the ratios of the standard deviations of return for the GMD versus actual performance histories, we discover that Manager B may be reporting as little as 15% of his actual monthly volatility.

With a Sharpe ratio of 4.99, traditional quantitative portfolio optimisation will highly favour this manager, while the GMD analysis reveals that investing with this manager is, at best, a highly risky proposition. The results could not be more different.

INSIGHTS FROM GMD

There are several lessons we can learn from the GMD analysis of these two managers. The first insight is that certain classes of managers have investment styles that contain large "short options" exposure. Both of these managers contained large short options exposures in their GMD models. Short-options exposure helped to create their high Sharpe ratios but also ultimately led to periods of poor performance because you cannot achieve something (higher returns) without incurring some cost (increased risk). Portfolio optimisation techniques will tend to over-allocate to these strategies because the risk inherent in shorting options did not manifest itself during these managers' brief histories, ie, the managers did not experience a "volatility event". We refer to the tendency of optimisation techniques to over-allocate in such situations as "short-volatility bias". It is worth emphasising that it is quite easy to construct an investment strategy based on the selling (short sale of volatility) of fairly valued options that gives the appearance of providing good risk-adjusted returns if the manager's track record just happens to exclude a period of sharply increasing volatility. To the extent that risk-adjusted returns are overestimated, traditional quantitative portfolio optimisation will over-allocate to such "short-volatility" strategies, and thereby systematically increase portfolio risk. This is a potentially serious issue, for our personal experience and research indicates that most hedge fund managers create some form of short volatility exposure to boost the consistency of their track records. As noted above, however, such temporary performance improvement is at the expense of increased exposure to a volatility event.

The second important insight is that there is a non-trivial tendency for managers to understate the periodic changes in the value of their portfolios. Certain over-the-counter securities can be rather difficult to mark-to-market because they are illiquid. As a result, there is a tendency for the owners of such securities to underestimate the periodic changes in value of their portfolios. If a manager systematically understates the volatility of his portfolio, then there will be an associated systematic overstatement of risk-adjusted returns. Using such returns for optimising a portfolio will result in an over-allocation to investment styles and managers who make use of less-liquid securities. This phenomenon is referred to as "illiquidity bias". The sad consequence of this form of bias is that the use of traditional portfolio optimisation techniques frequently results in a systematic tendency to decrease liquidity and underestimate portfolio risk.

1 An equity curve is a graphical or numerical representation of the value of (typically) a US$1,000 investment, over time, as a function of the manager's periodic (usually monthly) performance.

2 It is also worth conjecturing that, due to the substantial variation of the GMD relative to Manager B's reported performance, Manager B may be engaging in "marketing supportive" accounting practices. In particular, for August 1998, the performance between Manager B and his GMD strongly diverges. The GMD indicates that, based on the prevailing market conditions, Manager B should have experienced very poor performance in August. The GMD depicts a considerable sensitivity of Manager B to increases in volatility in the fixed income markets. It is interesting to note that Manager B reported a very large loss during the following month of September. However, GMD shows the loss occurring during the prior month of August.

BIBLIOGRAPHY

Alexander, Sharpe and Bailey, 1993, Fundamentals of Investments (Englewood Cliffs, NJ: Prentice Hall).

Edwards, M., 1988, "Commodity Fund Performance: Is the Information Contained in Fund Prospectuses Useful?", *Journal of Futures Markets* 8(5).

Elton, G.B., 1995, "Fundamental Economic Variables, Expected Returns, and Bond Fund Performance", *The Journal of Finance* 50(4).

Fung, H., and Hsieh, 1997, "Empirical Characteristics of Dynamic Trading Strategies: The Case of Hedge Funds", *The Review of Financial Studies* 10(2).

Glosten, J., 1994, "A Contingent Claim Approach to Performance Evaluation", *Journal of Empirical Finance* 1, pp. 133–60.

Liang, 1999, "On the Performance of Hedge Funds", *Association for Investment Management and Research*.

McCarthy, Spurgin and Schneeweis, 1997, "Informational Content in Historical CTA Performance", *Journal of Futures Markets*.

McCarthy, Spurgin and Schneeweis, 1998, "A Review of Hedge Fund Performance Benchmarks", *Journal of Alternative Investments*.

Michaud, 1999, "Investment Styles, Market Anomalies, and Global Stock Selection", The Research Foundation of The Institute of Chartered Financial Analysts.

Michaud, 1998, *Efficient Asset Management* (Harvard Business School Press).

Schneeweis and Spurgin, 1998, "Multifactor Analysis of Hedge Fund, Managed Futures, and Mutual Fund Return and Risk Characteristics", *Journal of Alternative Investments.*

Sharpe, 1992, "Asset Allocation: Management Style and Performance Measurement", *Journal of Portfolio Management* 18(2).

Silber, 1994, "Technical Trading: When It Works and When It Doesn't", *The Journal of Derivatives.*

Weisman, 1998, "Conservation of Volatility and the Interpretation of Hedge Fund Data", *Alternative Investment Management Association.*

5

Value-at-Risk for Asset Managers*

Christopher L. Culp, Ron Mensink and Andrea M.P. Neves

CP Risk Management LLC; State of Wisconsin Investment Board;
CP Risk Management LLC

Value-at-risk (VAR) is a probability-based metric for quantifying the market risk of assets and portfolios.[1] VAR is often used as an approximation of the maximum reasonable loss over a chosen time horizon. Its primary appeal – widespread among commercial bankers, derivatives dealers and corporate treasury risk managers – is its ease of interpretation as a *summary* measure of risk as well as its *consistent* treatment of risk across different financial instruments and asset classes.

VAR is not nearly as well accepted in the institutional investment community as it is elsewhere.[2] The main reason being that asset managers are typically in the business of *taking* risks, either to fund uncertain liability streams or to generate positive excess risk-adjusted returns. Not surprisingly, asset managers – mutual funds, private banks, hedge funds, pension plans, endowments and foundations – often view risk management in general and VAR in particular as inherently at odds with their primary business mandate.[3] Nevertheless, VAR *can be* a useful tool by which asset managers can better ascertain whether the risks they are taking are those they *want or need to be* taking and *think they are*. Investors, as well, are becoming increasingly aware of the benefits of VAR as a *monitoring* tool, thereby further prodding their fiduciary asset managers toward the regular calculation and disclosure of this measure of market risk.[4]

*This chapter was first published in *Derivatives Quarterly*, Winter, (1998), pp. 21–33 and is reprinted with the permission of Institutional Investor. The authors would like to thank Brian Heimsoth and Geoff Ihle for working with them on this project. The authors alone are responsible for remaining errors and omissions. The views herein do not necessarily represent those of the State of Wisconsin Investment Board or any CP Risk Management client.

In this chapter, some of the applications of VAR to asset management are explored, with particular attention on the importance of VAR for multi-currency asset managers.[5] We first explain what VAR is and why it is so appealing conceptually. In the subsequent section, the mechanics of calculating VAR are explained, including the importance of some of the assumptions underlying the most common VAR measurement methodology. Bearing in mind the measurement difficulties with VAR, we then summarise four concrete applications of VAR to asset management. These involve the use of VAR to:

❑ monitor managers, portfolios and hedging programmes;
❑ eliminate *ex ante* transactional approval requirements;
❑ define a formal system of risk targets and thresholds; and
❑ implement a risk budget.

WHAT IS VAR?[6]

VAR is a statistic that summarises the exposure of an asset or portfolio to market risk. VAR allows managers to quantify and express risk as follows: "We do not expect losses to exceed 10% of the fund's net asset value in more than one out of the next 20 quarters".[7] To arrive at a VAR measure for a given portfolio, a manager must generate a probability distribution of possible returns or changes in the value of that portfolio (or its component assets) over a specific time horizon. The distribution of possible portfolio returns or future values is called the VAR distribution.[8] The VAR statistic for the portfolio is the return or absolute dollar loss corresponding to some pre-defined probability level – usually 5% or less – as defined by the left-hand tail of the VAR distribution. Alternatively, VAR is the adverse return or dollar loss that is expected to occur no more than 5% of the time over the specified time horizon.

VAR is often considered a useful summary measure of market risk for several reasons. One feature of VAR is its *consistency* as a measure of financial risk. By expressing risk using a possible dollar-loss or adverse-return metric, VAR facilitates direct comparisons of risk across different portfolios (eg, equity versus fixed income) and distinct financial products (eg, interest rate swaps versus common stock). In addition to consistency, VAR enables managers or investors to examine potential losses over particular time horizons. Any measure of VAR requires the specification of such a risk horizon. A judicious choice of risk horizon can aid asset managers in numerous risk management and disclosure matters. An asset manager's choice of an appropriate risk horizon may depend upon the timing of events including the following: outside manager evaluations, board or trustee meetings, performance disclosures to investors, limited partners or third-party tracking services (eg, MAR or AIMR), regulatory examinations, tax assessments, key client meetings and the like.[9]

Another advantage of VAR traces to its roots in the probability theory. With whatever degree of confidence a portfolio manager wants to specify, VAR allows a specific potential loss over the risk horizon to be associated with that level of confidence. A 95% confidence level with a one-month risk horizon, for example, tells the portfolio manager, strictly speaking, that returns can be expected to dip below, say, X% in the next month with 95% confidence. Some often go on to assume that the 5% confidence level means they stand to experience returns below X% in no more than five months out of 100, an inference that is true only if strong assumptions are made about the stability of the underlying probability distributions.[10] Either way, VAR measures are *forward-looking* approximations of market risk unlike traditional backward-looking measures of actual historical performance, such as the *ex post* Sharpe ratio that is calculated for performance evaluation purposes using *realised* manager returns.[11] VAR thus complements rather than displaces such conventional methods.

As a related advantage of VAR, this measure of risk often appeals to asset managers because it is mostly tactically neutral. In other words, VAR is calculated by examining the market risk of the individual instruments in a portfolio, not using actual historical *performance*.[12] Whereas typical performance measurements reflect manager performance, VAR reveals the market risk borne by an investor based *solely* on the asset mix and current security holdings. Nevertheless, VAR is not totally neutral to *all* active strategies. If a manager loads up on a higher volatility sector (eg, technology), that strategy-induced volatility is picked up by VAR. Managers' tactical shifts and market time decisions, by contrast, are *not* reflected in VAR measures – nor, as we shall see later, should they be.[13]

THE MECHANICS OF VAR ESTIMATION

Creating a VAR distribution for a particular portfolio and a given risk horizon can be viewed as a two-step process.[14] In the first step, the price or return distributions for each individual security in the portfolio are generated. These distributions represent possible value changes in all the component assets over the risk horizon. Next, the individual distributions somehow must be aggregated into a single portfolio distribution then serves as the basis for the VAR summary measure.

Methods for generating both individual asset and portfolio VAR distributions range from the simplistic to the incredibly complex. The more realistic approaches to VAR measurement generate the VAR distribution by re-valuing all the assets in a portfolio for the most realistic market risk scenarios possible. These full re-valuation methods, however, can be very costly computationally. Accordingly, simpler approaches often make a number of statistical assumptions intended to reduce data requirements and computing costs. One such assumption is to assume that small changes in portfolio values around its current value are representative of larger potential value changes. This is known as the partial re-valuation approach to VAR measurement and is analogous to using a bond's duration as an approximation of risk while ignoring its convexity.[15] Other simplifications made with the intention of relieving computing costs include a variety of distributional assumptions, most of which will be discussed.

To date, most asset managers that implement VAR use the more simplified computational approaches. Accordingly, we explore in this section the mechanics of simplified VAR calculations using an international equity portfolio as an example. We begin with a simple historical calculation of VAR that relies exclusively on historical time-series data. We then discuss the most common method of VAR estimation – called variance-based VAR measurement – popularised by JP Morgan by its 1994 introduction of *RiskMetrics*. We conclude the section with short discussion of the shortfallings of the variance-based approach and a survey of other alternatives.

HISTORICAL VAR

One way to calculate VAR is simply to assume that the future will behave precisely like the past. VAR then can be calculated using a sample time series of past security returns. An example will help illustrate.

Figure 1 shows a frequency distribution of monthly returns on the FTSE 100 stock index from January 1988 to January 1995, as well as the summary statistics for that time series. The horizontal axis shows returns and the vertical axis shows the percentage of the total sample of historical returns

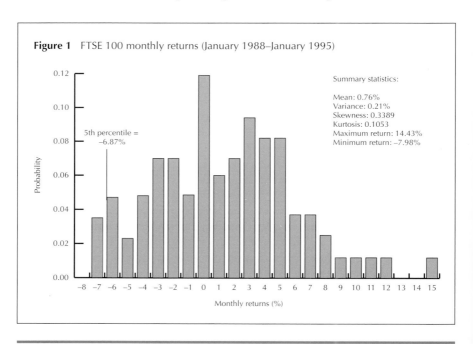

Figure 1   FTSE 100 monthly returns (January 1988–January 1995)

Summary statistics:

Mean: 0.76%
Variance: 0.21%
Skewness: 0.3389
Kurtosis: 0.1053
Maximum return: 14.43%
Minimum return: –7.98%

5th percentile = –6.87%

associated with each return interval on the horizontal axis. By assuming the future behaves like the past, we can call this frequency of past returns the "probability" that these same return levels will be realised in the future. The bar on the far right, for example, indicates that approximately 1% of historical monthly returns were greater than 14%.[16] Assuming the next month in the future behaves like prior months, we can interpret this to mean that there is a 1% probability of a return in excess of 14% next month.

As the summary statistics and Figure 1 show, this return distribution is positively skewed – more probability lies in the right-hand tail than the left-hand tail. In other words, the probability of a return X% above the mean is *higher* than the probability of a return X% below the mean. We also can see that the excess kurtosis is positive, indicating that the distribution shown in Figure 1 has fatter tails than the normal distribution.[17]

Suppose a British asset manager has an equity portfolio with a current market value of £1 million invested entirely in FTSE 100 stocks. Suppose further that the manager holds the equities in exactly the same proportion as their portfolio weights in the GTSE 100 index – ie, the fund is an index fund.[18] If the manager calculates the VAR for this portfolio at the 95% confidence level over a one-month risk horizon, the resulting VAR measure will reveal the value below which the portfolio is expected to exceed in five of the next 100 months. Using only the historical data in Figure 1, this VAR can be calculated as follows:

$$VAR = £1,000,000 \times R^{0.05}$$

where $R^{0.05}$ denotes the fifth percentile historical monthly return for the FTSE 100. This fifth percentile return, indicated with a bold vertical line on Figure 1, was –6.87% in the 1988–95 sample period. So, the sterling-dominated one-month VAR for this portfolio is £68,700.[19] We thus expect the net asset value (NAV) of this portfolio to decline by more than £68,700 in only five of the next 100 months.[20]

For large portfolios with numerous assets and exposures, the historical approach quickly becomes intractable. The data requirements alone can render this simplistic approach virtually worthless for large portfolios. Suppose, for example, we want to calculate the VAR of a portfolio comprised of FTSE 100 stocks but in which the portfolio weights for each stock are now different from the weights used to calculate the FTSE 100 index. In that case, each stock would need to be examined directly – ie, obtain historical time series for each of the 100 stocks and calculate the VAR using the new portfolio weights and the historical correlation matrix.

VARIANCE-BASED VAR

JP Morgan and Reuters greatly simplified the data problems of the pure historical approach by proposing a more simplified method of VAR measurement. This *RiskMetrics* VAR calculation methodology circumvents the data problems associated with using actual historical data in two ways. First, the *RiskMetrics* approach relies on primitive securities rather than actual security-level portfolio holdings. Primitive securities are securities intended to *represent* actual security holdings for the purpose of VAR calculations. The cash-flows on a given portfolio of actual securities are mapped into corresponding cash-flows on primitive securities in order to perform the VAR calculation. Second, *RiskMetrics* makes available the relevant data on those primitive securities so that virtually no historical data collection is required. As an example, *RiskMetrics* does *not* furnish data on coupon-bearing US Treasury securities, but it *does* on zero-coupon Treasuries. So, a portfolio of coupon-bearing Treasuries (ie, actual holdings) can be mapped into a portfolio of corresponding zero-coupon Treasury securities (ie, primitive securities) for which data are available. The primitive securities available through *RiskMetrics* include government bonds, swap rates (which double as corporate bond rates), exchange rates, equity index levels, commodity prices and money market rates, all of which are available for various countries and currency denominations.

Aside from addressing the data problem associated with historical VAR, the *RiskMetrics* approach makes a number of statistical assumptions that also simplify the *computational* side of the VAR calculation. Most importantly, the approach assumes that all primitive security returns are distributed normally. An attractive property of the normal distribution is that it is symmetric. Mean and variance are thus sufficient statistics to fully characterise a normal distribution – the variance of an asset whose return is normally distributed is all that is needed to summarise the risk of that asset.

So simplistic is Morgan's calculation method that many managers now use it with primitive securities of their own – ie, without using the *RiskMetrics* data set. The approach has thus come to be known more generally as the variance-based approach. Because this is by far the most predominant – and affordable – method of calculating VAR, the following subsections explore the mechanics of this methodology in more detail.

Single asset, single-period VAR

To calculate VAR using the variance-based approach, we rely on the fact that the probability in the left-hand tail of a normal distribution is a known function of the standard deviation of the distribution. For example, 5% of the normal distribution, lies 1.65 standard deviations below the mean. Again, the mechanics of this approach are best illustrated by example.

Consider again the FTSE 100 index portfolio from the standpoint of the sterling-based asset manager. From the summary statistics provided in Figure 1, we know that the average monthly return is 0.76% and the monthly variance is 0.21%. With a current portfolio NAV of £1,000,000, the one-month VAR at the 95% confidence level is calculated as follows:

$$VAR_e = £1,000,000 \times (0.0076 - 1.65 \times 0.045)$$
$$= £1,000,000 \times (-0.068) = £68,012$$

In Figure 2, the historical distribution of returns from Figure 1 is super-imposed with a normal distribution whose mean and variance are equal to the historical sample mean and variance. Figure 2 then depicts this vari-ance-based VAR estimate (expressed as a percentage return) with a vertical line. Note that the variance-based VAR expressed as a return is the same (to the second decimal) as the fifth percentile return of the actual frequency distribution. Not surprisingly, the variance-based £68,012 VAR is only triv-ially different from the £68,700 one-month VAR we calculated earlier using only the sample frequency distribution.

For a measure of the standard deviation used in the variance-based VAR calculation, we used the unconditional variance of the historical time series – ie, the standard deviation of all 85 monthly returns shown in Figures 1 and 2. Alternatively, we could have used a different method to estimate the volatility input to the variance-based VAR estimate.[21]

If we chose to re-calculate this number on a regular basis, for example, we might have used a moving average of return variance as our estimate for volatility.[22] Because moving-average volatility is calculated using equal weights for all observations in the historical time series, the calculations are

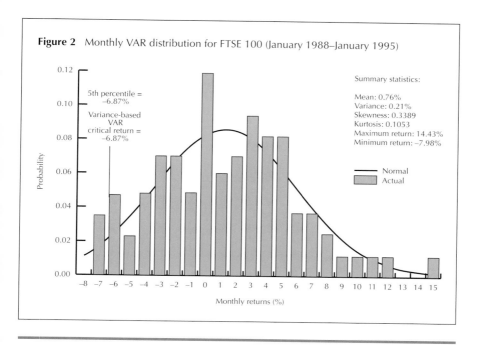

Figure 2   Monthly VAR distribution for FTSE 100 (January 1988–January 1995)

very simple. The result, however, is a smoothing effect that causes sharp changes in volatility to appear as plateaux over longer periods, failing to capture dramatic changes in volatility.

In order to remedy this problem, the *RiskMetrics* data sets provided by JP Morgan and Reuters include volatilities for all the supported primitive securities computed at both the daily and monthly frequencies using an exponentially weighted moving average.[23] Unlike the unconditional variance or the simple moving-average volatility estimate, an exponentially weighted moving average allows the most recent observations further in the past. This has the advantage of capturing shocks in the market better than the simple moving average and thus is often regarded as producing a better volatility for variance-based VAR.

Multi-asset, single-period VAR

The real savings in data and computing costs delivered by the variance-based VAR approach comes into play when the VAR is desired for a large portfolio of multiple assets and currency denominations. We can illustrate the simplicity of this approach – even in just the two-asset case – by assuming in our earlier example that the FTSE 100 portfolio is now run by a *dollar-based* asset manager. The total portfolio thus consists now of *two* positions – a sterling-denominated equity exposure, and a spot foreign exchange position to convert sterling into dollars.

Suppose the sterling price conversion is £1.629/US$. The equity portfolio then is worth US$613,874 at the prevailing exchange rate. The combined portfolio of the dollar-denominated investor thus includes a US$613,874 position in the FTSE 100 (the equity primitive security) and an equivalent spot exchange rate position (the FX primitive). The one-month VAR of the equity is now[24]

$$\text{VAR}_e = \text{US\$613,874} \, (0.0076 - 1.65 \times 0.045)$$
$$= \text{US\$40,915}$$

Because this considers the VAR of the equity portfolio *in isolation*, this risk measure is called the undiversified VAR of the equity position.

We now can calculate the undiversified VAR of the spot exchange rate position:

$$\text{VAR}_{fx} = \text{US\$613,874} \times (\mu_{fx} - 1.65\sigma_{fx})$$

where μ_{fx} and σ_{fx} are the mean and standard deviation of the monthly percentage change in the sterling/dollar rate. Again, using the unconditional standard deviation (from January 1988 to January 1995) as our volatility estimate, we calculate σ_{fx} as 0.0368 and μ_{fx} as –0.001. Substituting into the above equation, we ascertain that the undiversified VAR of the currency exposure is

$$VAR_{fx} = US\$613,874\ (-0.001 - 1.65 \times 0.0368)$$
$$= US\$37,888$$

We now can calculate the total portfolio VAR using the powerful property of a *bivariate normal* probability distribution.[25] Specifically:

$$VAR_p^2 = VAR_e^2 + VAR_{fx}^2 + 2\rho VAR_e VAR_{fx}$$

where ρ is the correlation between FTSE 100 returns and monthly percentage changes in the sterling/dollar rate. We estimate ρ to be -0.2136 from our 1988–95 sample – ie, the FTSE 100 varies *inversely* with changes in the sterling/dollar spot rate. Substituting that correlation coefficient and the other values into the above equation, we thus calculate the one-month portfolio VAR as follows:

$$VAR_p = [\{US\$40,915)^2 + (US\$37,888)^2$$
$$= + 2(-0.2136)(US\$40,915)(US\$37,888)^{1/2}$$
$$= US\$49,470$$

This number represents the *diversified* VAR, or the one-month VAR (at the 95% confidence level) that reflects *both* the equity *and* currency exposures, as well as the correlation between the two. The fund manager thus should expect the portfolio to lose 8% or more of its current NAV in five of the next 100 months from its combined FTSE 100 and sterling exposure. As one would expect, diversified VAR benefits from the lack of perfect correlation – and, indeed, the negative correlation in this case – and is considerably less than the sum of the two undiversified VARs.

Multi-period VAR

The previous examples use monthly data to generate VAR measures for a one-month risk horizon. Because *RiskMetrics* data are indeed available at the monthly frequency,[26] no further adjustments need to be made if we care about a monthly risk horizon. To compute the VAR for longer risk horizons, however, the one-period VAR must be adjusted. This calculation is performed with the aid of *another* simplifying assumption in the variance-based approach – namely, return distributions are assumed to be *independent* and *stable* over time (collectively, distributional stationarity). This means that the VAR distribution used to calculate one-month VAR is presumed *identical* to the distribution from which successive monthly returns are drawn. The multi-period VAR is then just the one-period VAR multiplied by the square root of the number of periods in the risk horizon.

Suppose we now wish to compute the diversified FTSE 100 portfolio VAR at the 95% confidence level for a *one-quarter* risk horizon. To accomplish this, we need only multiply the one-month diversified VAR by the square root of three – ie, US$49,470 × 1.7321 = US$85,685. So, we expect losses in our international equity portfolio not to exceed US$85,685 in 95 of the next 100 quarters.

ALTERNATIVES TO THE VARIANCE-BASED VAR APPROACH

As we see in Figures 1 and 2, the undiversified variance-based VAR is almost exactly the same as the undiversified VAR computed using actual historical data. At first glance, this may seem surprising. Figure 2 and the sample statistics for the actual historical show quite clearly, after all, that the frequency distribution does not resemble the normal distribution.[27] Nevertheless, even when the underlying data are not normally distributed, managers can sometimes get lucky – ie, the normal approximation is *sometimes* realistic *enough* for VAR calculations. But not always, and perhaps not even often.

Figure 3 shows the frequency distribution of monthly returns on the Nikkei 225 Japanese stock index from January 1988 to January 1995. As in Figure 2, a normal distribution is superimposed on the frequency distribution whose mean and variance come from the underlying historical return data. Figure 3 and the sample statistics show this distribution is negatively skewed and has even fatter tails relative to the normal distribution than the FTSE 100. Not surprisingly, the variance-based undiversified critical VAR

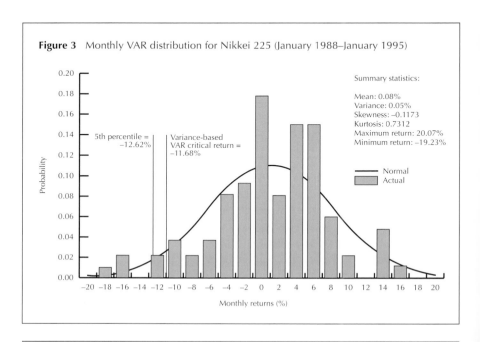

Figure 3   Monthly VAR distribution for Nikkei 225 (January 1988–January 1995)

return –11.68% when expressed as a return – is higher than the historical fifth percentile return of –12.62%. An undiversified VAR calculated using the assumption of normality thus *understates* the true risk of the Nikkei 225 portfolio.

As a general rule, variance-based VAR understates the risk of an asset or portfolio whenever the underlying distribution is negatively skewed and has tails fatter than the normal distribution (ie, leptokurtic). Quite a few asset classes fall into this category, including real estate, commodities, private placements and some bonds. Many asset managers, not surprisingly, are unsatisfied with the assumption that variance is a complete measure of risk for all asset classes. In addition, long-term asset managers with risk horizons of a quarter or more often are equally displeased with the assumption of distributional stationarity in the variance-based VAR approach. Some investors thus opt to calculate VAR using a measurement methodology that does not rely on variance and distributional stationarity.[28] Two such methods include Monte Carlo simulation and historical simulation.[29]

Non-variance-based VAR can be computationally quite expensive. Advanced VAR calculation systems that do not force the user to rely on the assumption of normally distributed asset returns often cost over US$1 million – sometimes US$1 million *per annum* in leasing fees. Beyond that purchase/leasing price, more advanced calculation methods also typically necessitate significantly more *data* (eg, historical security returns). In some cases, the cost of obtaining and maintaining this data can be as much if not more than the cost of the system itself.

Aside from the systems and data costs of advanced VAR measurement, the more complex the system the more costly it is to implement and maintain *from a labour-cost standpoint*. A very advanced system often necessitates the creation of a full-time job to manage the inputs and outputs of the system. And the more complex the system, the more savvy its user must be.

Asset managers thus often face a relatively unpleasant trade off between cost and precision/realism in their VAR estimates. Not surprisingly, many managers just eschew VAR altogether, especially when the *applications* of VAR are far from obvious for many asset managers. If the job of an asset manager is to *take risk* in order to fund an uncertain liability stream or earn a competitive return on invested capital, after all, why should the manager spend over a million dollars on a VAR measurement system? In the next section, we attempt to answer that question by proposing some applications of VAR that neither require a huge expenditure on a VAR system nor needlessly attenuate the investment autonomy of portfolio managers.

APPLICATIONS OF VAR TO ASSET MANAGEMENT

In order for VAR to make sense to most asset managers, the investment policy must first be accepted as sacrosanct. VAR should *complement* rather than *compete with* the primary investment management goals of the asset manager. It is a tool for helping managers determine whether the risks they *are* exposed to are those they *think they are*, and those they *want to be* exposed to. VAR will *never* tell an asset manager how much risk to take; it will only tell a manager how much risk *is being taken*. Taking the investment policy *as a given*, asset managers can apply VAR in at least four ways to the operation of their funds.

Monitoring

One of the primary benefits of VAR for asset managers is that it facilitates the consistent and regular monitoring of market risk. Institutional investors can calculate and monitor VAR on a variety of different levels. When done at the *portfolio* level, the risks taken by individual asset managers – whether internal traders and portfolio managers or external account managers – can be evaluated on an ongoing basis. Market risk also can be tracked and monitored at the aggregate fund level, as well as by asset class, by issuer/counterparty and the like. We now discuss three specific monitoring applications of VAR.

Internal manager/portfolio monitoring
Suppose that Pension Plan Dearborn is a defined-benefit plan with a current NAV of US$1 billion invested through internal *and* external fund managers in all traditional asset classes. Pension Plan Dearborn calculates the quarterly VAR once a week for all of its portfolio managers. Suppose that external account manager Rush manages a US$100 million international bond portfolio for Dearborn. If the VAR for account manager Rush is monitored each week, major departures of Rush's VAR from various established comparison risk measures should trigger an enquiry into Rush's recent investment activities – transactions that Pension Plan Dearborn's senior managers might otherwise have no reason to scrutinise.

Consider the specific case in which Rush has a quarterly diversified VAR that has averaged US$10 million (at the 95% confidence level) over the last two years. That means that Pension Plan Dearborn expects to lose no more than 10% of its total investment with manager Rush in 95 of the next 100 quarters. If the diversified VAR for manager Rush is re-calculated every week and suddenly jumps to US$50 million from the historical average of US$10 million, the senior managers of Plan Dearborn might be inclined to wonder – and to ask – why. Because VAR is strategy neutral, only two answers are possible. First, the volatility in Rush's international bond holdings went up (eg, as might have happened following the Asian currency crisis), in which case the risk of the position simply reflects the risks of the asset allocation decision. Alternatively, Rush may have acquired new securities that expose Dearborn to significant additional market risks that were *not* contemplated by the asset allocation decision.

Aside from monitoring a manager's risk relative to an historical risk profile, VAR also facilitates comparisons of the risks of one portfolio or manager with other portfolios or managers. To continue the above example, the increase in manager Rush's VAR might *not* appear problematic if the VAR of other international bond managers engaged by Plan Dearborn rise at the same time. The same is true of the VAR of the benchmark used to evaluate the performance of manager Rush rises proportionally. In these cases, Plan Dearborn may conclude that its market risk has increased because of its exposure to international fixed income as an asset class rather than because of its particular exposure to the investment strategies of manager Rush.

For VAR to provide a useful monitoring benefit, precision in the measurement of VAR is not absolutely essential. In fact, the primary benefit of VAR monitoring comes from examining relative VAR, or the VAR of a manager or portfolio compared to the VAR of a benchmark portfolio, peer group portfolios, other internal or external managers, or the same manager *over time*. Even if the actual levels of VAR – US$10 million and US$50 million above – are imprecisely measured, the same measurement bias may affect other portfolios in the same way.[30] The theory is that these measurement errors cancel out when *relative* VAR is the focus instead of the absolute level of the VAR measure in question. Consequently, asset managers can derive a surprising amount of marginal benefit from monitoring even a variance-based VAR.

External monitoring

The monitoring benefit of VAR is not restricted to internal and external portfolio management. Especially for asset managers whose portfolio holdings are not transparently available to investors at all times (eg, most hedge funds), a VAR reported to investors can help assuage any investors' concerns about market risk without necessitating disclosure of portfolio holdings. Similarly, regular reports of VAR to boards of directors or trustees can go a long way toward reassuring these bodies that market risk is within the specified risk tolerance of the investment pool.

Hedge effectiveness monitoring

Asset managers may use diversified VAR to monitor the extent to which their hedging strategies are accomplishing the desired objectives. To take a simple example, consider a US$500 million mutual fund invested in domestic and international equities that hedges its exchange rate risk using currency forwards and futures. Suppose the one-quarter diversified VAR for the fund is 15% of NAV *without* including the currency hedges in the VAR calculation. The mutual fund manager can evaluate the effectiveness of the hedge (and analyse the extent to which returns and risks are affected by currency risk) by re-calculating diversified VAR *with* the hedges. If the diversified VAR of the *hedged* portfolio is 14.5% of NAV, the fund manager might question whether the hedging is worthwhile *or* whether the hedges have been properly implemented.

The use of VAR to evaluate the effectiveness of a hedging programme depends strongly on the type of hedging programme in place *and* on how the investment policy defines the hedging objective. To see why, consider two different examples both of which concern a pension plan invested in international bonds and equities with a mandate to control its currency risk.[31] In the first case, suppose the pension plan specifies in its investment policy that no more than 1% of the current value *of any particular portfolio* can be exposed to exchange-rate risk and that portfolio managers are left to hedge those risks on their own. The effectiveness of each manager's hedge can be evaluated by examining the diversified VARs of each portfolio *separately* with and without the inclusion of the hedging contracts.

Now suppose the same pension plan specifies in its investment policy that no more than 1% of the current NAV *of the whole plan* can be exposed to exchange-rate risk. Suppose further these managers do not do their own hedging but rather the plan engages a FX overlay manager to hedge its *consolidated* currency risk. The effectiveness of the overlay plan can be evaluated by comparing the plan's *aggregate* diversified VAR with and without the overlay programme included.

Some interesting problems can arise when hedge effectiveness is monitored at a level different from the one specified in the investment policy as the hedging objective. Specifically, suppose the plan's international equity is invested entirely in Canadian dollar-denominated (CAD) equities and that its international bonds are denominated entirely in Austrian shillings (ATS).[32] These two currencies happen to be *negatively correlated*. Consequently, if the pension plan specifies a hedging policy *by portfolio*, the independent hedging decisions of the bond and equity managers may achieve the plan's desired VAR reduction on an individual portfolio basis but may also increase the plan's *aggregate* diversified VAR. By partially hedging two portfolios whose currency risks are negatively correlated, the natural hedge is removed and the plan's consolidated diversified VAR rises.[33]

An overlay manager could, of course, construct a partial hedge that incorporates the negative correlation between the ATS and CAD holdings. For a plan interested in hedging its *aggregate* exchange rate risk, the overlay manager thus can achieve the desired VAR reduction. At the same time, if an overlay manager is used and the diversified VARs of the individual portfolios are then evaluated, at least one of the portfolios will look riskier when the hedges are taken into account.

The usefulness of VAR in evaluating hedging programmes thus depends strongly on the particular hedging objectives specified by the asset manager in the investment policy. Some asset managers may be more concerned about currency risk at the manager level than at the aggregate fund level. The fund may, for example, want to control the independent currency bets made by outside managers and this may opt to require portfolio-specific hedging for *management* purposes. In that case, the fund would specify portfolio-level hedging requirements but then must monitor hedge effectiveness *at the portfolio level*. In the end, the plan *will* probably end up over-hedged (ie, speculating in currencies) in the aggregate when some of the currencies held are negatively correlated. Such plans thus should *also* carefully monitor their aggregate diversified VAR to ensure this residual FX exposure does not become an unexpected (and possibly significant) risk factor.

By contrast, an asset manager whose appetite for currency risk is defined at the aggregate level should both hedge at the aggregate level and monitor the management of that risk using aggregate fund-level diversified VAR.

"What-if" modelling of candidate trades

VAR also can be beneficial to asset managers that wish to eliminate transactional scrutiny by senior managers or directors and trustees. In this way, VAR can actually help give portfolio managers more autonomy than they might otherwise have without a formalised, VAR-based risk management process.

After the great derivatives disasters of the early 1990s, many directors and trustees of institutional investors became concerned with the risks posed by derivatives transactions. As a result, such transactions were prohibited in numerous investment policies and were subject to board-level approval in many others. Transactional monitoring using VAR can be an effective way of addressing this issue.

Suppose, for example, that the limited partners of a hedge fund are concerned about the possibility that the fund managers will engage in leveraged derivatives to augment their returns.[34] Because most hedge funds do not report their portfolio holdings on a regular basis, the limited partners might be inclined to ask the general partner to prohibit such investments. As a better alternative, the general partner might simply agree not to engage in any transactions that would increase the fund's VAR by more than X% of the fund's capital.

In order to minimise unnecessary scrutiny of particular trades, an asset manager need not require that VAR be calculated and reported *ex ante*. Especially if the cost of a VAR system is an issue, few affordable VAR systems allow for this type of real-time computation. Nevertheless, the requirement could be instituted and enforced *ex post*, with the corresponding requirement that any trades in violation of the maximum marginal VAR requirement will be liquidated or hedged within, say, a week of the deal.

As a cautionary note, asset managers must be attentive to the means by which the VAR of a particular transaction is calculated in order for this application of VAR to make sense. One VAR-like statistic, proposed by Mark Garman, is called "DelVar" and examines the impact of a particular trade on the VAR of a portfolio.[35] Although quite useful in its own right, DelVar would *not* be appropriate for the application of VAR discussed here. The particular measurement method proposed by Garman is useful for evaluating the impact of a particular security on the VAR of a portfolio *only for small presumed changes in underlying prices*. DelVar badly underestimates, however, the marginal risk of certain trades for *wide* price swings. In order to apply VAR in the manner discussed here, the portfolio VAR would have to be *fully re-estimated* with and without the candidate trade rather than simply approximated using a measure like DelVar.

Risk targets and thresholds

A third application of VAR to asset management involves measuring and monitoring market risk using a formal system of pre-defined risk targets or thresholds. In essence, risk thresholds take *ad hoc* risk monitoring one step further and systematise the process by which VAR levels are evaluated and discussed for portfolios or managers – or, in some cases, for the whole investment fund.

A system of risk thresholds is tantamount to setting up a tripwire around an investment field, where the field is characterised by a fund's investment policy and risk tolerance. This tripwire is defined in terms of the maximum tolerable VAR allocated to a manager or portfolio and then is monitored by regularly (eg, weekly) comparing actual VARs to these pre-defined targets. Investment managers are permitted to leave the field when they wish, but the tripwire signals senior managers that they have done so. When a tripwire is hit (ie, a VAR threshold is breached), an exception report is generated and discussions and explanations are required.

Risk targets can be specified in terms of absolute or relative VAR. A private bank might conclude, for example, that a particular client's capital should never be placed at risk above a certain amount *regardless* of the risks taken by other clients or managers. In that case, the traders on that client's account could be subject to an absolute VAR threshold. A mutual fund, by contrast, might prefer to specify its risk targets relative to the VAR of its benchmark portfolio or peer group.

The hallmark of a well-functioning risk target system is not that targets are never breached or that all exceptions are rectified through liquidating or hedging current holdings. Rather, the primary benefit of a risk target system is the formalisation of a *process* by which exceptions are discussed, addressed and analysed. Risk thresholds are thus a useful means by which asset managers can systematically monitor and control their market risks without attenuating the autonomy of their portfolio managers. Because the primary purpose of risk limits is to systematise discussions about actual market risk exposures relative to defined risk tolerances, huge investments in VAR calculation systems, moreover, typically are not required. Even an imprecise measure of VAR will usually accomplish the desired result of formalising the risk monitoring process.

Risk limits and risk budgets

A more extreme version of risk targets and risk thresholds is a system of rigid risk limits. This application of VAR is also known as a risk budget. In a risk budget, the fund's total VAR is calculated and then allocated to asset classes *and* specific portfolios in terms of absolute and benchmark-relative VAR, as well as shortfall-at-risk (SAR).[36] Managers are then *required* to remain within their allocated risk budget along these risk dimensions. So, whereas risk targets resemble a tripwire around a field that managers must account *ex post* for crossing, a true risk budget instead acts as an electric fence around the field that managers simply cannot cross *ex ante*.

A total risk budget defined across all portfolios can create numerous problems for an asset manager. First risk budgeting relies at some level on the absolute VAR of a fund and its portfolios. To the extent that the measurement methodology is flawed, the risk budget will be wrong. If the VAR measurement methodology is more biased for some asset classes or security types than others, some managers could be penalised or rewarded simply because of flaws in the measurement methodology. In the extreme, relatively riskier funds could be given a risk budget that is *too high*, whereas relatively safer funds could be allocated *too little* VAR.

Second, risk budgeting defined across both asset classes and portfolios can contradict and call into question the fund's asset allocation decision. This can be especially problematic when a fund manager's board must approve changes in the asset allocation *unless* hitting a risk limit in the risk budget triggers the change. Suppose a pension plan allocates capital into asset classes *annually* using traditional mean-variance asset allocation and portfolio optimisation techniques. Then suppose the plan defines a VAR budget for asset classes and portfolios, where VAR is measured using a variance-based approach. If the risk budget is enforced more frequently than annually, the risk budget will call into question the asset allocation *simply because volatility changes in the markets on a regular basis*. Variance-induced changes in VAR thus prompt a shift in the asset allocation through the risk budget. Even though the *practical* consequence is a change in the asset allocation itself, the *actual* trigger is the risk budget; the board may never be consulted.[37] To avoid this problem, risk budgeting should be limited to re-balancing funds between portfolios *within the same asset class*. Even then, asset managers contemplating a risk budget will need to allocate a considerable sum of money for the VAR calculation system to ensure that the calculation method is not biased against particular managers or financial instruments.

CONCLUSION

Many asset managers have avoided or criticised VAR based on the notion that systematic measurements and disclosures of risk serve only to attenuate the autonomous nature of the investment management process. On the contrary, measuring VAR and using it as the basis for internal monitoring and risk targets, external risk disclosures, and transactional risk evaluations can actually give the asset manager *more* autonomy than if investors or senior manages are unsure of what the fund's market risk exposures actually are. A sound VAR-based risk management system should take the investment policy as given and should seek only to help managers and investors ensure that the risks to which the fund is exposed are those risks to which it *thinks it is* and *wants*, or *needs, to be exposed.*

Most cost-effective systems for measuring VAR rely on simplistic and often unrealistic assumptions. Nevertheless, the benefit of most VAR applications for asset managers traces more to how the VAR estimate is used than to the calculation methodology. Especially for asset managers with exposures in multiple currencies, even simplified VAR can be an invaluable tool for distilling market risk into one summary statistic. It is no panacea, but an asset manager that measures its VAR may better be able to manage its primary investment business than one that is largely unaware of its consolidated market-risk exposures.

1 "Market risk" is the risk that the value of an asset or portfolio declines because of adverse movements in market prices such as interest rates, exchange rates and security prices. Market risk is distinct from other types of financial risk, such as default risk or liquidity risk. In this chapter, our attention is limited to market risk, primarily because that risk is the main financial risk that VAR was developed to measure.

2 See Culp, Miller and Neves (1998).

3 See Culp and Mensink (1999).

4 Throughout this chapter, we shall refer to managers as those who invest funds on behalf of outsiders. The outsiders placing capital with the asset manager are called investors. In a pension plan, for example, the managers are those internal and external portfolio managers (and their senior supervisors) who invest capital on behalf of retirees. The retiree beneficiaries, in turn, are the investors. At a hedge fund, mutual fund or private bank, the managers again represent the portfolio manager(s) or general partner(s), whereas the investors are the outside depositors/purchasers/limited partners.

5 For a more specific discussion of the used of VAR by pension plans, see Culp, Tanner and Mensink (1987).

6 Portions of this section draw heavily from Culp, Miller and Neves, *op. cit.*

7 For a general description of VAR, see Jorion (1997).

8 The VAR distribution may be expressed in returns or in dollars. Return distributions often are empirically more tractable, and these can always be converted to a corresponding potential dollar loss given the current portfolio value.

9 See Jordan and Mackay (1997).

10 This interpretation assumes that asset price changes are independently and identically distributed – ie, that price changes are drawn from essentially the same distribution every period.

11 See Sharpe (1994).

12 This is the source of some confusion in the institutional investment community. When the actual returns of a manager or portfolio serve as the basis for calculating a summary statistic, the resulting metric can be used for performance evaluation but *not* for VAR.

13 See Culp and Mensink, *op. cit.*

14 In practice, VAR is not often implemented in a clean, two-step manner, but discussing it in this way simplifies our discussion – without any loss of generality.

15 The full re-valuation and partial re-valuation methods are compared in JP Morgan, 1996, *RiskMetrics Technical Document*, Fourth Edition.

16 The x-axis labels on the Figure correspond to the upper tick. For example, the 15% label lies between two tick marks and the bar above that number implies that approximately 1% of the historical data was less than or equal to 15% and greater than 14%.

17 Excess kurtosis is the amount by which the kurtosis of a distribution exceeds the kurtosis of the normal distribution, which is three. A positive excess kurtosis statistic indicates that the distribution has as more peaked centre and fatter tails than the normal distribution.

18 For the purpose of this example, we thus treat the FTSE 100 portfolio as a *single asset*.

19 By convention, we drop the negative sign when reporting VAR.

20 VAR, however, does not give any indication of how far beyond this amount the portfolio could decline; it could be £68,701 or £1,000,000.

21 For a review of these methods, see Culp, Miller and Neves, *op. cit.* and Jorion, *op. cit.*

22 To get a moving average estimate of variance, the average is taken over a rolling window of historical volatility data. Given a 20-month rolling window, for example, the variance used for one-month VAR calculations would be the average monthly variance over the most recent 20 months.

23 The data sets also include correlations.

24 We could have come to the same result (save for rounding error) by taking our original equity VAR calculation and simply converting that VAR into US dollars at the prevailing spot rate.

25 The property on which we implicitly rely is that the variance of a portfolio of two assets whose returns are distributed bivariate normal is a linear function of the variance of each asset return plus twice the correlation of the two returns times the two standard deviations. This result can be extended to portfolios comprised of more than two assets if returns are distributed multivariate normal.

26 Volatility and correlation data are also available for the daily frequency.

27 Note in Figure 2 the fat tails of the actual distribution relative to the normal. This is consistent with the positive excess kurtosis statistic we examined earlier.

28 Some investors also avoid VAR for this reason, as well, choosing instead to focus on downside risk measures such as below-target risk or downside semi-variance. See Culp, Tanner and Mensink, *op. cit.*

29 For examples of these approaches, see Jordan and Mackay, *op. cit.*

30 This also may *not* be the case. Each situation should be evaluated on its own to identify sources of measurement error in the VAR statistic – and, in particular, whether measurement error is consistent across assets and portfolios.

31 This situation is explored in more detail in Ihle (1998).

32 This example follows from Ihle, *op. cit.*

33 This is illustrated numerically in Ihle, *op. cit.*

34 Not all derivatives are leveraged. Our use of the term here refers to *formula* leverage rather than margin. A swap in which the hedge fund receives a fixed rate of 8% and pays LIBOR against a notional amount of US$1 million would not be formula-leveraged. A swap in which the fund receives 8% fixed and pays LIBOR *squared* would be.

35 See Garman (1996).

36 SAR is directly analogous to VAR with the *net* asset/liability position subjected to the risk calculation and summary measure. See Culp, Tanner and Mensink, *op. cit.*

37 Ironically, a risk budget may be supported by a board, which thinks the budget reduces the need for board-level micromanagement. Yet, to the extent that the risk budget simply grants fund managers license to circumvent the board-approved asset allocation, the opposite intention will have been achieved.

BIBLIOGRAPHY

Culp, C.L., and R. Mensink, 1999, "Measuring Risk for Asset Allocation, Performance Evaluation and Risk Control: Different Problems, Different Solutions", *Journal of Performance Measurement* 4(1).

Culp, C.L., M.H. Miller and A.M.P. Neves, 1998, "Value-at-Risk: Uses and Abuses", *Journal of Applied Corporate Finance* 10(4).

Culp, C.L., K.T. Tanner and R. Mensink, 1987, "Risks, Returns and Retirement", *Risk* 10(10).

Garman, M., 1996, "Improving on VAR", *Risk* 9(5).

Ihle, G., 1998), "Forward Hedges that Increase Value at Risk", *Derivatives Quarterly* 4(4), pp. 67–72.

Jordan, J.V., and R.J. Mackay, 1997, "Assessing Value at Risk for Equity Portfolios: Implementing Alternative Techniques" in R.J. Schwartz and C.W. Smith, Jr. (eds), *Derivatives Handbook* (New York: John Wiley & Sons)

Jorion, P., 1997, *Value at Risk* (Chicago: Irwin Professional Publishing).

Sharpe, W.F., 1994, "The Sharpe Ratio", *Journal of Portfolio Management*, pp. 49–58.

Risk Budgeting for Pension Funds and Investment Managers Using VAR

Michelle McCarthy*

Deutsche Bank Group

Is there anything really new here? Is risk budgeting just a new way of saying asset allocation? Many investors find discussions of risk budgeting frustratingly mushy, being indistinct from investment practices they have been using for some time. This chapter intends to separate risk budgeting and VAR measurement from classic investment risk practices, such as asset allocation, and from classic investment risk measures, such as standard deviation. It will also show how these new techniques add to the investment process that is unique and valuable. This chapter will identify a set of key market risks for pension funds and asset managers, then describe a risk budgeting framework that addresses these risks. Finally, it will address a number of threats to the quality of a VAR measure, examine how these are addressed, and discuss the use of backtesting to validate the quality of the VAR measure.

DIFFERENTIATING VAR AND RISK BUDGETING FROM CLASSIC INVESTMENT RISK TOOLS

Risk measurement tools have been available to investors for some time now. The investment community actually introduced the first modern risk measures decades ago, these having developed through the work of Markowitz and Sharpe. So why is there a flurry of interest in "new" risk measures, such as VAR, originating from the world of banking? And how

*The author wishes to thank those who contributed to and reviewed this chapter, including Joseph Slunt, Sanjay Kohli, Maarten Nederlof and Kenneth Yip of Deutsche Bank; Kenneth Pennington of Zurich Capital Markets; and particularly Bob Maynard of the Public Employees Retirement System of Idaho who provided extensive comments and lively debate. The opinions expressed here are those of the author and do not represent those of Deutsche Bank.

do these measures differ from the traditional risk measures that have been honed and refined since the 1950s?

VAR is in fact part of the modern portfolio theory family of measures. As we will see in this chapter, however, VAR differs mainly in that it concerns the set of holdings currently in a manager's portfolio, not historical returns, and it has a very particular way of decomposing the risk characteristics of complex securities such as convertibles, mortgages, options and fixed income securities. These two differences give VAR more value as a supervisory tool than most applications of modern portfolio theory; it is able to provide a signal when a portfolio has shifted to a riskier position before performance has registered, rather than after. VAR provides a particularly extensible tool for risk budgeting. As we will see later in this chapter, it can be applied across asset classes, strategies and styles.

However, it is important to point out at this stage that there are a number of misunderstandings about VAR.

First, VAR is often understood to be computed on the assets of a portfolio only, when in fact measures relating to benchmarks and pension liabilities are clearly more important to investors. VAR can, and should, be computed relative to benchmarks and liabilities for investors.

Second, it is understood to forecast only to a short holding period (eg, potential loss in one day or 10 days), when in fact investors' decision horizons are longer than this time period. VAR can be computed for longer holding periods, including periods longer than a year.

Third, it is understood to forecast only the worst-case loss (eg, 99% worst case or 95% worst case), which many find a dubious figure – not least because VAR is based on historical datasets drawn mainly from ordinary markets, when in fact most practitioners know that markets are least likely to resemble ordinary markets in "crash" situations. In fact, VAR can be computed more reliably for lower confidence intervals. This provides a signal of what kinds of losses are possible under ordinary circumstances, and when the positions of a portfolio have been made riskier, this signal will increase. When the signal increases, it allows managers to take corrective action; VAR is useful even if it does not accurately measure the true "worst case" of a portfolio.

VAR methodologies vary; this chapter does not rest on a single approach for the calculation of potential loss. Methodologies can include the *"parametric"* approach, which looks at the volatility of key risk factors and their correlation to one another, and appears very similar to mean-variance models familiar in the asset management world; the *historical simulation*, which finds a portfolio loss at a particular confidence interval if a portfolio is re-priced through numerous actual historical scenarios; or the *Monte Carlo simulation*, which often looks like a blend of both these methods, re-pricing portfolios under simulated prices that have been constrained by historical volatility and correlation among risk factors.

VAR DEFINITION

In the examples which follow, we will frequently refer to "one-year 84% confidence VAR" and "Tracking Error". These have been chosen because they are convenient measures – they are very easy to compare to performance and relative performance, and will be recognisably close to the actual annual performance of ordinary portfolios. The 84% confidence interval represents the downside 1 standard deviation measure. VAR at one-year 84% confidence is a portfolio's possible loss, relative to its mean expected return, if the securities in the portfolio are held for a year. The 1 standard deviation confidence interval represents not some worst case, but rather the downside risk in an ordinary year. When this measure is computed on the securities in a portfolio minus the securities in its benchmark, the result is Tracking Error (also called "*ex ante* tracking error", "relative risk" and "active risk"). It becomes the possible loss of the portfolio in an ordinary year, relative to its mean expected outperformance (usually taken to be zero), if the position relative to the benchmark is maintained for a year. It is not the same as the standard deviation of past performance relative to benchmark, as it focuses on today's portfolio and benchmark, not the historical fund performance.

Preparing the portfolio for any of these models can be done in a number of ways which vary by product and asset class. There are products whose prices change with a great deal of certainty for a given change in a general market risk factor; for instance, the price of a given government bond is a function of the risk-free yield curve. Most high-quality fixed-income, derivative, commodity and foreign exchange products have this quality of being almost formulaically linked to a set of observable market parameters – their prices change instantly when the underlying risk factors used to model them change. A stock, on the other hand, may have general market factors that are associated with price change, but they are softer, and are often dwarfed by issuer-specific news. Equities are therefore often regressed against a set of indices or factors, rather than put through a pricing formula.

Given this, the equities in a portfolio are generally prepared by having their price histories regressed against the price histories of a smaller number of indices or factors. This simplifies the sheer number of risk factors needed to describe a portfolio, while still taking into account the security-by-security specifics of the portfolio.

Fixed income, derivative and foreign exchange instruments are less commonly treated through regression. As noted above, these instruments are usually priced formulaically as a function of market risk factors. Decomposing these instruments into their risk factors is usually just a matter of using their pricing models for an extra purpose; instead of solving given current market yields, curves and rates for an instrument's price, the instrument is stress-tested to find the sensitivity of its price to one or more states of the market. Consequently, this is used to find how much a portfolio is exposed to a given risk factor. For example, if a portfolio holds 1,000 call options on stock index ABC (each contract worth Eur 1), these options can be priced first at current market levels, then under an upward move of 1% in the price of the underlying stock index. If the option price moves +Eur 0.50 for a move of +Eur 1 in index ABC, holding that option is like holding $0.5 \times 1,000$ contracts of ABC. In a parametric VAR model, this position would register as an ownership of Eur 500 of index ABC.

To illustrate the contrasts between VAR and traditional measures and to explain risk budgeting, we will use a sample pension fund throughout this chapter. The fictitious "Acme"[1] Pension Fund will be a US defined benefit pension fund whose assets have a market value of about US$4.2 billion. Acme Pension is in surplus; the present value of its liabilities is nearly US$3.8 billion, leaving a surplus of US$400 million. Acme Pension has a high level asset allocation, which we will call its Policy: 50% Russell 3000 Index, 20% MSCI Europe/Asia/Far East Index, 25% Lehman Aggregate Bond Index and 5% Cash. Its asset managers have slightly different benchmarks, which are adjusted more frequently than the overall policy. These more specific, tactical targets are referred to in this chapter as the Benchmarks. The current set of benchmarks is as shown in Table 1.

Prior to discussing a risk budgeting framework, it is important to review what risks would need to be treated by such a framework. Risk budgeting

Table 1 The current set of benchmarks for Acme Pension Fund

Equity Managers

Large Cap Growth manager	Russell 1000 Growth	15%
Large Cap Value manager	Russell 1000 Value	13%
Small Cap Equity manager	Russell 2000	13%
"Equity Plus" S&P 500 Enhanced manager	S&P 500	5%
Technology Fund manager	S&P 500	4%
International Equity manager	MSCI EAFE	20%
Convertible Bond manager	50% S&P 500/50% Lehman Aggregate	4%
Total Equity benchmarks		74%

Fixed Income

"FixedFund", US Fixed Income manager	Lehman Aggregate	21%
International Fixed Income manager	Salomon WGBI	5%
Total Fixed Income benchmarks		26%

ordinarily covers the market risks in a portfolio; credit risks are still usually limited by name-by-name limits, and operational risks through policies and procedures. What, then, are the market risks that need to be considered for pension plans and asset managers?

WHAT ARE THE KEY MARKET RISKS FOR PENSION FUNDS?

Defined benefit plans
Surplus risk
The single key risk for a defined benefit pension plan is the chance that the assets in portfolio might underperform the pension liabilities it owes to its staff, causing the sponsor of the pension plan to have to unexpectedly contribute funds to make up the shortfall. In Acme's case, not only would it have to exhaust its US$400 million surplus before this were possible, but it might be given a number of years to make up a shortfall, so even if Acme were to realise a loss of US$600 million on the difference in performance between the assets and the liabilities, this does not mean it would need to raise US$200 million in cash immediately. Nonetheless, controlling the potential magnitude of this figure is an important goal for pension funds. They cannot control a number of pieces of the equation, but they can control their asset allocation and manager selection choices to help minimise the chance of a pension contribution.

Pensions commonly undertake periodic asset allocation studies to determine an asset mix which best meets their liability profile and risk tolerance. The lowest risk position may be to immunise liabilities using fixed income investments, but this is not entirely realistic, as there are insufficient long dated fixed income instruments to cover all liabilities. The closest match becomes the equity markets. Further, immunisation creates opportunity costs; if peer funds outperform their liabilities, they may be able to rest from making pension fund contributions. This then becomes a competitive strength. Straying too far from the liabilities, however, creates the risk of a shortfall.

Tracking error to planwide asset allocation
Once an asset allocation has been selected, it is now a proxy for the liabilities of the pension plan. If the pension staff decide to choose a mix of managers that differs significantly from the intended asset allocation, this risks ultimately underperforming the liabilities and causing a shortfall. If an individual manager invests a significant amount of his fund away from the benchmark eg, by shifting into cash, a different asset class or sector at some point that manager again risks failing to meet the pension fund's liabilities. This is why tracking error is a key risk measure for pension funds. While "you can't eat relative performance," you also do not want authority for your absolute risk being taken at a level which does not have the full

planwide perspective. For those who can only see a part of your plan, tracking error is the right measure of their risk. While tracking error limits can be quite broad, when they are well designed, such limits anchor managers to the portion of your asset allocation that you need them to fill.

Summarising the measures most important for defined benefit plans to monitor, they are "surplus at risk" and tracking error, at both plan and manager level.

Defined contribution plans/money purchase schemes

Inappropriate asset allocation
It is not entirely clear how directly this risk affects the company organising the plan; it is easier, however, to see how it affects the individual. If the asset allocation chosen by the plan participant is not in keeping with the future payments the participant will require during retirement, the participant will have a shortfall. If the participant chooses cash and short-term bond options, this risk is quite evident. There could be knock-on effects for the company organising the plan if there are lawsuits based on insufficient education for plan participants, or insufficient asset class choices in the plan; most companies have gone to great pains to provide education and a wide range of choices to minimise this risk.

Rogue manager
The next risk which could affect the participants and – more than likely because of lawsuits – the company organising a defined contribution plan would be a manager whose performance differed significantly from that expected for his asset class (tracking error), or who suffered a large absolute loss (total risk), or who had one or other of these sorts of losses from either poor controls or instruments deemed excessively risky.

In summarising the risks that the defined contribution manager may wish to monitor, the asset allocation risk is difficult to monitor at company level. It would require drawing up something like the liabilities that might be reasonable for the employees covered by the plan were they to be covered by a defined benefit plan, and then measuring the surplus at risk between these fictitious liabilities and the participants' asset allocation; rather a lot of work for a risk that, to the company, is something of a third order effect. There are a number of internet-based calculators available to measure this effect on the plan participant level; these do not attempt to break each mutual fund into its holdings but instead use the return histories of funds to show whether a given asset mix could meet a given participant's needs in the future.

Monitoring for managers who have strayed from an expected path cannot be done via these internet based calculators, as they use historical returns, not current fund holdings. It is very important to use current fund holdings to observe unexpected behaviour before it becomes a well established pattern. This can be done by measuring *ex ante* tracking error just as is done for a defined benefit plan.

WHAT ARE THE KEY MARKET RISKS FOR AN ASSET MANAGEMENT FIRM?

Like pension plans, asset managers have a number of important market risks; some are more controllable than others.

Variable fee income

As most asset managers are paid in fees relating to the size of assets under management, their fee income grows when the funds they manage have strong absolute performance, and shrinks when markets turn down in an absolute sense. This effect can be modelled partly as a function of market rates and partly as a function of redemption and sales patterns. This risk is very difficult to hedge. The core risks of every type of business have this quality; investors in publicly traded companies expect them to take their core risks, not hedge them away. If an asset management firm sells away its risk of having fee income drop when the main equity index drops, it has also normally sold away more upside than its investors would like, should the equity market rise.

Customer satisfaction; product integrity

There are a number of ways an asset management firm risks losing customers: poor absolute performance, poor performance relative to performance benchmarks, and poor performance relative to peers are key market-related risks that can cause a loss of customers. If any one of these situations is caused by an operational risk, a manager error or fraud, or by an instrument which fell within the letter of investment guidelines but which was perhaps riskier than their spirit, there is an additional risk that the asset management firm may have to make up a shortfall itself, or that it may be successfully sued for the shortfall amount.

VAR measures can be used to monitor the potential absolute and/or relative risk of each fund (see below for a discussion of risk relative to peers), in order to observe whether a fund's risk is unusual when considering how it has been communicated to clients, and to provide an ongoing communication mechanism. Benchmark-relative measures are more common than absolute measures, except for hedge funds; the benchmark chosen for the tracking error calculation will almost always be the same one used in periodic performance reporting. These measures can communicate to customers what kind of downturns are "business as usual" for a given strategy or asset class. They can also help senior management to monitor whether a portfolio manager is at a riskier position than he/she has historically taken, allowing them the chance to correct the course before unacceptable performance registers. In this way, the market-related product quality/customer satisfaction risk of a firm can be better managed.

WHAT IS "RISK BUDGETING" FOR AN INVESTOR?

Put simply, "risk budgeting" is the process of allocating an allowable measure of potential loss to different aspects of the investment process, monitoring whether those pieces of the investment process have exceeded their measure, taking corrective action (if deemed necessary) when a measure is exceeded, and using the risk measurement process to evaluate risk-adjusted return. The first step of risk budgeting is to determine which parts of the investment process need monitoring in this fashion, and set a risk tolerance level.

What to monitor

The following elements of the investment process (illustrated in Figure 1) represent the kind of items that might be subject to a risk budget. They are practical measures of the key risks we identified for pension plans and asset managers in the prior section.

Surplus-at-risk

Surplus-at-risk (SAR) is the amount by which the pension's policy asset allocation might underperform its pension liabilities, over a given time horizon (ie, one year) at a given confidence interval (ie, 95%). In the case of Acme, this would be the amount by which its policy could underperform its future liability cashflows, in present value terms, in the next year; the possible reduction in its US$400 million surplus, or the possible corporate contribution which might be required if the surplus is exhausted. In Acme's case, it could suffer a draw-down of US$1.141 billion relative to the mean expected return of assets versus liabilities in the 95% worst case; after subtracting a net mean expected return of 5% (or US$212 million) and subtracting the US$400 million surplus, there is a 5% chance that Acme might need to contribute US$529 million to its pension plan in the next year.

Implementation risk or tactical asset allocation risk

"Implementation risk" or "tactical asset allocation risk" is the degree to which the plan's tactical asset allocation might underperform its strategic asset allocation over, for example, one year at 95% confidence. In Acme's case, this is the difference between its policy and its asset managers' benchmarks. There is currently a 5% chance that the asset allocation pursued by Acme's pension staff might underperform the strategic asset allocation by more than 2.39% in the next year.

Active risk, planwide

"Active risk, planwide" is the amount by which the actual assets in which the plan has invested, across all its portfolios, could underperform its tactical asset allocation, usually in one year at 84% confidence (this is the same as tracking error, for the whole plan). In Acme's case, this would be the

Figure 1 Acme's current risk levels

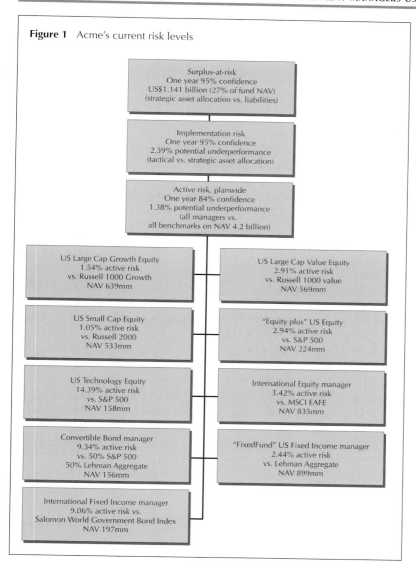

degree to which the assets invested could underperform the benchmarks at the total plan level. In an ordinary year, this group of investments might underperform the tactical asset allocation of the plan by 1.38%.

Active risk per manager

"Active risk per manager" is the amount by which a given manager might underperform their benchmark within the tactical asset allocation, usually at one year, 84% confidence (eg, tracking error). The highest tracking error among Acme's managers is currently the 14.39% tracking error of the US Technology Equity Fund manager, although this could be attributed to the unusual choice of the S&P 500 index as the benchmark for this fund; the lowest is the tracking error of the US Small Cap Equity manager to the Russell 2000 index.

You will note in Figure 1 that the active risk planwide is 1.38%, while if you sum the tracking error for each manager, weighted for the principal size of each portfolio, this totals 3.42%. This means that the managers' active risks are offsetting each other significantly; asking a single manager to revert to their benchmark could in fact raise planwide active risk, and this needs to be taken into account before taking actions at the manager level. In addition to a standalone or ("absolute") active risk figure per manager, VAR users often calculate another measure, sometimes called "incremental VAR", sometimes called "marginal VAR". It shows the change in planwide VAR which would result from each manager going flat to their benchmark, in order to help assess whether that manager's active risk is a key diversifier for the portfolio. If it is an important diversifier, this needs to be taken into account before the portfolio is significantly changed. Table 2 shows the incremental VAR statistic for each of the managers in this portfolio alongside the absolute active risk figure for each.

Interpreting Table 2, there are three managers with negative incremental risk: the Large Cap Growth, Large Cap Value and Small Cap Equity managers. If any one of these went flat to the portfolio benchmark, the planwide active risk would increase. If the Large Cap Growth manager indexed to their benchmark, planwide active risk would go up by 11 basis points, from 1.38% to 1.49%; that manager's active risk taking is balancing some other portion of the portfolio. The biggest adder of net risk is the

Table 2 Incremental VAR statistics compared to absolute active risk

	Principal in mm	Absolute active risk	Absolute risk Principal-weighted	Incremental risk Principal-weighted
Large Cap Growth manager	639	1.54%	0.23%	–0.11%
Large Cap Value manager	569	2.91%	0.39%	–0.07%
Small Cap Equity manager	533	1.05%	0.13%	–0.07%
"Equity Plus" Enhanced S&P	224	2.94%	0.16%	0.03%
Technology Fund manager	158	14.39%	0.54%	0.19%
International Equity manager	835	3.42%	0.68%	0.31%
Convertible Bond manager	156	9.34%	0.35%	0.16%
FixedFund US Fixed Income manager	899	2.44%	0.52%	0.17%
International Fixed Income manager	197	9.06%	0.42%	0.27%
	4,210		3.42%	0.87%

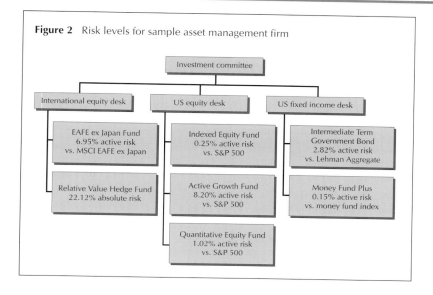

Figure 2   Risk levels for sample asset management firm

International Equity Manager; planwide active risk would go from 1.38% to 1.07% if that manager went flat to their benchmark.

Each layer of a given pension plan described above may be dealt with by different individuals. For example, the board of trustees should have a clear idea what kind of draw-down on the pension plan is unacceptably high, so they may focus on monitoring and establishing thresholds for SAR. The remaining risks, however, may be the domain of the pension staff.

In an asset management firm, only the active risk per manager is within the asset management firm's realm of responsibility, unless the firm bears some overall asset allocation responsibility for the investor. Monitoring this active risk per manager can help the firm to ensure consistency across different products, meaning that the risks taken in accounts are in keeping with customer expectations and performance goals. Asset management firms may have reasons to tally up risks across all of the portfolios they manage, to ensure product consistency and to understand how fee income could be affected by market movements. The risks they can most easily control, however, are at the "active risk per manager" level.

Figure 2 shows how the risk levels of a number of funds in a given asset management complex might appear.

Setting risk tolerance thresholds

Once an entity has decided which measures to monitor, the next step is to establish risk tolerance levels. This is more difficult: if the level is set too tightly, it eliminates the chance of outperformance and may make the fund perform less well than more aggressive peer funds. If set too loosely, large losses will be possible before the measure ever gives a signal that a corrective action is needed.

Setting these thresholds is the moment where *risk measurement* turns to *risk management*; the thresholds set an acknowledged, acceptable level of risk – in effect, an amount of loss that is tolerable in the pursuit of gain. The numbers used commonly come from historical experiences, and outperformance expectations combined with Sharpe or information ratio expectations.

For example, if Acme pension had underperformed its benchmark portfolio by 4% in some recent year and this was unacceptable to plan trustees, the plan may want to flag when its potential underperformance as a fund exceeds 4% at a given confidence interval. The trustees can provide Acme with the parameters it needs to monitor by stating that, for example, "we do not want more than a 10% chance of repeating that experience". That statement translates to a threshold of 4% for the year, 90% confidence active risk, planwide. While this may not seem like a very sophisticated approach to setting risk budgets, it is practical and tangible. It translates the experience of the trustees into the language of risk measurement.

Another way to arrive at a risk budget is to work from performance expectations. If, for instance, Acme hopes to outperform its benchmark portfolio by 5% next year, then it needs to be given sufficient off-benchmark room to do so. If Acme allows itself a tracking error of 10% and achieves its outperformance of 5%, then its information ratio will have been 0.5. If it allows itself a tracking error of 8% while keeping an outperformance goal of 5%, it is expecting its managers to achieve an information ratio of 0.625 – a more aggressive goal which may be harder to meet. If it allows itself a tracking error of only 5%, it further decreases the likelihood that the managers can achieve the 5% expected outperformance by forcing them to an information ratio of 1.0. Deriving the active risk budgets from Sharpe or information ratio expectations is useful in setting up a threshold that is in keeping with performance expectations. If Acme considers a ratio of 0.5 to be a good goal, then this will lead to setting each manager's active risk budget at twice their outperformance target. The budget for active risk, planwide, should also be twice that of the planwide outperformance goal.

Figure 3 shows what Acme might have arrived at as a budget at the end of its deliberations. The managers' individual tracking error budgets, when combined, sum to more than the total active risk budget for the fund – if summed in absolute, they would total a 5% potential underperformance. This is intentional, as it allows for the fact that there may be offsets across the managers. Downstreaming the portfolio-wide number helps to focus, however, on which managers present the fund with the best use of its scarce tracking error resource.

Asset management firms go through a similar process in establishing active risk per manager thresholds. Historical experiences and performance

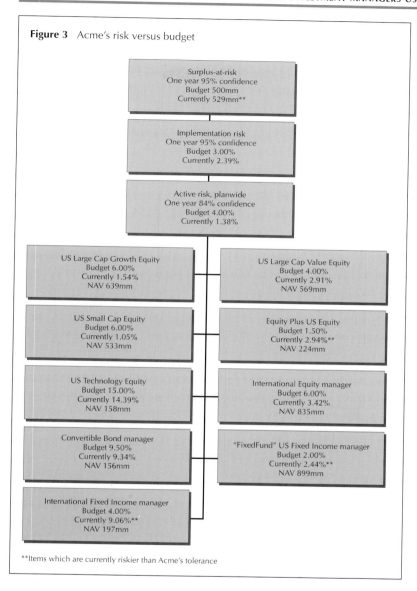

Figure 3 Acme's risk versus budget

Surplus-at-risk
One year 95% confidence
Budget 500mm
Currently 529mm**

Implementation risk
One year 95% confidence
Budget 3.00%
Currently 2.39%

Active risk, planwide
One year 84% confidence
Budget 4.00%
Currently 1.38%

US Large Cap Growth Equity
Budget 6.00%
Currently 1.54%
NAV 639mm

US Large Cap Value Equity
Budget 4.00%
Currently 2.91%
NAV 569mm

US Small Cap Equity
Budget 6.00%
Currently 1.05%
NAV 533mm

Equity Plus US Equity
Budget 1.50%
Currently 2.94%**
NAV 224mm

US Technology Equity
Budget 15.00%
Currently 14.39%
NAV 158mm

International Equity manager
Budget 6.00%
Currently 3.42%
NAV 835mm

Convertible Bond manager
Budget 9.50%
Currently 9.34%
NAV 156mm

"FixedFund" US Fixed Income manager
Budget 2.00%
Currently 2.44%**
NAV 899mm

International Fixed Income manager
Budget 4.00%
Currently 9.06%**
NAV 197mm

**Items which are currently riskier than Acme's tolerance

expectations are the touchstones for setting up a threshold level for a port-folio. Better yet, if customers explicitly request a risk guideline, this is more direct. It means that instead of guessing at customer risk tolerance, it becomes an agreed item. If the customer signs up for a given level of active risk, the asset manager can monitor whether the fund is within that level.

Risk thresholds are by no means guarantees that risk levels will not be exceeded. The very way they are structured means they will occasionally be exceeded – for an 84% confidence measure, underperformance should be worse than indicated for about 16% of the time. This needs to be explicitly acknowledged by all parties using these measures. Other, more traditional controls such as investment guidelines and standard deviation measures have the same flaw – they do not prevent unpleasant losses and, in fact, it is less clear under other types of controls what sorts of losses are possible as portfolios pursue gain. The greater clarity provided by VAR-based risk measures should not be mistaken for a guarantee, however.

Take as an example Acme's international equity portfolio. Acme might impose a limit in its guidelines to state that only 20% of the fund could be concentrated in Japan. It may suffer losses on Japanese stocks if there is a severe downturn in Japan, even in the presence of such a limit. A VAR limit would target a level of volatility for the portfolio. For instance, if Japan became more volatile, investments in Japan would use up more and more of such a limit, making a volatility based limit increasingly more restrictive. This limit is still reactive – Japan may only become more volatile *after* it has begun its descent – but it has a quicker feedback mechanism than the guideline and deals well with the complexity of limiting many countries' risks at once. VAR presents a portfolio's potential loss or tracking error implications far more clearly than guidelines do and allows Acme to monitor whether, since the last look at the portfolio, active risk has doubled from 3.4% to 6.8%. If no action is taken, the actual underperformance could be much more than 6.8% if some market crisis erupts – perhaps 10% or 12%. By moving from 3.4% to 6.8%, however, the VAR signal alerts Acme to a more significant off-benchmark position than had previously existed, allowing Acme to decide whether or not to initiate a change before performance has occurred. This clarity is the value of measuring VAR and comparing it to a budget threshold.

Trade-offs and peer comparisons

As is the case with tight investment guidelines, tight VAR budgets can constrain a portfolio's ability to outperform liabilities and/or benchmarks. Risk budgets are also difficult to reconcile with peer studies; peers with very different liabilities, or poor controls on risk, might outperform Acme pension fund in any given period. It is very difficult, and sometimes unwise, to manage to the dual constraints of being a top quartile fund in terms of returns relative to peers and in terms of risk adjusted returns permitted under an internal set of constraints. These two goals can have diametrically opposed investment processes; it is our belief that measurement relative to internal constraints is most likely to be well-matched to the business goals of a given pension fund, and should therefore be favoured over measures that do not adjust for different internal constraints.

If more data were gathered on the SAR, implementation risks and active risks borne by universes of pension funds, these data would be more fairly compared across the universe than return information alone. However, it will be some time before these measures are available in large scale for such comparisons.

A reminder of how this is different from asset allocation

Risk budgeting has two important qualities which differentiate it from asset allocation: *downstreaming* and *dynamic triggers*.

Downstreaming means that, in risk budgeting, there is a set of cascading limits which start with SAR and move all the way down to security selection; the risk budget addresses all of the risks at and between these points in the same units. This helps to ensure that the amount of discretion allowed to all those with risk–taking authority has been thought out ahead of time so that it fits together well with overall risk tolerance. Under classic investment management practice, individual managers may have tracking error limits or investment guidelines which can be "stress tested" in some fashion to their maximal parameters, but these are rarely related to some maximal tracking error for the plan, which in turn is rarely related to some maximum degree by which the asset allocation can differ from the stream of liabilities. Moreover, each of these points of risk may not be reviewed jointly, at the same time, under classic investment practices; risk budgeting puts in place a set of measures for these various levels of risk which are meant to be monitored concomitantly and on a regular schedule.

Dynamic triggers refers to the fact that the various risk-takers in a risk budgeting system utilise more of their risk budget as the assets they invest in become more volatile, and as correlations among financial markets change. In this way, the risk budget does not require a hard-coded allocation to each market, but instead is phrased as a unit of potential loss – and potential loss increases as a function of the size of a position, its volatility and its correlation with other portfolio risks.

Maintaining a quality VAR measure

Certain practices can dilute the quality of a VAR measure. If a pension fund asks its investment managers to conduct the "active risk per manager" measure individually, each manager may have a different approach – meaning comparisons may be impossible. This would make it extremely difficult to use these individual measures to pull together a meaningful "active risk, planwide" measure.

If anyone conducting a VAR measure does so using too limited a historical data sample, too long a historical data sample, or changing historical data to reflect their view of the markets, there is significant risk that their measure will have poor accuracy as a forecast. (More of this will be discussed below in the section on backtesting.)

Of the three VAR "errors" mentioned above, the third – whether or not historical data are changed to suit market views – is the most controllable.

If investment managers change the VAR methodology to reflect their current market views, this can distort the measure and falsely bury risk signals. Anyone executing a strategy in the markets has a forecast, which is usually different from what has occurred in recent history. Risk-takers develop a set of tools to measure their portfolios under their forecasts. It is important not to interchange these forecasts with the tools used for defence, such as the VAR measures monitored for risk budgeting. These tools must be kept separate from the forecasts used for "offence" – for risk-taking.

An example illustrates the dangers of mixing offence and defence tools: an investment manager might forecast that credit spreads will narrow – ie, that the correlation of corporate bonds and government bonds will be higher in the future than in the past. Perhaps in the past, the correlation of government and corporate yield changes was 0.80 and the manager believes it will move towards 0.90 as spreads narrow and the two sectors behave more similarly. They will purchase corporate bonds and sell government bonds to reflect its view. If those responsible for the VAR system also overwrite the historical correlation of 0.80 with the manager's forecast correlation of 0.90, the VAR figure for the portfolio is reduced. The VAR measure will fail to pick up the appropriate signals if the manager is wrong; it will lose on its strategy *and* have a VAR measure that understates just how risky that strategy can be. The rule among defensive VAR practitioners is to only change historical data in a direction that is certain to be conservative – in a direction which *increases* your VAR measure. Raising volatility estimates is always a conservative action, lowering them always reduces the VAR measure. Changing correlation estimates is not always straightforward: it can be difficult to determine whether the effect is truly uniformly conservative, and it should therefore be undertaken with great caution. Those who allow investment managers to conduct the VAR measure, and those who compute the measure themselves, need to be satisfied that the quality of the VAR measure has not been compromised by overwriting historical data with a view that is more "rosy".

Taking corrective action

Once a plan has established what to monitor and determined how much risk may be excessive, a set of actions needs to be put into place for whenever these risk thresholds are exceeded. Different institutions will have different approaches to this. Some will require a set of procedures to which there are no exceptions; others may prefer the risk budget excess to be a starting point of a conversation, which need not necessarily lead to a change in portfolio composition.

Because VAR measurement is newer than other risk measures, more institutions currently fall into the second category. Such institutions are not looking for an automatic process that forces actions without discussion; they are looking for a signal that will assist them in identifying what to investigate. They need to study all the information brought out by the VAR measure, understand the manager's intentions, and look at whether they believe the future in a given asset class is likely to be so different from the past that the VAR signal is rendered invalid. The value of using a measure and a threshold, in this case, is to help the pension staff or the investment committee at an asset management firm identify funds that may have a more extreme profile than usual, and which are therefore worthy of looking into in more detail.

The advantage of this conversational approach is that a black box is not making a decision; it is rare that market participants are willing to give a simple, statistical model that much power. The disadvantage to this softer process is that the players may convince one another that a problem does not exist when in fact it does. If thresholds are never enforced or are always moved higher when a breach occurs, they lose their utility.

When a VAR threshold is exceeded, the following types of actions are examples of possible steps to be taken.

Surplus-at-risk (see Figure 4)
❑ Elevate the information to the board;
❑ If decisionmakers agree that the change which has triggered the risk threshold is persistent and important, shift the strategic asset allocation to reduce the potential threat to surplus.
❑ If the change is thought to be technical or temporary, take no action. If the change persists beyond a given time period, the item should be raised again.

Implementation risk (see Figure 5)
❑ Elevate the information to the investment committee.
❑ If decisionmakers agree that the gap between the tactical and strategic asset allocations has widened beyond their comfort zone, bring the tactical asset allocation closer to the strategic.
❑ If the change is thought to be technical or temporary, take no action but continue to monitor its severity and revisit if it does not self-correct.

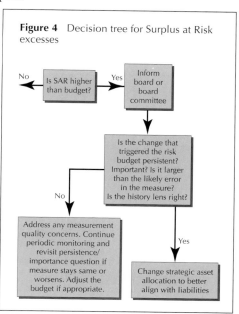

Figure 4 Decision tree for Surplus at Risk excesses

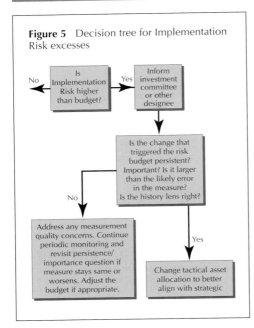

Figure 5 Decision tree for Implementation Risk excesses

Active risk, planwide (see Figure 6)

❑ Elevate the information to the investment committee or a responsible individual.

❑ Determine the drivers of the off-benchmark risk.

Could it be the combined effects of different managers, none of whom is at an unacceptable tracking error level? This is not uncommon, particularly since the individual managers' tracking error limits usually sum to a higher figure than the planwide risk tolerance. If they summed arithmetically to the planwide figure, there would be no opportunity to take advantage of diversification across the managers' tracking errors, and the plan would

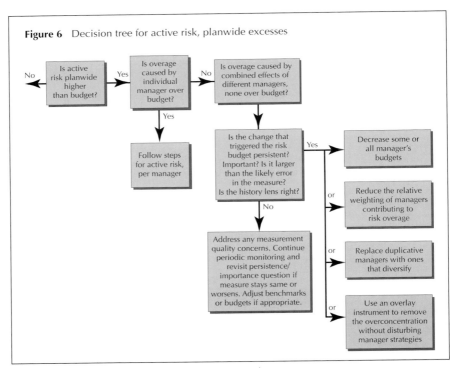

Figure 6 Decision tree for active risk, planwide excesses

take insufficient risk to meet its outperformance goals. In this case, if the investment committee deems the risk budget excess to be persistent and important, managers' tracking error thresholds in the affected asset classes could be decreased. Managers could also be asked to take on different sector weightings, a duplicative manager could be replaced by one which diversifies better, or the plan could even put in place an overlay to reduce the concentration without disturbing managers' portfolios.

❑ The investment committee might consider the effect not to be significant or persistent, but might closely monitor this measure to ensure it does not increase or persist longer than expected.
❑ If the overage is caused by a manager or managers who are at too high a risk level relative to their risk budget, see the "active risk per manager" section below.

If the overage is caused by a combination of managers who are all under their individual risk budgets, the committee may:

❑ revise some managers' budgets lower and ask them to trim positions;
❑ replace some managers with others who diversify the fund better; or
❑ use an overlay strategy.

Active risk, per manager (see Figure 7)
❑ Elevate the information to the investment committee or a responsible individual.

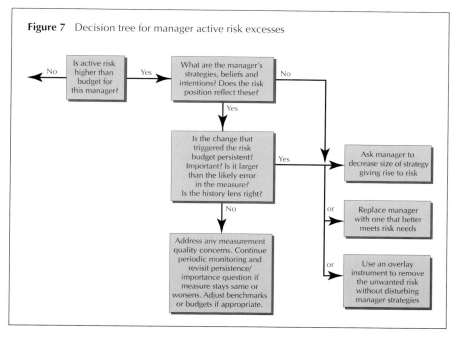

Figure 7   Decision tree for manager active risk excesses

❏ Determine the drivers of off-benchmark risk.

❏ Understand manager's beliefs and intentions.

❏ Decide whether the historical dataset which gave rise to the VAR signal should be ignored in favour of a forecast; the investment committee could decide to accept the portfolio and raise the Active Risk budget or employ other measures to monitor the off-benchmark strategy.

❏ The benchmark could be changed to one which better accommodates the manager's strategy.

❏ If the off-benchmark risk is thought to be unacceptable, the investment committee could:

- request a shift in the manager's portfolio to reduce active risk to an acceptable level;
- replace the manager; or
- put in place an overlay to reduce the off-benchmark position without disturbing the manager's portfolio.

Evaluating risk-adjusted performance

Evaluating performance and performance attribution data about managers and the plan as a whole closes the loop; it helps solidify whether the VAR measures were predicting accurately what they were meant to predict. VAR by necessity will be less precise than performance reporting; it is trying to forecast possible return, and sources of return, given the holdings in a portfolio and the risk factors which represent those holdings. Breaking holdings into risk factors is sometimes called "risk decomposition" or "risk attribution". Risk decomposition restates a portfolio as a set of factors that should drive a large percentage of performance – but risk decomposition is mute on information such as manager skill and frequency of portfolio rebalancing.

Performance measurement starts with the "answer", a known amount of performance, and works backwards to identify what variables caused it. The more similar the tools used for performance attribution and risk attribution, the better these tools can be used together, to make a forecast and then to see if it becomes a reality. Risk measurement may be less accurate than performance measurement, but unlike performance measurement, it provides an early warning of unacceptable portfolio characteristics before they can be crystallised as unacceptable losses.

Risk-adjusted performance measures are widely recognised to be superior tools to evaluate managers; if performance alone is observed, managers will have no incentive to minimise risk while maximising return.

VAR can be used as the denominator in the risk-adjusted return fraction, but is inferior to using the standard deviation of returns in some circumstances, and superior in others.

VAR does not give any credit for manager skill, but standard deviation of returns does. For instance, in a simplified case where Acme's

"FixedFund" Fixed Income manager buys and sells bonds but whose port-folio persistently has the duration of a four-year government bond, VAR will consider FixedFund to have the return volatility of a four year government bond. In a sense, VAR will assume the fund has average market volatility. If the FixedFund manager executes and times trades consistently better than the market, they will earn higher than average returns and have lower than average volatility. VAR might register an annual volatility of 4% for such a portfolio, when the volatility of the manager's actual returns might be 3%. VAR is an inferior risk-adjusted performance measure when manager skill is significantly different from the market average.

When portfolios use options, however, a well-executed VAR measure can be superior to standard deviation in adjusting return for risk. For example, in Acme's "Equity Plus" Enhanced S&P 500 fund, we have Equity Plus sell put options on the S&P 500 index to increase return. If the S&P declines significantly, these options will cause losses for the portfolio. However, at the time of writing, the S&P has been in a secular upturn for the last several years; these options would show very little volatility in an upward-trending market. The S&P has an annual standard deviation of 18.24% at the time of writing, and the standard deviation of Equity Plus historical returns will effectively be equal to this. The premium the man-ager is earning would appear to be met with very little risk were the denominator in the fraction to be the volatility of returns. A VAR measure, however, weighs equally the chance that the market will go up as well as down, and if used as the denominator in the risk-adjusted return fraction, would "charge" volatility against this manager for the potential losses he would sustain in a downward market move. The VAR figure might be 21%, which better captures the manager's potential option losses than the 18.24% standard deviation of returns. Some VAR measures will not pick up this effect (notably the mean-variance, parametric or "delta-normal" methods), but those using the historical simulation or Monte Carlo methodologies will usually reflect option risk in this fashion.

RISK BUDGETING VERSUS ASSET ALLOCATION

Risk budgeting rests most easily on a framework of VAR measurement. The VAR of a portfolio can be estimated at an asset class level, and this is a key component of traditional efficient frontier asset allocation studies and asset/liability studies. The inputs to classic mean-variance optimisers are the standard deviation for the benchmark representing an asset class and its correlation with other such benchmarks. The classic analysis of Acme's portfolio would use the managers' benchmarks – ie, their mean expected returns, standard deviations around those returns, and correlations to one another as the basis of a risk analysis.

VAR measurement builds on this framework by taking the analysis to the security level rather than remaining at the benchmark level. Rather than assuming that the manager of the Equity Plus fund has the same volatility as the S&P index, VAR analysis breaks down the equity put options he has sold to show that his potential loss is, in fact, higher than that of the S&P.

It is costly in terms of time and system resources to conduct this security level analysis; for portfolios that have limited fixed income risk, exposure to foreign exchange and limited exposure to derivatives, mortgages or convertibles, security-by-security analysis and asset class-level analysis may yield very similar results. For portfolios that have fixed income, foreign exchange, derivatives, mortgages or convertibles, the two styles of analysis may differ. And if an account has just begun to depart from its usual style of investing and has just begun to look a great deal different from its benchmark, only analysis of current holdings will pick up this signal.

In the end, the costs and benefits of thorough risk analysis have much in common with the measurement of performance. Much of a portfolio's performance could probably be explained by knowing its allocation to broad asset classes and knowing how much those asset class benchmarks changed in a given period. Yet few are satisfied with that approach to marking a portfolio to market; the potential errors are too numerous to mention. For the same reasons that it is unsatisfactory as a performance analysis (for the measurement of actual gain or loss), asset class-based analysis is insufficient for risk measurement (the estimate of potential gain or loss).

RISK BUDGETING VERSUS INVESTMENT GUIDELINES

VAR measures came about in banking institutions to address the problems caused by principal limits and limits on risk sensitivities (eg, duration limits). Investment guidelines can be ineffective risk controls when they use these same sorts of limits: they can be evaded by a change in a product name, thereby failing to prevent "bad" risk-taking, yet can hamper good risk-taking by preventing the use of hedging instruments that could achieve portfolio goals cheaply and effectively.

Reviewing the history of banking risk limits reveals why principal limits and sensitivity limits did not achieve adequate risk control.

Principal limits – limiting how much a portfolio can purchase of particular categories of securities – have a lot of merit but do not achieve good risk control for certain kinds of portfolios. Portfolios best served by them are those which only purchase simple assets and never use short strategies or complex assets. Portfolios which use overlays, short sales, derivatives or products embedding derivatives (eg, convertibles, corporate bonds, mortgages) can end up with very different risk profiles with the same portfolio net asset value. These limits perform particularly poorly in keeping up with product innovation, especially with products which embed any sort of leverage. They also fail to capture the different risks of fixed income – for example, that a 30-year fixed rate note may have the same principal as a 30-day floating rate note, but that these notes are affected by interest rate changes in very different ways.

Principal-based rules also have little ability to flexibly allow a portfolio to own more of an asset if it hedges or diversifies other assets, or to allow less of an asset if its price is more volatile (eg, Turkish equities versus Canadian equities). The asset proportions allowed under these limits tend to be hard-coded and complex; the complexity of these rules increases enormously with multi-asset class, multi-country portfolios. Under them, portfolios of more variable risk may be assembled than originally intended.

To accommodate hedging and fixed income duration risk, banks and investors began to include risk controls that specified *risk sensitivity* limitations. These are based on the profit or loss of a portfolio under a given risk factor change. For instance, a portfolio might be limited with a duration of no more than half a year, plus or minus, relative to the benchmark. This ensures the portfolio will have a loss similar to that of the benchmark if interest rates rise 0.01% across the entire yield curve and across all bond market sectors. But what if the portfolio has offset a large, long 30-year position with a duration-weighted, short one-year position? This would register a net duration measure of zero and, in the absence of other controls, the manager could keep adding to the position without restraint. This position will have no net loss for a parallel yield curve shift, but could have large off-benchmark losses for a non-parallel shift. To counter this, the guidelines might set rules by segment of the yield curve and by market sectors – however, the complexity of maintaining these rules, particularly across international portfolios, is sobering. And if you add to this picture all the different ways investors set such rules, you can see that asset managers could end up with an excessively complex set of rules for their portfolios.

VAR measures combined the best aspects of sensitivity based measures with historical volatility and correlation. If, instead of setting a limit of ±0.5 years duration for a fixed income portfolio, the investor set a limit of active risk being no greater than 2.00%, this rule would capture yield curve and sector positions as well as duration positions, while remaining capable of accommodating international investment. An Argentinean off-benchmark position might count more heavily than a pound sterling off-benchmark position because it is more volatile.

VAR measures get to the heart of risk and are more easily comparable than other types of controls after all, it is potential performance that we actually want to control with market risk limits, not the names of instruments in a portfolio. Traditional measures can make it difficult to determine which portfolio is actually taking the most risk; is it riskier to have an equity portfolio beta of 1.1 or a foreign fixed income portfolio with a duration one year higher than its benchmark? It is hard to say. But a portfolio with an active risk or tracking error of 8% is definitely riskier than one with a tracking error of 0.30% – it has a greater chance of performance being significantly different to its benchmark, and this chance should normally be given to the managers and markets with the greatest ability to significantly outperform their benchmarks.

Leverage

VAR and risk sensitivities are useful measures in monitoring leverage. In the case of an S&P portfolio, where cash positions are "equitised" using futures, a sensitivity measure can be used to ensure that the equity futures have not been used to lever the portfolio. For example, if a portfolio was invested 5% in cash, 95% in stocks matching the S&P, leverage would occur if equity futures covering an underlying amount of 8% of the portfolio had been purchased. Risk sensitivity measures would show an exposure of 103% to the S&P in this portfolio, revealing the existence of leverage.

VAR adds a further element: showing the potential impact of leverage. An account which is 103% invested in the S&P has taken greater risk than an account which has invested 103% in 30-day commercial paper. The tracking error for the first fund will be much higher than the second because of the volatility of the item that leverage has been used to invest in.

Derivatives, foreign exchange

VAR and risk sensitivities deal much better with derivatives than traditional clauses in investment guidelines. Investment guidelines ordinarily forbid their use, or permit the managers "only to hedge" without defining what a hedge is, or is not. Does it include an overhedge? Does it include a hedge denominated in a different currency to the item being hedged? What about foreign exchange forwards of very different terms – which therefore bear different interest rate risk?

Risk sensitivities measure whether an item can be defined as a hedge. To be so defined, a hedge's sensitivity must be opposite to, and no greater than, the portfolio's sensitivity to the underlying risk being hedged. If the portfolio loses US$1 million if the euro/US dollar foreign exchange rate increases 1%, while the hedge gains US$1 million in the same event, this would be considered a hedge. However, if the hedge gains US$1.5 million as the euro/US dollar rate increases 1%, this would not be considered a hedge. And if the hedge gains US$1 million as the pound sterling/US dollar rate increases 1%, while the portfolio's loss occurs if the euro/US dollar rate increases, this would not be a hedge.

VAR controls go further to allow more leeway in hedging, if necessary. If the portfolio were exposed to a number of small currencies, each of which would be costly to hedge, the portfolio manager might instead want to use a more liquid, highly correlated currency to execute a broad hedge.

If the portfolio VAR was reduced after application of this "hedge", it could truly be considered a hedge. But if the VAR increases, the hedge is risk-increasing and, therefore, not a hedge at all, but another form of speculation.

VAR and risk sensitivities can monitor strategies and products that are difficult to cover in investment guidelines; this can help investors find a broader range of value-added strategies and can also avoid them unintentionally owning unwanted risk.

RISK BUDGETING VERSUS STANDARD DEVIATION

In the section on evaluating risk-adjusted performance, we discussed a number of differences between VAR and standard deviation of a portfolio's returns. When comparing the two as a risk control, the key difference between them is that VAR provides a more sensitive early warning. Typically, standard deviation is computed on five years' of monthly returns. This is because if a manager has just altered their strategy a great deal, it will take many months before this signal will come through the return history and reflects in the performance analysis. VAR takes the current set of holdings in his portfolio and looks at the history of those holdings, rather than the history of the managers' old holdings. If they have invested very differently from their benchmark, the current set of holdings will have a large tracking error to the benchmark. Therefore, VAR will sound a signal more quickly when a large change in strategy has taken place.

VAR is also more readily available for new managers and new strategies: the only requirement is a set of current holdings which can be well proxied with market risk factors. Standard deviation requires some years to pass before the manager's return history is available, which limits its use for new strategies.

RISK BUDGETING VERSUS BETA

Beta uses similar measures to those used in computing VAR: it expresses the relative volatility between a portfolio and "the market", usually an equity benchmark. VAR differs mainly in that it instead computes tracking error, which is related to beta but not identical. Tracking error measures the degree of potential underperformance between a portfolio and its specific benchmark, while beta is often assumed to use a single benchmark to represent the market. Tracking error is extensible across equity, fixed income, balanced, domestic and international portfolios, where there is no single benchmark for the market.

RISK BUDGETING VERSUS DURATION

Duration sensitivity shows how sensitive a fixed income portfolio is to a 0.01% rise in interest rates across the yield curve. It does not address how likely a 0.01% move is or in which segments of the yield curve it will occur, nor for which fixed income sectors or country markets it will occur. VAR blends duration information with the volatilities of the various segments of the market and various countries, and their correlation to one another, to weigh the potential loss in a portfolio where non-parallel shifts may occur. Alternatively, two portfolios might have the same duration and bear different risk. If Acme's International Fixed Income fund focused in emerging markets, and its "FixedFund" was a US fixed income fund, they could have the same duration, yet the VAR of the emerging market portfolio would be higher than the VAR of the developed market portfolio, capturing the role of volatility and the higher risk of emerging markets.

CONTROLLING LIQUIDITY, CREDIT, CONCENTRATION RISK

This is an area where investment guidelines work better than VAR and are an excellent companion to VAR.

On its own, VAR fails to distinguish the higher risk of a position that is too large for market liquidity versus one which could easily be liquidated. VAR breaks positions down into risk factors and measures the volatility of these risk factors over the desired holding period to arrive at a potential loss. Volatility is the standard deviation of periodic price or yield changes. For example, a single stock, XYZ Co, trade one million shares on an average day and the volatility of this stock's price changes is 15%. If Acme's equity plus manager owns 15 million shares of XYZ, the historical volatility of this stock does not apply to them; they will move the market well beyond the normal volatility if they decide to sell their 15 million shares. VAR does not have any easy way to adjust for positions which outstrip market liquidity; indeed, seasoned observers are often surprised by how much market behaviour can change when large positions come into the market. It is very difficult to predict with any great accuracy.

To avoid the VAR measure being so seriously wrong, there are a couple of approaches, one of which is already well covered by investment guidelines as they are commonly written. Investment guidelines seek to restrict concentrations in individual stocks or bonds and country markets, to prevent them becoming too large a share of the portfolio. By doing so, they ensure a reasonably well-diversified portfolio, so that VAR can be a valid measure. This approach does not tackle the fact that a single individual at an asset management firm may manage many such portfolios and these may be cumulatively too concentrated in certain issues, such that they risk moving the market by their actions. On the other hand, by limiting the amount in each portfolio, this reduces the impact one security can have on each portfolio's results, even if that security has an unusually bad day.

Another approach is to measure the VAR of liquid and illiquid assets over different holding periods, reflecting the longer period of time it would take to liquidate a holding which is too large for market liquidity, or whose market is natively illiquid. This is often used by banks or hedge funds who turn portfolios over more rapidly; it results in a matter of days to liquidation for the portfolio and should use a VAR estimate that has been holding-period adjusted to show the extra risk of illiquid investments.

A third approach is to keep the holding period constant but to adjust the VAR measure upward to reflect illiquidity. This is done when:

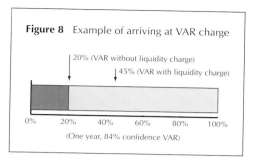

Figure 8 Example of arriving at VAR charge

20% (VAR without liquidity charge)

45% (VAR with liquidity charge)

0%   20%   40%   60%   80%   100%

(One year, 84% confidence VAR)

❏ a portfolio manager has a position that is large with respect to daily market turnover (even if it is not exceeding portfolio concentration rules);
❏ a market has clear illiquidity;
❏ a market is so new that it has no data history and therefore might appear to have zero volatility; or
❏ a market has low volatility for structural reasons (as managed currencies sometimes do), but where there are clear risks, such as the risk of devaluation, which cannot be perceived through volatility information.

This approach adds an extra charge to the VAR measure to correct the perceived difference between an instrument's volatility over a given holding period and the actual loss that the position might sustain if it needed to be liquidated in that holding period, or, in the case of a managed currency, the potential devaluation that could occur with a given probability in that holding period. This is more art than science but at least acknowledges the extra risk that illiquidity can bring.

Figure 8 provides an example of arriving at a VAR charge; if the annual volatility of a holding is 20%, but the portfolio manager holds significantly more of the share than can easily be traded in during the holding period, their potential loss lies somewhere between 20% and 100%. By modelling the market moves a position of his size might cause were it to be liquidated over the course of their one year holding period, the risk measurement group has arrived at a VAR of 45% which reflects the effect of illiquidity.

USING BACKTESTING TO CALIBRATE THE VAR MODEL

VAR measurement is a bundle of assumptions and it is not hard to find examples where actual markets exceeded VAR's "worst case" projections. So how do users gauge whether their VAR measure is a good predictor of potential performance?

Backtesting is the tool to which VAR users turn to calibrate their models. It can only be performed, however, on portfolios that have reasonably frequent VAR and performance measurement, otherwise changes to the portfolio occurring in between the backtest observations can throw the results. Banking institutions using their internal VAR models to assess market risk

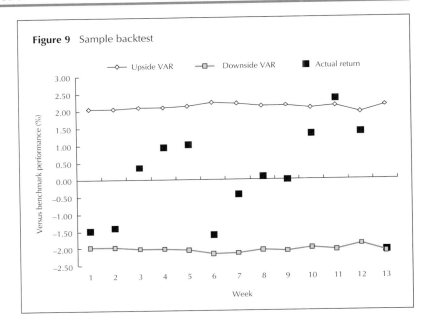

Figure 9 Sample backtest

capital conduct daily backtests. Weekly backtests are also possible and, for portfolios with very limited turnover, monthly backtests are possible.

Figure 9 shows a sample backtest. At the beginning of week one, a VAR "prediction" is made: the portfolio's worst case potential underperformance of its benchmark, in the next week, at 95% confidence. The first week's VAR prediction is a loss of 2.00%. At the end of the week, actual performance relative to the benchmark is measured; it registers that week at 1.50% below the benchmark. As the portfolio composition changes, the risk and performance figures will shift around but if the model has predictive value, only 5% of the actual results should be worse than their VAR prediction. These "outlier" data points may be enormous; as long as they are 5% of the data points or fewer, the model is doing what is purports to do.

In Figure 9, 5%, or 0.7, of the data points should have been worse than the downside VAR prediction; none are. The same number (0.7) should have exceeded the upside VAR prediction; one did. This tiny sample would thus be a reasonably successful backtest; a much larger sample is preferable to truly draw conclusions about a VAR model's robustness.

---

1   The name "Acme" has been chosen to resemble a fictitious company. Any resemblance to an actual company is entirely coincidental.

7

Risk Budgeting for Active Investment Managers
The Green Zone... Assessing the Quality of Returns*†

Robert Litterman, Jacques Longerstaey, Jacob Rosengarten and Kurt Winkelmann

Goldman Sachs Investment Management

In golf it is the "fairway". In baseball it is a "fair ball". In football it is "in bounds". In portfolio management we also have a name for it. It is the "green zone".

Portfolio managers are in the business of producing distributions of returns. In so doing, they take risk on behalf of their clients. If, over time, they take too little risk, they may not be earning their fees; if they take too much risk, they may be putting their clients' assets in jeopardy.

The green zone is our name for the range for risk taking which is agreed upon as appropriate in the context of a porfolio management assignment.

In most investment contexts the returns portfolio managers create are compared to those of an index of the returns of the relevant market. This is a reasonable standard if the relevant index returns are available to the client at relatively low cost. In this context tracking error[1] measures the relevant risk – the risk relative to such a benchmark – that the portfolio manager is taking in order to add excess return. Clients have a responsibility as well to discuss risk expectations not only about the absolute returns of a portfolio, but also to provide clear guidance about how much risk relative to a benchmark (sometimes referred to as "active risk") they expect the portfolio manager to take.

---

*This chapter is reprinted with the permission of Goldman, Sachs & Co.
†(This chapter contains simulations. Simulated results do not reflect actual trading and have certain inherent limitations. Please see appendix for further disclosures.)

Why do we need a green zone?[2] After all, isn't maximising portfolio return against the relevant benchmark the ultimate objective of investing? The relative return statistic, which measures the *quantity* of performance, only reflects the mean of the distribution of returns. It is in itself not enough information to judge performance. We also need to be able to assess the *quality* of the returns. In this chapter we suggest that a portfolio management assignment should include an understanding between the client and the portfolio manager which defines the appropriate range for tracking error. We also assert that one important measure of the quality of performance is the consistency with which the portfolio tracking error stays within this range.

Traditionally, portfolio manager performance has been monitored on the basis of returns, either in terms of excess returns relative to a benchmark, returns relative to competitors, or on a risk-adjusted return basis. This is certainly an appropriate focus. Increasing expected return for a given level of risk is the objective of portfolio management.

However, there are two major problems in trying to judge performance based only on the level of returns. First, the mean is a very imprecise statistic. We never observe the mean of the distribution directly; we only infer it from realisations of returns. It takes a long time to distinguish between luck and skill. In any interval of time measured in years rather than decades, the noise in an estimate of the mean of the distribution of returns is likely to be large relative to the difference in means that would distinguish between great talent and mediocre skills.

Moreover, there is widespread recognition that what matters to investors is not simply return, but risk-adjusted return. Increasingly there is an awareness that a risk-adjusted return such as an information ratio (the ratio of annualised mean excess return relative to benchmark divided by tracking error) is a better statistic to focus on than the raw return.[3]

Investors should insist that managers agree upon a range for tracking error
Unfortunately, while the risk adjustment of returns is an important refinement, it does not really address the first issue raised previously, which is the significant noise in the mean return statistic. It still takes much too long – many years if not decades – to generate risk-adjusted performance statistics that can meaningfully separate skill from luck.

Most investors recognise the need to take some risk in their investments. After all, taking risk is the source of returns.[4] But risk is a scarce resource for an investor. It is becoming common these days for fund managers and other investors to recognise that they need to efficiently manage a "risk budget" for their investments. In a carefully drawn business plan there will be pressure to reduce expense allocations up to the point where return objectives justify the marginal use of capital. This point is true not only for expense budgets, but for risk budgets as well. Having determined a risk budget and capital allocations to different investments, processes must exist to avoid material variances from budget. We believe managing the active risk in a fund's risk budget effectively can be accomplished only if portfolio managers are capable of providing a relatively stable, agreed-upon range for tracking error.

In this chapter we suggest that an additional dimension ought to be used to measure portfolio manager skill. Portfolio managers should be concerned not only with increasing their mean return, but also with managing their risk, and in particular, managing the range within which the tracking error of their portfolio fluctuates.[5] Most portfolio managers do attempt to produce consistent, risk-adjusted performance relative to a benchmark.[6] This means they must develop the skills needed to manage their tracking error. In judging performance it certainly would seem to make sense to have metrics which monitor how well they achieve this goal.

There is another, perhaps more subtle, but also perhaps more important reason that we may wish to monitor the risk management capabilities of a portfolio manager. Not only is the ability of a portfolio manager to manage the risk of the portfolio of direct benefit to the client, but it is also likely to correlate strongly with the ability of the portfolio manager to consistently outperform the market. Success in portfolio construction depends on the ability to understand and quantify the sources of risk in the portfolio, to be able to determine the appropriate sizing of intended exposures, and to be able to avoid unintended risks. The mastery of these critical skills is required in order to optimally allocate the portfolio manager's limited allotment of risk, and therefore to be consistently successful in the attempt to increase the mean level of return.

Over any short-term period, risk is easier to manage and measure than is the mean of the distribution of returns

But these same risk management skills are the ones that allow a portfolio manager to stay consistently in the green zone. Thus, our view is that while carefully managing a target level of risk may not seem particularly important to the client, at least relative to adding additional return, we think the ability to do so is nonetheless a very significant indicator of portfolio management skill that should be used by investors and consultants in picking and retaining portfolio managers.

In addition to being an important skill, a manager's ability to stay in a range around a targeted volatility can be much more accurately measured than can be the ability to generate higher mean returns. The reason for this is that over any short or even intermediate period of time the volatility of a distribution from which returns are drawn is much easier to manage, and is also much more accurately measured, than is the mean of that underlying distribution.

We propose a simple approach to monitoring the tracking error of a portfolio relative to a target range. The basic idea is to define three ranges of outcomes for realised tracking error. The first range of outcomes represents those that are close enough to target to be considered a successful result. This is the "green zone". Another range, the "yellow zone", represents outcomes that are not successful. These outcomes will occur sometimes even for the best managed portfolios simply because the realised tracking error is a random process. A skilled manager should operate in the yellow zone only occasionally. Outcomes in this range should be viewed as a warning signal, but they may often have a reasonable explanation. Finally, we will define a range of bad outcomes, the "red zone". Events in this range should occur very rarely, if at all, for a portfolio manager who understands the sources of risk in the portfolio. These events are not only warnings, but are likely indications of lack of control in the portfolio construction process.

The green, yellow and red zones are a quality control tool to help manage the risk budget
We believe portfolio managers should be judged, at least in part, by their ability to keep their portfolio tracking error in the green zone an appropriately high percentage of the time. On the other hand, we recognise that there can be no simple formula for measuring success. As is true for any sport that involves attempting to hit a target, the frequency of success is a function not only of the skill of the athlete, but also of environmental factors. In the case of portfolio management, the environmental factors will differ across markets, and will include for example, time-varying volatilities, the degree of liquidity, the transparency of security valuations and the transactions costs associated with changing portfolio exposures.

While we have intentionally tried to create a simple, colour-coded approach, we also recognise that the apparent simplicity of this approach may be deceiving. The random influences of the environmental factors in different markets, as well as the complexities of portfolio construction, of statistical estimation, and so on, lead quickly to a thicket of complicated issues when one attempts to apply this approach in practice. We will only scratch the surface with respect to some of these issues in this chapter. Nonetheless we wish to highlight that when a yellow or red warning does occur, such issues are very relevant in interpreting the cause and implications of the signal.

One of the most difficult questions which arises in trying to manage tracking error within a target range is the issue of how large to make the range. Obviously, the larger the target, the easier it is to stay within it. On the other hand, for the client, the larger the target range, the less precise is the risk management, and for any given sized mandate, the larger is the usage of the risk budget. Also, with a larger target range, a departure from the range clearly represents a stronger signal. Thus, there will always be a tension that needs to be balanced in setting the size of the target range.

Despite these difficulties in interpretation, the investment management industry faces the need to better define and communicate its risk management obligations to its clients. Our view is that portfolio managers ought to discuss and establish targeted ranges for tracking error with clients at the inception of a mandate, and then discuss the reasons for and actions required or taken when exceptions occur. We have also found it helpful to ask the manager to identify the types of market conditions that may be difficult for his investment approach – and the types of risk profiles to expect. If the manager can identify *ex ante* the types of environments that may cause his tracking error to drift out of the green zone, one may have a higher degree of confidence this is a short-term event rather than a long-term one. Such clear and quantitative communication should provide the basis for a more informed relationship between the client and the portfolio manager – one that will be less likely to lead to disputes when performance is disappointing.

WHAT IS THE STANDARD BY WHICH TO MEASURE SUCCESS IN MANAGING PORTFOLIO RISK?

Unfortunately, as discussed above, there can be no single standard for measuring success in managing portfolio tracking error. There are too many different contexts to expect any one standard evaluation of success. Some managers invest in very liquid instruments, such as financial futures contracts. These managers can usually adjust exposures very quickly and at very little cost. Other managers invest in relatively illiquid securities such as emerging market securities and will have to pay heavily to adjust position sizes. An investor should not expect or want the latter type of manager to try to manage his or her tracking error as tightly as might be the case with the former type of manager.

Clear communication between the client and the portfolio manager are essential to setting risk and return expectations
Another consideration may be a manager's style. Some managers may follow an investment process that explicitly targets a given, constant level of volatility every day. Other managers may have a process that requires judging the level of opportunity in the market and adjusting the risk of the portfolio to be higher when opportunities are greater. Clearly, one should expect the variability of returns from the latter process to be greater over time than the former.

For these reasons, and many others, we do not think it is reasonable to expect there to be one formula that defines the appropriate range of tracking error outcomes. Although we think the ability to manage portfolio risk is central to the service an asset manager provides, we cannot justify a suggestion, for example, along the lines that every manager should be expected to keep their tracking error within a particular range around their target a given percentage of the time. Rather than try to come up with such a formula, later in this chapter we provide an example of what might be expected in one particular context. In so doing, we hope to stimulate portfolio managers and clients to think carefully about these issues so that both can discuss them more knowledgeably and have a better understanding of what can and cannot be expected.

MONITORING REALISED TRACKING ERROR

In general, the term "tracking error" refers to the volatility of the excess returns of a portfolio relative to a benchmark. In this chapter, however, we use the term "tracking error" in four different contexts that are important to distinguish. Thus, we differentiate between the following concepts.

❑ *Realised tracking error:* one of many statistical measures of the volatility of actual realised excess returns over a previous period of time.
❑ *Target tracking error:* a target level for tracking error against which we can measure the success of realised tracking error.
❑ *True tracking error:* the unknowable volatility of the distribution from which actual excess returns will be drawn at a point in time.
❑ *Estimated tracking error:* one of many possible statistical (or other) forward-looking measures or guesses of what the true tracking error of a portfolio might be at a point in time.

Given these definitions, we specify the following steps that we would expect a portfolio manager to take, highlighting the different tracking error concepts:

❑ at the inception of a mandate, agree with a client on the appropriate lever or range for *targeted tracking error;*
❑ on an ongoing basis, use the historical *realised tracking error* of the portfolio as well any other relevant information to form the best possible measure of the *estimated tracking error* of the portfolio going forward;
❑ take whatever actions are appropriate (taking transactions costs and other relevant issues into account) to attempt to keep the *true tracking error* in line with the *targeted tracking error;* and
❑ if the investment process suggests that the *targeted tracking error* be adjusted, do so, and if appropriate, notify the client.

Given these definitions, we can also specify which actions we could expect a client to follow:

❑ at the inception of a mandate, agree with the portfolio manager on the appropriate level or range for *targeted tracking error;*
❑ on an ongoing basis, monitor the *realised tracking error;* and

❏ if the *realised tracking error* strays outside of the agreed-upon range in an unusual manner, discuss this discrepancy with the portfolio manager.

In particular, we want to emphasise that the concept of tracking error a client should hold a portfolio manager responsible for is the *realised* tracking error. It is perhaps obvious that neither the portfolio manager nor the client can ever know what the true tracking error is. Less obvious, perhaps, is the fact that while the portfolio manager should know what his or her best estimate of tracking error is, and that estimate may be a point of discussion or even a part of the investment process, ultimately what matters to the client is not the expected, but the realised distribution of returns.

It is a good idea to reflect your tracking error policy in the plan's Investment Policy and Guidelines
Unfortunately, confusion often arises over a failure to distinguish among these different concepts. For example, we have seen cases where a portfolio manager has followed an investment process in which positions are adjusted until a model gives an estimated tracking error consistent with the client's expectations. Although this may seem like a reasonable investment policy, the weakness of the approach is that it does not include a contingency for dealing with model failure. All risk models are approximations, and realised tracking error often turns out to be consistently much higher than a model's estimated tracking error. Portfolio managers should not blindly manage according to the forecasts of risk models. While portfolio managers should use models, they need to understand the limitations of those models and to take responsibility for the actual outcomes.

DEFINING THE GREEN, YELLOW AND RED ZONES
When a consumer makes a major purchase, there are generally clear standards for quality. No one would be happy with a purchase that does not perform within reasonable parameters of those expectations. Similarly, we believe that there should be clear standards for portfolio managers as well. The purpose of creating zones for tracking error is to provide expectations for the client and the portfolio manager ahead of time, with respect to the size of the risks to be taken.

Unfortunately, the whole set of issues related to monitoring the quality of portfolio manger performance is complex and poorly understood. One large source of confusion is the uncertainty in the measurement of tracking error. After all, tracking error is a statistical quantity that requires estimation. Let us try to sort through the issues by assuming for the moment that tracking error is an observable quantity, and not an uncertain statistical estimate.

If tracking error were observable, it would be relatively straightforward to monitor a portfolio manager's success in managing the risk of the portfolio. A portfolio manager could agree to keep the tracking error within a band, say between 300 and 500 basis points of annualised volatility, and the client could monitor this. There may be any number of reasons why the tracking error might go outside of the band. Such an event might initiate a conversation between the client and the portfolio manager. This conversation might focus on the obvious fact that tracking error is only partially under the control of the portfolio manager. Changes in the volatilities and correlations of the underlying securities, together with the costs of adjusting positions, all create a non-trivial control problem. The issues worthy of discussion might be whether the band is wide enough and whether there is an apparent reason for the manager to end up outside the band. The situation would be a little like an aeroplane pilot who is directed to fly at a particular altitude. What that really means is that the pilot should try to stay close to that altitude, but of course air traffic control recognises that air currents and other random effects will cause some movement around that target. Ahead of time the pilot and air traffic control agree that what that instruction really means is that the pilot should keep the plane within a specified band around the target.[7]

Daily performance data feeds from managers can help investors better identify potential tracking error issues before they have a significant impact on performance

Unfortunately, risk is not observable, but rather is a statistical measure that is only observed subject to sampling noise. Different statistical estimators will have different properties. Tracking error estimators that attempt to track changing volatility more quickly will be subject to higher degrees of sampling noise. Thus a balance must be struck. *Realised* tracking error (the output of the statistical estimation process) will fluctuate in a band around whatever the true, unknown level of tracking error is. Unfortunately, because of these measurement issues, the adequacy of risk management is often difficult to assess and the clarity of the communication between portfolio manager and client with respect to these quantitative measures of risk is often low. In several recent highly publicised cases, such lack of clarity has no doubt been a factor which has led to litigation over the manager's alleged mis-management of risk and potential responsibility for losses.

The measurement problem discussed in the previous paragraph is significant, but if recognised and understood, it does not present a serious impediment to adequate risk management. Going back to the aeroplane analogy, it is as if our radar can only measure the altitude of the plane subject to a certain band of uncertainty. As long as the uncertainty is recognised, and the agreed upon altitude band within which the plane is supposed to fly is large enough, then that uncertainty in observing the altitude is a manageable issue.

In portfolio management the target tracking error range needs to be relatively wide because the realised tracking error is constantly buffeted by the changing volatilities in the market. The measurement problem needs to be understood in the context of this range. The issue is not whether we can measure tracking error precisely; we cannot. The issue is whether we can measure it with enough accuracy and in a timely enough fashion, to be able to identify and respond to problems that might otherwise adversely affect the overall performance of the fund. We will see that daily performance data provide considerable information about true tracking error. The sampling error resulting from using a short moving average tracking error estimator based on daily data creates a band of uncertainty around the true tracking error which is not ideal, but which certainly should be adequate for monitoring purposes relative to the width of a target tracking error range that is reasonable in the context of overall fund risk budget allocation.

It is important to measure what is going on at the time it is going on
Interestingly, most portfolio managers have not focused on short moving average measures of tracking error based on daily performance data. The standard investment management industry measure for realised tracking error is a long moving average of relatively infrequently measured returns. A typical measure might be a three-year average based on monthly returns. Unfortunately, such a measure is relatively imprecise, and when observed, is out of date. Returning to our aeroplane example, think of this measure as the equivalent of using obsolete technology for estimating the altitude of an aircraft. It is akin to two observers using protractors to estimate the angles between them and the plane and then triangulating to come up with an estimate. The estimate has a huge uncertainty band, and in any case, by the time the estimate is ready the plane is long gone. Air traffic control could not manage their airspace this way, and one should not try to manage the risk in investment portfolios that way.

We suggest using tracking error estimates based on 20- and 60-day moving averages of squared daily returns, because they are the fund manager's equivalent of radar-based measures of altitude – they give a relatively quick and relatively accurate measure of what is going on at the time it is going on. If something is going wrong with the volatility of a portfolio's returns relative to its benchmark, we will find out about it relatively quickly, perhaps in time to do something to correct the situation.

We wish to separate two issues associated with managing tracking error. The first is the uncertainty of the volatility estimator. The second is the time variation of the true volatility itself. The statistical uncertainty of volatility estimators is well understood and can be easily illustrated. Figure 1 shows examples that illustrate what the time series properties of the 20-day and 60-day moving average estimators of tracking error[8] look like when the true tracking error is constant. The use of daily performance data provides much more information over a short time than weekly or monthly returns,

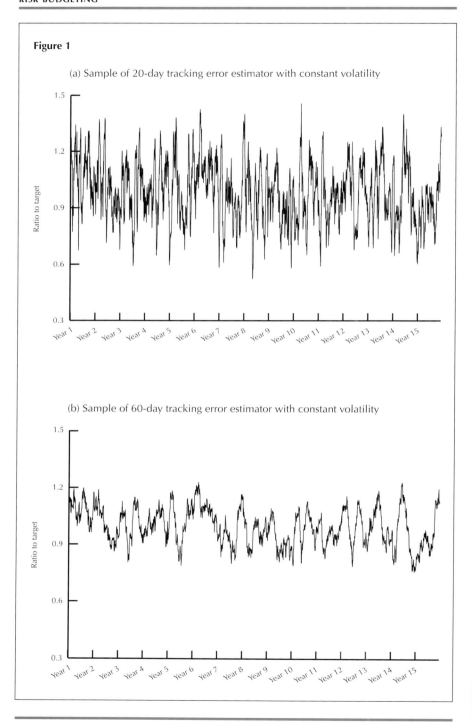

Figure 1

(a) Sample of 20-day tracking error estimator with constant volatility

(b) Sample of 60-day tracking error estimator with constant volatility

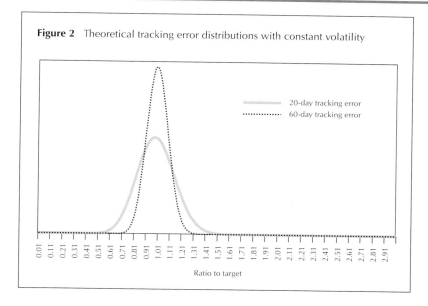

Figure 2 Theoretical tracking error distributions with constant volatility

20-day tracking error
60-day tracking error

Ratio to target

but there is still a clear reduction in the estimation noise from increasing the number of days from 20 to 60. In these figures we have assumed that the true tracking error is constant and equal to the targeted level.

If you could imagine drawing many examples of simulated times series such as those displayed in Figure 1, and keeping count of how often the realised tracking error falls in a particular ratio to target, we could create a histogram which would provide a graphical representation of the distribution of outcomes for these two tracking error measures.[9] These distributions are shown in Figure 2.

In these distributions we can see that the benefit of using more data in the 60-day moving average is to reduce the sampling variability of the estimator. Notice, however, that we have assumed that the true tracking error is constant. If the true tracking error is changing over time, then the longer interval incorporated in the 60-day estimator will create a larger bias relative to where the true tracking error is at each point in time. For example, if volatility has been decreasing over the 60-day period, then the 60-day estimator will be biased upward. The bias could potentially create more error on average than is created by the increased sampling variability in the 20-day moving average. One might want to search for the optimal estimator, but we are not particularly interested in finding a single best estimator for tracking error. By monitoring both the 20-day and the 60-day measures we hope to obtain reasonably clear and up-to-date indications of how much risk is embedded in the portfolio at each point in time. We focus primary attention on the 60-day estimator, but we use the 20-day estimator in order to get a sense whether volatility seems to be changing in the most recent

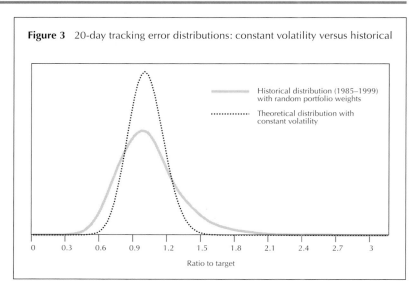

Figure 3 20-day tracking error distributions: constant volatility versus historical

Historical distribution (1985–1999) with random portfolio weights

Theoretical distribution with constant volatility

Ratio to target

period relative to the 60-day measure. Nonetheless, we also recognise the larger sampling variability that is associated with it and the likelihood that such differences are simply due to sampling noise.

Having focused on the properties of our estimators in an idealised environment, we now turn to their properties when applied to data from the real world in which volatility varies over time. In Figure 3 we compare the distribution[10] of the 20-day tracking error estimators for returns based on actual historical data with those for estimators in an artificial constant

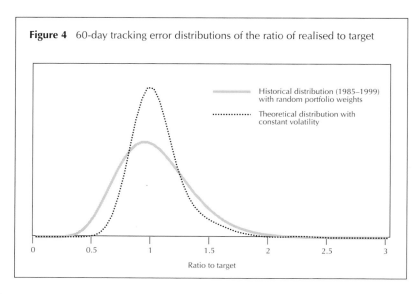

Figure 4 60-day tracking error distributions of the ratio of realised to target

Historical distribution (1985–1999) with random portfolio weights

Theoretical distribution with constant volatility

Ratio to target

volatility world. We see that the range of outcomes for the estimator based on historical data with time-varying volatility is considerably spread out relative to the sampling variability of the estimator when the underlying volatility is constant. This comparison gives a sense of the clear evidence for and importance of time variation in tracking error. In Figure 4 we show the same comparison for the 60-day tracking error estimator. There is a similar pattern of historical data leading to tracking errors in a much wider range than would be predicted in a constant volatility environment. Thus, volatility in the markets is a reality that managers have to deal with and clients have to be prepared for.

In Figure 5 we compare the time series properties of the 20-day and 60-day tracking error estimators from one of our 500 historical simulations. We see that the 60-day tracking error estimator is much smoother than the 20-day estimator. The longer average eliminates some estimation noise, but it also slows the adjustment of the estimator to changes in the true underlying tracking error of the portfolio. This effect is particularly obvious in the months following the stock market crash in 1987. By following both of these measures over time, however, we can obtain a relatively clear picture of the range, the current level and the recent changes in the tracking error in the portfolio.

The bottom line is that there are two issues to deal with. There is significant sampling variability in any tracking error estimator and there is significant time-variation of the underlying risks in the markets. Daily performance data can give us a better handle on measuring the underlying tracking error, but given these two issues, managers will understandably find it difficult to keep realised tracking error within any tight band around a targeted level.

How, then, can we use a tracking error to monitor portfolio risk management? We suggest a simple approach based on our previously mentioned green, yellow and red zones, from which we generate signals that indicate when something unusual is going on. When a signal is generated, there may or may not be a problem, but a process can be created to follow-up and make such a judgment. The idea is to create bands and a monitoring process in such a way that when a portfolio manager is managing the portfolio in a manner consistent with expectations, the realised targeted tracking error should be in a green zone most of the time. Ideally in this circumstance the signals of potential problems will occur only during unusual market conditions.

The three-zone approach will generate signals that indicate when something unusual is going on

Although it is clearly somewhat arbitrary, we suggest defining "unusual" as something that would be expected to happen no more than twice per year. In other words, we want to make the zones wide enough that false

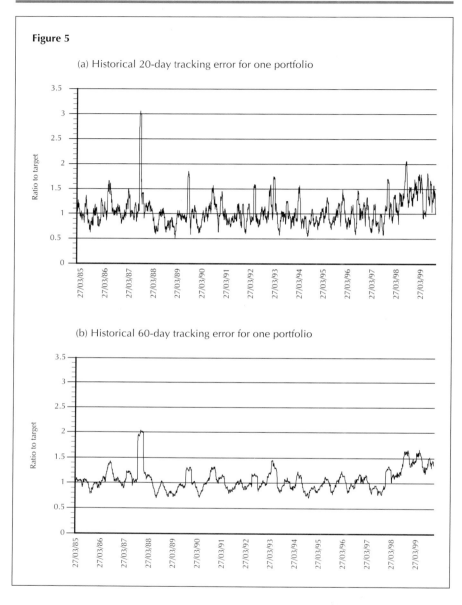

Figure 5

(a) Historical 20-day tracking error for one portfolio

(b) Historical 60-day tracking error for one portfolio

signals of potential problems occur only occasionally. In particular, we suggest creating the green zone as a region wide enough so that the random fluctuations in tracking error of a portfolio with fixed weights (but on average at the targeted tracking error) would cause the realised tracking error to exit the zone no more than twice per year, once each on the high side and on the low side.[11]

Clearly, we need to recognise that most of the time (even when something unusual is occurring) it is not necessarily an indication that there is a problem, or that some action needs to be taken. The yellow signal, which switches on when the realised tracking error moves out of the green zone, is most likely simply a signal that something unusual, but not serious, is going on. By design, we expect a fixed portfolio that has a true tracking error on target will nonetheless create such signals twice a year. Of course, in practice portfolio managers will be changing exposures – sometimes to generate higher return, but also potentially to offset changing volatilities in their markets. In markets with low transaction costs, managers might easily offset the market conditions that would otherwise cause their tracking error to hit the green zone boundaries and thus they might be expected to observe even fewer signals.

However, we would also like to signal another set of conditions where realised tracking error is so far off-track that we expect such circumstances to be extremely rare unless portfolios are being managed in a manner inconsistent with the targeted tracking error. Above we defined "unusual" as something occurring no more than twice per year. Here we similarly suggest defining "extremely rare" as something that should occur no more than twice in five years, once each on the high side and on the low side.

As with the green zone, we attempt to define the yellow zone such that when a passive portfolio is constructed consistently with targeted risk levels, the underlying changes in market volatility and the statistical noise associated with risk monitoring will be expected to create a red signal; that is, a realised tracking error moving beyond the yellow zone on the high side no more than once in five years, and on the low side, no more than once in five years.

The process of establishing zone ranges in advance will set expectations between the client and manager appropriately
Recognising the difficulty of defining zones according to these probabilistic criteria and the fact that the zones would have different widths in different markets, we provide some guidance based on our historical simulations with US equity data and realised tracking error based on 20- and 60-day moving averages. These simulations, the details of which are discussed in the appendix, show how wide the regions would have had to have been historically to have provided the required probabilities of creating false signals for the 20- and 60-day estimators in these markets. Experience with different investment styles and markets will certainly require modifications of these guidelines in other contexts.

Figures 6 and 7 show the distributions of tracking error estimators in our simulations using the past 15 years of daily US equity returns. The portfolio weights for each simulation were chosen randomly, but within the simulation the weights were held constant over time. Each 15-year simulation

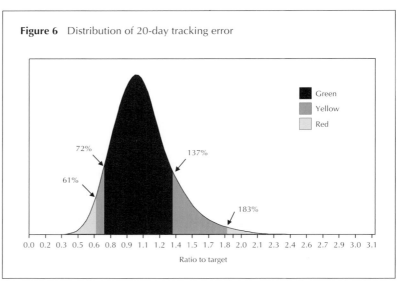

Figure 6 Distribution of 20-day tracking error

is based on a different set of portfolio weights. The histograms average results from over 500 simulations. We have identified the ranges for the green, yellow and red zones which in these historical simulations would have created signals of entry into the yellow and red zones, as defined in footnote 11, consistent, respectively, with the probabilities defining "unusual" and "extremely rare" events mentioned above. In Figure 8 we superimpose the coloured zones for the 20- and 60-day estimators, respectively, over sample time series of tracking error from our historical simulations.

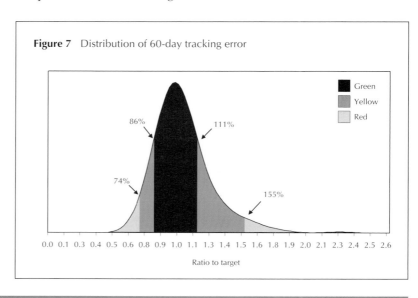

Figure 7 Distribution of 60-day tracking error

Figure 8

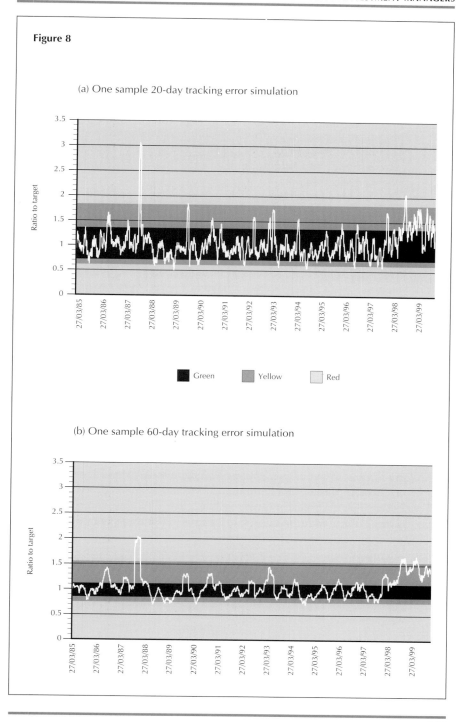

(a) One sample 20-day tracking error simulation

Green   Yellow   Red

(b) One sample 60-day tracking error simulation

One observation about Figure 8(b) is that the tracking error for this portfolio has remained in the yellow zone for most of the past two years. Of course, this is just one particular portfolio with random exposures, but it is actually quite representative of other sample portfolios. As many observers have noted, the past two years have been unusual in terms of their cross-sectional volatility of returns, which in turn, increases tracking error. It might be prudent for a portfolio manager in this environment to trim back the portfolio exposures. In these simulations we have not done so. However, in the appendix we show that such active risk management may have the ability to significantly reduce the probability of moving into the yellow or red zones.

Having discussed these coloured zone concepts with many portfolio managers during the past year and having tried to provide some guidance based on historical simulations, we are well aware of the difficulty in specifying the appropriate bounds for the green, yellow and red zones. In the next section we discuss some of the obvious issues.

Nonetheless, we are convinced of the usefulness of this approach. The important point of this chapter is not that a particular zone can be precisely and correctly established for every circumstance, but rather that portfolio managers and their clients should recognise ahead of time that there will be fluctuations in tracking error, and should agree upon what is a reasonable expectation for the range of realised tracking error outcomes. The fact that such ranges cannot be set with precise probabilities is not particularly important. The process of attempting to establish such ranges in advance, which should then set expectations appropriately, is very important.

LIMITATIONS TO THE APPLICATION OF THE GREEN ZONE

Absence of a tracking error target
An argument can be made that targeting a fixed level of tracking error is not necessarily a desirable component of an investment process. While not endorsing this argument, we recognise that different managers follow a variety of different investment processes and may react to opportunities differently. In particular, some managers may profess an ability to identify situations with particularly large return opportunities. They may, in these situations, wish to increase their tracking error, intentionally creating periods of lower tracking error followed by periods of higher tracking error. Such managers might argue that trying to target a fixed level or band for tracking error is not efficient and is not part of their investment process.

Despite some real issues surrounding the use of tracking error, there are solutions that still make the green zone approach viable
No doubt some investors may prefer such an approach. However, even in this case, the implication is not that targeting a tracking error is irrelevant

or impossible, but rather that the range of expected tracking error outcomes needs to be made wider. The investor in this case may be willing to live with a fairly wide, but not unlimited, amount of variation over time in the tracking error. An appropriate discussion might concern what percentage of the time the portfolio tracking error might be expected to be in different ranges.

The absence of a benchmark

Many portfolios do not have a benchmark. This is not really a problem, simply a change in orientation. Instead of tracking error relative to a benchmark, the issue becomes a targeted level for volatility of excess returns relative to a risk-free rate of interest.

Benchmark deficiencies

While certain sectors of the market have clear and generally accepted benchmarks, others are harder to represent using existing indices. Since we most often strive to use benchmarks which are recognisable by investors, we often compromise on whether the index really represents the portfolio manager's investment philosophy. To adjust for that, we often provide a higher tracking error allowance. That in turn often leads to portfolios having significant biases versus their stated benchmarks and results in estimated tracking error that may be more inaccurate and a realised tracking error that has the potential for higher volatility and may be less manageable.

Transactions costs

Some portfolio managers operate in liquid markets in which adjusting the exposures can be accomplished at relatively low cost. Others operate in illiquid markets and the transaction costs created by trying to adjust exposures to changing market conditions would be prohibitive. Such considerations mean that there can be no one standard for the degree of control of tracking error expected of portfolio managers. However, the approach of targeting a band for tracking error is still valid. The important difference is that the band for managers operating in less liquid markets may be made wider and the interpretation of results and appropriate actions will differ. Because of the costs associated with changing exposures, the portfolio manager with high transactions costs should be expected to adjust less quickly to changing market volatilities. Nonetheless, note that we have proposed establishing tracking error ranges such that the probabilities of exiting are calibrated to portfolios with constant weights. Thus, lack of ability to trade efficiently should not be viewed as an automatic excuse for a high frequency of realisations outside of an agreed-upon range.

Valuation issues

In some markets, valuation transparency is low and it is difficult to accurately estimate daily performance. In such circumstances, portfolios have historically been valued on a monthly or less-frequent basis. Clearly, in such circumstances our approach of using daily performance to monitor tracking error cannot be used. However, liquidity and pricing transparency is increasing in global capital markets very quickly. For example, trading desks at investment banks generally mark their positions to market every day.

Although requests for daily performance data may be new for some managers, such data are becoming more and more readily available
In many portfolios, positions are marked every day but with some significant degree of noise (for whatever reason) relative to the benchmark returns. In this case, the simple moving average of squared daily excess returns will overstate annualised tracking error because the noise component will impact daily volatility, but will wash out over time. The impact of such noise in the tracking error estimate, to create an upward bias and increased variability, can be significantly reduced by averaging the daily returns; a simple example would be through the use of weekly returns. Of course, such averaging is not a panacea; the estimate is still less accurate but the impact of the noise may be significantly reduced.

EXAMPLES USING THE GREEN ZONE
In this section we illustrate the usefulness of the green zone concept through two examples. These examples are based on real applications developed this past year in the Investment Management Division at Goldman Sachs.

Example 1: allocating active risk across multiple managers
Why should an investor care about the range of tracking error outcomes? The basic answer is that tracking error is a scarce resource that the investor should attempt to allocate efficiently. Just as a consumer must be concerned about the cost of purchases because one must live within an income budget, the investor must be concerned about the tracking error of his or her portfolio managers because inevitably the investor must live within a risk budget.[12]

Some managers are not sensitive to the tracking error component of the investor's risk budget. This lack of sensitivity is understandable, if regrettable, because for most investors the major component of risk is the market risk, not the tracking error. As long as this is the case and when tracking error has a low correlation with market risk, small changes in realised tracking error will not have a large impact on the overall risk of the portfolio. Nonetheless, a rational investor will allocate risk first between market exposure and active risk in order to maximise expected return, and will then allocate the active risk among different portfolio managers in order to similarly maximise expected return. In this context the investor should not be indifferent to managers' usage of this scarce resource.

In an investor's portfolio, the total tracking error from all managers can be viewed as part of the overall asset allocation of the risk budget

In an investor's portfolio, the total tracking error from all managers can be viewed as a part of the overall asset allocation of the risk budget. The dominant risk in most investors' portfolios is equity risk. The allocation of risk to tracking error can usefully be viewed as a part of the overall risk allocated to assets uncorrelated with equity markets. To the extent that such an allocation to uncorrelated risk can generate expected return, it is a very useful component of the portfolio. Given its low correlation to equities, the component of risk should not add much to the overall risk of the portfolio. There is, of course, a limit to the size of the overall allocation of risk to uncorrelated assets. If that allocation gets too big, it becomes a dominant source of risk in itself. In choosing a set of managers, an investor is either explicitly, or implicitly, making an allocation of risk to tracking error. To the extent that the manager does not provide the expected level of tracking error, the manager is changing the investor's intended allocation of portfolio risk.

Creating too little tracking error to client expectations is a different issue, but still a problem for the investor. In this situation, there are two concerns. First, fees will have been charged without creating sufficient opportunity to generate excess return. In addition, there is the opportunity cost. The risk allocation that is given to one portfolio manager and not fully utilised by that manager is an allocation that could have been given elsewhere.

Shown on the following page is an example based on the report that we use to monitor managers in one of our fiduciary assignments (Figure 9). Together with normal performance data, we have added "normalised return" – the excess return relative to benchmark divided by the targeted tracking error over that period of time. Thus, the units of normalised return are standard deviations. Any normalised return greater than 2 in absolute value, whether positive or negative, and over any period of time, would be unusual if the portfolio tracking error is on target. Thus, normalised return provides a quick signal if unusual events are occurring.

In addition, this weekly risk report also includes agreed-upon green, yellow and red target zones for the tracking error of each manager. These zones were negotiated at the time the mandate was agreed upon. Not all zones are the same width. The realised tracking error is monitored on a 20- and 60-day basis, based on daily performance figures provided by the managers. When the realised tracking error leaves the green zone for a significant period of time, we arrange to have a conversation with the manager about what is going on.

Figure 9 ABC pension fund risk and performance report

Portfolio	Benchmark	Normalised return			Annualised tracking error				Annualised gross targets			Yellow zone TE (bps)	Red zone TE (bps)	Prior Week			Month to Date		
		Week	MTD	3Mb	Last 20D (bps)	Last 60D (bps)	Last 20D /target	Last 60D /target	ER (bps)	TE (bps)	IR			P (%)	B (%)	D (%)	P (%)	B (%)	D (%)
US Active Equity – Large Cap	S&P 500	0.43	1.38	(2.36)	517	544		1.20		442		517	628	3.30	1.65	1.65	1.44	(0.24)	1.68
Manager A	S&P/Barra Value			3.02	745	718	1.24	1.20	300	600	0.50	700	900	2.36	1.94	0.43	2.73	0.96	1.77
Manager B	S&P/Barra Growth	2.49	1.60		1,215	1,184	1.35	1.32	450	900	0.50	1,000	1,100	4.64	1.40	3.25	1.74	1.30	3.04
Manager C	S&P/Barra Growth	2.23	0.46	1.02	963	952	1.38	1.36	350	700	0.50	850	1,000	3.67	1.40	2.27	(0.52)	(1.30)	0.78
US Active Equity – Total Small Cap	Russell 2000				529	545				397		542	605	5.56	3.96	1.59	1.02	0.61	0.41
US Active Equity – Small Cap Growth	Russell 2000 Growth				945	992	1.57	1.65		601		806	920	7.18	5.38	1.81	0.57	0.49	0.09
Manager D	Russell 2000 Growth	1.65	0.68		1,465	1,435	1.46	1.44	450	1,000	0.45	1,200	1,500 (2)	7.79	5.38	2.42	2.02	0.49	1.53
Manager E	Russell 2000 Growth	1.31	(0.84)		1,130	1,243	1.74	1.91	300	650	0.46	900	900	6.63	5.38	1.26	(0.48)	0.49	(0.97)
Manager F	Russell 2000 Growth	1.62	0.13		1,000	940	1.18	1.11	500	850	0.59	1,150	1,400	7.42	5.38	2.04	0.91	0.49	0.42
US Active Equity – Small Cap Value	Russell 2000 Value				623	529		1.31		452		648	705	3.38	1.92	1.46	1.64	0.78	0.85
Manager G	Russell 2000 Value	1.19	0.49		546	655	1.09	1.09	200	500	0.40	600	600 (2)	2.80	1.92	0.88	1.35	0.78	0.56
Manager H	Russell 2000 Value	3.00	1.09		1,100	880	1.76	1.41	300	625	0.48	1,150	1,350	4.62	1.92	2.70	2.26	0.78	1.48
Non-US Active Equity – Developed	FT/S&P EuroPac				667	511		1.37		556		748	837	2.97	1.93	1.04	(2.87)	(2.60)	(0.26)
Manager I	FT/S&P EuroPac	1.79	(1.44)	2.79	1,207	889	1.86	1.70	325	650	0.50	750	1,000 (1)	3.64	1.93	1.70	(4.34)	(2.60)	(1.73)
Manager J	FT/S&P EuroPac	(2.11)	(0.43)	(1.67)	690	564	1.38	1.13	250	500	0.50	700	800	0.50	1.93	(1.44)	(2.93)	(2.60)	(0.33)
Manager K	FT/S&P EuroPac	2.64	0.49	5.51	1,111	876	1.59	1.25	350	700	0.50	1,000	1,000 (2)	4.61	1.93	2.67	(1.78)	(2.60)	0.83

(1) Based on a rolling 20 day TE.
(2) Based on a rolling 120 day TE.

Legend: ■ Green   ■ Yellow   ■ Red

Example 2: GSAM – monitoring risk in the asset management group
Monitoring portfolio manager performance requires a number of different metrics. For example, there is total return, there is return relative to a benchmark, there are peer group rankings, and there are measures of risk adjusted returns. In addition, for managers who have tracking error targets, there needs to be monitoring of the degree to which those targets are met. It was in this context that we originally developed the approach of monitoring the ratio of 20- and 60-day realised tracking error to target. Moreover, it was in the context of trying to understand when and to what degree we should respond to deviations from target, that we recognised the need for signals based on realised tracking error crossing out of prede-fined regions.

The "green sheet" has proved useful to GSAM in setting expectations and providing useful feedback which can foster better quality control
Figure 10 shows an example of a portion of one of our weekly performance reports (using hypothetical products). This report, known internally as the "green sheet", has columns that are coded for easy recognition of signals of tracking error concerns. For example, we have defined the green zone for a hypothetical set of US equity portfolios, including all ratios of realised 20-day tracking error to target between 0.7 and 1.4, and have defined the red zone as ratios below 0.6 or above 2.0. For the 60-day tracking error we define the green zone as the range between 0.8 and 1.3. The red zone is defined as ratios below 0.7 or above 1.8.

As can be seen, the internal monitoring report includes very similar data to the report used for monitoring external managers. The predefined green, yellow and red zones provide clear expectations for the asset management division portfolio managers. When portfolios move into the yellow or red zone, which will happen every so often, it may be time for a discussion of what is going on. We never expect portfolio management, or risk monitor-ing, to be reduced to a formula, but these types of quantitative tools have proved to be useful in setting expectations and in providing useful

Figure 10 Goldman Sachs asset management – the green sheet

■ Green   ■ Yellow

Portfolio	Benchmark	Week	MTD	YTD	3Mo	12Mo	Last 20D	Last 60D	Last20D /Target	Last60D /Target	Target TE	Prior Week P	B	D	Month To Date P	B	D
Net Performance		*Normalised return versus target*					*Annualised tracking error*					*Prior Week*			*Month To Date*		
US Equity Fund Group																	
Fund 1	S&P 500	-1.21	-0.22	-0.16	-0.19	0.45	263	260	1.05	1.04	250	0.76	1.18	-0.42	-1.02	-0.91	-0.11
Fund 2	R 1000 Growth	0.37	0.91	1.70	2.14	0.91	526	390	1.75	1.30	300	2.13	1.98	0.15	0.62	0.06	0.56
Fund 3	R 1000 Value	0.26	0.85	1.44	1.22	1.36	226	240	0.90	0.96	250	1.32	1.23	0.09	-0.39	-0.83	0.44
Fund 4	R 2000	0.28	-0.12	0.37	-0.07	-0.68	300	288	0.86	0.82	350	4.39	4.25	0.14	1.68	1.76	-0.08

feedback which can foster better quality control of the investment management process.

CONCLUSION

We have tried to create a simple, yet powerful approach to monitoring the realised tracking error of portfolios. We assume a portfolio manager has a target tracking error for each mandate, and we use daily performance to estimate two statistics, a 20-day and a 60-day moving average estimators to measure realised tracking error. We suggest that portfolio managers create and discuss with clients the appropriate ranges of outcomes – our green, yellow and red zones – with which to interpret such statistics.

We recognise that the complexities of portfolio management prevent there from being any one standard for assessing success in managing tracking error, especially over a short time. Issues such as different investment processes, different characteristics of different markets, differing transactions costs, and so on will cause the interpretation of the outcomes for different portfolios to vary. Moreover, managers' understanding of and judgments about the sources of volatility, of the likelihood of episodes of higher volatility to persist, and of the costs of adjustments to the portfolio exposures, will all affect their appropriate course of action.

Portfolio managers have a responsibility to provide clients with their intended tracking error range and investors should monitor the outcomes
Nonetheless, portfolio managers have a responsibility to provide their clients with an understanding of the range of tracking error they intend to be taking, and clients should monitor the distribution of outcomes they receive to ensure it is consistent with the agreed-upon range. Portfolio managers should communicate to clients what they consider their green, yellow and red zones to be, and clients may wish to discuss situations when the realised tracking error goes outside the green zone. Whether any action is necessary at these times will depend on the circumstances causing the deviation.

Our view is that the ability to define and articulate tracking error targets, to monitor and manage the tracking error of the portfolio over reasonably long intervals, and to know when and how to incur transactions costs in order to do so, is all part of the skill that defines excellence in portfolio management. Hopefully the use of these colour-coded zones will help in the process.

APPENDIX: SIMULATION METHODOLOGY AND RESULTS

We use historical returns on US equities for the past 15 years to simulate the statistical behaviour of the tracking error of US equity portfolios managed relative to an S&P 500 benchmark. We sample from 500 historical simulations, each based on a different random portfolio with 100 overweight and 100 underweight positions. The stocks in each portfolio are chosen randomly from the 385 stocks in the current index for which data exists over the entire 15-year period. The active exposures are randomly drawn from a uniform distribution, (0.5, 1) for overweight positions, and from a uniform distribution, (–1, –0.5) for underweight positions. The active weights are adjusted so that each portfolio has a beta of 1 with respect to the benchmark. Finally, all active exposures are scaled so that the median tracking error of the portfolio on average over the entire period is equal to the target tracking error.

In each simulation we create measures of 20- and 60-day tracking error based on the moving average of squared excess returns relative to the benchmark. For each sample path of tracking error and definition of green, yellow and red zones we identify yellow and red zone signals as outlined in note 10 in the text. We find that letting the green zone region stretch from ratios of a low end at 72% of target to a high end at 137% of the target for the 20-day estimator leads to signals of entry into the yellow once per year on the low and high sides. Letting the yellow zone region stretch from ratios to target of 61% to 72% on the low side and 137% to 184% on the high side, leads to signals of entry into the red zone once in every five years.

Following the same approach, we find that letting the green zone region stretch from ratios of 86% to 111% relative to target for the 60-day estimator and letting the yellow zone region stretch from ratios of 74% to 86% and 111% to 155% relative to target leads to yellow zone signals once per year on the low and high sides. As above, red one signals occur once in every five years, given these definitions.

In addition to creating this base case result, we undertook two experiments to see how sensitive these results were – first to the number of active positions in the portfolios, and second to the assumption that the portfolios were managed passively.

The first set of experiments adjusted the number of random-active exposures between 10 and 100. As expected, we found the locations of the lower and upper zones spread out as the number of exposures declined, reflecting the higher variability of tracking error in less diversified portfolios. The degree of spread, however, was relatively small, suggesting that our results may have general applicability with respect to US equity portfolios. For example, the upper end of the yellow zone increased from 184% for random portfolios with 100 overweight and 100 underweight exposures to 197% for random portfolios with only 10 overweight and 10 underweight exposures. The lower end of the yellow zone was even less sensitive. There the border with the red zone only decreased from 61% of target to 59% of target as the total number of exposures dropped from 200 to 20.

The second experiment we tried was to see how much benefit could be obtained by actively adjusting portfolio exposures to compensate for observable signals of higher or lower volatility in the market. In looking for relevant signals, we observed that the recent level of cross-sectional volatility of stock returns – that is, the standard deviation of the distribution of stock returns in a given day – is a good predictor of higher tracking error in the next few months. We followed a simple procedure of continually scaling exposures back (or up) by 75% of the degree to which a simple exponentially decaying moving average of recent cross-sectional volatility is above (or below) its median value. Of course, such daily scaling is not intended to be cost effective or realistic, but the results may be instructive in suggesting to what extent active risk management might be capable of reducing the range of tracking error outcomes. Following this simple procedure decreases the top of the yellow zone for the 20-day measure of realised tracking error from 184% of target to 148% of target. For the 60-day measure the results are even more dramatic. In this case the top of the yellow zone decreases from 155% to 124% of target.

1   "Tracking error", usually measured in basis points, refers to the annualised volatility of the returns of a portfolio relative to its benchmark. In some cases a portfolio may not have an explicit benchmark, or the benchmark may be a risk-free rate; in those contexts tracking error refers to the volatility of the excess returns relative to the risk-free rate.

2   The concept of attributing a colour coding to define ranges in risk management was first coined by those who drafted the market risk capital supervisory framework of the Basle Committee on Banking Supervision. Over the past few years, certain banks have been allowed to calculate the amount of capital required to cover market risk in their trading businesses based on their internal models (namely value-at-risk type calculations). However, to encourage banks to use the best possible models, supervisory authorities have associated a multiplier with the capital requirement. The value of the multiplier depends on how well these internal models forecast risk.

   Given the statistical limitations of backtesting, the Committee defined three potential ranges results. The green zone corresponds to backtesting results that do not suggest a problem with the quality or accuracy of a bank's model. The yellow zone encompasses results that do raise questions in this regard, but where such a conclusion is not definitive. The red zone indicates a backtesting result that almost certainly indicates a problem with a bank's risk model.

   For more details on this methodology, the reader may want to refer to "Supervisory framework for the use of 'backtesting' in conjunction with the internal models approach to market risk capital requirements", January 1996. (This document is available from http://www.bis.org/publ/index.htm.)

3   There have been additional refinements suggested, such as the recognition that volatility, per se, is not the appropriate measure of risk. See, for example, "How to rate management of investment funds", by Jack Treynor, in the Harvard Business Review, January/February 1965. In particular, risks which can be diversified away should not create a return premium. Modern portfolio theory suggests that the primary source of a risk premium should be from returns that correlate with the market portfolio. One implication is that at the same level of volatility, portfolio managers who create excess returns in commodities, long/short portfolios and other uncorrelated assets, should be valued more highly than those who create the same mean return in a portfolio that is positively correlated with equities. Note that negatively correlated returns are even more valuable. A portfolio manager who creates consistently positive returns while investing in a portfolio of short equity positions, for example, would be especially valuable. But of course creating such returns consistently

would be a very significant achievement given the wind-in-your-face environment created by the long-term positive average return to equity risk.

4   Returns can be positive or negative.

5   For the reasons discussed in note 3, it may also make sense for portfolio managers to target a low correlation between the returns of the broad market and the excess returns of the portfolio relative to its benchmark.

6   Even if a manager outperforms his benchmark, a client may not remain invested with the manager if unacceptably high levels of tracking error are needed to generate these returns. Excessive use of risk budget might cause the client to lose confidence in the manager.

7   Even though altitude is easier to measure than tracking error, there are also variations that depend on circumstances. Vertical separations between aircraft may depend on whether there is adequate radar coverage (air traffic controllers have a clear idea of what happens over the Midwestern United States but can only infer where aircraft are over the Atlantic). Our views on where the green, yellow and red zones should be may also depend on a variety of factors, such as how closely the benchmark represents the investment philosophy of a manager. While we may have strong views on the control parameters of some managers, we may need more flexible ranges for those sectors of the market where the benchmarks are either not as clear or not completely investable.

8   Note that none of what we discuss in this chapter depends on the absolute level of tracking error; our approach works whether the targeted tracking error is 1% or 5%. What interests us, and therefore the way we will express all our results, is the ratio of realised tracking error to the targeted level.

9   In fact, in the simple, idealised situation in which the excess returns are normally distributed with constant volatility, the true distribution of the square of these tracking error estimators, appropriately scaled, is well known to be chi-squared with degrees of freedom equal to the number of observations.

10   This distribution is based on the simulation methodology described in the appendix. It represents an average over many historical simulations of portfolios with randomised exposures.

11   To be a little more precise, we need to address a couple of details. First, there are many possible regions with the property that realised tracking will remain within them a fixed percentage of the time. For example, one region would be centred around the target, or other regions could be created that include the entire top or bottom of the distribution of outcomes. We suggest an approach which defines the green zone as that region where, if the exposures of the portfolio were held constant, we would expect the tracking error to signal a divergence on the high side once per year and on the low side once per year.

Second, we need to define exactly what constitutes a "signal". We do not want to count as a signal a single day in which tracking error crosses from inside to outside of a given region. To do so might create many signals whenever the tracking error is near the edge of the green zone region. Rather, we suggest defining a signal as an event where for two consecutive weeks the average tracking error lies within the green zone followed by a period of two consecutive weeks in which the average lies outside of the green zone. Also, to be precise, we would not record another "signal" if there has already been a signal at that boundary within the previous month.

12   See Kurt Winkelmann's chapter "Risk Budgeting: Managing Active Risk at the Total Fund Level" also included in this volume.

Additional Notes

General

Opinions expressed are current opinions as of the date appearing in this material only.

In the event any of the assumptions used in this chapter do not prove to be true, results are likely to vary substantially from the examples shown herein. These examples are for illustrative purposes only and do not purport to show actual results.

With respect to targeted tracking errors and risk levels, there can be no assurance that such targets will be met.

Simulated, modelled or hypothetical results

Simulated performance results have certain inherent limitations. Such results are hypothetical and do not represent actual trading, and thus may not reflect material economic and market factors, such as liquidity constraints, that may have had an impact on the Adviser's actual decision-making. Simulated results are also achieved through the retroactive application of a model designed with the benefit of hindsight. The results shown reflect the reinvestment of dividends and other earnings but do not reflect advisory fees, transaction costs and other expenses a client would have paid, which would reduce return. No representation is made that a client will achieve results similar to those shown.

Risk management

The portfolio risk management process includes an effort to monitor and manage risk, but should not be confused with and does not imply low risk.

8

Risk Obsession: Does it Lead to Risk Aversion?

Amy B. Hirsch

Paradigm Consulting Services, LLC

This chapter will explore the various methods by which investors define, quantify and "obsess" over portfolio risks. Although the issues we will discuss are applicable to risk management in general, the focus will be on alternative investment portfolios and, in particular, hedge funds, since they are gaining tremendous institutional interest.

Risk obsession starts with the simple notion that most investors want to achieve a certain return with little downside risk or loss in their portfolio. Investors attempt to create portfolios that will achieve optimal results: high positive returns with low standard deviation. This goal is both reasonable and sensible, depending upon how you define high and low.

When asked to define their risk/reward targets, many investors immediately determine a certain target return. When asked to complete the equation and define their risk tolerance, investors will often say something off hand like "little to no risk". Unfortunately, most people cannot define their own risk tolerance. Conversely, some investors will think they can tolerate risk, but, when faced with a portfolio loss, they immediately panic. In both cases, however, investors often become obsessed with risk and risk measurements, making them their portfolios' own worst enemy. I will discuss the meaning of risk obsession, give a brief overview of why investors have become more obsessed with risk, and then review some of the myths and realities about risk measurement tools used by investors.

It is not possible to incorporate all of the statistical, economical and psychological aspects of risk obsession into one chapter. The intention, therefore, is to open the reader to different ways of viewing portfolio risks without becoming obsessed, and to illustrate that understanding different strategies and risks requires more than a few statistics to create a solid portfolio.

At Paradigm Consulting Services, LLC, a consultancy firm focused solely on alternative investment portfolios, it is our job to find investments that complement our clients' broad equity and bond portfolios. Over the past 20 years in alternative investments, including eight years consulting, I have personally seen the "smartest" risk managers and investors fooled by their own obsession with risk. In this chapter, we will examine some common mistakes and myths, and perhaps some different approaches to mitigate these mistakes. The chapter will primarily be a mix of both anecdotal and "bubbled-up" evidence based on our experience with institutions, family offices and individuals.

We start with a simple premise: that it is appropriate to include alternative investments (specifically hedge funds and managed futures) in your asset allocation to provide a return stream that is non-dependent on rising equity and bond markets, and is therefore non-correlated to your equity and bond holdings. Further, alternative investments often provide a better risk-adjusted return than traditional investments in equities and bonds.

In the quest for risk-adjusted returns, however, investors often become obsessed with the notion of risk reduction and risk measurement. During the past 20 years, I have witnessed a cadre of portfolio abuses. The greatest abuse is the widespread use of various statistics to "optimise" and "monitor" portfolios of alternative investments. While some of the fault lies in academia and some with industry professionals, it is the investor who has created the demand for the "ultimate risk measurement". Investors need to count on one or two key statistics to create an optimal portfolio. It is reminiscent of the most sought-after weight loss programme: take a pill, eat all you want, do not exercise and become thin. Apply this to the portfolio: buy the track record, diversify among 50 managers and conduct no due diligence. Throw in some VAR calculations, track your standard deviation and go to the beach.

This basic human flaw (coupled with flawed quantitative tools) leads investors to varied results. If you travel down one risk obsession path, you may become risk averse and performance poor, resulting in very low standard deviation but also low returns. If you travel down another risk obsession path, you inadvertently increase risk and destroy your portfolio, resulting in negative returns coupled with high standard deviation. In both cases, you miss the bigger portfolio picture. In this chapter, I will try to wind my way down these paths, exploring the resultant effects on portfolio performance. In some cases, the paths become one, and the investor is left with poor performance and huge risk.

To understand why this happens, we will examine the common risk tools available to investors, apply these tools to real world situations, and attempt to make an educational assessment of the mistakes made by obsessing about risk.

WHAT IS RISK OBSESSION?

Risk obsession in portfolio terms means something very different from risk obsession in everyday life. While some are obsessed with taking physical risks such as rock-climbing or skydiving, investors are obsessed with *avoiding* risk in their portfolio. Investors typically associate high standard deviation with excessive risk and have been taught to avoid investments with track records that indicate low return/risk ratios. At the extreme, investors have been known to faint when hearing the words "derivatives" and "futures", as they associate them with high volatility and excessive risk.

In the past 10 years, equity investors have been lulled into a false sense of security by a raging bull market in US equities, and subsequently did not feel the need to diversify their holdings into other assets. The notion that their holdings could depreciate simply did not occur to many; even institutions fell prey to the bull market hype and fanaticism.

The summer of 1998 was the first wake up call for many investors. First, they received quite a shock when Long Term Capital Management needed the assistance of the Federal Reserve to ensure the safety of the worldwide markets. Second, this happened at the same time that Russia declared they would not pay their bond obligations to foreign holders. The S&P 500 declined by 14.44% in August 1998 and investors, reeling from these events, started to examine the risk side of the equation more carefully.

In the search for portfolio insurance, hedge funds and managed futures subsequently attracted significant interest. Attempting to mitigate potential losses, investors now increasingly look to these two asset classes to get them through the turbulent times in the stock and bond markets. However, the problem is that many investors approach risk management with limited tools and limited experience. This leads them to focus on, or obsess about, certain quantitative notions that are meant only to be a small part of the risk management tool kit. It is this obsession that I will focus on, along with the following key risk management fallacies:

❏ standard deviation;
❏ Sharpe ratio;
❏ exclusion of high standard deviation investments;
❏ track record obsession; and
❏ replacing due diligence with statistics.

MEASURES OF RISK: MYTHS AND REALITIES

First the bad news: you have to take risk to achieve returns. You may not see these risks and they may never harm your portfolio, but they certainly exist. Sophisticated high-net-worth investors have been investing in hedge funds and managed futures in an attempt to mitigate downside risk during extreme market moves with the expectation of "absolute" returns in both bull and bear markets. As alternative investments gain acceptance, institutions are becoming significant investors in hedge funds and managed futures. Historically, high-net-worth investors have based their investment decisions on the recommendation of other investors. Sometimes, they even conduct a cursory review of the manager and their track record. Unlike many high-net-worth investors, however, institutions rely much more upon quantitative analysis, benchmarks and standard risk measurements.

The most commonly used tools in portfolio construction and manager analysis are the Sharpe ratio and standard deviation. Standard deviation is a statistical measure of the distance a quantity is likely to lie from its average value. In portfolio or manager analysis, standard deviation is applied to the annual rate of return of an investment, to measure the investment's volatility, or "risk".

The accepted definition is:

$$StdDev(r) = [1/n * (ri - rave)2]^{1}/_2$$

Where, in the case of manager performance the terms:

ri are actual annual rate of return, for the fund;
n is the number of values of ri used; and
rave is the average value of the ri.

Clearly, large tails or excessive standard deviation damages the compounding affect on annual performance. Lower downside deviation of returns allows you to achieve your performance results in a better risk-adjusted manner. This assumes that the standard deviation in the investment or portfolio is on both sides of the mean performance.

The Sharpe ratio is a measure of risk taken to achieve performance reward. The accepted statistical definition of the Sharpe ratio is:

$$S(x) = (r(x) - r\$)/StdDev(x)$$

Where, in the case of manager performance:

x is the performance of the fund;
r(x) is the average annual rate of return of x (the fund);
r$ is the rate of return of a "riskless" security (ie, cash); and
StdDev(x) is the standard deviation of r(x).

The Sharpe ratio is often used in constructing portfolios with little or no due diligence to the underlying strategies and reasons for profits and losses. Portfolio construction by Sharpe ratio can be very costly to investors. In hedge funds, in particular, it is more important to isolate the "alpha" of the return and the environment in which it was produced than to assume a Sharpe ratio will predict future performance.

The point I want to make about the obsession with these statistics is that standard deviation, and therefore the Sharpe ratio, does not distinguish between downside deviation and upside deviation. Both measures are indifferent to whether or not the deviation from the mean results in positive or negative returns. In the case of Managed Futures investments, which act as portfolio protection essentially by being long volatility, the resultant Sharpe ratio will be penalised by the upside return and appear to be a low or "bad" Sharpe. This does not help the investor in creating an "optimal" portfolio.

To see the application of these statistics and the results of their misuse, we will review a potential portfolio using actual manager data from the Paradigm Consulting Services, LLC database, but removing the names for confidentiality purposes.

POTENTIAL EFFECTS OF STANDARD DEVIATION AND SHARPE RATIO OBSESSION

Our obsession with standard deviation is frightening. Perhaps the biggest mistake an investor can make is to conflate standard deviation and risk. While standard deviation may be a measure of risk, it does not represent the entire risk of an investment. In fact, it may not even represent risk at all if you do not mind upside deviation.

An understanding of standard deviation is critical if you are to truly protect your portfolio. Most importantly, investors must be aware that standard deviation will differ at the strategy level. For example, event-driven strategies, such as merger arbitrage or distressed investing, will probably experience lumpy returns or tails, since events do not occur on a consistent basis. A manager will set up his or her portfolio with the expectation of a catalyst in the future such as a take-over, spin-off, or restructuring. When these events occur and the manager's assumption is correct, they will have a staggering positive effect on the company's stock or bond price. This, in turn, will create a higher standard deviation at the manager performance level. In addition, as more cash merger deals are being done, hedging is difficult to impossible thus increasing the standard deviation of the manager's return as well. It does not, however, define the risk in the portfolio.

On the other hand, "market neutral" arbitrage strategies should have a very consistent return pattern and low standard deviation. Usually highly hedged, these strategies attempt to maintain certain neutralities to the broad stock and bond markets. This may be in the form of dollar neutrality, sector neutrality, etc. While a defined risk is still taken in order to achieve the return, the standard deviation should be low on both the up and down side.

In any case, investors should not obsess about the standard deviation number, rather, they should focus on its appropriateness *vis-à-vis* the strategy they are investing in. We will take this to an extreme and study the potential effects of standard deviation obsession.

Table 1 Alternative investment managers – January 1995 to June 1998

	Sharpe ratio	Annual risk (%)	Annual return (%)	Worst draw-down (%)
Manager Set '"A"				
Mgr 1	2.84	3.18	14.89	–2.69
Mgr 2	0.38	9.65	9.32	–14.80
Mgr 3	2.66	3.02	13.86	–2.84
Mgr 4	2.48	3.57	14.71	–1.86
Mgr 5	5.37	3.21	23.53	None
Manager Set "B"				
Mgr 1	0.52	15.47	13.90	–7.88
Mgr 2	0.67	12.71	14.39	–14.00
Mgr 3	0.52	20.45	16.51	–17.54
Mgr 4	0.94	18.01	23.23	–10.40
Mgr 5	0.23	27.94	12.09	–28.93

Case study

If an investor were sitting in his office on July 1, 1998, saddled with the task of creating a non-correlated hedge fund portfolio to complement his equity and bond holdings, which of the sets of managers in Table 1 would he be likely to invest in?

The investor already knows that he does not want anything to do with the managers in set "B": the Sharpe ratios are terrible (all being below 1.0), and the draw-down numbers are enough to give a board of trustees a heart attack. He would pass on these investments without a single thought, and this is where the problem begins.

There has been no discussion of strategy, style or risk. The investor has simply conducted a cursory analysis of track records, accepting the manager's own style description without question. It never ceases to amaze me when a manager tells me about a client who wired money in without visiting or conducting telephonic due diligence – they simply "liked the track record". Let us stay on this course, however, and look at the pure economics of the statistical biases.

Next, we will create an equally weighted portfolio and see whether the investor's intuition is correct. That is, we will give the same allocation to each of the managers and review the portfolio results. If given the choice between the two portfolios in Table 2, which would he invest in?

Given the propensity of investors to abhor standard deviation, it is probable that the investor would have invested in Portfolio A (comprised of Manager Set A). Although the average annual return may be slightly lower (15.29% versus 16.86%), the draw-down is significantly lower (–2.54 versus –7.61). Furthermore, in the search for risk-adjusted returns, investors would clearly favour a Sharpe ratio of 3.22 over that of 0.74. After all, the historical standard deviation of Set B does not even warrant a second look – or does it?

Obsession with achieving a low standard deviation often hurts a portfolio. The investor was naturally drawn to the relative statistical health of Manager Set A. In fact, for the entire period of their existence

Table 2 Equal weighted portfolio of managers – January 1995 to June 1998

	Portfolio A	Portfolio B
Annual return (%)	15.29	16.86
Annual risk (%)	2.92	14.71
Sharpe ratio	3.22	0.74
Worst draw-down (%)	(–2.54)	(–7.61)

prior to June 1998, only one manager could have been suspected of potential harm. The others each had annual returns in excess of 13.00% and standard deviations below 3.6%. Two of the managers had over 10 years' worth of track record. What the investors did not see were the hidden risks behind the numbers. In each case, there was a reason not to invest with this set of managers. Only due diligence and reference checks could have saved you from three of them. In the case of two, you may still have been fooled. Let us stay with this line of statistical thinking and turn the clock ahead.

It is now December 1998 and the investor is conducting his annual portfolio review. Was he correct in constructing a portfolio based on Sharpe's and standard deviations? Did each manager perform as the investor expected based on his or her individual track records? Table 3 shows the manager results extending the performance record starting in January 1995 (like our former statistics), but ending in December 1998.

Having been fearful of seemingly harmful standard deviation, the investor let his obsession lead him directly into the worst portfolio scenario thinkable. His top producing manager (Manager 5), who had an annual return of 23.53% prior to July 1998, finished the year by damaging his

Table 3 Manager results – January 1995 to December 1998

	Sharpe ratio	Annual risk (%)	Annual return (%)	Worst draw-down (%)
Manager Set '"A"				
Mgr 1	0.90	52.12	–43.67	–93.57
Mgr 2	0.55	17.59	–4.84	–43.72
Mgr 3	0.44	7.27	8.74	–10.10
Mgr 4	0.03	9.16	5.67	–24.52
Mgr 5	0.35	32.23	–6.29	–66.26
Manager Set "B"				
Mgr 1	0.54	15.07	13.82	–7.88
Mgr 2	0.84	13.89	17.60	–16.51
Mgr 3	0.70	22.80	22.06	–18.30
Mgr 4	0.84	17.72	21.00	–10.40
Mgr 5	0.65	32.05	27.29	–28.93

Table 4 Equal weighted portfolio of managers – January 1995 to December 1998

	Portfolio A	Portfolio B
Annual return (%)	−5.42	21.36
Annual risk (%)	20.01	16.05
Sharpe ratio	0.51	0.95
Worst draw-down (%)	−52.67	−7.61

Table 5 Overall change from June 1998

	Portfolio A	Portfolio B
Annual return (%)	−20.71	4.50
Annual risk (%)	17.09	1.34
Sharpe ratio	−2.71	0.21
Worst draw-down (%)	−50.13	0.00

annual return (−29.82%) thereby creating a negative (−6.29%) average annual return. This same manager, who had never had a negative month until that point, now had a worst draw-down of (−66.26%). The results of the other managers were equally disturbing.

How would his portfolio have fared had he held it until the end of 1998? Let us take a fresh look at the change in statistics of the two portfolios by changing the ending period to December 1998 (Tables 4 and 5).

The investor actually managed to create a negative average annual return, increased his maximum draw-down by 50.13%, increased his standard deviation by 17.09%, and lowered his Sharpe ratio by 2.71. In fact, in the six months from June to December 1998 there was a (−20.71%) change in the average annual return of the portfolio. Good job! Meanwhile, portfolio B increased its average annual return by 4.5%, increased its Sharpe ratio by 0.21, and only increased its standard deviation by 1.34%.

Perhaps I am being a bit unfair. After all, these are very different strategies. One consists of steady, arbitrage hedge fund strategies, while the other consists of very volatile managed futures strategies. Unfortunately, all the VAR analysis in the world could not have saved you from mistaking the relative safety of the two strategies. In fact, prior to August 1998, when we experienced a global liquidity crisis in the wake of the Russian debt debacle and the crisis at Long Term Capital, even VAR looked like a reasonable measure. Unfortunately, VAR is only as good as the number of devastating events that it includes.

The investor could not have known that Portfolio A was a group of arbitrage strategies and Portfolio B was a group of managed futures strategies if he were seeing the results for the first time in December 1998. Had we started the portfolio construction process, again using only statistics, beginning in December 1998, he would have chosen Portfolio B. This would have created completely different results in the two years to follow, since managed futures have had a very difficult performance period.

The exclusion of Managed Futures investments, however, is a common mistake made in the name of low standard deviation and high Sharpe ratios. Let us examine the effect of including a 20% allocation of managed futures to Portfolio B in light of the events of August 1998 to see how much

Table 6 Managed futures – January 1995 to December 1998

	Portfolio 'A'	80% Portfolio 'A' 20% Portfolio 'B'	Alpha or value added
Average annual return (%)	−5.42	5.10	10.52
Annual risk (%)	20.01	11.89	−8.12
Worst draw-down (%)	−52.67	−29.80	22.87
Sharpe ratio	0.51	0.02	(0.49)

an obsession with risk measurements hurts the portfolio. Could managed futures have contributed any significant protection to the hedge fund portfolio? The results are shown in Table 6.

By decreasing the Sharpe ratio, the investor actually averted risk. He would have increased his annual return by 10.52%, decreased his annual standard deviation by 8.12%, and chopped his worst draw-down by 22.87%. In August 1998 (for the insanely curious), Portfolio A was down (−21.60%), Portfolio B was up +14.73%, and the 80/20 combined portfolio was down (−8.16%). Not stellar results, but a huge difference, and one that many investors would understand in view of the financial and political climate at the time.

Our job is to think about risk at the portfolio level which automatically includes all the risks associated with all the underlying strategies. It is imperative that investors start to think "outside the box" when evaluating their portfolio goals and their actual risk tolerance. Reliance on Sharpe ratios and standard deviation numbers clearly does not work.

What about diversification? If you cannot construct portfolios solely using Sharpe ratios and standard deviation, can you simply diversify across managers to mitigate risk?

DIVERSIFICATION: ALL ROADS LEAD TO A CORRELATION OF ONE!

Let us move on to another common misconception among risk-obsessed investors: diversification will save me during times of market dislocation. Well, yes, it may. Certainly, one must actually have diversified the reward path as well as the risk components to achieve this. The most common mistake, however, is to diversify the number of managers and not the number of styles and strategies. Can an investor eliminate due diligence by massive diversification? Do you lower your risk through diversification? Let us examine a popular industry index to conduct the first test of the theory of diversification.

The most popular hedge fund strategy (and largest percentage of the hedge fund universe) is equity hedged or equity long/short. Do investors obtain any protection by diversifying among equity hedge managers? To answer this, let us examine the results of the HFRI index for Equity Hedge.

Table 7 Composition of index in number of funds and average size

Year	Number of funds	Average assets (US$)	Return (%)	Worst month (%)
1995	90	41,000,000	31.04	−1.44
1996	102	70,000,000	21.75	−2.87
1997	133	76,000,000	23.75	−0.93
1998 (to June)	227	100,000,000	9.30	−1.27

For the period from January 1995 to June 1998, the HFRI Equity Hedge Index had a total return of 115.20%, an annual return of 24.48%, and an annual risk of 7.11%. The composition of the index in number of funds and average size was as in Table 7.

Our investor is once again sitting in his office in July 1998 attempting to diversify his portfolio. Looking at the statistics above, he would guess that he could not go too wrong by randomly choosing managers by throwing darts at the index. In fact, our investor probably thinks he cannot do better than the index. I, however, have chosen to conduct due diligence and create a portfolio of only five managers. My portfolio versus the index is shown in Table 8.

It appears from Table 8 that I am doing better than the index. The question is, will it save me in extreme risk scenarios?

Along comes August 1998 and the financial markets meltdown. The S&P 500 Index is down (−14.44%), the Russell 2000 Index is down (−19.42%), MSCI EM Index is down (−28.03%), and Nasdaq Composite Index is down (−19.93%). Thank goodness our investor has all those diversified managers. Right? Surely his diversification will protect him much more than my measly portfolio of five managers.

Let us now review the August 1998 results: HFRI Equity Hedge Index is down (−7.65%), while my portfolio is down (−4.11%). How is this possible? Perhaps I did a bit of cherry picking, which is certainly appropriate considering what we do for a living. That in itself, however, does not explain the alpha.

Table 8 Due diligence portfolio

Year	Number of funds	Average assets (US$)	Return (%)	Worst month (%)
1995	5	na	31.30	−0.78
1996	5	na	28.78	−1.43
1997	5	na	35.15	0.09
1998 (to June)	5	na	10.47	−0.07

The reality is that in a raging bull market, many hedged equity managers forget to short. Others are simply long-biased managers who want to charge an incentive fee. This does not provide diversification at the portfolio level. In fact, the systematic risk in the index is much higher than the small portfolio of five managers. I know, because I did due diligence on the five managers. They traffic in different cap sizes, varying sectors and actually hedge their portfolios.

Had the investor chosen the wrong managers from the index, the results could have been devastating. The average always hides the tails! The bottom line is that you must understand the underlying instruments and profit and loss attribution of the managers you invest with to obtain true diversification.

To exemplify the need for strategy and style diversification, let us go back to the portfolio of five hedge fund managers we chose earlier in the chapter and examine what happened to correlations before and after August 1998.

For the period from January 1995 to June 1998, the correlation among the managers and to the major indices was as follows in Table 9.

As you can see from the correlation chart in Table 9, it appears that we have selected a diverse group of managers that gives us non-correlation to the broad indices as well as to each other. It seems our obsession about risk is about to payoff. Right? Wrong.

As is shown in Table 9, the lowest correlation among managers prior to the August 1998 event was 0.05 between Manager 5 and Manager 2. After the event, the correlation to December 1998 as shown in Table 10 jumped to 0.59. Consequently, we did not achieve our desired non-correlation through diversification among managers. This occurs for many reasons, but in the case of 1998 we saw a confluence of events that resulted in massive correlation. Among the many reasons were:

❑ many managers were in the same trade;
❑ many portfolios had to sell into a massive liquidity squeeze at fire-sale prices;

Table 9 Correlation analysis, hedge funds/indices – January 1995 to June 1998

	Mgr 1	Mgr 2	Mgr 3	Mgr 4	Mgr 5	LB Bond	MSCI EM	S&P 500
Mgr 1	1.00							
Mgr 2	0.36	1.00						
Mgr 3	0.31	0.13	1.00					
Mgr 4	0.42	0.07	0.58	1.00				
Mgr 5	0.08	0.05	0.22	0.26	1.00			
LB Bond	−0.41	−0.24	0.00	−0.15	−0.10	1.00		
MSCI EM	0.37	0.49	0.28	0.42	0.20	−0.07	1.00	
S&P 500	−0.05	0.23	0.05	0.02	−0.03	0.42	0.57	1.00

Table 10 Correlation analysis, hedge funds/indices – January 1995 to December 1998

	Mgr 1	Mgr 2	Mgr 3	Mgr 4	Mgr 5	LB Bond	MSCI EM	S&P 500
Mgr 1	1.00							
Mgr 2	0.75	1.00						
Mgr 3	0.86	0.55	1.00					
Mgr 4	0.93	0.72	0.86	1.00				
Mgr 5	0.44	0.59	0.16	0.50	1.00			
LB Bond	−0.10	−0.31	0.01	−0.13	−0.22	1.00		
MSCI EM	−0.09	0.27	−0.11	0.10	0.51	−0.15	1.00	
S&P 500	−0.08	0.18	−0.16	0.02	0.51	0.20	0.73	1.00

❑ many portfolios were not really non-correlated to begin with; and
❑ all portfolios got marked down and therefore had directional correlation.

Let me expand upon this last point.

When times are good, margin calls are low and managers mark their portfolios liberally. When times are bad, all managers mark their books conservatively. Some may have to deal with margin calls. Their performance will suffer in the same way and funds will become more correlated. Clearly, the pricing of a fund during good times is vastly different from bad times. Thus, correlation will appear very different. Investors should always look at tail correlations when creating portfolios. That is, identify the correlation of managers during extreme market moves as opposed to normal environments. You will find that many managers who appear non-correlated on "average" become extremely correlated during tail events.

ATTEMPTING TO REDUCE RISK BY "WAITING" FOR A DEMONSTRATED TRACK RECORD

In an effort to avoid or dampen risk, investors often wait for a manager to have a demonstrated track record of a period between two and five years. This is typically enough for them to justify an investment. Their theory is that a demonstrated track record proves that the manager can make money, can manage an office, and has demonstrated that he or she is indeed good at the strategy he or she purports to employ. The basic flaw in this assumption is that the investor is confusing a proven ability with future viability. Furthermore, without empirical proof of this ability (ie, audited financial statements), investors should be hesitant in believing the manager's claims.

To further complicate the issue, we are at an interesting crossroad in the alternative investment "industry". Investors are being forced to make investment decisions at a breakneck pace due to a growing trend in hedge funds to "close" to new investors quickly. In many cases, however, hedge funds only close until they reopen. This could be months or years, but rarely is it a permanent condition. Not wanting to risk being shut-out, investors feel they no longer have the luxury of watching the growth of a manager from the side-lines before investing. This creates a problem in portfolio construction since new managers do not have track records. Furthermore, many mutual fund managers who have never shorted stock are entering the hedge fund arena. Investors are being asked to take a leap of faith that these managers can indeed run a long/short portfolio.

Conversely, many investors will need to watch a manager grow, and only invest after they have exhibited solid performance for a certain period of time. In many cases, this investment is carried out regardless of lack of information, little understanding of the underlying strategy, or little comfort with the manager himself. Investors continue to fall prey to the almighty track record because investors truly believe (because of their obsession about risk) that they can lower or avoid risk by investing with managers who have a proven record. Unfortunately, they are often indifferent to strategy and the need for information beyond performance numbers. Always remember this: *nobody will market to you whilst exhibiting a bad track record – they all look good at first.*

At the beginning of 1998, a client of ours insisted that we conduct a due diligence on a manager because of his stellar numbers. We quickly advised him that "if it looks too good to be true, it probably is". The numbers, however, were too compelling, and the client was searching for the perfect "market neutral" strategy because he was obsessed about systematic equity risk. Here is an example of investors waiting for a proven five-year record, and those who invested because the statistics told them the manager "must be good".

If you had seen the track record exhibited in Table 11, you too would have been very tempted to invest, with your decision based solely on the numbers. Table 11 appears to show a brilliant track record. Not one down month, meaning great standard deviation and Sharpe ratio figures.

Once again our investor is sitting in his office in July 1998 looking for the perfect non-correlation to equity and bond markets with solid absolute returns. For the period in Table 11, the average annual return on this fund is 24.97%, the standard deviation is 3.06% and the Sharpe ratio is 6.20. Our investor insists that this must be real, due to the numbers but we still do not recommend an investment in this fund for three basic reasons:

❏ the manager refused to disclose information about the portfolio and could not articulate his strategy;
❏ we were not comfortable with the accounting methods; and
❏ we simply did not believe in the manager.

Unfortunately, past performance is not indicative of future results. By 1999, this fund was out of business. By the time the fund closed, the average annual return and standard deviation numbers basically flipped. The

Table 11 Global fixed income manager "X"

Year/month	Return (%)	Year/month	Return (%)	Year/month	Return (%)
1993/11	1.41	1995/09	1.62	1997/07	2.27
1993/12	2.36	1995/10	1.47	1997/08	1.99
1994/01	2.12	1995/11	1.20	1997/09	1.02
1994/02	2.25	1995/12	1.20	1997/10	2.08
1994/03	2.90	1996/01	0.65	1997/11	1.04
1994/04	3.87	1996/02	1.60	1997/12	0.40
1994/05	1.30	1996/03	1.61	1998/01	1.17
1994/06	2.37	1996/04	1.01	1998/02	3.69
1994/07	2.28	1996/05	3.01	1998/03	2.78
1994/08	2.46	1996/06	4.73	1998/04	3.61
1994/09	1.95	1996/07	1.65	1998/05	0.76
1994/10	2.02	1996/08	2.47	1998/06	0.50
1994/11	1.97	1996/09	2.93	1998/07	
1994/12	1.18	1996/10	2.50	1998/08	
1995/01	1.26	1996/11	1.04	1998/09	
1995/02	1.27	1996/12	2.28	1998/10	
1995/03	1.60	1997/01	1.75	1998/11	
1995/04	1.60	1997/02	2.64	1998/12	
1995/05	1.60	1997/03	2.29	1999/01	
1995/06	1.60	1997/04	2.43	1999/02	
1995/07	0.55	1997/05	1.35		
1995/08	0.84	1997/06	1.72		

new average annual return was 1.09%, and the standard deviation was 28.01%. The Sharpe ratio dropped to 0.14 (during the period November 1993 to February 1999).

How could an investor be obsessed with risk and let this happen? They searched for the perfect market neutral strategy and ended up rearranging the deck chairs on the Titanic. Well, in their quest to avoid risk, investors often become risk averse. This limits the scope of the investments, and investors desperately need to believe the statistics despite their natural instinct. Let me repeat myself, if something looks too good to be true, it probably is. You end up adding risk to your portfolio and threatening the portfolio returns.

By waiting for a run-up in returns, investors lose sight of the fact that risk typically increases as assets under management grow. If a manager exhibits good results, he or she attracts capital quickly. Often, what works for a strategy in terms of assets may not match the manager's desire to manage larger amounts of capital. As assets increase through both asset raising and appreciation of profit, the risks in the portfolio increase. This can be caused by several factors. First, the manager may increase his position size to accommodate increased assets. Second, the manager may seek other strategies to allocate the assets to, and simply trade outside his or her area of expertise. This may include a geographic shift from being a purely

US investor to suddenly including emerging markets in the portfolio. While this may seem harmless, it proved to be disastrous to some managers in 1998 when they got caught in the Russian debacle. Lastly, simple mathematics tells you that performance becomes diluted when you spread it across a greater asset base.

As investors wait and wait to see that proven track record (in an effort to avoid risk), they are actually increasing the probability of losing money. We have now seen the demise of some of the greatest hedge fund managers of all time: Steinhardt, Robertson and Soros. All were too big when they died and all were unable to deploy their assets in a fashion necessary to maintain good risk-adjusted returns.

CONCLUSION

In the final analysis, we all need to be aware of the risks in our portfolios and observe the changes in statistics of our managers and at the portfolio level, yet must pay greater attention to finding the hidden risks through more due diligence. Investors must understand the methods by which profit and loss is achieved, understand the difference between good and bad leverage, and never expect past performance to repeat itself.

The most important lessons in this chapter are the following few facts.

❑ Statistics are a tool, not an absolute measure of risk.
❑ Understanding the underpinnings of your investments is the only way to diversify your portfolio and mitigate risk.
❑ Standard deviation may be your friend, not your enemy, as in the case of Managed Futures.
❑ You are loaning people your money in return for a floating rate of return, which has no guarantees. You are therefore entitled to information about the investments in your portfolio. If you invest without this knowledge, then you should obsess about risk. If you receive this information, you can be thoughtful about risk. The latter is much better for a good night's sleep.

Alternative investments remain an excellent complement to an investor's equity and bond portfolios. Hedge funds remain an appropriate investment to diversify your overall portfolio. Portfolio construction requires intense due diligence and analysis of the underlying investments. If you lack the experience to complete the review yourself, we advocate investing in a fund-of-funds (which may give you broad exposure to different types of managers), or hiring a consultant to guide you through the labyrinth of strategies and styles.

9

Market Neutral and Hedged Strategies*

Joseph G. Nicholas

HFR, Inc.

"Market neutral" and "hedged" investing refers to a group of investment strategies that seek to neutralise certain market risks by taking offsetting long and short positions in instruments with actual or theoretical relationships. These approaches seek to limit exposure to systematic changes in price caused by shifts in macroeconomic variables or market sentiment.

The market neutral and hedged strategies discussed in this chapter (convertible arbitrage, fixed income arbitrage, merger arbitrage, equity market neutral, statistical arbitrage, and equity hedge) invest in very different asset classes, ranging from equities to Treasury bonds to options to convertible bonds. Thus, if we look at these strategies in a conventional manner – by asset type – they bear little resemblance to one another. Convertible arbitrageurs take long positions in convertible securities and short positions in common stocks while fixed income arbitrageurs take long and short positions in different kinds of fixed income instruments and merger arbitrageurs take long and short positions in the stocks of companies involved in mergers. Yet all of these strategies are described as market neutral. How can these apparently disparate investment strategies fall into one grouping? *Market neutral and hedged strategies all derive returns from the relationship between a long and a short component of the portfolio, whether that relationship takes place at the level of individual instruments or at the portfolio level.*

By taking long and short positions in amounts that neutralise market risks, market neutral strategies trade exposure to the *market* for exposure to the *relationship* between the long and short sides of their portfolios.

*This chapter is from *Market-Neutral Investing: Long/Short Hedge Fund Strategies*, published by Bloomberg Press. Copyright 2000 Joseph G. Nicholas. This material appeared in slightly different form as a paper originally commissioned by the Alternative Investment Management Association (AIMA), entitled "Market Neutral and Hedged Strategies".

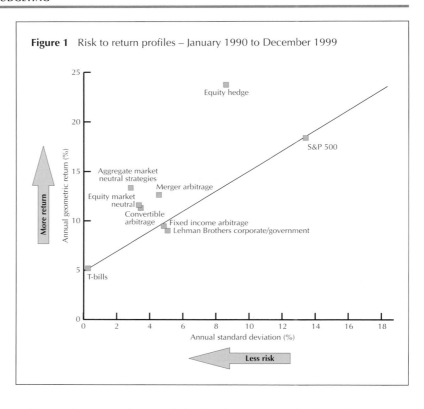

Figure 1 Risk to return profiles – January 1990 to December 1999

The performance characteristics for these approaches have been attractive (see Figure 1). The risk to return profiles of market neutral and hedged strategies over the past decade outperformed long-only strategies, with almost all of the market neutral and hedged indices residing above a straight line drawn from the risk free rate offered by Treasury bills through the profile for the S&P 500.

Relationship investing

There are many definitions given for market neutral investing. In general, the term indicates an approach to investing that includes constructing a portfolio with offsetting long and short exposures in neutralised through the use of short selling or otherwise obtaining an offsetting exposure to a long position. This may be done in a general sense, for example, by hedging interest rates, or in a subset, such as neutralising exposure to stocks in a market sector such as technology. The most common technique is to take a short position in an instrument closely related to a long exposure, thus hedging out exposure to "market risks" that affect both securities. Market neutral strategies are intended to "neutralise" these systematic market risks through the use of offsetting long and short positions.

Relationship investing involves a non-directional approach with the return to the strategy coming from the net result of the long and short components. However, the return does not always come solely from a non-directional exposure. In some cases this assessment is accurate, with returns being generated from changes in value of matched long and short positions (such as in explicit pairs trading). But, in many cases the short component hedges, or neutralises, part of the long exposure, leaving an unhedged, residual directional exposure. When such a position is leveraged the result is a leveraged directional exposure. Market neutral and hedged approaches do not eliminate risk entirely but, rather, they allow managers to reduce unwanted risks and retain the exposures they wish to maintain.

Understanding market neutral approaches

The key to understanding market neutral approaches is to identify the different risk exposures, hedge relationships, sources of return, and the possibility of repeating those returns. The return may come from the net change between the hedged components of the position, or from a change in value of the directional exposure outside the hedge, or a combination of both.

These distinct exposures within a strategy can be evaluated independently to develop a clearer picture of the potential return outcomes. The total risk/return characteristics of a market neutral approach will be reflected in a combination of the hedged components' analysis and that of the non-hedged aspects of the strategy.

For an over-simplified example, consider convertible arbitrage where the long position is a convertible bond which has both stock and bond characteristics, and the short position is the underlying equity. The risk/return characteristics of the strategy are a combination of the hedge relationship between the equity component of the long convertible bond and the short equity position, and the un-hedged fixed income characteristics of the convertible bond.

To understand how leverage affects risk exposures in a market neutral position one needs to understand the relationship of the long position to the short position. Leverage multiples the risk associated with residual directional exposures. Theoretically, the risk to perfectly hedged components is not increased by applying leverage. However, perfect hedges are not always available nor are they always desirable. Imagine how much harder they are to construct at the portfolio level when a manger has a universe of thousands of instruments from which to choose.

Linear analysis of returns

A common way of examining a stream of returns is by comparing the returns with those of a benchmark. The most common is to compare them to a proxy for the overall stock market such as the S&P 500. Using traditional linear regression analysis we can determine the relationship between the returns generated by a strategy (the dependent variable) and the market return (the independent variable). The relationship is described by the regression line that is the best linear fit between the two streams of returns. The equation of the line takes the form $y = a + bx$, where y is the strategy return less the risk-free interest rate, a is alpha (the y-intercept), b is beta (the slope of the line) and x is the market return less the risk-free rate. The risk-free rate is subtracted from total return in order to represent the return that is attributable to the additional risk of a passive investment in the stock market, or an actively managed market neutral strategy.

There are three important indications produced through linear regression analysis. First, this analysis produces a correlation statistic, referred to as r, which indicates the direction and strength of the relationship between the two streams of returns. Thus, a correlation of 1 would indicate that a 1% increase in the stock market return would be accompanied by a proportional increase in the strategy return. Second, beta indicates the magnitude of that relationship, and is generally accepted as a proxy for systematic stock market risk. For example, a beta of 2.0 indicates that for a 1% increase in the stock market return we would expect the portion of the strategy return explained by market return (as indicated by the correlation statistic) to increase by 2%. Lastly, alpha indicates the residual portion of the strategy return that is unexplained by fluctuations in the stock market return. It is widely accepted as a measure of the value added through active portfolio management.

As indicated in Table 1, market neutral strategies tend to have low correlation and low betas to the stock market. Thus, their returns are largely independent of stock market fluctuations. The portion of the return unexplained by stock market fluctuations, alpha, should be highlighted.

Table 1 Statistical profiles: January 1990 to December 1999 (with risk-free rate subtracted)

Strategy	Average monthly rate of return	Monthly standard deviation	Correlation to S&P 500	Beta to S&P 500	Alpha
S&P 500	0.8620	3.870	1	1	0
Convertible arbitrage	0.5159	1.019	0.4027	0.401	0.425
Fixed income arbitrage	0.3609	1.429	–0.0956	–0.100	0.393
MBS arbitrage*	0.4838	1.337	–0.0310	0.040	0.499
Equity hedge	1.4256	2.527	0.6453	0.645	1.063
Equity market neutral	0.5178	0.973	0.2548	0.253	0.463
Statistical arbitrage	0.5273	1.088	0.4735	0.472	0.413
Merger arbitrage	0.6054	1.339	0.5040	0.502	0.456
Relative value arbitrage	0.7213	1.191	0.3477	0.346	0.630

*Data only available January 1993 to December 1999

Although alpha is commonly thought of as management skill, it should be emphasised that some portion is attributable to the strategy itself. Market neutral strategies are designed to take advantage of pricing inefficiencies in financial markets, and as such, are alpha oriented.

In the following sections, it will be demonstrated that by adding market neutral strategies to a traditional portfolio of stocks and bonds, volatility – as measured by standard deviation – and systematic risk – as measured by beta – can be reduced without a corresponding reduction in returns. This pleasant paradox suggests that inefficiencies exist in financial markets and that astute money managers armed with investment strategies designed to take advantage of these pricing inefficiencies, may be able to produce higher risk-adjusted returns than the market. The excess return at each level of systematic risk is largely attributable to the alpha generated by each of the market neutral strategies.

Adding market neutral strategies to a traditional portfolio of stocks and bonds

Market neutral and hedged strategies offer competitive returns with lower volatility than traditional long-only investments in equities. In addition, they have low correlation to traditional investments in stocks and bonds. Both of these characteristics allow investors to improve risk-adjusted returns by diversifying a portion of a traditional portfolio of stocks and bonds into low correlation market neutral and hedged strategies.

The riskless (variance in returns) of a portfolio depends on the correlation between its holdings rather than the average variance of the separate components. Thus, adding an allocation that is highly correlated to an existing portfolio will not generally reduce overall portfolio volatility, because it will move in lockstep with the existing contents. On the other hand, adding a low correlation allocation, particularly one that exhibits low volatility as a stand-alone investment, can reduce overall portfolio volatility. The idea is to make allocations to strategies that will perform well in different market environments. Table 2 details the correlation of each of the market neutral and hedged strategies covered in this chapter to the S&P 500 and the Lehman Brothers Government/Corporate Aggregate Fixed Income Index, as well as to each other.

Note that the market neutral and hedged strategies are not highly correlated with one another (except in cases, such as equity market neutral and statistical arbitrage, where the two strategies overlap) or with the major stock and bond indices. This indicates that a portfolio of market neutral and hedged strategies will produce returns with less variance than traditional investments. Using mean variance optimisation, it can be illustrated that adding an allocation to market neutral and hedged strategies to a portfolio of stocks and bonds can reduce risk while maintaining competitive returns.

Table 2 Correlation matrix: January 1990 to December 1999

	Convertible arbitrage	Equity hedge	Equity MN	FI arbitrage	Merger arbitrage	Statistical arbitrage	Bonds	Stocks
HFRI convertible arbitrage	1							
HFRI equity hedge index	0.516	1						
HFRI equity market neutral	0.183	0.466	1					
HFRI fixed income arbitrage	0.124	0.036	0.067	1				
HFRI merger arbitrage index	0.482	0.473	0.149	−0.082	1			
HFRI statistical arbitrage index	0.187	0.252	0.577	0.096	0.244	1		
Lehman Brothers government/ corporate aggregate index	0.230	0.137	0.184	−0.274	0.114	0.427	1	
S&P 500 with dividends	0.398	0.642	0.246	−0.100	0.499	0.483	0.395	1

Mean variance optimisation uses quantitative models to maximise output given a certain level of input or, alternatively, to minimise input given a certain desired level of output. The result of the model is what has come to be called an "efficient frontier" or the set of possible portfolio allocations that maximise expected returns for a given level of variance (risk) or minimise variance (risk) for a given level of return. The model reveals mathematically the risk-reducing benefits of diversification. Mean variance optimisation provides some interesting insights into asset allocations that include stocks, bonds and market neutral and hedged strategies.

The market neutral and hedged strategies covered in this chapter derive returns from relationships between securities rather than the directional bias associated with traditional investments in stocks or bonds. While those relationships are subject to volatility, as a group, the returns they produce have generally been more stable than traditional stock and bond indices over the past decade. Moreover, they have low correlation with these indices. This point is illustrated in Figure 2 using mean variance optimisation. For each level of risk (standard deviation) the efficient frontier maximises historical returns given the allocation options (market neutral and hedged strategies, stocks and bonds). All of the points on the curve represent "efficient portfolios" – that is, they maximise return for a given level of variance or they minimise variance for a given level of return. No combinations of the inputs can be put together that would have yielded a result to the left of the curve. The set of all possible allocations, including a 100% allocation to bonds and a 100% allocation to stocks, resides on or inside the frontier. The point with the highest risk adjusted return, as measured by the Sharpe ratio, is referred to as the most efficient allocation.

In this case, 100% allocations to stocks or bonds represent the upper and lower bounds of the frontier. The most efficient allocation would have been nearly 88% to the aggregate market neutral index and about 12% to bonds. This can be explained by the fact that the market neutral index aggregates a

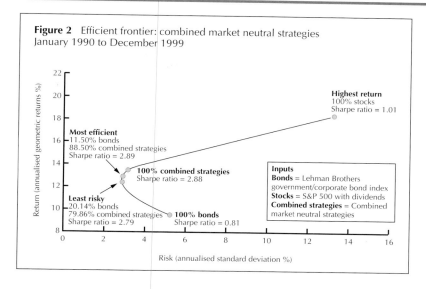

Figure 2 Efficient frontier: combined market neutral strategies January 1990 to December 1999

number of different strategies that include exposures to a wide range of somewhat uncorrelated asset classes. However, while this graph is not meant to recommend allocating 88% of a portfolio into market neutral and hedged strategies, the magnitude of improvement in risk adjusted returns by adding market neutral and hedged strategies should not be overlooked. To further illustrate the point, Figure 3 shows how overall portfolio volatility is reduced (without a corresponding proportional reduction in returns)

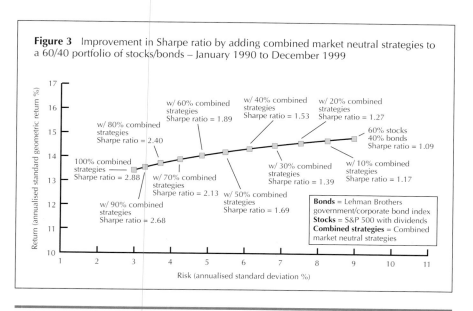

Figure 3 Improvement in Sharpe ratio by adding combined market neutral strategies to a 60/40 portfolio of stocks/bonds – January 1990 to December 1999

by adding market neutral and hedged strategies to a traditional portfolio in 10% increments. The proportion of stocks to bonds remains fixed at 60/40 (eg, 20% market neutral + 48% stocks + 32% bonds = 100%).

By adding market neutral and hedged strategies to a traditional portfolio of stocks and bonds, volatility could have been reduced dramatically without a proportional decrease in returns. The 100% market neutral and hedged portfolio had only a third the volatility of the traditional portfolio with only a tenth less return.

Market neutral and hedged strategies can be used to reduce exposure to systematic stock market risk

Market neutral and hedged strategies, when added to a portfolio of traditional assets (assumed to be 60% stocks and 40% bonds) can reduce the overall portfolio's exposure to systematic risk in the market. Systematic risk, referred to as market risk and measured largely by beta, is the risk common to all securities in a similar asset class (in this case, the stock market). Systematic risk is driven by macroeconomic and investor factors and, therefore, is more difficult to remove from portfolios by traditional diversification tactics such as the number of investments, different industries, market-capitalisation or investment mix. However, because market neutral and hedged strategies derive their returns from relationships between securities rather than the directional fortunes of an asset class, such as traditional investments in stocks or bonds, the risk to return profiles of such strategies have a low correlation to those of the overall market.

As discussed earlier, the investment returns generated by traditional portfolio structures can be enhanced on a risk-adjusted basis by allocating a portion of the investment funds to market neutral and hedged strategies. In addition, such an allocation can reduce exposure to stock market risk, as measured by beta.

With a traditional portfolio consisting of 60% stocks, represented by the S&P 500, and 40% bonds, measured by the Lehman Brothers Aggregate Government/Corporate Bond Index, the historical return over the last ten years has been 14.73% with an accompanying beta of 0.66. By adding a portfolio of market neutral and hedged strategies to this traditional 60/40 fixed portfolio mix in 10% increments (eg, 20% market neutral + 48% stocks + 32% bonds = 100%), Figure 4 illustrates the reduction in market risk, as measured by beta, while maintaining competitive portfolio returns.

At each level of systematic risk incurred, the portfolio with an allocation to the market neutral and hedged strategies offers higher returns than the traditional portfolio. Figure 4 shows that while increasing the allocation to bonds reduces systematic risk, it does so at a greater cost to returns than increasing the allocation to market neutral and hedged strategies while holding the remainder at a constant 60/40 stocks/bonds mix. At any level to the left of the traditional portfolio mix, a combination of the market neu-

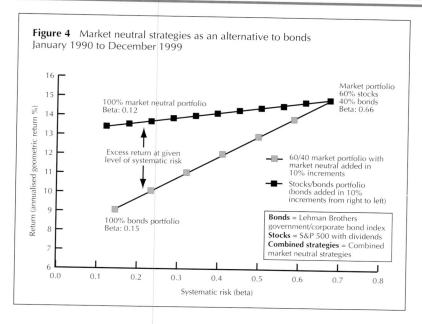

Figure 4 Market neutral strategies as an alternative to bonds
January 1990 to December 1999

tral and hedged portfolio with the traditional mix described above produces a superior risk to return profile for the combined portfolio by reducing the systematic risk incurred. The combined portfolio return is reduced by just over 9% (from 14.73% to 13.38%) along this sample of portfolios. However, along this same frontier, systematic risk, as measured by beta, is reduced by over 80% (from 0.66 to 0.12). This is only possible because the market neutral and hedged strategies extract excess returns from pricing inefficiencies in the market.

The return to risk attributes produced by combining a market neutral and hedged portfolio with the traditional portfolio mix is superior to that of the traditional portfolio. The Treynor measure is used to gauge this factor in Figure 5, which is quite similar to the Sharpe ratio but replaces variance with beta in the denominator:

$$\text{Treynor measure} = \frac{\text{Portfolio return} - \text{Risk-free rate}}{\text{beta}}$$

In Figure 5, as exposure to stock market risk is reduced by adding a larger allocation to the market neutral and hedged portfolio, beta declines at a faster rate than the combined portfolio return. This results in the strong upward movement in the Treynor ratio shown here. In addition, the rate at which the Treynor measure improves as beta is reduced is much higher than if the bond allocation is increased. By adding a market neutral and hedged portfolio to that of a traditional 60/40 portfolio mix, it may be

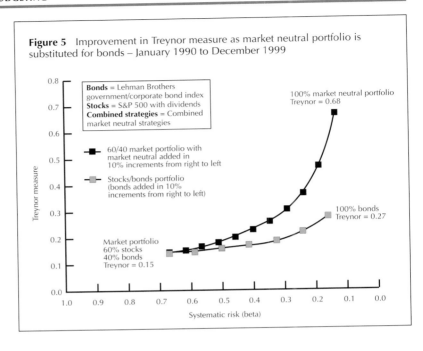

Figure 5 Improvement in Treynor measure as market neutral portfolio is substituted for bonds – January 1990 to December 1999

possible for investors to generate returns similar to that of a traditional 60/40 stock/bond portfolio mix with reduced exposure to systematic stock market risk.

Similar results can be obtained when a stock/bond portfolio is compared to a stock/market neutral portfolio. Again, the S&P 500 is used to represent a portfolio of stocks and the Lehman Brothers Aggregate Government/ Corporate Bonds Index as a proxy for bonds. Over the past decade, the S&P 500 has posted an average annual return of 18.45%, which is, of course, accompanied by a beta of one. The bond index has posted returns of 9.14% with a beta of 0.1506 as compared to the S&P 500 Index.

Traditionally, investors would use an allocation to bonds to diversify equity market exposure and achieve less variance in returns. By replacing the allocation to bonds with an allocation to a portfolio of market neutral and hedged strategies, investors may be able to produce higher returns at a given level of stock market risk.

Figure 6 shows the two sets of returns at specific levels of systematic risk (beta). The lower line is the traditional mix of stocks and bonds while the upper line replaces bonds with a portfolio of market neutral and hedged strategies. As the graph shifts to the right, the allocation to stocks (which increases market risk) increases in 10% increments from zero to 100%.

At any level of market risk in Figure 6, the portfolio consisting of stocks and the market neutral and hedged strategies provided better return/risk

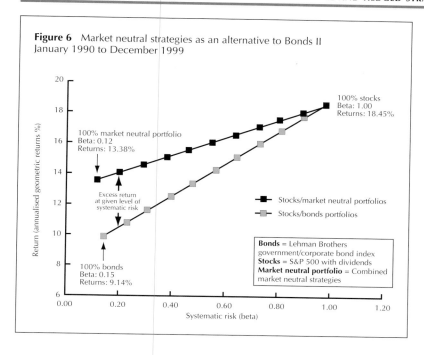

Figure 6 Market neutral strategies as an alternative to Bonds II January 1990 to December 1999

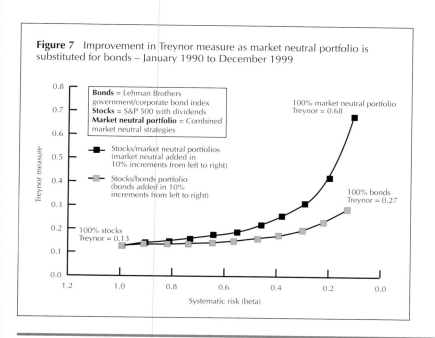

Figure 7 Improvement in Treynor measure as market neutral portfolio is substituted for bonds – January 1990 to December 1999

characteristics than the stock and bond portfolio allocations with the obvious exception of owning the S&P 500, or all of the market risk.

Again, using the Treynor measure, Figure 7 indicates that the portfolio of stocks and the market neutral and hedged strategies produces more return given a certain level of risk than combinations of stocks and bonds. As the graph shifts to the right, the allocation to stocks (which increases market risk) decreases in 10% increments from 100 to 0%.

The marginal improvement in the Treynor measure increases significantly at higher levels of market neutral and hedged allocations revealing the historical benefit of replacing the bond portfolio with a portfolio of market neutral and hedged strategies. Beginning at the 70/30 allocation of stocks and the diversifying asset (bonds or the market neutral and hedged portfolio) and then increasing the diversifying asset allocation (moving right along the graph) increases the marginal return for a given level of market risk incurred of the market neutral and hedged combination over the traditional portfolio mix of stocks and bonds. This indicates that by replacing the allocation of a bond portfolio with an allocation to a portfolio of market neutral and hedged strategies, investors may be able to produce higher returns for a given level of stock market risk.

The various market neutral and hedged strategies offer returns that are higher than those of fixed income, but with lower volatility than equities. In addition, these strategies exhibit low correlation to equity and fixed income indices in most market environments. Of particular interest, given the hedged nature of these strategies, is performance during periods when the stock market is down. During the 1990s there were 37 months during which the S&P 500 registered negative returns. The average monthly return of the S&P 500 during these periods was –3.01%. The aggregate market neutral and hedged strategies were down by only 8, or 22%, of these months, and registered an average return during the 37 periods of 0.47%.

The pages that follow provide an in-depth look at five important market neutral and hedged strategies: convertible arbitrage, equity market neutral and statistical arbitrage, equity hedge, fixed income arbitrage and merger arbitrage.

CONVERTIBLE ARBITRAGE

Convertible arbitrageurs construct long portfolios of convertible securities and hedge the equity element of these positions by selling short the underlying stock of each bond. Convertible securities include convertible bonds, convertible preferred stock and warrants, but the analysis here is confined to convertible bonds. Convertible bonds are bonds that can be converted into a fixed number of shares of the issuing company's stock. They are hybrid securities that have features of a bond and of a stock and, therefore, their valuations reflect both types of instruments. Generally, the price of the convertible security will decline less rapidly than the underlying stock in a falling equity market and will mirror the price of the stock more closely in a rising equity market. Typically, convertible arbitrageurs extract arbitrage-like profits from these complex pricing relationships by purchasing the convertible bond and selling short its underlying stock.

Convertible bond valuation

Before delving into the kinds of trades that convertible arbitrageurs execute, it is important to understand the different components that determine a convertible bond's value and the sometimes complex models that managers use to value them.

Statistical advantage

If an investment manager can identify a convertible bond with a favourable total return profile, then that manager can make arbitrage profits by purchasing the convertible bond and selling short the underlying stock. The pricing of a convertible bond with a favourable return profile will decline less rapidly than the price of the underlying stock. In a rising equity market, the price of the convertible will be more highly correlated to the price of the stock. The comparative returns in Table 3 illustrate these relationships.

In this example, the total return profile of the convertible bond is favourable because it captures most of the upward movement of the underlying equity but escapes a lot of the downside. For the sake of simplicity, we will assume for now that the equity does not pay a dividend, so it returns 0% if its price does not change. On the other hand, the convertible returns 5% because it pays a coupon. In addition, the equity and the convertible do not respond equally to changes in the price of the equity. These two features give the convertible a statistical advantage.

Mathematically, the investment manager who invests in a non-dividend paying equity security gets a risk to reward relationship that has no inherent edge. This is not to say that good stock pickers will not make money on stocks, only that everything else held equal, statistically speaking, a stock has just as much potential to decline as it has to appreciate. This simply means that a 10% movement in either direction produces a similar percentage gain or loss, and is expressed as a 1:1 reward to risk potential. The convertible bond's reward to risk potential in the above example is 4:1

Table 3 Total annual return profile

Change in price of underlying equity	Down 10%	Unchanged	Up 10%
Common stock percent change	−10%	0%	+10%
Convertible bond percent change (with coupon)	−2%	+5%	+8%

because a 10% move in either direction produces gain potential that is four times the potential loss.

Convertible valuation components
Investment value

The valuation of convertible bonds is a hybrid of stock and bond valuation because the convertible combines features of both the stock and the bond. The value of the bond component of a convertible is known as the investment value. In spite of the name, investment value should not be confused with the market value of the convertible security. It refers solely to the fixed income component of the security, which is the value of the bond stripped of the option to convert to stock.

The investment value represents a sort of floor for the investment. The price of the convertible will not normally fall below its investment value because, even if the stock component falls significantly, the convertible retains its value as a bond. The only exception is when the issuing company runs into fundamental difficulties that cause the stock price to fall rapidly and cause the credit quality of the bond component to come into question. These types of securities, known as busted convertibles, will be discussed later in this strategy segment. Convertible arbitrageurs will use the tools of conventional fixed income analysis, such as fundamental analysis, coupon and maturity date, credit quality, and yield to maturity, to determine the investment value of a convertible bond.

Theoretically, the investment value of a convertible bond will remain stable over a wide range of stock prices so long as interest rates remain unchanged. If the stock price approaches zero, the investment value will generally follow, as plummeting stock prices are a sign of financial distress within the company, leading to possible bankruptcy and default on its debt. On the other hand, the investment value of the bond should not be influenced by increasing stock prices although the overall market price of the convertible will be affected. This is based on the assumption that the creditworthiness and financial condition of issuing companies, which are key factors in determining the investment value of the convertible bond, will change slowly and the investment value should remain unchanged so long as the company's creditworthiness remains intact. In practice, this is usually the case, but dramatic changes in company fundamentals do sometimes occur. A negative earnings surprise will have a negative effect on the investment value of a convertible bond in the same way that a rating downgrade will negatively affect the value of a corporate bond. Deteriorating fundamentals signal an increased risk that the company will not be able to pay the coupon or the principal.

Changes in interest rates will affect the investment value of a convertible bond in the same fashion that they affect normal corporate bonds of similar credit quality. Interest rates represent the price of borrowing money. When rates increase, lenders will be attracted to the higher rates and the value of debt issued at a lower rate will decline. Thus, an increase in interest rates will result in a decline in the investment value of a convertible bond. A decrease in interest rates will have the opposite effect.

It is worth noting once again that a convertible bond's valuation is dynamic and that certain components of that price may have more influence under certain circumstances than others do. Thus, in a rising interest rate environment, when the investment value of the security is falling, that decline may be overshadowed in the overall price of the convertible because the price of the underlying stock is rising. Typically, a convertible trading at or near its investment value will be more sensitive to changes in interest rates than a convertible trading at a premium to that value (which will be more sensitive to changes in the price of the underlying stock).

Investment premium

A convertible bond's investment premium is the difference between the market value of the convertible and its investment value. It is expressed as a percentage of the investment value. The calculation disaggregates the embedded bond component of the convertible from the aggregate convertible, and isolates the amount, above and beyond the investment value, that an investor must pay to receive the aggregate hybrid security. For a convertible bond with a par value of US$1000 and an investment value of US$800, the investment premium would be $(1000 - 800)/800$, or 25%. This value is an important measure of downside risk that can be monitored as prices and other variables change.

$$\text{Investment premium} = (\text{Market price} - \text{Investment value})/\text{Investment value}$$

Generally, a large investment premium means that a convertible will be very sensitive to changes in the price of the underlying stock. Large investment premiums reflect a large difference between the market value of the convertible and its investment value caused by a high stock price. As discussed in more detail later on in this strategy section, when the price of the underlying stock increases, convertibles tend to trade more like the stock than the bond. Thus, if the stock price begins to tumble, the convertible will continue to reflect the decline of the underlying stock until it gets closer to the investment value and begins to reflect the bond component rather than the stock component. By the same logic, a convertible with a small investment premium will be relatively more bond-like and more sensitive to factors that affect the price of bonds, such as changes in interest rates.

Conversion price

The conversion price is the price the investor pays to convert the bond to stock with the convertible bond at par. When it is issued, a convertible will specify the amount of common stock equivalent to the value of the convertible bond at par. This is known as a conversion ratio. The conversion price is essential because it determines the number of shares that each bond can be converted into at par (the conversion ratio). However, convertibles rarely trade exactly at par, and the price of the underlying stock is prone to fluctuation. The conversion ratio always remains the same.

Conversion ratio
The conversion ratio is the number of shares of common stock a convertible bondholder would receive per bond upon converting the bond to the underlying stock. As stated above, at issuance it is the number of shares the bondholder would receive at the conversion price if the bond were trading at par. The conversion ratio is fixed for the life of the bond.

$$\text{Conversion Ratio} = \text{Par Value}/\text{Conversion Price}$$

Conversion value
The conversion value of a convertible bond represents the value of the equity side of the convertible. It is simply the value of the bond, at any given time, if it were converted to the underlying common stock at the current market price. The value is equal to the number of shares each bond can be converted to (as specified at issuance) multiplied by the current market price of the common stock. The conversion value, like the investment value, represents a price floor that the convertible should not trade below.

$$\text{Conversion Value} = \text{Conversion Ratio} \times \text{Price of Common Stock}$$

Premium over conversion value
Investors are usually willing to pay a premium above a convertible bond's conversion value because the bond features of a convertible provide downside protection and usually provide higher current income, in the form of interest payments, than the stock dividend. The premium is calculated by taking the difference between the market price of the convertible and its conversion value and dividing it by the conversion value.

$$\text{Conversion Premium} = (\text{Price of Convertible} - \text{Conversion Value})/ \text{Conversion Value}$$

A convertible bond's premium over conversion value is the amount the investor pays for the convertible bond in excess of the amount that he would receive if he converts it into the underlying common stock. In essence, it represents the value of the option to convert the bond to stock. For example, if a bond trading at US$1,000 (normal par value) can be converted into 50 shares of a US$14 stock, then the conversion value would be US$700. The premium is the difference between the price at which the bond is trading when it is purchased and the conversion value, or US$300 (1000 – 700). The conversion premium is usually expressed as a percentage of the conversion value. Thus, in this example the convertible bond had a 42.9% conversion premium (300/700).

Generally, the higher a convertible bond's conversion premium, the less the price of the convertible bond will correlate with the price of the under-lying common stock and the more it will correlate with its investment value. Following the logic described above, it makes sense that the value of the investor's option to convert the bond to stock decreases and the pre-mium paid for that option decreases when the price of the underlying stock rises and the bond trades more like the stock. As a bond trades closer to its investment value the equity component becomes less valuable. However, it is important to keep in mind that various factors affect a con-vertible bond's conversion premium. For example, convertibles with higher yields have a higher conversion premium, because the convertible acts more like a bond as it trades closer to the level where the issuer could issue non-convertible debt. Thus, in such cases, investors pay more for the current income component than the equity component regardless of the price at which the common stock may trade.

Dynamic relationship of the components

The six separate components described in the preceding sections – invest-ment value, investment premium, conversion price, conversion ratio, con-version value and premium over conversion value – are embedded in the market price of a convertible security. Because it is a hybrid security, a con-vertible bond will respond to different market forces than its underlying common stock. It fact, there is almost never a one-to-one correspondence between the price of a convertible bond and the price of its underlying common stock. For example, the price of a convertible bond will tend to move inversely to changes in interest rates because of its bond characteris-tics, while its underlying common stock will react to the perceived macro-economic causes and effects of such interest rate fluctuations.

There is no single formula for calculating the movement of a convertible security as a function of the price of its underlying equity, only a range of factors that have varying levels of predictive value. Convertible bond spe-cialists make arbitrage profits by identifying pricing disparities between convertible bonds and their underlying equity and tightly monitoring the factors that will change these relationships.

Figure 8 is an example of a convertible price curve, with the price of the underlying stock on one axis and the price of the convertible security on the other. This curve is representative of the types of curves that convert-ible arbitrageurs create and examine; however, these curves are not fixed.

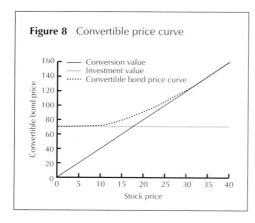

Figure 8 Convertible price curve

Conversion value
Investment value
Convertible bond price curve

Convertible bond price

Stock price

When the underlying variables contributing to the price of the convertible change, then the shape of the curve can change. In addition, different managers may create different curves for the same security, depending on how they evaluate the relevant variables.

Convertible arbitrage approaches

Quantitative screens

Most convertible arbitrage managers start with a universe of convertible issues and apply a quantitative screen to that universe in order to identify investment opportunities. Many managers use data obtained from Value Line, for example, or from internally generated databases. Managers may screen for different criteria, such as price, coupon, current yield, dividend yield, premium, issue size, duration or credit rating. Given these and other variables, arbitrage opportunities are identified using evaluation models that locate "theoretically cheap" convertible securities. To identify theoretically cheap securities, managers compare the market value of convertible securities with mathematically calculated expected values of the same convertible given the market price of the underlying equity securities and other variables such as interest rates, credit quality, implied volatility and call probability.

Kinds of hedges

Once arbitrage opportunities are identified, managers determine what the appropriate hedge will be for that security. The standard convertible arbitrage position is neutrally hedged based on a calculated delta. Delta refers to how the price of a convertible security will respond to a movement in the price of the underlying stock. It is calculated by taking the slope of the tangent line to the convertible price curve at the current price. As noted previously, different managers may create different curves for the same security, so the appropriate delta to maintain neutrality may differ from one manager to the next. Bullish and bearish hedged trades use the same basic strategy but sell short either fewer or more shares of the underlying stock than is necessary for delta neutrality. In the course of fundamental research, a manager may determine that an issuing company will outperform or underperform the market and build this opinion into the hedge by selling short either more or less shares than required for delta neutrality.

Setting up a market neutral hedge

In the context of convertible arbitrage a neutral hedge usually means selling short enough shares of common stock so that, ideally, the position will not incur losses from equity price fluctuations in either direction. Convertible arbitrage managers use sophisticated valuation models and "what if" scenarios to determine the correct number of shares to sell short to establish a neutral position. Some of the valuation methodologies that managers use are described later in this strategy section as well as the dynamics of maintaining neutrality in real time trading. For now, it should be emphasised that managers compare the market value of securities with mathematically calculated, expected values given the market price of the underlying equity securities.

The sources of return on a neutral hedge include the following:

❑ interest income from the convertible security purchased;
❑ interest earned on cash proceeds from the short sale of the underlying common stock;
❑ the value of the option to convert, or conversion premium; and
❑ trading profits from rebalancing the position due to a decline in price of the underlying common stock and/or a rise in the convertible market price.

Setting up a bullish hedge

Sometimes known as a long-biased hedge, a bullish hedge refers to a hedge in which the manager has sold short fewer shares than are required to maintain neutrality to movements in the price of the underlying stock. By doing so, the manager increases the downside risk but is able to participate more fully in increases in the price of the convertible resulting from increases in the price of the underlying stock. Managers will uncover information while doing fundamental research that leads them to believe that the company's stock price will increase. Such information typically may include earnings growth potential, increased cashflow, or indications of solid management. It is important to note that, for most arbitrageurs, a bullish hedge would be justified only when such positive fundamental information was identified as well as a statistical mis-pricing between the convertible and its underlying equity.

The sources of return for a bullish hedge are similar to those for a neutral hedge except that a bullish hedge position will participate disproportionately in gains resulting from an increased stock price and losses resulting from a decreasing stock price.

Setting up a bearish hedge

Sometimes known as a short-biased hedge, a bearish hedge is one for which the manager has sold short more shares than are required to maintain neutrality to movements in the price of the underlying stock. By selling more shares short, managers decrease their participants in increases in the price of the convertible resulting from increases in the underlying stock. At the same time, they also increase their participation in declining stock prices. Essentially, the manager trades some of the convertible upside for a short stock exposure that will benefit from declines in the stock price. As noted in the preceding discussion of bullish hedges, managers often uncover information while doing fundamental research on the company that leads them to believe that the company's stock price will move, in this case, decline. Such information may include indications of management shortcomings, accounting problems or increased competition.

The sources of return for this type of hedge are similar to that of a neutral hedge except that a bearish hedged position will participate disproportionately in gains resulting from a decreasing stock price and losses resulting from increasing stock prices.

RISKS AND RISK CONTROL

Fundamental analysis

The degree to which a manager engages in fundamental analysis is one factor that defines a convertible arbitrage manager's style. Certain portions of the convertible market (for example, so-called busted convertibles) and some kinds of hedges (such as bullish or bearish hedges) demand that managers engage in in-depth, traditional fundamental analysis of the issuing company. If the credit quality of the company is dubious, traditional credit analysis is needed. In cases where a company shows signs of explosive growth traditional fundamental stock analysis is generally required. Some managers may carry out fundamental analysis on every security in their portfolio. In any case, fundamental analysis is usually one part of a larger process. How much fundamental research managers are able to carry out, is usually a function of the number of securities in their portfolio and the amount of resources at their disposal.

Traditional credit analysis applicable to convertible arbitrage
Some convertible managers perform traditional credit analysis on issuing companies that are under consideration. The purpose of this analysis is generally to review the credit quality of the issuing company in order to ensure that coupon and principal payments will be made and to determine whether this probability is accurately reflected in the price of the convertible security. Stable or improving trends in both cashflow and interest coverage are generally indicators of the ability of the issuing company to service its debt. These variables are often compared with the corresponding figures for competitors and even across industries to determine whether current trends will continue. Some forward-looking managers will run rigorous "what if" scenario tests to determine the effect of changes in different variables on the issuing company's credit quality.

It makes sense that managers who invest in higher yield, high conversion premium issues, that is those bonds trading near their investment value that generate very high current income (also known as busted convertibles), will want to protect that income stream by researching the issuing company's ability to continue to pay it. The more a convertible trades like a bond, the more important traditional fixed income credit analysis becomes.

Traditional fundamental equity analysis applicable to convertible arbitrage
Some convertible managers carry out traditional qualitative and quantitative fundamental equity analysis on issuing companies that are under consideration. Generally, managers study industry and company dynamics that may act as catalysts for stock price appreciation. In some cases, managers may also be interested in dynamics that would indicate stock depreciation. These kinds of traditional fundamental equity analysis are particularly important if the issue trades – or the manager expects it to trade – in a more equity-like fashion. Common points of analysis include accelerating earnings momentum, upward trends in earnings estimate revisions, cashflow return on capital, price to earnings and price to book value ratios, changing industry dynamics, new product developments and corporate developments such as spin-offs, restructurings and potential merger or acquisition involvement.

It behoves managers who invest in more equity-sensitive convertible issues – those defined by low conversion premium convertibles with a large investment premium – to engage in fundamental equity analysis. In addition, managers who put on bullish and bearish hedges typically attempt to justify these directional plays with some form of fundamental research.

Hedge analysis
Determining the appropriate hedge
Once arbitrage opportunities have been identified, convertible arbitrage managers must determine the appropriate number of shares to sell short to maximise the reward to risk ratio of each opportunity. In many cases, managers seek to implement a delta-neutral hedge. As detailed previously, delta refers to the change in the rice of the convertible resulting from a change in the price of the underlying stock. A delta-neutral position, ideally, does not incur losses from equity price fluctuations either up or down.

In order to determine the correct hedge ratio, managers compare the current market price of the convertible to a mathematically calculated expected value. This expected value can be generated using proprietary valuation models or binomial models. Some managers also use the Black–Scholes option pricing model. Managers may even consider estimates from multiple models as a check. The valuation models take into account different variables that affect the price of a convertible security. The most common and powerful are the stock price, interest rates, volatility and time to expiration. Generally, managers will run extensive "what if" scenarios for changes in these major variables to determine how the price of the convertible would act under such circumstances and how changes would affect the hedge. This information is used to establish target values for the convertible.

Maintaining the appropriate hedge

Maintaining the appropriate hedge requires constant attention. As different variables affecting the price of the convertible change after the initial position has been set, the manager may have to adjust the hedge in order to maintain delta neutrality. The manager does this by selling more shares short or covering some of the initial short. The hedge is determined by examining the slope of the convertible price curve and determining the appropriate delta, (ie, slope of the tangent), at the current price of the convertible. Different managers will come to different conclusions about what the appropriate hedge is depending on where on the curve that particular security is trading and whether or not they are incorporating an opinion about future price directions into the hedge.

Portfolio construction

Overall risk/reward

In addition to assessing the risk-to-reward potential of each particular position, managers usually assess the risk/reward implications of the portfolio as a whole. Riskier positions will often be counterbalanced by less risky positions. Bullish hedges will be balanced by bearish hedges; investment-grade positions will be paired with non-investment-grade positions.

Diversification

Convertible managers often try to diversify their risk. By spreading their exposure across risk factors, they reduce the possibility that all of their positions will depreciate at once. For example, it is quite unlikely that a group of companies in the technology sector and another group of companies in the energy sector will be affected equally by a drop in the price of oil. Therefore, managers limit their risk exposures by careful consideration of exposure to factors such as:

❑ Industry;
❑ Sector;
❑ Market capitalisation of issuer (liquidity);
❑ Bond sensitive convertibles (interest rate risk);
❑ Stock sensitive convertibles (stock market risk);

❏ Credit quality (bankruptcy);
❏ Implied volatility; and
❏ Event risk.

Sell disciplines
Positions are "unwound" by selling the convertible bond and buying back the stock sold short. The following list presents the most common reasons to unwind positions.

❏ A theoretically undervalued or cheap position is no longer undervalued.
❏ An event (for example, a spin-off) occurs that affects the valuations of the two securities in a fashion that is out of line with the manager's expectations.
❏ New negative information is uncovered that causes the manager to change expectations.
❏ Forced selling arises as a result of unexpected redemptions or a liquidity squeeze.
❏ The issuing company calls the bond, forcing conversion.

Liquidity
The convertible market is prone to bad performance during "flight-to-quality" scenarios when global financial markets are unstable and equity prices free fall. Spreads relative to Treasuries increase when investors pull money out of stocks, convertibles, high yield debt, and corporate debt in favour of the safety provided by Treasury bonds. These kinds of situations can result in a lack of trading liquidity in the convertible market that negatively affects convertible prices. The third quarter of 1998 provides a good example. With convertible prices falling quickly in late August and early September, bid/ask spreads opened to abnormal levels because few investors were buying these securities. The only sellers were either those in a panic or managers who were forced to liquidate positions in order to fulfil redemption requests or respond to margin calls from brokers. Certain dealers also refused to make markets in securities they had actively traded in the past. The lesson to be learned is that no matter how theoretically attractive a security may be, one must always consider: the extreme, can the position be unwound, and, if so, at what cost?

Leverage
Leverage, when it is employed prudently, can amplify returns available from capturing mispricings between convertible securities and their underlying equities. It can be thought of as a form of interest rate arbitrage, whereby funds are borrowed at a rate lower than the combined yield of the convertible bond and the short interest received, less any dividends paid on the common stock. However, leverage increases the volatility and

overall risk of a portfolio. Because the amount of capital required to support leverage on any given position is determined by the conversion premium, managers using high delta positions that require high hedge ratios only have to put up a small amount of capital. For the most part, this is a way to amplify returns on low risk positions. In the unusual circumstance when such convertibles start trading down the curve towards their investment value, as they did in the third quarter of 1998, both the risk of the position and the cost of leveraging increases. At the extremes, leverage can force a manager to sell a security at an inopportune time in order to meet margin requirements.

SOURCE OF RETURN

No single asset class can be shielded from all financial market risks. Certain strategies that balance short and long positions in related securities do, however, have the ability to shield an investor from particular, targeted risks, and thus reduce the volatility of returns and correlation to the market. Under normal market conditions, a delta-neutral convertible strategy will ideally not incur losses if the price of the underlying stock moves up or down within a defined range.

In a normal market environment, convertible arbitrage returns are based on the relationship between convertible securities and their underlying stock rather than the direction of the stock market. This is because convertible arbitrageurs take long positions in convertible securities and sell short the underlying stock in a ratio that benefits from the differing return profiles of the two securities under different market scenarios. Convertible arbitrage returns, therefore, are not strongly correlated to overall stock market movement under most market conditions. This statement is less true, however, in periods of extreme stock market movements. In addition, the convertible market has its own valuation cycles, independent of stock market movements, that are driven by supply and demand for convertibles. Nonetheless, convertible arbitrage specialists can achieve ample and stable returns over time based on their ability to evaluate and select undervalued convertible securities and hedge them with the underlying stock, as opposed to the far more random nature of most directional investment strategies.

RECENT GROWTH AND DEVELOPMENTS IN CONVERTIBLE ARBITRAGE

Convertible arbitrage as a strategy quadrupled from 0.5% of hedge fund assets in 1990 to over 2% in 1999. To put this in perspective, one must remember that the current convertible market is not large enough to support the huge amounts of assets that make up the equity and fixed income markets.

Because the convertible market is much smaller than either the equity or fixed income markets, it has its own distinctive characteristics. As the

Table 4

No. of funds	Average size (US$ mm)	Year	Jan	Feb	Mar	Apr	May	Jun	Jul	Aug	Sep	Oct	Nov	Dec	Ann- ual*
4	5	1990	−1.47	−0.92	1.26	1.48	1.75	1.72	1.15	−0.18	−0.47	−1.56	−0.05	−0.49	2.16
7	6	1991	0.44	1.61	1.39	1.49	0.94	0.98	1.57	2.09	1.31	1.22	1.66	1.63	17.60
11	7	1992	2.12	0.94	0.99	0.80	1.70	0.71	1.85	1.65	1.46	1.24	0.70	1.09	16.35
22	14	1993	0.93	0.86	2.19	1.50	1.24	1.04	1.41	1.40	1.03	1.29	0.60	0.77	15.22
27	20	1994	0.66	0.24	−2.11	−2.79	0.03	0.15	1.55	0.80	0.12	−0.09	−0.79	−1.48	−3.73
32	21	1995	0.55	0.98	1.83	1.90	1.88	2.32	2.13	0.96	1.55	1.25	1.58	1.33	19.85
33	28	1996	1.82	1.06	1.17	1.88	1.73	0.44	−0.37	1.40	1.23	1.27	1.40	0.66	14.56
35	60	1997	1.01	1.11	0.59	0.68	1.40	1.71	1.61	1.14	1.11	1.19	0.09	0.41	12.47
52	67	1998	1.91	1.52	1.58	1.35	0.40	0.22	0.49	−3.19	−1.07	−0.48	3.33	1.60	7.77
55	83	1999	2.11	0.25	1.53	2.66	1.40	1.09	1.05	0.42	0.93	0.90	1.80	0.64	15.80

*Annual represents geometric compounded average

hybrid smaller sibling of these larger markets, the convertible market is particularly sensitive to nervousness and fears that affect these other markets. In contrast to the stock market, which draws a more diffuse investor base, the convertible market is peopled almost entirely by professional investors. As a consequence, when one convertible arbitrageur wants to sell, chances are that others do too. The professional nature of the convertible market is contrasted by the presence of both more total investors and a lower percentage of sophisticated investors in the stock market, with the result that the two markets have, on occasion, de-coupled and will likely do so occasionally in the future. September 1998 was a perfect example of this phenomenon; the equity markets rebounded from huge losses in August while the convertible market stayed flat after experiencing similar losses in August of that year. Upward pressure from the stock market on convertible prices was counteracted, in this case, by forced selling within the convertible market to reduce risk and maintain normal levels of leverage.

Higher quality convertible issues returned to normal spread relationships in the first quarter of 1999, and convertible arbitrage performance has also rebounded, as illustrated in Table 4 and Figure 9. As in any market downturn, there are ample opportunities available to those managers who made it through the difficult period unscathed.

MERGER ARBITRAGE

Merger arbitrage usually involves buying the common stock of a company that is being acquired or merging with another company and selling short the stock of the acquiring company. Some managers may use options rather than stocks if it is cheaper to put on the trade that way.

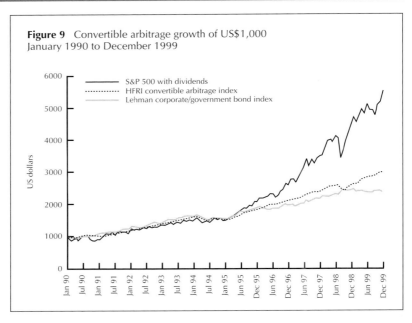

Figure 9 Convertible arbitrage growth of US$1,000
January 1990 to December 1999

The target company's stock will typically trade at a discount to the value that it will attain after the merger is completed for two reasons:

❏ corporate acquisitions are generally made at a premium to the stock price of the target company prior to the announcement of the proposed merger; and
❏ all mergers involve event risk, which is risk that the transaction will fail to be completed as announced.

If the transaction fails to go through, then the price of the target company's stock usually declines, sometimes dramatically. Merger arbitrage specialists make profits when they correctly anticipate the outcome of an announced merger and lock in the spread between the current market price of the target company's stock and the amount offered by the acquiring firm.

An impending merger creates a pricing disparity between the price of the acquiring company's stock and the price of the target company's stock that can be referred to as the merger arbitrage spread. As noted above, corporate acquisitions are generally made at a premium to the stock price of the target company prior to the announcement of the proposed merger. Later in this section, we will discuss some of the factors that affect how large of a premium an acquiring firm is willing to pay. Common sense tells us, however, that most companies would not accept less than their present market value, as represented by their stock price, and thus, acquiring companies must pay a premium to that stock price.

If the announced deal goes through, stock in the target company will become an ownership interest in the acquiring company – so, in theory, the two stocks can be seen to represent ownership interests in the same company. Until the deal is consummated, however, the prices of the two stocks will usually reflect the market's uncertainty about whether the deal will go through. Uncertainty can be generated by any number of factors including, but not confined to, financing difficulties, regulatory roadblocks, complicated deal structures, management disagreement, market sentiment and the emergence of new negative information about one of the two firms. Often, this means that the target company's stocks will trade at a discount to the value it will attain if the deal is completed.

Merger arbitrage specialists usually translate an arbitrage spread into an annualised rate of return, estimate the probability that the deal will go through, and then determine whether the returns to be derived from the spread if the deal is completed offer sufficient compensation for the estimated risk of the deal failing. As a general rule, friendly deals involving larger capitalisation companies will produce tighter spreads and moderate rates of return, while more complex deals and those involving small capitalisation firms will usually produce wider spreads and higher rates of return due to increased risk.

Merger arbitrage specialists do not try to anticipate possible merger activity, because trying to anticipate mergers is to invest on the basis of rumours. Instead, they research announced mergers and acquisitions in order to reduce uncertainty about each of the possible outcomes. Before taking a position, they will consider public corporate documents of the firms, historical financial statements for each of the firms, Edgar fed filings, analyst reports, standard media releases, conference calls and conversations with the companies' management and industry contacts. If arbitrageurs feel that the rate of return implicit in the spread is significantly more than the accrual risk of the deal not being completed, they will put on a position. Generally, they will enlarge positions as more non-negative information becomes available, market sentiment towards the deal solidifies, and the outcome of the transaction becomes more certain. A merger arbitrage manager will liquidate an investment position when new negative information is uncovered and the return no longer offers sufficient rewards for the perceived risks of holding the position. But if all goes as planned, the position will not be liquidated until the merger is consummated.

MERGER ARBITRAGE APPROACHES
Cash mergers or tender offers
The simplest example of a merger arbitrage opportunity is a company being acquired for cash. The target company's stock will typically trade slightly below the price proposed by the acquiring company. An investor

who purchases the target company's stock will receive this discount when the deal is completed. In effect, the investor receives an "insurance premium" for accepting the risk that the transaction could fail to occur. The source of return in cash merger situations is derived solely from the premium the acquiring firm decides to pay, because the dollar amount of the cash payment will not change between the time the deal is announced and the time the deal is completed. Merger arbitrage specialists will buy the stock of the target company or an option on that stock to lock in this differential.

Thus, the manager must research the balance sheets of the two companies in detail to ensure that the acquiring firm will be able to support the combined entity. The risk to the investor is solely event risk and is unrelated to the price of the two stocks. Possible stumbling blocks include legal and regulatory issues, market sentiment and questions about whether the acquiring firm has sufficient cashflow to finance the acquisition.

Stock swap mergers

In stock swap mergers, or stock for stock mergers, the holders of the target company's stock receive shares of the acquiring company's stock. The majority of mergers during the past few years have been stock for stock deals. A merger arbitrage specialist will sell the acquiring company's stock short and purchase a long position in the target company in the same ratio as that of the proposed transaction. (If the purchasing firm is offering a half share of its stock for every share of the target company, then the merger arbitrageur will sell half as many shares of the purchasing firm as he buys of the target company.) By going long and short in this ratio, the manager ensures that the number of shares for which the long position will be swapped is equal to the number of shares sold short. When the deal is completed, the manager will cover the short and collect the spread that has been locked in.

As with all mergers, stock swap mergers involve event risk. Any number of factors can cause a deal to fail to be completed. In addition to the normal event risks, stock swap mergers involve risks associated with fluctuations in the stock prices of the two companies. Since the terms of the deal involve an exchange of shares and are predicted on the prices of the two companies' stock at the time of the announcement, drastic changes in the share prices of one or both of the companies can cause the entire deal to be re-evaluated. Merger arbitrageurs derive returns from stock swap mergers when the spread or potential return justifies the perceived risk of the deal failing.

Stock swap mergers with a collar

Stock swap mergers are often even more complex when the exchange ratio is based on the price of the acquiring company's stock when the deal is closed, or in a more extreme case, when the target firm can call off the merger if the acquiring firm's stock price falls below a certain floor or collar. Because the merger completion is explicitly linked to the stock price of the acquiring firm, stock swap mergers with collars are more sensitive to stock market volatility than other merger arbitrage opportunities.

In deals that can be called off if the acquiring firm's price falls below the collar, market risk is explicitly translated into event risk. A spate of stock market volatility can cause merger arbitrageurs involved in such deals either to adjust their hedges to reflect new exchange ratios or to unwind positions that are no longer attractive or which have fallen through on the basis of a movement in the stock price of the acquiring company. On the other hand, a collar can be structured to ensure that the target company receives a fair price, and thus the collar may actually decrease the risk of the deal falling through. The outcome of more complex mergers is generally more uncertain, and therefore the spreads will usually be larger in these cases.

Merger arbitrage managers will generally look at collar deals in one of two ways. The first way is to assign probabilities to each possible scenario and then to calculate a rate of return based on the exchange ratios and the probabilities. For example, if a collar stipulates three possible scenarios, with a different exchange ratio for each, then the manager could look at the rate of return that would occur in each of the three scenarios and then multiply those rates of return by the probability of that scenario occurring, in order to come up with a rate of return calculation for the deal as a whole. The second way to analyse a collar is as an option. If the acquiring company trades down through the bottom of the collar, then the manager loses the optionality and the position becomes directional – that is, the manager now holds an unhedged long position in the target company.

Leveraged Buyouts and hostile takeovers

Leveraged Buyouts (LBOs) are a type of merger that was created in the 1980s. Michael Milken became the most prominent financial persona of the decade by financing corporate raids with the issuance of junk (high yield, low credit quality) bonds. Notable corporate raiders such as Ron Perelman, Boone Pickens, Nelson Peltz and Sir James Goldsmith sold junk bonds through Milken's Drexel Burnham Lambert to raise the money to take over companies such as Revlon, TWA, Disney and Union Carbide. As Edward Chancellor has noted, "The purpose of the leveraged buyout... was to acquire a company with the maximum amount of debt. The interest and principal on the LBO debt was to be paid off as quickly as possible with the cashflow generated by the company".[1] Debt was said to force the new owners of the company to "trim the fat" off the company, which often meant replacing existing management. Conventional valuations gave way to calculations of how much cashflow a company could generate and how much debt it could service. If the company could generate enough cashflow to service the debt, then the raider had effectively bought a company with borrowed money, and financed the borrowing with the cashflow generated by that same company. Notable so-called arbitrageurs in the 1980s, such as Ivan Boesky, would try to identify companies that were vulnerable to a leveraged takeover and take a stake in that company, in hopes of receiving the premium paid by the corporate raider. In retrospect, arbitrage was a misnomer for these individuals' behaviour which was highly speculative.

The era of leveraged buyouts and corporate raiders came to a halt in the early 1990s beginning with the failure of a number of prominent thrifts, and culminating in Milken being sentenced to jail for ten years. The loopholes that allowed Milken to issue large amounts of junk bonds to finance raids have been closed. But, although LBOs have become less common, the form still persists. Disciplined merger arbitrageurs will only consider announced deals and refrain from the speculative behaviour exhibited by Boesky and other so-called arbitrageurs in the 1980s.

In an LBO the acquiring company will still use leverage (borrowed funds) to produce the cash necessary to buy the target firm. To attract the funds necessary to finance the acquisition, the acquiring company may issue junk bonds. Because LBOs are not generally friendly transactions, the target company will often fight the deal and demand larger premiums. These deals involve risks that are entirely different from cash or stock mergers, such as the financial strain on the acquiring firm created by borrowing funds at high interest rates and the unwillingness of the target company's management to accept the takeover bid. Since LBOs are often financed by issuing debt, a merger arbitrageur must do fundamental credit analysis on the firm to determine whether servicing that debt endangers the completion of the acquisition. LBOs and hostile takeover situations create larger spreads which promise greater returns than standard mergers, but they also create a flood of risks that the merger arbitrageur may or may not be willing to analyse.

RISKS AND RISK CONTROL

Risks

Event risk

The primary risk to all merger arbitrage strategies is event risk. When an announced deal falls through, the merger arbitrageur's long position in the target company will generally drop significantly, erasing the expected premium. The merger between Ciena and Tellabs announced on June 3, 1998, and annulled September 14, 1998, is a good example of a high profile deal that a lot of merger arbitrage strategists liked, but which fell through.

Dead flow

The quantity of announced deals is cyclical and can be affected by economic conditions. For example, in the fall of 1998 very few deals were announced as potential buyers waited to pursue mergers or acquisition until uncertainty about global financial and political stability had waned. Merger arbitrageurs are constrained by the quality and quantity of announced deals.

Liquidity

Liquidity is not usually a problem, because all merger arbitrage trades involve equities. However, deals involving smaller capitalisation companies may be subject to some liquidity risk.

Risk control

Diversification

One way that merger arbitrage managers control event risk is through the diversification. If they can put together a diversified portfolio of merger arbitrage trades, then the failure of one deal will not spell disaster for the portfolio as a whole. Many managers use position limits to control the size of any one position in their portfolio. The ability to diversify is somewhat dependent on the quality and quantity of announced deal flow.

Leverage

Many merger arbitrage managers use some amount of leverage. When used prudently, leverage increases the risk of these trades in proportion to the amount of leverage used. But, as witnessed in the third quarter of 1998, when a portfolio of merger arbitrage trades is supported almost entirely by borrowed funds, it can become very risky. Nobody knows exactly how extensive Long Term Capital Management's merger arbitrage book was, but it is clear that it was large and supported almost entirely by leverage. The firm was eventually forced to unwind these positions, many of them at huge losses, in order to provide liquidity to support other parts of its portfolio.

Source of return

In a normal market environment, merger arbitrage returns are event driven rather than market driven. This is because merger arbitrageurs take long positions in target companies and sell short acquiring companies in a ratio that locks in the spread between the two companies that will eventually become one company. In doing so, they receive the premium paid by the acquiring company for taking the risk that the deal may fall through. Merger arbitrage returns, therefore, are not strongly correlated to overall stock market movement under most stock market conditions because they are derived from *the relationship between the stock prices of two companies.*

However, this general statement about source of return must be qualified. Merger arbitrage returns are determined by deal spreads and the amount of deal flow, both of which are related to the directional fortunes of the stock market. Deal flow can slow down or disappear in market corrections. Similarly, acquiring companies are more likely to pay larger premiums during bull markets when high stock prices provide ready currency for mergers and acquisitions.

The strategy is subject to its own set of risks. Generally, these are event risks having to do with *the relationship between the target company and the buyer* rather than directional risks having to do with the systematic direction of stock market prices. Nonetheless, merger arbitrage specialists can achieve ample and stable returns over time based on their ability to anticipate the probable outcomes of specific transactions, as opposed to the far more random nature of most directional investment strategies.

The research process that merger arbitrageurs use to examine possible investment is the same in any market. Managers examine publicly available documents to assess synergies between acquiring and target companies, estimate the probabilities of possible outcomes of announced deals, analyse possible regulatory roadblocks to deal completion and value the stock of involved companies.

GROWTH AND RECENT DEVELOPMENTS IN MERGER ARBITRAGE

Merger arbitrage as a strategy more than doubled from less than 1% of hedge fund assets in 1990 to over 2% in 1999. This growth has come despite the fact that the strategy is constrained by the number of announced deals and the regulatory environment.

Deal flow and other factors affecting volume
While merger arbitrage returns are not highly correlated to overall stock market movements, they still depend on the overall volume and nature of merger activity at any given time. When deal flow dries up, as it did during the third quarter of 1998 because of worries about global financial and political instability, it becomes much more difficult for merger arbitrage managers to put together a diversified portfolio of trades. As evidenced by the spate of stock for stock mergers in the fourth quarter of 1998 and throughout 1999, rising stock prices create opportunities for companies whose stock has been carried upward to use the value of that stock as currency for acquisitions.

Internet related stocks in 1999 were an excellent example of stock values increasing acquisition activity. The demand for Internet stocks was such that investors were willing to pay previously unheard-of prices to own the stock of companies that had yet to register a profit. Big name companies in the sector, such as America Online and Yahoo!, with relatively low earnings and relatively high stock prices, have been able to use their stock prices to acquire other large companies such as Netscape, Broadcast.com and most recently Time-Warner.

The current bull market has also influenced the nature of announced deal flow. While the overall volume of mergers exploded in the 1990s, as discussed previously, the number of leveraged buyouts and hostile take-overs funded by junk bonds decreased significantly. The majority of merg-ers today are strategic and non-competitive. The acquiring company generally has a sound business reason for the merger.

The number of such transactions has increased in recent years for two reasons:

❏ bull market stock prices provide readily available currency for stock swap mergers; and
❏ companies that are looking to expand increased their efficiency in the early 1990s and are now enjoying high profitability and strong cashflow.

These companies often want to expand into related niches and find that it is cheaper to buy market share than compete for it through its existing business structure.

Companies are also consolidating in response to global competition in a world where foreign markets are of increasing importance to domestic business health. Regulatory changes can also prompt mergers and acquisi-tions. A good example is the banking industry, which continues to consoli-date as the barriers to interstate commerce collapse. Major deals include First Chicago-Bank One, Deutsche Bank-Bankers Trust and Bank of America-Nations Bank Montgomery.

Another factor affecting the volume and type of mergers are changes in management compensation packages. Stock options have become almost expected. It is logical, then, that managers' interest should be more closely aligned than ever with shareholders' interest because of the high percent-age of their total compensation that is represented by stock options. They are more willing to consider business moves, such as selling or merging their firm, that will create shareholder value and in the process increase their personal wealth.

All of this has had a mixed effect on merger arbitrage specialists. While there are more opportunities, strategic non-competitive mergers generally lead to smaller arbitrage spreads, although firms with high stock prices have been willing to pay relatively high premiums in order to take advan-tage of their stock price as ready currency. In hostile takeover and multi-ple-bidder situations buyers tend to be less disciplined and more inclined to overpay for an acquisition.

Returns
Merger arbitrage managers recovered nicely in the fourth quarter of 1998 and continued to perform well in 1999. Deal flow for 1999 hit record highs,

Table 5

No. of funds	Average size (US$ mm)	Year	Jan	Feb	Mar	Apr	May	Jun	Jul	Aug	Sep	Oct	Nov	Dec	Ann-ual*
7	5	1990	-6.46	1.71	2.90	0.98	2.28	0.73	0.02	-0.82	-4.58	0.73	2.19	1.21	0.44
8	5	1991	0.01	1.59	2.30	2.83	1.55	1.12	1.44	0.64	1.10	1.41	1.38	1.20	17.86
8	5	1992	1.96	0.96	1.34	0.14	0.00	0.30	1.45	0.12	1.34	0.40	-2.22	1.91	7.90
10	5	1993	2.12	1.64	0.49	1.30	1.17	2.25	1.54	1.67	1.85	2.05	0.86	1.65	20.24
11	11	1994	1.50	-0.41	1.37	-0.25	1.22	0.89	0.68	1.99	0.59	-0.26	-0.22	1.48	8.88
17	30	1995	0.86	1.45	1.49	0.35	1.26	2.47	1.35	1.35	1.63	0.91	2.13	1.31	17.86
20	41	1996	1.57	1.29	1.51	1.62	1.46	0.78	0.81	1.64	0.81	1.23	1.38	1.37	16.61
19	55	1997	1.04	0.39	1.05	-0.70	1.92	2.13	1.60	1.04	2.13	0.84	2.02	1.90	15.79
28	61	1998	0.96	1.89	1.05	1.59	-0.60	0.50	-0.57	-5.69	1.74	2.14	2.33	1.94	7.23
40	72	1999	0.71	0.25	1.05	1.31	2.04	1.61	1.38	0.52	1.28	0.93	2.37	1.08	15.52

*Annual represents geometric compounded average

offering ample opportunities for the strategy. In addition, the proportion of failed deals remained close to its historical average. Historical returns for the strategy are shown in Table 5 and the growth of US$1000 invested in merger arbitrage (as measured by the HFRI Merger Arbitrage Index) in 1990 is shown in Figure 10.

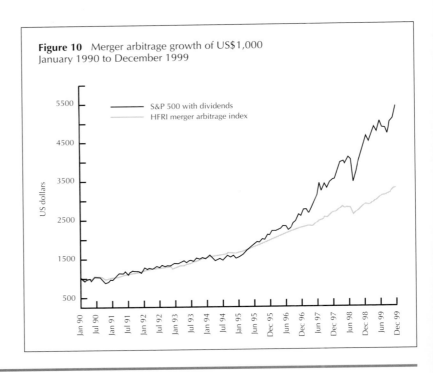

Figure 10 Merger arbitrage growth of US$1,000 January 1990 to December 1999

FIXED INCOME ARBITRAGE

Fixed income arbitrage strategies involve investing in one or more fixed income securities and hedging against underlying market risk by simultaneously investing in another fixed income security. These trades seek to capture profit opportunities presented by (usually small) pricing anomalies while maintaining minimum exposure to interest rates and other systematic market risks. In most cases, fixed income arbitrageurs take offsetting long and short positions in similar fixed income securities, which are mathematically or historically interrelated, when that relationship is temporarily distorted by market events, investor preferences, exogenous shocks to supply or demand, or structural features of the fixed income market. These positions could include corporate debt, US treasury securities, US agency debt, sovereign debt, municipal debt or the sovereign debt of emerging market countries. Often, trades involve swaps and futures.

By purchasing cheap fixed income securities, and selling short an equal amount of expensive fixed income securities, fixed income arbitrageurs protect themselves from changes in interest rates that systematically affect the prices of all fixed income securities. If they select instruments that respond to interest rate changes similarly, then an interest rate rise that adversely affects the long position will have an offsetting positive effect on the short position. In fixed income terminology, they do not make directional duration bets. They realise a profit when the skewed relationship between the securities returns to a normal range. Rather than try to guess which direction the market will go, they neutralise interest rate changes and derive profit from their ability to identify similar securities that are mispriced relative to one another. Because the prices of fixed income instruments are based on yield curves, volatility curves, expected cashflows, credit ratings, and special bond and option features, they must use sophisticated analytical models to identify true pricing disparities. The complexity of fixed income pricing is actually essential to fixed income arbitrageurs. They rely on market events, investors with different incentives and constraints, investors with different modes of analysis and investors less sophisticated than themselves to create relatively over and undervalued fixed income securities, and thus, profit opportunities.

FIXED INCOME ARBITRAGE APPROACHES

Most fixed income arbitrage trades fit into one of five categories: basis trades, asset swaps, TED spreads, yield curve arbitrage and relative value.

Basis trades
A basis trade involves the purchase of a government bond and the simultaneous sale of futures contracts on that bond. Bond futures have a delivery option; that is, several different bonds can be delivered to satisfy the futures contract. At expiration, the price of the "cheapest-to-deliver" bond

will converge with the price of the futures contract. Because it is not certain which bond will become the cheapest-to-deliver at maturity, this uncertainty, along with shifts in supply and demand for the underlying bonds can create profit opportunities.

With a borrowing and a lending component, basis trades are profitable when the borrowing becomes cheap relative to the lending. Fixed income arbitrageurs will usually seek out those bonds with a price relatively low to the price of the relevant future, establish a position and then wait for the cheapest-to-deliver bond to change, knowing all the while that the worst case scenario is to deliver the currently held bond into the futures contract. Alternatively, a fixed income arbitrageur would profit if he is able to sell short the second or third cheapest-to-deliver bond at a positive net basis (ie, through cheap financing) and subsequently the net basis was forced to zero at the expiration of the futures contract because of insufficient supply of the cheapest-to-deliver bond. In this example, the insufficient supply of the cheapest-to-deliver bond caused the prices of the second and third cheapest-to-deliver bonds to converge with that of the futures contract. Thus, the fixed income arbitrageur has sold the delivery option for more than it is worth.

Asset swaps

An asset swap involves an exchange of cashflows between two parties. Usually, the fixed income arbitrageur purchases a bond and simultaneously swaps the bond's fixed-rate cashflows for the floating-rate cashflows of another, usually less liquid, security. The difference between the two rates represents the profit opportunity. The risk is that an increase or decrease in interest rates will adversely affect the spread. The trade works only if the floating rate is higher than the financing costs. So, as with basis trades, the trade involves both borrowing and lending and profit is contingent on the borrowing being cheap relative to the lending.

When the trade is made with a low-risk bond such as US Treasuries or sovereign issues of major developed nations that are, in essence, default-free, then the relationship between the bond and the swap is likely to be relatively stable. However, changes in tax laws or a financial or political debacle in a country can cause such relationship to change. Swaps based on less certain bonds are inherently more risky. Generally, the lowest risk swaps involve swapping a very liquid bond for a less liquid security. Thus, the manager is paid to hold a security in his portfolio for which there is little demand. If the demand were to increase, then the manager can exist the position at a greater profit than anticipated. Otherwise, the security is held to maturity in order to realise the return from the positive spread relative to financing. Because this spread is often quite small, asset swaps are often highly leveraged to produce the desired return.

TED spreads

The "TED" originally referred to Treasuries over Eurodollars but now often refers to all global government bonds hedged against par swaps in the same currency. These trades, which are also called international credit spreads, seek to take advantage of the differences in yields between government securities and LIBOR (London Inter-Bank Offering Rate) contracts of similar maturity.

In the case of Treasuries over Eurodollars, the manager takes a long position in US Treasuries and a short position in Eurodollar contracts of the same maturity. The spread between the two yields is constantly changing and is affected by turmoil or uncertainty in the international financial markets. Generally speaking, positions are established when such spreads are narrow.

For example, if a manager takes a position when the spread is 10 basis points on a three-year bond, the worst case scenario is that the manager loses 10 basis points per year over the three years. However, the trade anticipates that the spread will widen between the date of the trade and maturity allowing the manager to exist the trade at a profit. Thus, the manager, in essence, purchases an "option" for 10 basis points to participate in the upside deriving from events that may cause the spread to widen, particularly "flight-to-quality" situations. These situations occur when a larger number of investors seek the safety and stability of government securities to escape from turmoil in international stock and bond markets. The resultant buying of government securities generally causes the credit spread to widen. A notable example of a flight-to-quality event occurred in 1998 when Russian defaulted on its debt.

Yield curve arbitrage

Yield curve arbitrage refers to an array of trades that involve taking long and short positions at different points on the US treasury yield curve in order to profit from relative pricing disparities. Supply and demand for treasury securities, as well as exogenous factors such as central bank policy actions, government issuance cycles, liquidity preference and futures hedging affect the shape and steepness of the yield curve. These factors may create anomalous kinks in the yield curve or spread differentials that represent profit opportunities for yield curve arbitrageurs.

The trades can be categorised by the maturities of the long and the short positions. Trades involving securities of very close maturities will usually be driven by structural or issuance cycle factors. Often, these issue-driven yield curve arbitrage trades make use of three securities (referred to as a butterfly) or more over a small range of maturity. Issue-driven yield curve arbitrage trades seek to profit from "kinks" in the yield curve rather than the steepness of the curve. By using multiple securities, managers can minimise the effect of changes in the slope of the yield curve on the trade.

A classic example of an issuance driven trade is "on-the-run" treasury bonds versus "off-the-run" Treasury bonds. Newly issued 30-year Treasury bonds (on-the-run) will usually have lower yields than old 30-year Treasury bonds (off-the-run) because they are more liquid and often carry a premium in the financing market. A manager buys the off-the-run Treasury bond and sells the on-the-run Treasury bond with the expectations that, over time, the yields of the two bonds will eventually converge. If the expected convergence occurs, then the manager makes profits in proportion to the original spread between the two securities, less financing costs. The risk is that conditions can change dramatically and unexpectedly between the current and future dates (for example, a fundamental change can occur in the debt structure of the federal government). Alternatively, this trade can be initiated in the opposite direction based on anomalies and changes in liquidity or financing conditions between the two issues.

At the other end of the yield curve arbitrage spectrum are trades where the difference in maturities of the two securities is larger and thus the relationship is often dependent on broader market factors (such as macroeconomic conditions) rather than being due to pure quantitative misalignment. A classic example is two-year notes versus 10-year notes. Many observers would classify these trades as relative value plays rather than yield curve arbitrage. But it is important to note here that there is a spectrum of yield curve arbitrage trades.

Relative value trades

Relative value trades, in the fixed income realm, are trades in which the long and the short component are on different parts of the yield curve or in different fixed income sectors, but their values are still linked in some manner. In almost all cases, there is no structural or technical factor in the fixed income market that will force a convergence of value. The opportunities are driven by relative misvaluations. Typically, the trade has a positive carry and a positively skewed distribution of expected returns. By "positively skewed" we mean that the expected returns are not evenly distributed around the average (in other words, a bell curve), but rather, more returns fall on the positive side.

Often, opportunities for relative value trades are the result of temporary credit anomalies and the returns are derived from riding out the credit anomaly and obtaining advantageous financing. A manager might take a long position in a bond and short a swap at one point on the yield curve and do the inverse at a different point on the curve. The relative pricing disparity between the two points is driven by investors' preference for securities offered at different points on the curve. An example of such an unusual anomaly occurred in 1998 when the liquidation of Long Term Capital Management's positions produced a 40 basis point difference between four and five-year bonds in the United Kingdom (the historical range was closer to 0–10 basis points). The manager who enters this kind of trade correctly takes profits when the credit anomaly works itself out.

In other cases, the relationship between the components is much more subjective. For example, a manager might go long securities in the corporate sector and short securities in the government sector if he felt that the spread between the two would tighten. Because the relationship between the components is often somewhat subjective, in many relative value trades there is no way to force a convergence of value.

RISKS AND RISK CONTROL

Risks
Interest rate or market risk
The value of almost all fixed income instruments is influenced directly by interest rates (which can be thought of as the price of borrowing money). If interest rates drop, the prices of existing fixed income securities will rise because their fixed coupon payments stay the same. The change in the price of the security reflects the increased value of that fixed stream of cashflows, given the lower levels of interest being offered currently. Interest rate changes initiated by the central bank or otherwise can realign the values of the entire fixed income sector. In the United States monetary (more specifically, interest rate) policy is linked to the real economy. The central bank sets targets for two key short-term interest rates (the federal funds rate and the discount rate) and will use interest rate policy to promote growth or rein in inflation. It tends to raise interest rates when it perceives inflationary pressures and lower interest rates when the economy needs stimulation. Thus, fixed income investors will watch indicators of the real economy such as the Consumer Price Index, the Producer Price Index, Hourly Earnings, the Unemployment Rate, Gross Domestic Product and Retail Sales to try to determine how changes in wages, labour, output and price levels will affect interest rates in the future.

Central bank policy is by no means the only factor affecting interest rates. We want to draw attention to two other factors at this juncture. First, perceptions of happenings in the real economy, and perceptions of what future central bank policy will be are as important, if not more, than the fundamental events themselves. By the time the Federal Bank raises or lowers interest rates, the rate change has often already been factored into prices through investor perceptions. Secondly, it is important to note that the central bank does not have a monopoly on interest rates. Its interest rate policies reflect perceptions of the domestic economy, and increasingly, the global economy. The two rate cuts in the fall of 1998 were an excellent example of how events that were exogenous to the US real economy set off a liquidity crisis in US financial markets that threatened to disrupt the real economy, and thus, prompted the Federal Bank to inject liquidity into the system.

Credit risk

The value of a fixed income security is contingent upon the credit quality of the issuer, in other words, the issuer's ability to continue to repay interest and principal. A security issued by a company that defaults on its debt becomes almost worthless.

Fixed income securities in the United States are rated by two major rating agencies: Standard & Poor's and Moody's. The ratings of these two agencies provide a guide to the credit quality of issuing entities. In addition, managers can compare the credit quality of a particular issuer with that of similar issuers. For example, the debt of an energy company that is rated B must pay a higher coupon that the bonds of the rest of the companies in its peer group, which are rated BBB-. Even though the entities are similar, the B security pays a higher coupon and thus may represent a good value relative to its peer group. Managers may try to avoid credit quality exposure by being long and short equal amounts of similar credit quality issues.

Residual currency exposure

In trades that involve securities denominated in foreign currencies, a manager must hedge the trade back into domestic currency in order to avoid unwanted currency bets on top of the fixed income trade. This is done using currency futures contracts. In practice, currency hedges are not always perfect and thus, residual currency exposure is a risk.

Counterparty risk

Most fixed income arbitrage trades involve both borrowing and lending (going long and short), so they require the manager to be both borrower and lender. The relationship with other entities, either as a borrower of securities or a lender, is called a counterparty relationship. By entering into such relationships, the manager runs the risk that the counterparty will, in effect, default on its end of an arrangement. This possibility requires managers to research the creditworthiness of counterparties before entering into relationships with them. Counterparty risk generally reveals itself in crisis situations, as evidence by the fall of 1998. Since that time, dealers and managers alike are doing a great deal more due diligence on their counterparts in order to insure their creditworthiness.

Model risk

Many fixed income arbitrage managers depend heavily on quantitative models to identify pricing anomalies in fixed income markets. In order for these managers to be successful, their quantitative models must accurately predict pricing relationships. There is always the risk that a model that has exhibited predictive value in the past will fail to do so in the future. Thus, the use of quantitative models requires constant vigilance and reassessment to ensure their predictive accuracy.

Tail risk

Even when quantitative models work, they usually identify opportunities within a 95% confidence interval. Managers, therefore, must be wary of the other 5%. 95% accuracy may imply that a particular occurrence will only happen once in a lifetime, but not when in that lifetime. It was just such a "multiple standard deviation" occurrence that caused the Long Term Capital Management debacle.

Government policy risk

As previously mentioned, the role of the central bank in changing or not changing interest rates is a risk factor. Other government policy moves, such as changes in tax laws or issuance of new treasury securities, can have equally significant effects on the value of fixed income securities. Managers must be aware of political as well as financial happenings in order to control these risks.

Liquidity risk

As with any asset class, managers must pay a premium for the most liquid fixed income securities. If they choose to hold less liquid securities, they will usually receive a higher yield than if they hold more liquid securities, but run the risk of having a security in their portfolio they cannot sell whenever they choose. In a normal market scenario, some of the liquidity premium is embedded in the bid/ask spreads for different securities. Furthermore, in a stress period, the value of illiquid securities can drop, on a mark-to-market basis, in the case of a flight-to-quality situation. In addition, the liquidity of a particular instrument can change as the overall demand for liquidity in the market changes. Thus, in the liquidity squeeze in August and September 1998 corporate bonds that were normally judged to be very liquid became increasingly less so, particularly when compared with the liquidity provied by treasuries. Managers must be aware of and control for implicit liquidity bets embedded in seemingly innocuous spread trades.

Measuring and controlling interest rate risk
Duration

Fixed income arbitrageurs insulate themselves from market risk by taking offsetting long and short positions in similar securities whose values are historically or statistically interrelated when that spread relationship is temporarily out of sync. "Statistically interrelated" most often refers to duration.

Duration is a measure of how sensitive a bond's price is to a shift in interest rates. For example, if a bond has a duration of two years, then the bond's value will decline approximately 2% for each 1% increase in interest rates, or rise approximately 2% for each 1% fall in interest rates. Such a bond is less interest rate sensitive than a bond of similar credit quality with a five-year duration, which will decline in value approximately 5% for each 1% increase in interest rates and rise approximately 5% for each 1% decrease. Roughly,

$$\text{Duration} = \frac{\text{Change in price/price}}{\text{Change in interest rates}}$$

Duration is equal to the average maturity of bonds for which a particular price/yield relationship holds. Bonds with longer maturities will be more affected by a change in interest rates because that change will be felt over a longer period of time. For example, if I have a five-year bond with a coupon rate of 6% and a 10-year bond of similar credit quality with a similar rate of 6% and interest rates rise 1%, then both of my bonds are now less attractive than they were when I bought them, because I could now get the same interest rate for less money. The price of the five-year bond, however, reflects the present value of its now less favourable rate over only five years, whereas the 10-year bond reflects the present value of its rate over ten years. Accordingly, the price of the bond with a longer maturity will be more sensitive to changes in interest rates than the bond with the shorter maturity.

Fixed income arbitrageurs buy one bond and sell short another bond with similar duration. That way, if interest rates change, the effect, in dollar terms, on the long position will be offset by the short position because both bonds respond the same way to the change. If the total duration of the long side of a portfolio is equal to the total duration of the short side of the portfolio, then the portfolio is said to have zero duration. Fixed income arbitrageurs try to eliminate market risk by structuring their trades and portfolios to be at or near zero duration. Any foreign currency risk is hedged against in a similar fashion using currency futures contracts.

Parallel and rotational shifts of the yield curve
Fixed income arbitrage managers often attempt to insulate their portfolios from both parallel and rotational shifts in the yield curve. Parallel duration calculations estimate the sensitivity of the price of the portfolio with respect to parallel shifts of the yield curve of different magnitudes. Rotational duration calculations estimate the sensitivity of the rice of the portfolio to yield curve pivots of various magnitudes (a pivot is achieved by holding one point on the curve constant while changing anther). The pivot points are usually bellwether points such as the three-month yield and the 10-year yield.

Sources of return
Although few pure arbitrages still exist, fixed income arbitrage strategies have a non-directional philosophical orientation that qualifies them to be

included in discussions of market neutral strategies. Fixed income arbitrageurs make bets on *the relationship between two or more securities* rather than on market direction. They construct trades involving securities whose relationship is temporarily out of sync. In some cases, managers construct a "synthetic option", such as in a basis trade, that allows them to buy the potential upside at a limited and defined cost that represents the worst case scenario.

In normal market environments, fixed income arbitrage shows very little correlation to general market indices, indicating that returns are derived from other sources. Nevertheless, as with many investment strategies, in serious downturns, many relationships that have held historically can become dislocated in a way that works against fixed income arbitrageurs. Thus, the relationship between securities is not necessarily a more stable source of return than the market, but certainly a different and non-directional one.

In a normal market environment, fixed income arbitrage returns are based on the relationship between two or more fixed income securities rather than on the direction of the fixed income markets. Fixed income arbitrage returns, therefore, are not strongly correlated to overall fixed income market movement under most market conditions. As we will discuss further on in this section, this statement is less true in periods of extreme market movements. Generally, fixed income arbitrage specialists can achieve ample and stable returns over time by evaluating and selecting undervalued fixed income securities and hedging them with related securities, as opposed to submitting the far more random nature of most directional investment strategies.

While we have touched on some of the sources of return for particular kinds of fixed income arbitrage trades, some more general categories apply across all of them.

Financing
Because most fixed income strategies take the form of spread trades in which the spread is not particularly large, the trades must be leveraged, often many times, in order to produce a competitive return. Therefore, fixed income arbitrage managers must be able to obtain attractive financing. In order to establish the credit lines and counterparty relationships that fixed income arbitrage strategies require, a manager must have a relatively large minimum amount of capital under management (generally US$25 to US$50 million).

Repurchase agreements
Repurchase agreements, or REPO, refers to the financing of specific bonds long or short. Due to fluctuations in supply and demand for a particular bond, the market for financing a position in that bond can vary widely.

A bond whose supply is tight is said to be "on special". That is, a short seller of such a bond will receive less than market rates on the short proceeds, making any arbitrage involving that bond less profitable. The ability to get good REPO quotes is a driving factor behind many arbitrages.

Technology
Fixed income managers sometimes refer to "complexity premiums". These are the costs of the complex quantitative modelling and large amount of computer modelling needed to analyse fixed income securities. Many managers feel that they are paid to understand relationships that others do not. Often, such understanding becomes a matter of technology. Managers can spend hundreds of thousands of dollars on computer systems that can analyse and manage a fixed income portfolio. Some of the returns, therefore, are attributable to the investment in technology. However, technology has become a factor that is necessary but not sufficient to ensure success. Technology can bring better data to the manager faster and make it easier to analyse, but the analysis is still the manager's realm.

Liquidity
More liquid securities command a premium over less liquid but similar securities. Thus, managers who are willing to hold less liquid securities may derive some of their profit from "capturing" the liquidity premium by holding the less liquid security and simultaneously selling the more liquid security short. However, they run the risk of getting stuck with a security for which, at any given time, there are few buyers. Managers should be aware of their overall exposure to liquidity in their portfolio. For example, a manager could have a portfolio of trades that was diversified in all other aspects, but in which the short positions were all in less liquid securities. In a liquidity squeeze, this exposure would override all other factors.

Events
Some fixed income arbitrages result from extraordinary market events or from the perceived possibility of a forthcoming event. Fixed income arbitrageurs may invest in these situations in a hedged fashion in order to profit from a perceived or actual credit anomaly created by the event. An example of such an event would be a perceived risk of tax law changes.

Manager skill and hard work
Fixed income arbitrage involves a great deal of sifting through data to find arbitrage or arbitrage-like situations. As fixed income markets become more and more efficient, arbitrage-like opportunities become fewer and harder to find. In addition, the number of managers chasing these arbitrage profits can narrow the spreads. With the downfall of Long Term Capital Management and scaling back of their large players in the third and fourth

quarters of 1998, the field has thinned. Those managers who have been able to survive have exhibited a good measure of skill and hard work.

GROWTH AND RECENT DEVELOPMENTS IN FIXED INCOME ARBITRAGE

Fixed income arbitrage as a hedge fund strategy tripled from 0.6% of hedge fund assets in 1990 to about 1.8% in 1999. This increase masks the negative returns and pullback that occurred in the second half of 1998. In addition, many relative value arbitrage and mortgage-backed securities managers are engaged in forms of fixed income arbitrage. Thus, the above figure probably understates the amount of assets in the strategy.

In spite of negative performance by the fixed income markets as a whole in 1999, the performance of managers in the HFRI Fixed Income Arbitrage Index in 1999 returned to a level commensurate with their historical average as illustrated in Table 6 and Figure 11.

EQUITY HEDGE

Equity hedge managers build equity portfolios by combining core long holdings with short sales of stock or stock index options. Their net market exposure (long positions-short positions) varies depending on the manger's preference and market conditions. Ideally, they increase long exposure in bull markets and decrease it or even go net short in a bear market. While the short exposure is often intended to act as a hedge against a general stock market decline, many managers also hope to generate an ongoing positive return from their short positions.

In a rising market, well-chosen long positions increase in value as fast or faster than the market, and well-chosen short positions will increase less

Table 6

No. of funds	Average size (US$ mm)	Year	Jan	Feb	Mar	Apr	May	Jun	Jul	Aug	Sep	Oct	Nov	Dec	Ann-ual*
4	35	1990	2.25	2.10	−0.21	2.23	0.32	0.15	0.68	0.03	0.49	1.22	0.55	0.57	10.84
4	37	1991	4.00	2.42	1.52	1.88	2.34	1.39	1.96	−0.82	−2.58	−0.03	−1.17	1.46	12.89
5	43	1992	4.70	2.53	2.53	2.26	0.62	−0.45	−0.08	0.84	−0.79	3.33	2.18	2.62	22.11
9	56	1993	0.25	0.89	1.47	1.45	1.94	0.37	1.99	1.50	0.70	0.96	2.12	1.87	16.64
13	97	1994	2.32	1.63	0.93	0.98	0.75	1.32	0.36	0.71	0.88	0.65	0.76	0.06	11.94
21	99	1995	0.64	0.34	1.79	0.64	−0.54	−1.18	2.49	0.92	−1.89	1.58	−0.01	1.22	6.08
24	115	1996	0.95	0.69	0.58	1.39	1.15	1.35	1.30	0.63	0.52	1.18	−0.37	1.94	11.89
23	130	1997	1.43	1.17	0.54	0.98	0.34	0.67	0.58	0.40	0.51	−0.37	−0.14	0.71	6.87
25	203	1998	0.39	1.28	1.34	1.03	0.19	−1.31	1.69	−1.18	−6.45	−6.09	−1.42	0.15	−10.29
23	103	1999	1.17	1.09	1.31	0.11	−0.03	1.32	0.65	−0.34	0.39	0.51	1.18	1.19	8.87

*Annual represents geometric compounded average

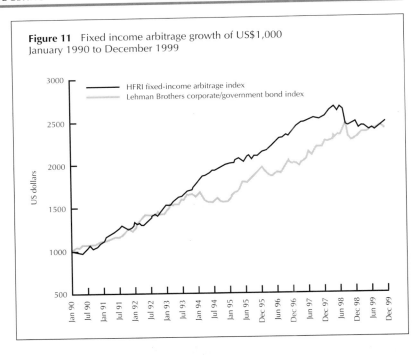

Figure 11 Fixed income arbitrage growth of US$1,000 January 1990 to December 1999

than the long positions or even decline in value. Similarly, in a declining market, well chosen short holdings tend to fall more rapidly than the market falls and well chosen long holdings fall less rapidly than the market or even increase in value. While underperforming short positions reduce returns in a rising market, equity hedge managers accept this reduction in returns in exchange for the protection the short positions provide in the case of a declining market.

The source of return for the long side of the portfolio is similar to that of traditional stock pickers, but the source of return for the strategy as a whole differs in the use of short selling and hedging to outperform the market in a declining or downward trending market. Thus, in a bull market, equity hedge managers should achieve positive returns, but smaller returns than if they held only long positions. Likewise, in a bear market they may make negative returns, but lose less than if they held only long positions. Therefore, one can expect equity hedge managers to make returns over time that are similar to long-only managers but with less volatility.

INVESTMENT THEMES AND FUNDAMENTAL ANALYSIS

Equity hedge approaches incorporate, to a greater or lesser extent, two techniques: investment themes and fundamental analysis. Investment themes incorporate ideas about macroeconomic trends – broad notions that will affect share valuations in the future. Fundamental analysis is a method of assessing a particular company's financial health and future prospects. It can be sub-divided into quantitative and qualitative aspects.

Investment themes

Most equity hedge managers try to be early in identifying economic trends – sometimes referred to as investment themes – that will have a major impact on the market. Identifying what industries and technologies will come into demand and remain so is an important part of identifying candidates for long positions.

After identifying what portions of the market to focus on, equity hedge managers look for companies that are well positioned to take advantage of these economic and technological developments. In different industries the factors that come into play usually differ. For example, Dell Computer Corporation has vaulted to the forefront of the personal computer industry by implementing a direct-sales, build-to-order strategy. A manager who identified the competitive advantage of this innovative sales strategy early would have taken a long position in Dell and benefited from the subsequent rise in its share price.

Another good example involves the debate about whether the massive potential of the Internet for voice, data and video services and products will be delivered to consumers in the future by way of cable-modem or fibre-optic cables or other media such as satellites. A manager who feels that cable-modems will win out would probably take a long position in telecommunications giant AT&T. AT&T has positioned itself to dominate the cable-modem market by acquiring two of the four largest cable television companies.

These are just two examples of how an equity hedge manager might use macro-ideas about the economy to locate good long candidates. Further, managers may look for an identifiable catalyst that will focus the investment community's attention on the company, such as better-than-expected earnings or positive press releases.

On the short side, equity hedge managers look for the inverse. Short ideas often emerge within the framework of long investment themes when managers attempt to identify good long candidates. While trying to determine what company has a competitive advantage in an area, the manager often finds a competitor that suffers from a competitive disadvantage such as bad management, accounting difficulties, insufficient cashflow, or excessive debt. Even more than on the long side, managers try to identify a catalyst, such as a negative press release or earnings report, that will accelerate negative sentiment within the investment community.

Investment themes may seem to be a logical part of "growth" investing, but most "value" managers are also making use of macro-ideas about where the economy is headed next (these two key investment styles, growth and value, are discussed later in this chapter). Managers who favour value weigh these macro-ideas about economic trends against the valuations of the companies that will be affected by them. Companies that are currently out of favour, but positioned to take advantage of an emerging trend are ideal long candidates for equity managers who favour value stocks.

Fundamental analysis

As it applies to the investment world, fundamental analysis refers to the elementary or essential components of a company that can potentially affect its stock price. Generally, fundamentals can be broken up into two categories: quantitative and qualitative.

Quantitative

Quantitative fundamental analysis collects quantifiable statistical indications of a company's financial well-being. Classic examples of such indicators are price-to-earnings ratios and price-to-book value ratios. Because these statistical indicators are produced uniformly across the entire industry they help make sometimes very different companies readily comparable. Equity hedge managers can arrive at most of the commonly used quantitative fundamentals by examining a company's publicly available financial documents.

Qualitative

Qualitative fundamentals are far more subjective than quantitative ones. For example, it would be difficult to assign an objective measurement to the quality of a company's business plan, but this is an essential factor in the company's success or failure and thus worthy of attention. Qualitative analysis involves assessing those factors that cannot be quantified yet are integral to the future success of the company. Examples of these factors include business plans, quality of management, competitive position and public sentiment towards the company. Often, qualitative analysis involves projecting the future path of the company.

Equity hedge approaches

A number of key factors make up an equity hedge strategy and these factors are essential to distinguishing between different equity hedge managers. The seven most important factors are: quantitative analysis versus qualitative analysis mix, investment universe, investment style, liquidity, net market exposure, research and use of leverage. Each of these factors is defined briefly below; in-depth discussions of investment style, net market exposure and research follow.

Quantitative versus qualitative mix

Managers value quantitative and qualitative analysis differently. At one end of the spectrum are managers who are highly dependent on quantitative analysis, and these bear a close resemblance to equity market-neutral and statistical arbitrage managers. These managers may rely solely on modelled statistical indications to guide their investment decisions. At the other end of the spectrum are managers who rely on qualitative analysis to generate their ideas by talking to industry contacts, listening to conference calls, and making on-site company visits. They run the numbers only as a check on what they have discovered "in the field". It is possible to find managers anywhere along this spectrum.

Universe of stocks

Because managers have a limited capacity to conduct fundamental research, they must concentrate on some segment of the equity market. The screening process may be driven by market capitalisation, manager expertise or particular investment themes. Most managers actively track a relatively small group of companies or ideas and keep a larger group "on the radar screen".

Style

There are two major styles of equity investing: value and growth. At the extremes are managers who solely follow the one or the other and in between are a variety of mixes of the two. In recent times the line between the two styles has become blurred as "value" and "growth" often describe ways of thinking about stocks rather than succinct investment styles.

Value

Value investors buy out-of-favour stocks that are priced cheaply because of low profits or under-utilised assets and which the manager believes will perform well in the future. The managers then hold these positions until their underlying strength returns the stock price to expected levels. On the short side, value investors find stocks whose underlying fundamentals do not justify the prices the stocks are fetching and sell those stocks short.

Quantitative measures of value assess a company's current capital value and its future earnings prospects. Then the manager determines how much investors have to pay to realise this future value. Many of these measures are "bang for your buck", that is, some key measure of value over the stock price.

❑ Price/Earnings (P/E) – how much do I pay for the company's earnings stream?
❑ Price/Book Value (P/B) – how much do I pay for the company's assets?
❑ Price/Sales – how much do I pay for the company's revenues?
❑ Total Assets/Sales – how much revenue is being generated by assets?
❑ Discounted Cashflow

❑ Dividend Discount Model – this measure assumes the current price is equal to the present value of all future cashflows
❑ Changes in Operating Margins
❑ Return to Equity – how well is equity utilised?
❑ Excess Cashflow – this measure reflects the company's ability to support future earnings and service current debt.
❑ Dividend Yield – this figure is the amount of current income generated by the stock.

What is undervalued and what is overvalued? In the past, managers would often have strict P/E or P/B rules for inclusion in their portfolios, such as a P/E ratio of 12 or under. The 1990s bull market has challenged such rules and made value managers think long and hard about revising such rules upward. But while valuations are a hot topic for debate, it is clear that what constitutes a good value is a moving target that varies by sector and industry. Older, established industries in which companies have established earnings streams, such as the automobile industry, are generally subject to traditional valuation rules. In newer industries, such as the Internet, in which companies are fighting to establish a market presence, the old valuation rules appear to be more dubious at the current time. However, these rules are sure to regain their importance after the initial rush to buy these stocks at any price pushes valuations to levels unjustified by the underlying businesses. As has happened in other notable extended bull markets (Japan's stock market of the late-1980s provides a good example), investors who have reaped huge gains from increasing share prices tend to focus on the future and earnings potential. But when the momentum slows or even reverses that emphasis tends to shift to the present and current earnings.

Growth
Growth investors buy the stocks of rapidly growing companies whose fundamental business is so strong that they feel it justifies almost any valuation. The classic growth stock at the time of writing is Amazon, which has yet to register a profit, but whose innovative Internet retailing business and name recognition have chased its stock price up to heights that cannot begin to be justified by the company's revenues and net income. On the short side, growth investors look for companies that are fundamentally flawed and whose stock price will be carried down by these shortcomings.

Quantitative measures of growth are generally measures of a company's growth potential as reflected in future earnings and changes in investor expectations. The usual assumption is that stock prices are driven by investor expectations, which can be quantified in analyst earnings estimates. Thus, revisions of these estimates, either up or down, can be a powerful indicator of a company's growth trend. Common growth measures include the following.

❏ Earnings Growth – how rapidly are earnings growing?
❏ Earnings Growth Forward to Price/Earnings – this figure measures growth relative to P/E Ratio.
❏ Earnings Estimate Revisions – these signal changes in expectations:
  • Consensus among analysts – how much diffusion is there among the analyst community?
  • Change in estimate relative to price;
  • Magnitude and direction of changes in individual estimates; and
  • Likelihood of future revisions.
❏ Earnings Surprises – these chart earnings relative to expectations.

Qualitative measures of growth are perhaps more important to this style than quantitative ones. The bottom line for growth investors is whether or not the company in question will be successful in the future. Thus, this style of investing is sometimes thought of as having a more subjective or qualitative bent to it than value investing. Qualitative growth factors, such as business plan, management, competitive position and the like, are key pieces of information for growth managers to evaluate.

As with value, what constitutes growth differs by industry. It would be illogical to expect traditional cyclical stocks to experience the explosive growth seen recently in information technology stocks. Many managers compare a company with other companies within the same industry to determine how quickly that company is growing.

Liquidity
In equity hedge strategies, liquidity is a function of the market capitalisation of the companies in the portfolio and the size of the manager's position in each company. Larger capitalisation (large-cap) companies whose stocks are actively traded are considered more liquid. In addition, a position in a large-cap company is more liquid than a position of an equal dollar amount in a small-capitalisation (small-cap) company because the position represents a smaller percentage of the outstanding shares. The average market capitalisation of an equity hedge portfolio serves as an indication of its liquidity.

Net market exposure
Net market exposure is a rough indication of a manager's exposure to systematic rises or declines in the overall level of stock prices. Ideally, managers have more exposure in bull markets than in bear markets. A simplified version of the formula commonly used to calculate market exposure is shown below.

$$\text{Market exposure} = \frac{(\text{Long exposure} - \text{Short exposure})}{\text{Capital}}$$

For example, a fund manager has US$1,000,000 in capital to invest and borrows a further US$400,000. The manager then takes long positions worth US$800,000 and short positions worth US$600,000. The manager's net market exposure is 200,000/1,000,000, or 20% net long. Conservative fund managers generally keep market exposure between 0 and 100% or even go net short. More aggressive funds may magnify risk by using leverage to exceed 100% exposure.

Some managers adjust net market exposure to reflect a macro view of the direction of the market. For other managers, net market exposure is simply a function of whether they find better investment opportunities on the long or the short side. These managers take short positions primarily as stand-alone opportunities to make investment returns, rather then as a hedge against market decline (the position still serves as a hedge, but this is a secondary effect). This kind of a position is sometimes referred to as a trading position to distinguish it from short positions taken as part of an overall portfolio hedge. While net market exposure is usually an indication of how aggressive or conservative a manager is, it is important to analyse the nature of the underlying positions to determine whether market exposure is a result of an overall hedge or of trading positions.

Research

Managers must base investment decisions on the analysis of information about companies. Ideally, this information is accurate, timely, and has some level of predictive power. With this in mind, it is important to ask where a manager obtains information because the possible sources of company information are myriad and vary in quality and perspective. Some of the most important information sources are listed below.

❑ *Trade journals and newspapers:* most managers read *The Wall Street Journal*, *The Financial Times* and other more specialised publications in order to keep abreast of news and events that may lead to investment ideas.

❑ *Data feeds:* various electronic sources of financial information are available to managers, including Bloomberg, Reuters, Edgar Online and other providers of more specialised information.

❑ *Industry contacts:* managers (or their analysts) build networks of contacts within the financial industry and the various industries that interest them. Some analysts may have formerly worked in a particular industry and use their industry expertise to analyse stocks in that industry.

❑ *Conference calls:* many companies schedule conference calls to communicate with a large number of investors and potential investors at one time. Participating in such calls can be a way to gain access to company management or become familiar with the company without having to expend the resources to make an on-site visit.

❑ *Company visits:* many managers rely on on-site visits and conversations with customers, suppliers, and competitors, to supply the details about a company that may not be apparent from its publicly available documents and press releases. Site visits also allow managers to get a "hands-on" feel for how the company operates on a daily basis.

❑ *Street research:* some managers rely on specialised analysts at large brokerage houses to assess companies. Most of these analysts follow a small number of companies or a single industry, and thus, some managers argue, they have a high level of expertise in that particular area. Street research, however, must always be viewed with caution because it is often designed to create brokerage commissions rather than objectively portray the company in question. The prevalent analyst rating scale is inflated to the extent that sell recommendations are rarely issued.

❑ *Newsletters:* the number of industry newsletters available is rapidly increasing.

❑ *Internet:* the Internet has become a fertile source of information. Company Web pages, news searches, newsgroups, and other links have become important data sources, particularly with the coming of electronic brokerage. In addition, many financial publications are now offered online with searchable archives.

Leverage

Most equity hedge strategists use leverage, which allows a manager to invest more than the amount of contributed capital by borrowing funds. Leverage increases risk, but allows managers to add new stocks to the portfolio without having to sell another stock first. Aggressive equity hedge managers use leverage to move quickly in order to exploit investment opportunities. Although conservative equity hedge managers use leverage more sparingly, the deployment of some amount of leverage is a standard characteristic of equity hedge funds.

RISKS AND RISK CONTROL

Stock picking risk

When managers pick a stock for the long or short side of their portfolio, they take on risks specific to that company. These risks include but are not limited to: regulatory issues, threats to market share or proprietary position, decreasing profit margins and other significant industry trends, continuity of management, dilution of current business due to future expansion, the emergence of new technologies, and the possibility that the company will be involved in a merger or acquisition. While company-specific risks are inevitable, a manager should be able to say with conviction that these risks are acceptable given the potential for the share price to increase (for long positions) or decrease (for short positions). The essential tool for managing these risks is in-depth fundamental research and analysis that allows managers to make predictions about the future based on all the currently available information.

In addition, equity hedge managers may counter specific risks with short, specific hedging positions. For example, a manager might hedge against exposure to a specific industry by pair trading. A manager that trades in pairs takes a long position in a company with a favourable outlook in a particular industry and a corresponding short position in another company in the same industry (often a competitor). In the case of a systematic drop in the prices of the industry as a whole (eg, bad news for a large company in an industry is often taken as indicative of the entire industry), the long and short positions will offset each other.

Market risk

The stock market as a whole is vulnerable to changes in the financial community or in the overall economy that can affect all companies and, thus, can cause directional changes in the overall level of stock prices. Interest rates are a good example of a directional change. An easy monetary policy (lower interest rates) usually causes share prices to increase because of the liquidity it creates. Conversely, a monetary tightening (higher interest rates), which is usually intended to keep inflation in check, reduces liquidity by raising the cost of money and makes bond markets more attractive to investors and thus, causes share prices to fall.

Equity hedge managers can mitigate the risk of systematic changes in stock prices by monitoring macro-factors relative to stock market valuations and carefully adjusting their long and short exposures as the market dictates. This process is by nature imperfect, but many managers attempt to avoid getting caught too net long in a market decline or too net short in a market rally. While the portion of an equity hedge portfolio that is "within the hedge" may approximate market neutrality, at any given time managers can lose money on both their long and short positions. The portion of the portfolio that is not hedged is, of course, susceptible to all the directional caprices of the market.

Universe of stocks

It is widely held that the stocks of larger, more readily tradable companies trade differently than those of smaller, less liquid companies. More information is available about large companies and large-cap stocks than about smaller companies and their small-cap stocks. The more information that is available and the more analysts at big brokerage houses who follow the company, the less likely it is that a single manager will have an informational advantage over other investors. The market for large-cap stocks is thus said to be more efficient than the market for small-cap stocks. Managers must weigh the informational disadvantage associated with large-cap stocks against the gain to be had from liquidity. In addition, there is a risk associated with the size of a position relative to the total market capitalisation of a company. As mentioned earlier, a position in a large-cap company will be more liquid than a position of an equal dollar amount in a small-cap company because the position will represent a smaller percentage of the outstanding shares. The average market capitalisation of an equity hedge portfolio is an indication of its liquidity.

Managers looking for undiscovered stock stories tend to focus on middle and small-cap stocks. Generally speaking, the smaller the capitalisation, the more risky the stock. Small-cap stocks are often unknown companies with unproven earnings streams that do not pay dividends. As evidenced in the fall of 1998, small-cap stocks are more adversely affected by a liquidity squeeze. The Russell 2000 index of small-cap stocks lost more than 33% from its peak in July 1998 to its trough in October 1998. In spite of 19.62% returns in 1999, the index was still only 9.76% above its 1998 low. On the other hand, the S&P 500, which lost 19% from peak to trough, was up 27.92% from its July 1998 level to the end of 1999.

Diversification

Mean variance optimisation has shown that, everything else being equal, a diversified portfolio of stocks experiences less volatility than a concentrated one. This theory is an extension of the old adage "don't put all your eggs in one basket". Ideally, in a portfolio of lowly correlated stocks, when one position is dropping, another one is gaining, therefore reducing the volatility of the overall portfolio. Most equity hedge managers also diversify their portfolios across industries and sectors to ensure that happenings in any one sector or industry will not have too much effect on the portfolio as a whole and ensure that a particular level of diversification is always present in the portfolio. If a position grows in market value and thus achieves a larger than intended weighting in the portfolio, then the manager may trim that position back.

Sell disciplines

Many managers determine a target valuation for a stock when they purchase it based on what they think it should be worth. When the stock reaches the target, they either sell the position or reassess the target value. Managers may sell positions before the stock reaches its target value if new information causes them to lose conviction about the underlying growth or value qualities that originally prompted the purchase of the position. When the price of a stock does not behave as expected, the manager reassesses the position. Generally, equity hedge managers are more tolerant of unexpected price moves in core long-term holdings than in trading positions.

Leverage

Most equity hedge strategists use some amount of leverage. Leverage allows managers to add new stocks to a portfolio without having to wait to sell another one. Alternatively, managers may also use leverage to increase the size of favoured positions. Aggressive equity hedge managers use leverage to move quickly to exploit investment opportunities. More conservative equity hedge managers use leverage more sparingly, but the deployment of some amount of leverage is a characteristic of equity hedge funds in general.

SOURCE OF RETURN

The prices of individual stocks can, and often do, move in response to company specific factors that are unrelated to the macro-movements of the overall stock market. Thus, an equity hedge manager drives returns, to some extent, from an ability to pick stocks that will outperform or underperform the market. On the long side this is no different from traditional long-only managers. The strategy differs in the use of short positions to derive returns from the manager's ability to identify fundamentally flawed or overvalued companies whose stock prices will fall in the future.

Theoretically, an equity hedge strategy allows managers to make money in both up and down markets because they retain the flexibility to go both long and short. In practice, short positions often reduce returns in up markets. Though equity hedge portfolios may not outperform a traditional long-only stock portfolio in a bull market, over time, they should outperform the stock market on a risk-adjusted basis because short positions allow the strategy to significantly outperform the stock market in down or sideways markets.

Picking individual stocks is an important source of return for equity hedge managers, but it is not the only source of return. Another key source of return is derived from the *relationship between stocks in the portfolio* and in particular, the relationship of long positions to short positions. Just as constructing a portfolio of correlated stocks dilutes the volatility-reducing gains from diversification, hedging for the sake of hedging dilutes the effectiveness of the technique and may end up being nothing more than a drag on returns. Constructing hedges that target specific risks involves very careful attention to the relationships between the contents of the portfolio. At the portfolio level, equity managers can mitigate market risk, and profit from declining markets, by adjusting net market exposure. For individual positions, industry-specific risks can be hedged by shorting another company in the industry. Needless to say, balancing hedging objectives for the overall portfolio with company or industry-specific hedges is more art than science.

RECENT GROWTH AND DEVELOPMENTS IN EQUITY HEDGE INVESTING

Equity hedge as a strategy has grown from 5% of hedge fund assets in 1990 to over 11% in 1999. Record growth in the equity markets and the outstanding performance of the equity hedge strategy have fuelled the dra-

Table 7

No. of funds	Average size (US$ mm)	Year	Jan	Feb	Mar	Apr	May	Jun	Jul	Aug	Sep	Oct	Nov	Dec	Ann-ual*
12	44	1990	−3.34	2.85	5.67	−0.87	5.92	2.52	2.00	−1.88	1.65	0.77	−2.29	1.02	14.43
26	48	1991	4.90	5.20	7.22	0.47	3.20	0.59	1.41	2.17	4.30	1.16	−1.08	5.02	40.15
37	33	1992	2.49	2.90	−0.28	0.27	0.85	−0.92	2.76	−0.85	2.51	2.03	4.51	3.38	21.32
59	29	1993	2.09	−0.57	3.26	1.30	2.72	3.01	2.12	3.84	2.52	3.11	−1.93	3.59	27.94
78	42	1994	2.35	−0.40	−2.08	−0.37	0.41	−0.41	0.91	1.27	1.32	0.40	−1.48	0.74	2.61
90	41	1995	0.30	1.68	2.09	2.64	1.22	4.73	4.46	2.93	2.90	−1.44	3.43	2.56	31.04
102	70	1996	1.06	2.82	1.90	5.34	3.70	−0.73	−2.87	2.63	2.18	1.56	1.66	0.83	21.75
133	76	1997	2.78	−0.24	−0.73	−0.27	5.04	1.97	5.05	1.35	5.69	0.39	−0.93	1.42	23.05
210	100	1998	−0.16	4.09	4.54	1.39	−1.27	0.50	−0.67	−7.65	3.16	2.47	3.84	5.39	15.98
226	122	1999	4.98	−2.41	4.05	5.25	1.22	3.80	0.61	0.04	0.45	2.74	7.23	11.30	46.14

*Annual represents geometric compounded average

matic growth during this period. Equity hedge managers, as measured by the HFRI Equity Hedge Index, have produced returns comparable to the S&P 500 at a much lower level of volatility. The strategy is appealing to investors who worry that the current level of valuations in the equity market is untenable and, in turn, seek the protection of a hedged equity portfolio.

1999 saw the US equities resume their upward path. As mentioned previously, the Nasdaq composite was up 84% for the year, and all other indices registered significant gains as well. Equity hedge managers participated in these gains to a large extent, with managers included in the HFRI index gaining 46.14%. This performance continued stellar returns for equity hedge strategies throughout the 1990s, as shown in Table 7 and Figure 12.

EQUITY MARKET NEUTRAL AND STATISTICAL ARBITRAGE

Equity market neutral managers strive to generate consistent returns in both up and down markets by selecting positions with a total net exposure of zero. They hold a large number of long equity positions and an equal, or close to equal, dollar amount of offsetting short positions for a total net exposure close to zero. A zero net exposure, referred to as "dollar neutrality", is a common characteristic of all equity market neutral managers. By taking long and short positions in equal amounts, the equity market neutral manager seeks to neutralise the effect that a systematic change would have on values of the stock market as a whole.

Some, but not all, equity market neutral managers extend the concept of neutrality to risk factors or characteristics such as beta, industry, sector, investment style and market capitalisation. In all equity market neutral

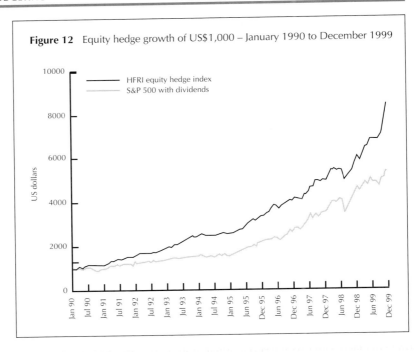

Figure 12   Equity hedge growth of US$1,000 – January 1990 to December 1999

portfolios, stocks expected to outperform the market are held long, and stocks expected to underperform the market are sold short. Returns are derived from the long/short spread, or the amount by which long positions outperform short positions. Thus, equity market neutral managers, in theory, are able to achieve stable returns, regardless of the overall direction of the stock market.

Some detractors of this strategy refer to equity market neutral investing as "black box" investing. The proverbial black box is a quantitative computer-based model. Many, but not all, equity market neutral managers rely on multi-factor models to rank stocks relative to one another according to expected returns and exposure to risk factors. Well-constructed quantitative models consolidate large quantities of information about a company into an ordinal ranking that can be compared to a large number of other stocks. In comparison, managers who construct an equity market neutral portfolio without the aid of a quantitative model are constrained by the amount of time and resources they have available to analyse and trade stocks.

It is no coincidence that equity market neutral investing emerged as a prominent strategy in the 1990s. The philosophical ideas that underlie the strategy have been in circulation for at least fifty years, but the rapid advances of the past decade in information technology and financial data availability have made the strategy more practical to implement. The cost of building the necessary infrastructure to analyse thousands of stocks and monitor hundreds of positions has been drastically reduced, allowing small, boutique money management firms to implement the strategy.

While most equity market neutral managers are highly dependent on quantitative models, it should be emphasised that there is a whole spectrum of approaches, which range from qualitative fundamental stock picking that is quite similar to equity hedge management to statistical arbitrage, which involves a minimum of human input. Equity statistical arbitrage can be considered a sub-strategy of the equity market neutral strategy. Similar to equity market neutral, equity statistical arbitrage managers construct portfolios consisting of equal dollar amounts of equities held long and short. However, there are distinctions between these two strategies. At a general level, the amount of manager discretion involved in statistical arbitrage strategies is far less than in equity market neutral strategies.

Different managers allow for different amounts of human discretion, but even in the case of the most quantitatively oriented managers there is art involved in building and refining models and in the constant process of review that is required to keep the model dynamic and accurate. The different strategic approaches of equity market neutral and statistical arbitrage managers all involve equal dollar amounts of stocks on the long and short sides to protect the portfolio from systematic, directional moves in the prices of the stocks. Individual managers can achieve this goal in many different ways.

EQUITY MARKET NEUTRAL APPROACHES

There are generally three main steps in the equity market neutral investment process: the initial screen, stock selection and portfolio construction. Portfolio construction is described in the "Risks and Risk Control" section of this chapter, but it is important to note that this step is not simply a check on stock selection but rather, an interaction with stock selection to produce a portfolio that maximises expected returns while optimising risk exposures.

Initial screen: universe of investable stocks

Managers use models to eliminate stocks from the beginning that would be difficult to trade in large blocks. Out of a possible 8,000 stocks traded on US exchanges, the manager winnows the group down to a more manageable number (400 to 2,000) of stocks using particular criteria. The most common criteria include liquidity, ability to short the stock, potential impact on market price, involvement in mergers and acquisitions and excluded sectors or industries.

Liquidity

The universe of investable stocks is usually, but not always, made up of large, very liquid companies because smaller, less liquid stocks are not always available to borrow and sell short. Market neutral portfolios often experience high turnover, so it behoves managers to trade stocks that are readily available to borrow and easy to sell. A small number of managers build small and middle-capitalisation equity market neutral portfolios, but the size of such portfolios is limited. For the most part, equity market neutral managers limit their universes to the 1,000 or 2,000 most liquid domestic stocks.

Also related to market capitalisation is the number of Wall Street analysts who follow a firm. Generally, the larger the firm, the more analysts who follow it. Most managers agree that increases analyst coverage results in more efficient pricing for the largest stocks. Some equity market neutral managers avoid such efficiently priced stocks by screening out the largest names, or, more commonly, by using a different factor model to analyse the largest names.

Ability to short

Equity market neutral managers must be able to sell stocks short. They often eliminate from consideration stocks included on brokers "hard-to-borrow" lists. Shorting stocks can also present logistical difficulties because of the uptick rule that states that short sales can be executed only after an upward movement in the stock price. Thus, managers often implement the short side of their portfolio before the long side, so that they do not end up with long positions that they cannot match with short positions.

Market impact

Equity market neutral managers who are moving large amounts of stock attempt to measure the impact their purchases will have on the market price of the security. If the purchase of a large block of a certain stock would adversely affect the market price of that stock, then the manager may eliminate that stock from their universe of investable stocks. Some managers measure this as a percentage of average daily trading volume. Others calculate how long it would take them to liquidate a particular size position.

Stocks involved in mergers and acquisitions

Many equity market neutral managers eliminate stocks involved in mergers and acquisitions from consideration because the pending merger may affect the stock's price in a way that confounds the ranking assigned to it by the manager's stock selection model. The price of a stock that would normally rank well may be held down by the uncertainty of the outcome of a pending merger. Managers prefer to apply their models to those stocks for which they have the most predictive power; therefore, merger stocks may be eliminated.

Excluded sectors and industries
Some managers may exclude particular industries or sectors that they believe behave differently or for which their model has less predictive power. For example, managers who have heavily weighted traditional measures of value in their models might exclude Internet stocks from their investment universe because traditional measures of value have little or no predictive power for that group of stocks. For the same reason, some managers use sector-specific models with greater predictive value for certain stocks.

Stock selection
Once managers limit their investment universe, they can begin choosing individual stocks for their portfolio. The second component of equity market neutral investing in which a market neutral manager can add value is their stock selection models. Philosophically, managers are looking for quantifiable inputs that are indicative of investor behaviour. For the most part, the result is a multi-factor model that ranks stocks relative to one another on the basis of expected return. Building an effective model involves choosing factors that will have predictive value over a broad range of stocks and combining scores on each factor into a composite ranking that has a meaningful predictive value.

Technical and price momentum factors
Technical factors are generally the measure of a stock's price momentum that is related to investor's reactions. Most investors tend to overreact to both good news on the upside and bad news on the downside. Price momentum factors reflect the fact that some investors believe that recent price movements may help predict future price movements (perhaps a strange perversion of the tendency of a body in motion to stay in motion). Examples of technical and price momentum factors include:

❑ volume on uptick relative to volume on downtick;
❑ DAIS Static Relative Strength – price relative to market;
❑ one month relative strength – four-week change in price relative to the
   market as a whole;
❑ six-month relative strength value; and
❑ moving average price.

Fundamental factors – quantitative
Value factors Value factors seek to emulate the behaviour of fundamental value investors. The measures assess a company's current capital value, historical earnings stream, and future earnings prospects and then

determine how much investors have to pay to attain this "value". Many of these measures are "bang for your buck", that is, some key measure of value over the stock price.

❑ Price/Earnings – price of current earnings
❑ Price/Book Value – price of current capital
❑ Price/Cashflow
❑ Discounted Cashflow
❑ Dividend Discount Model – the current price as equal to the present value of all future cashflows
❑ Price/Sales – price of current revenues
❑ Total Assets over Sales
❑ Changes in Operating Margins
❑ Earnings Relative to Industry over Price
❑ Return on Equity – how well is equity utilised
❑ Excess Cashflow – ability to support future earnings and current debt
❑ Dividend Yield – amount of current income generated by the stock

Growth factors
Growth factors are measures of a company's growth potential as reflected in future earnings and changes in investor expectations. The usual assumption is that stock prices are driven by investor expectations, which can be quantified in analyst earnings estimates. Thus, revisions of these estimates, either up or down, can be a powerful indicator of a company's growth trend. These are commons measures of growth:

❑ Earnings growth
❑ Earnings growth forward to P/E
❑ Earnings estimate revisions – changes in expectations
  • Consensus among analysts – how much agreement or disagreement exists among analysts
  • Change in estimate relative to price
  • Magnitude and direction of changes in individual estimates
  • Likelihood of future revisions
❑ Earnings surprises – earnings relative to expectations
❑ Current return on equity versus five-year range

Fundamental factors – qualitative
Many equity market neutral managers do not have a qualitative component to their models, but some make use of qualitative data in addition to quantitative data. This information might include data gathered through industry contacts or conversations with company management. In general, this kind of qualitative information is used as an overlay, or check, on model results. The complete lack of qualitative elements is the distinguishing factor between statistical arbitrage and the more general category of

equity market neutral. Statistical arbitrage managers seek to eliminate the human element by depending completely on their quantitative models.

Corporate signals

Equity market neutral managers are also wary of sudden moves made by employee owners of company stock. These sudden moves may include buybacks and inside trading, which may be indications that public announcements of important information are forthcoming. There is no way for managers to account for this type of information in their models.

Putting it all together: creating relative rankings

The general form of most multi-factor stock selection models is a linear equation of n terms that takes the form: $r = B_1f_1 + B_2f_2 + \ldots + B_nf_n$, where r is a measure of expected return for a stock, and B (Beta) is the sensitivity of the expected return to changes in the value of its corresponding factor f. Conventional multi-factor models typically use regression analysis to construct a predictive formula linking the values of each of the chosen factors for each stock with that stock's subsequent return. Thus, particular factors are assigned weightings in the equation based on their estimated predictive value. The regression coefficients for each of the independent variables usually become the factor weights in the multi-factor stock-ranking model.

Figure 13 illustrates the structure of a hypothetical four-factor model where

$$B_a = 0.4 \ B_b = 0.3 \ B_c = 0.2 \ \text{and} \ B_d = 0.1$$

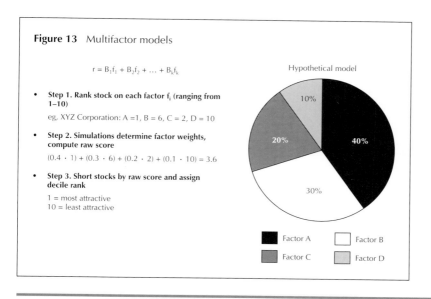

Figure 13 Multifactor models

$r = B_1f_1 + B_2f_2 + \ldots + B_kf_k$

Hypothetical model

- **Step 1. Rank stock on each factor f_i (ranging from 1–10)**

  eg, XYZ Corporation: A =1, B = 6, C = 2, D = 10

- **Step 2. Simulations determine factor weights, compute raw score**

  $(0.4 \cdot 1) + (0.3 \cdot 6) + (0.2 \cdot 2) + (0.1 \cdot 10) = 3.6$

- **Step 3. Short stocks by raw score and assign decile rank**

  1 = most attractive
  10 = least attractive

10%

20%

40%

30%

Factor A   Factor B

Factor C   Factor D

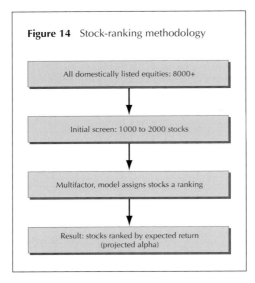

Figure 14   Stock-ranking methodology

All domestically listed equities: 8000+

Initial screen: 1000 to 2000 stocks

Multifactor, model assigns stocks a ranking

Result: stocks ranked by expected return
(projected alpha)

The first step is to analyse every stock on each of these individual factors and assign a factor ranking from 1 to 10 (1 = best, 10 = worst). For example, applying these four factor measures to XYZ Corp. might show that its stock has a rank of 1 for Factor A, 6 for Factor B, 2 on Factor C and 10 for Factor D. Our simple model would then evaluate XYZ Corp. as $(0.4 \times 1) + (0.3 \times 6) + (0.2 \times 2) + (0.1 \times 10) = 3.6$, giving XYZ Corp. a score of 2.6 on the multifactor model. After going through the same process for every stock, the model would sort the stocks according to their computed scores and assign them decile (10% of the universe) rankings from 1 (most attractive) to 10 (least attractive).

The entire method by which stocks are ranked is summarised in Figure 14.

Buy and sell rules

Buy and sell decisions are usually a function of the relative ranking system. Stocks held long are usually added to the portfolio when they achieve a certain ranking in the stock selection model and satisfy the risk parameters set for the portfolio as a whole. They are sold when their ranking drops below a certain point. On the short side, stocks ranked below a certain level are sold short and covered when they rise above a particular ranking. Some managers may have more absolute targets for stocks. Buy and sell rules generally work within the framework of risk optimisation; therefore, a buy or sell rule might be violated in order to maintain proper portfolio balance. Indeed, the third key element of the equity market neutral strategy is proper portfolio construction.

Mean reversion-based approaches

Some statistical arbitrageurs use a different method to select their stocks based on mean reversion (a statistical anomaly). Managers utilising mean reversion strategies work under the assumption that, while in the short term, anomalies among stock valuations may occur, in the long term, these anomalies will correct themselves as the market processes information. Thus, in a group of stocks that historically trades similarly, short-term events and the tendency of investors to overreact to unexpected news can create pricing disparities (that is, stocks that are over and under-valued relative to the group) that should not hold in the long term. One stock's statistical price anomaly that reverts back to the mean price of its group of stocks is known as mean reversion. It is a common discrepancy exploited by statistical arbitrageurs. The strategy tries to take advantage of related securities whose prices have diverged from their historical norms.

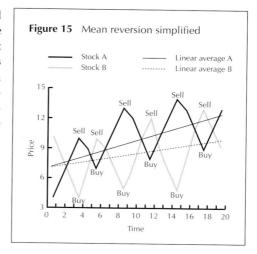

Figure 15 Mean reversion simplified

Managers who use mean-reversion based strategies search for groups of stocks whose values, over the long term, are positively correlated. There is usually a common theme within each group that links the individual equities together. Sector, industry, or a particular risk factor may define a group. In addition, most managers look for negative correlation with other groups.

As displayed in Figure 15, the long-term trend line for the group is relatively smooth while the short-term individual stock lines are full of peaks and troughs. Mean reversion managers try to sell short the stocks in the group that are at their peaks and buy those that have bottomed out.

Many mean reversion managers use a relative value system to determine buy and sell decisions. Stocks sold short are usually added to the portfolio when their prices are sufficiently higher than the rest of the group. They are covered when their price drops back closer to the mean of the group. On the long side, stocks that are valued below a certain level are held long until they rise above the mean of the group. Other managers may have more absolute targets for stocks. How managers choose to set up their rules determines how much trading they do, how much turnover the portfolio experiences and their transaction costs. Transaction costs and trade impact on market price are often included in mean reversion models, allowing managers to forgo trade opportunities when the cost of completing the transaction is greater than the potential gains.

Buy and sell rules usually work within the framework of risk/return optimisation. Exceptions include stocks that are involved in announced mergers or in other corporate events.

Due to the ever-changing markets, the factors that unified a group in the past may not always continue to do so. Statistical arbitrage managers must determine when and if to drop stocks from their groups and/or add new ones. For example, in the flight-to-quality situation of the third quarter of

1998, market capitalisation and credit quality became powerful drivers in the market that could confound formerly effective themes. If the goal is to create a model based on coherent groups with unifying themes, then keeping a model dynamic requires a certain level of vigilance. Deciding which factors are driving which groups, the essential component of model building, is the skill of the individual manager.

By buying the relatively undervalued stocks in the group and selling short the relatively overvalued stocks in the same group, a manager achieves the dual objectives of buying the stocks with the higher expected returns and selling the stocks with the lowest expected returns, while minimising net exposure to a group of stocks that share a particular driver. Some examples of stock groups follow:

❑ *Sector* – stocks within a sector often move together, the fortunes of one in the group affecting the outlook for the sector as a whole. Thus, statistical arbitrage managers may avoid making sector bets by being long and short equal amounts within a sector.

❑ *Industry* – stocks within an industry often move together, the fortunes of one in the group affecting the outlook for the whole group (eg, a bad earnings report for Compaq affects Dell and Gateway as well). Thus, statistical arbitrage managers may avoid industry bets by being long and short equal amounts within the industry. The bet becomes whether the longs are better than the shorts, rather than whether the industry as a whole will move in a particular direction.

❑ *Market capitalisation* – in liquidity-driven markets the prices of large liquid stocks will do better than smaller less liquid stocks. Alternatively, in some market cycles, large-cap stocks become overvalued relative to small-cap stocks and small cap may be up while large cap is flat. In any case, stocks of similar capitalisation are subject to systematic directional price moves.

❑ *Interest rates* – companies that are sensitive to interest rate changes include those that are highly leveraged (ie, those that pay a lot of interest) and those that are big lenders (ie, receive a lot of interest income). The stock prices of these companies may show a correlation to changes in interest rates.

❑ *Oil prices* – companies that are dependent on oil (such as airlines) may be sensitive to changes in oil prices. The stock prices of these companies may show a correlation to changes in oil prices.

❑ *Labour* – companies with large labour forces, particularly large union labour forces, are subject to disruption by labour strikes. Statistical arbitrage managers may try to neutralise this risk by being long and short equal amounts of such companies.

RISKS AND RISK CONTROL

Portfolio construction and optimisation

The goal of portfolio construction is to balance reward and risk. After evaluating the defined universe of stocks for both expected return and risk, the market neutral manager creates the optimal bundle of equal amounts of highly ranked and lowly ranked stocks while maintaining as close to a net zero exposure to the chosen systematic risk factors as possible. Many equity market neutral managers utilise sophisticated computations known as quadratic optimisers in this process. Common optimisers include APT and BARRA, and many managers have developed their own proprietary optimiser. The reduction of risk associated with neutralising systematic risk factors must always be weighted against forgone returns. Depending on their assessment of the magnitude of the risk and the possible returns, a manager might either violate a buy or sell rule in order to maintain proper portfolio balance or allow risk factor exposures to stray from neutrality.

Risk ractors

At the most general level, equity market neutral managers go long and short equal dollar amounts of equities to insulate their portfolios from unexpected directional moves that affect stocks as an asset class. Some managers extend this logic to other more specific, systematic risk factors. The logic is the same: by balancing long and short exposure to a risk factor, the risk factor can be theoretically neutralised. The optimisation process involves balancing the dual objectives of buying the stocks with the highest expected returns and selling the stocks with the lowest expected returns while minimising net exposure to selected risk factors. Some common risk factors are listed below.

❏ *Beta* – a measure of how sensitive the price a specific stock, or portfolio of stocks, is to changes in the price of the stock market (as measured by the S&P 500). Thus, a beta-neutral portfolio should be relatively insensitive to stock market swings.

❏ *Sector* – stocks within a sector often move together, the fortunes of one in the group affecting the outlook for the sector as a whole. Thus, equity market neutral managers may avoid sector bets by being long and short equal amounts within the same sector.

❏ *Industry* – similar to sectors, stocks within an industry often move together (eg, a bad earnings report for Compaq affects Dell and Gateway as well). Thus, equity market neutral managers may avoid industry bets by being long and short equal amounts within the same industry. The bet becomes whether the longs are better than the shorts, rather than whether the industry as a whole will move in a particular direction.

❏ *Market capitalisation* – in liquidity-driven markets the prices of large liquid companies do better than smaller, less liquid companies. Alternatively, in some market cycles, large-cap stocks become overvalued relative to small-cap stocks and small-cap stocks may be up while large-cap stocks are flat or down. In any case, stocks of similar capitalisation are subject to systematic directional price moves driven by liquidity preferences or changes in investor sentiment; therefore, equity market neutral managers may try to eliminate capitalisation bets.

❏ *Interest rates* – companies that are sensitive to interest rate changes include those that are highly leveraged (ie, those that pay a lot of interest) and those that are big lenders (ie, those that receive a lot of interest income). The stock prices of these companies may show a correlation to changes in interest rates. Thus, equity market neutral managers may try to eliminate interest rate bets from their portfolios.

❏ *Commodity prices* – companies that are dependent on oil or another such commodity (such as airlines with oil) may be sensitive to changes in prices of that commodity. The stock prices of these companies may show a correlation to changes in prices of that commodity. Therefore, equity market neutral managers may try to eliminate commodity price bets from their portfolios.

❏ *Labour* – companies with large labour forces, particularly large union labour forces, are subject to disruption by labour strikes. Equity market neutral managers may try to neutralise this risk by being long and short equal amounts of such companies.

❏ *Transaction costs* – the cost of executing a trade is often incorporated in the risk factor optimisation process.

❏ *Market impact* – the change in a stock's market price that executing a trade will create is often incorporated in the risk factor optimisation process.

❏ *Price/Earnings* – an equity market neutral manager may try to eliminate implicit P/E bets.

❏ *Price/Book value* – an equity market neutral manager may try to eliminate implicit P/B bets.

Optimisation

After evaluating the defined universe of stocks for expected return (sometimes referred to as projected alpha), most market neutral managers utilise an optimiser to create a bundler of highly ranked and lowly ranked stocks. In doing so, the manager attempts to maximise expected return while maintaining as close to a net zero exposure to the chosen systemic risk factors as possible. As previously mentioned, common optimisers include APT and BARRA and some managers have developed their own proprietary optimiser. Many managers optimise their portfolio on a daily basis in order to oversee risk exposures, but most managers rebalance the portfolio only on a weekly or monthly basis in order to avoid the transaction costs that they would incur if they were to rebalance the portfolio daily.

Execution and trading

Once the model produces a buy and sell list for the portfolio these trades remain to be executed. Equity market neutral managers devise systems to ensure that their traders execute the trades correctly and at the lowest possible cost. Three main costs must be considered in the trading process:

❑ *Opportunity costs:* the cost of not getting their best ideas into the portfolio in a timely fashion.
❑ *Market impact:* the impact implementing a position can have on the market price of that particular stock.
❑ *Commissions:* the cost of the trade.

Manager styles – putting it all together

An equity market neutral or statistical arbitrage manager's style is dictated by the way that the manager puts the different components of their equity market neutral strategy together. It is not simply a matter of which factors the manager chooses for the model, but how many factors (some managers believe that more factors are better, while others warn against dilution of predictive value or "overfitting"), how those factors work together, which risk factors are neutralised and so forth. In the end, an equity market neutral strategy becomes a balancing act. Equity market neutral managers must harness the power of quantitative models without erasing any advantage through their overuse. Managers must periodically question how well the model creates an optimal bundle of risk and reward.

In addition to methods of initial screens, stock selection, and portfolio construction, there are a number of other points that can differentiate one manager from the next.

First, the method and frequency with which managers rebalance their portfolios can distinguish equity market neutral managers from each other. As discussed earlier, buy and sell rules are usually based on the relative rankings produced by the multi-factor model of expected returns. How a manager chooses to set up their rules (eg, does the manager sell long positions that slip into the second decile, or wait until they fall into the third decile) determines how much trading the manager does, how much turnover the portfolio experiences and what the transaction costs will be.

These rules also reflect the time horizon for positions. Managers who are looking to exploit short-term price moves reflect this strategy in which factors they use as well as in a higher rate of turnover compared to a manager with a longer term outlook.

Transaction costs and impact on market price are often part of the optimisation process. Trade opportunities can be foregone when the cost of completing the transaction is not merited by its potential benefits. Buy and sell rules usually work within the framework of risk/return optimisation. Exceptions include stocks that are involved in announced mergers or in other corporate events.

Another key point of differentiation among equity market neutral managers and more quantitatively oriented statistical arbitrageurs is the level of human discretion they allow in their investment process. Another way of describing this is to ask what level of qualitative analysis the manager performs on top of the analysis of the quantitative model. Common qualitative factors involving manager discretion include reviewing buy and sell lists to identify anomalies that the quantitative model would not pick up, such as pending involvement in merger or acquisitions, late breaking news, stocks subject to excessive rumours or faulty data.

Because markets are always changing and stock prices are driven by different factors, some factors that had predictive power in the past may lose their predictive power in the future. Equity market neutral managers and statistical arbitrageurs must determine when and if to drop factors from their models and/or to add new ones. If the goal is to create a model that will approximate investor behaviour, then keeping a model dynamic requires a certain level of vigilance. Deciding which factors to use and how to weight them is an important part of any equity market neutral or statistical arbitrage strategy.

Source of return

Equity market neutral managers derive returns from the performance of their long portfolio relative to their short portfolio; in other words, from their long/short spread. This *relationship between* stocks may not necessarily be less volatile than the stock market as a whole, although it has seemed to be so over the past few years. It is important to note that although equity market neutral managers invest in equities, their source of return is entirely different from that of a traditional long-only manager. The risk to an equity market neutral strategy is relative stock-picking risk, rather than absolute stock-picking risk. The strategy does not require all long positions to go up and all short positions to down. Rather, it is only necessary for the long positions to outperform the short positions. Equity market neutral managers feel that with the aid of powerful quantitative models they can manage this relationship between securities better than they can predict the fact of any particular stock or the market as a whole.

Many managers describe equity market neutral as unemotional. The models that determine the portfolios make it possible for managers to make decisions devoid of personal problems and the occasional bad day. Equity market neutral managers believe that in the long-term, a system based on factors that have proven to have predictive value is more disciplined than a system that involves human emotion and intuition. These managers go to great lengths to eliminate systematic market risks and isolate their quantitative models. By doing so, they take on model risk – the risk that their quantitative system is flawed or does not have the predictive power it was thought to have.

The stock market is dynamic. Quantitative models and the managers who create them require time to react to changes in the market. These two facts periodically create situations in which static factors in quantitative models must be reconsidered in light of rapid and dynamic changes in the factors driving stock prices. Managers must ask model-specific questions, such as whether the model's traditional value factors will have any predictive power for Internet stocks.

Recent growth and developments in equity market neutral investing

Equity market neutral and statistical arbitrage have grown from 2% of hedge fund assets in 1990 to over 10% in 1999. This dramatic increase has been fuelled by record growth in equity markets, consistent risk-adjusted performance and investors seeking the downside protection offered by a fully hedged equity portfolio. In addition, improved quantitative models and technological innovations have reduced infrastructure costs and made equity market neutral strategies an option for smaller money managers.

Equity market neutral and statistical arbitrage managers had a difficult year in 1999. Anecdotal evidence suggests that some managers have since adjusted their models to reflect the emphasis on momentum investing (as evidenced by the rebound in the second half of the less quantitatively oriented Equity Market Neutral Index). On the other hand, stock market valuations have continued to defy traditional valuation rules, which has resulted in poor performance for statistical arbitrageurs. A return to more

Table 8 HFRI equity market neutral returns

No. of funds	Average size (US$ mm)	Year	Jan	Feb	Mar	Apr	May	Jun	Jul	Aug	Sep	Oct	Nov	Dec	Ann-ual*
8	14	1990	1.23	1.23	0.82	0.73	0.50	1.37	0.77	1.80	1.81	1.37	0.83	2.01	15.45
10	19	1991	2.51	0.04	2.70	−0.01	−0.02	0.56	2.50	0.28	1.92	0.97	1.17	2.07	15.65
15	22	1992	0.36	0.96	0.58	−0.03	0.11	0.62	1.24	−0.35	1.17	1.04	1.18	1.54	8.73
19	22	1993	1.91	1.06	1.67	−0.14	0.58	2.37	0.63	0.91	2.44	−0.10	−1.45	0.77	11.11
25	89	1994	0.78	0.58	0.44	0.92	−0.95	0.58	0.37	−0.35	0.02	−0.12	−0.45	0.82	2.65
31	75	1995	0.22	1.42	1.77	1.86	0.60	0.92	2.23	0.98	1.85	1.58	0.78	1.03	16.33
34	70	1996	2.18	0.95	0.86	0.35	1.39	1.37	1.62	0.78	0.66	2.10	0.16	0.95	14.20
38	133	1997	1.20	0.12	0.43	0.96	1.49	1.54	2.17	0.21	2.18	1.36	0.53	0.67	13.66
78	136	1998	0.54	0.76	1.26	0.66	0.48	1.69	−0.27	−1.67	0.81	−0.61	0.85	3.59	8.30
48	185	1999	0.15	−1.33	−0.76	−0.65	0.17	2.02	1.91	0.70	0.89	1.00	1.10	5.26	10.80

*Annual represents geometric compounded average

Table 9 HFRI statistical arbitrage returns

No. of funds	Average size (US$ mm)	Year	Jan	Feb	Mar	Apr	May	Jun	Jul	Aug	Sep	Oct	Nov	Dec	Annual*
		1990	0.83	1.02	0.48	−0.18	1.72	1.61	0.98	−0.31	−0.33	0.81	2.18	1.88	11.19
		1991	4.46	1.81	1.21	1.06	1.79	−0.50	2.39	0.44	1.01	0.30	−0.19	2.85	17.84
		1992	0.16	1.84	1.68	0.85	−0.07	0.51	1.53	−0.38	0.55	−0.17	0.96	2.86	10.77
		1993	2.24	1.47	1.97	−0.38	0.62	2.85	0.86	1.15	2.08	−0.89	−0.98	1.04	12.62
		1994	1.52	−0.19	−0.40	1.08	−0.70	0.21	0.87	0.86	−0.75	0.55	−0.03	1.59	4.67
		1995	0.33	1.99	1.16	1.59	1.58	1.08	2.01	0.59	1.80	0.87	0.63	−0.21	14.25
		1996	2.42	1.32	1.30	−0.08	1.11	1.96	1.20	0.45	1.42	3.44	2.28	1.28	19.63
		1997	1.04	0.91	0.49	2.23	1.21	2.16	3.60	−0.25	2.21	1.31	1.44	1.53	19.36
		1998	−0.05	1.47	1.85	0.52	1.11	1.90	−0.39	−1.03	0.15	0.60	1.38	2.24	10.14
27	45	1999	−0.98	−1.14	−2.00	−0.23	0.49	1.98	1.23	0.02	0.12	0.46	−0.45	−0.76	−1.32

*Annual represents geometric compounded average

rational valuations in the future would benefit these strategies. Tables 8 and 9 show the returns for the HFRI Equity Market Neutral and the HFRI Statistical Arbitrage indices. Figures 16 and 17 show the growth of US$1,000 invested in each of the strategies in 1990. Please note that

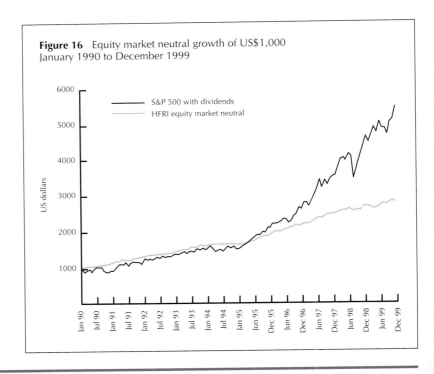

Figure 16 Equity market neutral growth of US$1,000 January 1990 to December 1999

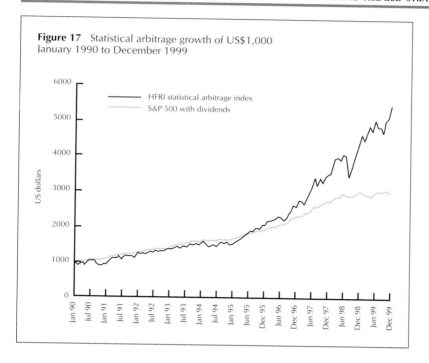

Figure 17 Statistical arbitrage growth of US$1,000
January 1990 to December 1999

Statistical Arbitrage was disaggregated from Equity Market Neutral in
1999 in order to more accurately reflect the highly quantitative nature of
this sub-strategy. The Statistical Arbitrage index returns for 1990 to 1998
were calculated based on the historical returns for the managers in the
index.

1   Edward Chancellor, 1999, *Devil Take the Hindmost: A History of Financial Speculation* (New
    York), p. 255.

10

The Infrastructure Challenge: Empowering the Stakeholder through the Successful Deployment of Technology and Data

Gabriel Bousbib

Reuters America Holdings

This chapter is about deploying and using technology for the delivery of time-critical risk information to various participants in the investment management community. We look at this challenge from the point of view of an asset management firm, providing investment management services to individual customers and plan sponsors. We first look at the technological framework necessary to deliver and support the risk budgeting process throughout an investment management firm and its stakeholders. We analyse the traditional technology infrastructure of an investment management firm and assess how event-driven technology will enable firms to move from linear cyclical processing to hub-and-spoke "many to many" system frameworks. We then review the transaction and market data flows across the organisation, and assess the key procedural challenges for ensuring quality transaction, real-time market and historical data. Finally, we gaze into what the technology of the future will bring us. In early 2000, many attributed the stunning uninterrupted growth of the American economy starting in March, 1991, to the 10-year two trillion technology investment made by American businesses over the period, which represented more than 40% of all business investment in the United States. This level of investment showed no sign of levelling off, as it grew more than 20% only in 1999. The extraordinary technological progresses of the last decade of the twentieth century, as well as new advances in the wireless and connectivity areas, will help transform the industry into a truly real-time enterprise, connecting and informing all of its stakeholders. Risk budgeting will then take its full significance. It will provide investors with the ability to assess in real-time, through any kind of device, the risk return attractiveness of any given investment/pension product, hence allowing for efficient capital allocation decisions. In turn, this will create further transparency and the need for efficiency throughout the entire supply chain in the capital markets industry.

THE STAKEHOLDERS OF RISK BUDGETING

The needs of the stakeholders

Investment management is about either managing risk, operational and market-driven, or providing tools to make risk-return investment decisions. The internal and external stakeholders of an investment management firm have varying information needs, both in terms of content and timeliness. We review briefly the risk budgeting needs of the various stakeholders in an investment management firm before outlining a potential technological framework for addressing them.

End-user retail client (external)
Whether as a plan participant or as an investor in mutual funds or individual securities, the retail client needs to understand the sensitivity of his/her holdings to particular market variables, industrial sectors, and geographies, as well as to given economic/political scenarios. In addition, the retail client requires comprehensive performance information and performance attribution across the same risk variables previously mentioned. Finally, the retail client needs information and research with respect to the different investment alternatives available. The client is then able to assess how these alternatives can impact his/her overall asset and liability situation, based on the client's expected future needs (college education, house purchase, etc) and goals (planned retirement age, lifestyle, etc).

End-user institutional client (external)
Plan sponsors for defined benefit or contribution plans best illustrate this type of player. Their role is to oversee the performance of the investment management firm tasked with managing the plan, based on investment guidelines and principles defined by the plan. Risk information is becoming critical as plan sponsors alter their investment philosophy. In recent years, indexing has made up a significant portion of plan sponsors' investment strategy (particularly of a public funds strategy). However, studies have shown that active managers will provide a higher return at a lower-than-market risk level. In 1996, public funds put 59.2% of their portfolios into indexed funds; in 1997, public funds devoted only 30.1% of their portfolios to indexed funds. At the same time, fund allocation to levered investments has grown dramatically. In addition to risk and performance information and investment alternatives (discussed above), an institutional

client will require compliance data, aimed at ensuring that the investment management firm is not breaching any of the investment guidelines (eg, type of security, sector, country) defined by the institutional client.

Portfolio manager (internal)

A portfolio manager is responsible for making investment decisions on behalf of the firm's institutional or retail clients. Portfolio managers require risk, performance and research tools similar to their customers, albeit usually far more sophisticated and more comprehensive across security types. In addition, portfolio managers need portfolio construction tools – ie, the ability to re-balance an existing portfolio based on given risk and return considerations – as well as compliance constraints. Finally, portfolio managers increasingly require transaction impact models to help them assess the market impact certain transactions may have on current prices, thereby affecting the potential performance of given portfolios. In effect, considering the size of given investment management firms, the trading impact of portfolio managers' decisions can no longer be attributed only to traders. Rather, a portfolio manager needs to make transaction decisions based on risk, return, investment objectives and compliance factors, as well as market impact estimates.

Research analyst (internal)

A research analyst provides both qualitative and quantitative analyses to the portfolio manager, and hence requires very similar tools as a portfolio manager.

Trader (internal)

A trader in an investment management firm is responsible for providing best execution for the transaction choices made by the portfolio management, with the caveat briefly discussed earlier. Hence, a trader will require optimal and efficient information about and access to liquidity pools, both for order transmission and trade confirmations. The automation of order and transmission and trade confirmation provides for a paperless, error-free environment, enabling the trading staff to focus on finding the best sources of liquidity and determining the impact of given trades.

Risk manager (internal)

A risk manager provides oversight in terms of the investment management firm's exposure to various market factors and economic/political scenarios, as well as possible counterparty default. He/she also ensures that market and credit exposure levels do not breach any internal or client-defined limits. The analytical tools required by a risk manager are quite similar to the ones discussed for a portfolio manager. The challenge then remains to provide the risk manager with a comprehensive view of the entire firm's positions, with the ability to slice the data across markets, sectors, individual companies, asset classes and customers.

Operations and back-office (internal)

Operations and back-office staff are responsible for the processing, clearing and settlement of trades. Whilst the settlement of securities in the US is now fairly efficient, thanks to organisations such as the DTCC, the same cannot be said about overseas markets. The spectacular growth in cross-border trading is fuelled by the rapid privatisation of assets around the world, which increased from US$25 billion to US$200 billion in the period 1990–99. The rapid growth of overseas markets strains the existing execution facilities, which were created for much lower trading volumes. Today 20% of cross-border trades fail to complete as agreed, with the attendant costs, loss of information and control; 40% of the operating costs are related to these fails. Over the last decade, operational risk has emerged as a critical challenge for financial institutions, particularly investment management firms. Operational risk can be tackled by a combination of policies, procedures and a technology platform capable of providing efficient transport of and access to transaction data.

Client support (internal)

Client support staff respond to retail and institutional client inquiries, trade requests, account changes, etc. In the context of risk budgeting, their challenges and needs are very similar to the ones faced by the operations and back-office departments. In addition, since these are client-facing situations, meaningful reputational risk exists, rendering the timely access to procedures and policies critical, while providing an event driven environment so that customers can be automatically alerted to circumstances relevant to their portfolios.

Management (internal)

Management needs information related to the firm's ability to attract and grow its asset base, the firm's compliance with internal and client-defined restrictions. In order to determine pay and commission levels, management also needs to understand the performance of its portfolio managers and liquidity providers, as well as the cost performance of its operations versus competing providers.

The transaction lifecycle

These stakeholders are part of a continuum of activities, which cover the entire life cycle of an asset management firm, as illustrated in Figure 1. The role of a technology platform is to empower the different actors throughout the value chain, whilst minimising the total costs – ie, operating and resulting risks – of doing so. In this section, we review the various activities

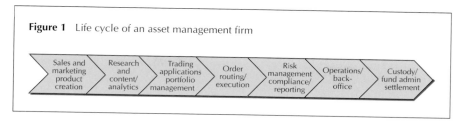

Figure 1 Life cycle of an asset management firm

taking place within an asset management firm, and try to outline some of the most critical limitations resulting from the lack of an adequate technology platform.

Sales and marketing/product creation

This sector creates investment products for various client segments, with the products promoted through direct and indirect channels (mostly brokerage firms). The rapid growth of assets under management has been mostly due to the unprecedented economic growth experienced by the United States over the last 10 years, as well as the rapid growth of 401 thousand retirement plans. This may in turn have become investment management firms' biggest challenge: their technology platforms are not capable of coping with such rapid growth, while investors' objectives and investment needs are rapidly changing. Most investment products are designed today around single classes of assets (eg, equity or fixed income), using qualitative measures (eg, value, growth). Going forward, the major challenge for investment management firms will be the ability to design cross asset class products, which provide a desired, clearly quantified risk return profile for given types of investors. Typically, the design of such products has been partially hindered by vertically designed technology platforms, able to cater to single asset classes.

Research and content/analytics

The aim here is to understand growth prospects for given companies, sectors and geographies, determine economic values of given securities/assets and calculate their sensitivity to given market variables versus projected returns. Traditionally, asset management firms have focused on providing superior research and information to their portfolio managers on given securities and companies, probably a reflection of the traditional bottom-up approach to investment followed by a significant proportion of active managers. The single security bias may have slowed down the adoption of portfolio management and order management systems, which are becoming so critical in $T + 1$ and $T + 0$ worlds, or near real-time security settlement and processing.

Trading applications and portfolio management
This sector exists to assist in the shift from single security to multi-security analysis, to construct portfolios which meet client-defined investment objectives, and to monitor the value of the portfolio's existing and potential positions. Automation in the portfolio management arena remains a significant challenge, particularly with respect to pre-trade compliance and trading cost analyses. In late 2000, most buy-side firms do not have automated pre-trade compliance capabilities – that is, the ability to assess any internal (eg, client defined) or external (eg, 5% SEC public declaration rule) before sending an order or completing a trade. When they exist, their portfolio management systems are usually single asset class capable, and hence do not provide portfolio managers with the ability to select the best available type of security in order to achieve a given investment objective.

Order management and execution
Excluding personnel expenses, commissions and direct execution costs represent the largest expense item for investment management firms. Annual expenses for direct execution costs represent, on average, 12 basis points (bp) of the assets under management, sometimes going as high as 25bp for active equity orientated firms (revenues are about 95bp of assets under management). Once assets under management exceed, for example, US$5 billion, it is likely that the portfolio management function will be dissociated from the trading and order execution function. Hence most firms are faced with a dual challenge: to properly automate the transmission of orders and executions between portfolio managers to traders as well as between traders and external execution venues (ie, broker dealers, alternative trading systems such as ECNs, etc).

Thanks mostly to third-party software vendors, firms have been able to adequately automate the order management and execution process between portfolio managers and trading staff. Unfortunately, these software products tend to be single asset-class enabled and hence may limit asset management firms' expansion beyond the mono-asset class paradigm for their product offerings. Moving on to the trader to execution venue connectivity, it is clear that, at least in the US equity markets, the acceptance of the FIX protocol[1] has helped automate the post execution process. However, it has yet to bring about similar benefits in the transmission of orders to execution venues. Traders' reluctance to electronically transmit orders to execution venues is the direct result of firms' inability to measure accurately and in real-time the transaction costs resulting from "market impact". Market impact represents the actual transaction costs resulting from a given order that impacts on an existing liquidity pool and potentially affects the price at which the transaction can be completed. Instead, traders are left with their own judgement and market timing – ie, the timing decision of sending an order to an execution venue – to determine the optimal process for executing a large order. Market impact and market timing are all but two illustrations of "indirect" execution costs, which, by some industry estimates, represent in some cases more than 80% of the true execution costs borne by an asset management firm.

The analytical framework for measuring and decomposing execution costs is well understood, thanks to the work of a number of academics and practitioners; however, the technology platforms required to measure these costs and provide recommended trading strategies have yet to be deployed. The concentration of the asset management industry will make the issue of execution costs more acute, and the solution adopted by some firms to simply close given funds to new investors cannot be a long term one. The rapid growth of Alternative Trading Systems, both in the equity (ECNs) and fixed income arenas, has multiplied the choice of execution venues, potentially easing the challenge of executing large orders. However, until consolidated order books are available, such multiplication of trading venues may lead to a fragmentation of the liquidity pools available, and further complicate the analytical and technology framework required to determine optimal trading decisions. Parallel to the rapid transformation of trading venues they have in some cases helped jump start, investment management firms are also faced with the challenge of optimising internal order flow, for example, internal order crossing, order grouping, etc. Overall, the automation of the order execution process through the more accurate determination of trading strategies, choice of venues, and measurement of "indirect" transaction costs represents one of the most significant technology and analytical challenges for investment management firms.

Risk management, compliance and reporting

As a non-leveraged financial institution, an asset management firm will pursue risk management objectives that are quite different from a sell-side firm's goals. Ultimately, a sell-side firm depends mostly on short-term financing to carry its asset inventories. A sudden change in market conditions or the firm's credit worthiness, or unexpected market losses, can lead to the firm's counterparties withholding their short-term financing, thus forcing the company into a fire sale of its assets to remain afloat.

The concept of value-at-risk (VAR) became very popular in the mid-1990s, thanks to its acceptance by sell-side firms as well as a majority of bank regulators around the world. VAR measures the maximum unfavourable change in the portfolio mark-to-market that can be expected to occur over a specific time period and confidence interval due to the movements of economic variables. Ignoring the theoretical limitations of the concept (fat tails and non-normal distributions, validity of historical data series, etc), VAR is perfectly adapted to a leveraged sell-side institution, since it provides the firm with the maximum mark-to-market loss required to be potentially covered by the firm's equity and long-term debt capital.

An investment management firm (putting aside hedge funds) is not levered; it does not live in a mark-to-market world. Rather, it operates in a relative world of spread versus a benchmark. Moreover, while sell-side firms operate in the instantaneous world of current market value, a buy-side firm will measure its performance over one or several calendar periods, which account for both past and future cashflows. In this respect, VAR should not be the primary risk indicator of a large buy-side firm. A buy-side firm needs first a measure of spread-at-risk, ie, the likelihood that the performance of a given fund or client will under-perform the relevant index or benchmark by more than a given threshold. It also needs to determine the contributions of market variables and particular securities to such potential under-performance. Although relative performance is the key measurement driver of an investment management firm, it ought not to neglect absolute exposures, and, therefore, VAR can be used as a secondary firm-wide metric to protect the firm from unacceptable levels of exposure to given market variables, geographies, sectors, etc. Such exposure levels may directly impact a given group of clients or hurt the firm's performance across a wide range of investment products, consequently affecting its ability to grow its asset base. In the risk management world, the buy-side industry should be able to benefit from the significant investments made by sell-side firms in third-party risk management applications. These applications typically offer the required underlying analytical capabilities, but tend to lack the relative value bias sought by investment management firms. On the post-trade compliance side, buy-side firms have always been aware of the need for strong compliance capabilities, for obvious reasons. The batch environment in which most of these firms operates provides an acceptable technology platform, although it is rapidly being challenged by more complex compliance rules and/or new asset classes.

Operations and back-office

Investment management firms have built strong operations and back-office platforms, which are usually well integrated into the post-execution trading process. Technology challenges in the operations arena are most likely to result from new asset classes combined with unabated growth of assets under management, which will most likely cripple existing back-office infrastructures that are still highly dependent on manual processes. Such manual inefficiencies are usually the result of the lack of connectivity between or within firms. Increasingly, investment management firms will come to realise that operations and back-office are not core to their strategic thrust, and will look to outsource these functions to independent third-party providers, thus facilitating the connectivity they need to streamline their operations departments. Improvements in technology, as well as the rapidly decreasing cost of bandwidth provided through secured IP networks, will facilitate the growth of back-office application service providers. These providers will enable investment management firms to completely outsource their operations and back-office departments, thereby avoiding the duplication of information and reducing the inefficient processes which plague today's back-office departments. As a corollary, this will also transform what has historically been a fixed cost into a variable cost, with firms required to pay a transaction charge.

Settlement and custody

A number of initiatives have taken aim at improving the notoriously inefficient settlement process, particularly in the overseas markets. Foreign investments by US investment management firms are expected to represent 15% of assets under management by 2007, versus 8% in 2000. Foreign markets are not adequately equipped to cope with this significant growth in volumes. Foreign security trading involves up to 10 different players, including two asset management firms, two broker-dealers, four global and sub-custodians as well as two agent banks. An odd combination of telex, SWIFT and various electronic means of communications are used today by these firms to complete the settlement and payment processes, with a considerable margin of error. More than 20% of foreign settlements require some form of manual correction, at significant cost for all institutions involved. A number of industry-wide initiatives, as well as new entrants, are developing solutions to improve the settlement process, and in particular to reduce the percentage of fails. These initiatives mostly leverage newly available middleware technology and help enrich the transaction – ie, add and compare the information necessary for settlement – in real-time.

Proposed framework

The previous two sections helped to define the needs of the various stakeholders in an asset management firm and outline some of the technology challenges existing within the various elements of the transaction lifecycle. In this section, we attempt to define the critical building blocks in terms of the application and infrastructure technology necessary to address those needs and limitations.

Although the various stakeholders are playing different roles and have different needs within the transaction lifecycle, we can find significant commonality in terms of the application and infrastructure technology required to define a common framework. Such a framework can be articulated around five building blocks:

❑ *Information*: providing market data (real-time, snapshot and historical), static data (fundamental, counterparty, terms and conditions), trade and position/portfolio data;

❑ *Analytics*: providing valuation, calculated exposures, performance and attribution measures, compliance parameters, limits;

❑ *Processing*: generating accounting, payment and settlement entries based on corporate actions, security events, etc, to update customer accounts;

❑ *Transactions*: providing transaction capabilities across the firm's entire value chain, from a customer changing the asset mix of his/her retirement fund, to a portfolio manager re-balancing a portfolio to account for new market developments, to a trader receiving trade execution confirmations; and

❑ *Events*: generating alerts and actions based on market-driven events (eg, stock price hitting a pre-defined target, total exposure exceeding given thresholds). Event-driven management and monitoring of all participating applications in a distributed systems environment plays a critical role in bringing together the information, analytical, processing and transaction layers outlined above.

The optimal implementation of this framework would be an environment that stores any piece of information only once, makes it available to the rest of the environment in a seamless fashion, minimises manual intervention, and enables analytical and processing engines to determine new data required by the firm's various stakeholders. Finally, the implementation of such a framework is event-driven and is capable of alerting stakeholders of relevant market events or abnormal patterns (eg, in the settlement process) likely to lead to failed trades.

On an enterprise-wide level, these five building blocks form the essence of an integrated enterprise solution that can provide the following attributes, possibly in real-time:

❑ market data and news;

❑ fundamental and securities data;

❑ valuation, risk exposures, performance and attribution;

❑ portfolio construction and optimisation;

❑ limit monitoring and allocation;

❑ pre- and post- trade compliance;

❑ notifications and updates;

❑ orders, transactions, indications of interest and delivery confirmations; and

❑ back office, settlements and accounting entries.

Underpinning such a framework is the ability to "transport" or access any kind of data (market, transaction, account, counterparty, security or events on the aforementioned) across the enterprise. This data can then be presented in a timely fashion to the relevant individuals within the firm, or externally to the firm's customers. The timeliness of such data presentation is becoming of critical importance as markets move towards T + 0 settlement and 24-hour global trading. The traditional batch world, with an end-of-day concept, is rapidly giving way to a real-time environment with no beginning and no end. Extended trading hours in the US and the rapid demise of traditional floor trading operations are only the tip of the iceberg, illustrating the complete transformation that the investment management industry, and more generally the financial services industry, will be experiencing over the next decade.

More importantly, the need for connectivity is about making the enterprise a real-time enterprise, which manages events in real-time, assesses exposures in real-time and consequently understands in real-time the usage of capital and optimal ways to allocate it. In many ways, the financial services industry played a major role in helping bring some convergence between economic and regulatory capital requirements. The financial services industry must become capable of managing in real-time how it deploys and consumes capital. Let us take the analogy of the airline industry. Ten years ago, airlines figured they could improve their bottom line by squeezing more seats in to the coach section, putting one olive as opposed to two in the business class tray, etc. Today, thanks to technology, airlines are making money by optimally managing their fleets and their seats. They can in real-time change the pricing structure on any flight based on usage factors, etc, thereby maximising the dollars they can extract from the perishable inventory. Our industry is faced with a similar challenge today, ie, the move towards a "connected" environment providing real-time capital management capabilities. After all, we have it easier than the airline industry: our inventory is not perishable the way an airline seat is. This does not mean that investment patterns will become more volatile and that portfolio managers and their ultimate clients will have more propensity to shift assets based on newly available information. It will simply create an extra layer of investment discipline and accountability both for the investment manager and the fund's fiduciaries.

The connectivity challenge will be tackled by the adoption of middleware smart technology, able to act given certain events, together with the wider acceptance of data protocols. FIX was an early illustration of such protocols. XML and many of its variations are further illustrations of the benefits offered by "tagging" data in a common reference language, so that a firm's internal or external software applications can easily exchange data and communicate smartly through event-driven messaging. Hence, an execution occurring on the Tokyo Stock Exchange would be transmitted via the common transaction protocol to the relevant back office, accounting and risk systems, etc, located in the United States, together with the corresponding events (eg, generate confirmations, payment instructions, re-calculate VAR, etc).

Financial transaction protocols are not new, they have been around for about 25 years and there are hundreds of them. Object-oriented software technology was not available when most of these protocols were developed. However, with the recent advent of object oriented software technology, it is now possible to put advanced functionality into a protocol and make the protocol object available as the protocol specification. In 2000, the development of specialised protocols is likely to accelerate, for the traditional lack of cooperation in the cold-war society of the past 100 years is rapidly being transformed by a new spirit of "coopetition", ie, cooperation among competitors. The plethora of industry consortia which characterised the first half of 2000 in most industrial sectors illustrates that, at long last, we have understood the age old prisoner's dilemma of favouring cooperation over competition, whilst staying clear of any monopolistic/oligopolistic tendencies.

Financial information technology will become more readily available with the advent of standard financial protocols, accelerating the trend towards outsourcing. Current systems are large and often proprietary with customised protocol interfaces to other systems within an organisation. Installations take years and software systems are expensive as vendors are recovering profit from the slim margins of consulting to install their products. The next generation of financial transaction servers will come from the database manufacturer with a pre-existing data model to support one or several standard financial protocols. Products which currently require custom development will be available as packages from vendors. Improved interconnectivity between IT systems will lead to wider sharing of business intelligence inside the organisation with reduced costs. The applications of such standard universal financial protocols (UFP) would be multiple, as illustrated below.

❑ A new regional electronic exchange is set up in Nagasaki. The exchange purchases a computer and a database software package with an order match system. They connect this system to the secure Internet and because the database server has UFP compliance, they are ready to do electronic business with any registered institution in the world. Not only are orders and reports processed, but clearing records, quote data and corporate actions are also managed by the protocol.

❑ The same regional exchange purchases a UFP compliant market surveillance system which they plug in and install with their order match system. This comes on line within one week of the purchase date.

❑ A new listing is to occur on this exchange. The institution makes their balance sheet and other such information available to the world financial community via the UFP protocol. The IPO time is reduced by four months.

❑ An asset manager in San Francisco buys a UFP compliant FOREX dealing system and plugs it in. After configuring their server, they are able to participate fully in several of the existing FX consortia virtually overnight.

❏ An investment management house in Chicago wishes to change back office/clearing partners due to excessive charges. They simply change their UFP-compliant interfaces to point to another clearing firm and they are on-line in less than two days.

❏ A bank in Paris has 20 offices in various cities in the world. They pay a huge cost for telecommunications to maintain a private secure network for order/report transactions when some offices are submitting as few as two futures orders per day. The bank puts these smaller offices on the internet using a secure, UFP-compliant trading system and reduces their network overhead by 50%.

❏ An asset manager in Hong Kong wants to find a market for an exotic interest rate derivative. They put out indications of interest on their UFP-compliant database server and receive interest from firms in Madrid and Sao Paulo.

❏ A small financial engineering company in London develops a pricing model for a digital option. They make the model UFP-compliant and are able to guarantee its operation in any world financial centre without localisation for pricing bus or the local trading system.

❏ A respected London bank receives the daily transaction activity of its Singapore and Osaka offices via UFP in to a UFP compliant risk management system. Using this, they detect some dangerous trading activity and stop a potentially embarrassing event.

THE DATA CHALLENGE

Data are critical to the success of endeavours such as the risk budgeting process. Garbage in will result in garbage out. Data need to be sourced, captured, transmitted, provided in a timely fashion, enriched and, finally, stored for later retrieval.

For the purpose of providing some background, we review the critical importance of data and data management, including a comparison between the benefits of centralised and decentralised data management. We then review the different sets of data required, namely transaction, market, historical, securities terms and conditions, as well as counterparty. We determine the relevant data dependencies and data flows. Finally, we analyse the procedures and processes required to obtain and maintain clean data.

Background

With respect to data, investment management firms are faced with the following two major challenges.

1. To distribute and link effectively data they have sourced from external sources. Linking means, in particular, the firm's ability to provide the data to the user when they need it and in relation to the analysis the user

is conducting at that point. We all know that excess information is no information.

2. To maintain and store internal and external data, to allow for easy drill-down access, through multiple search criteria.

On the first point, such ability is dependent upon an event-driven technology infrastructure, which we discuss in detail in the next section. On the second point, a number of industry experts have been advocating the development of "data warehouses" – ie, central data depositories integrating the entire transaction universe of the firm – from existing legacy systems. Data warehouses became particularly popular in the mid-1990s, when firm-wide risk management projects took centre stage in most sell-side firms. The approach was to build point-to-point connections between the central data depository and a number of legacy systems which provided transaction, counterparty, securities terms and conditions, calculated data, etc. A risk engine was then "applied" to the aggregated data, helping produce firm-wide risk management numbers, and hopefully providing management with the ability to drill down and find trouble spots. This data warehouse concept was then extended to other areas of the firm. In light of rapidly decreasing hardware costs, data warehouses were seen as an elegant way to solve the never-ending reconciliation issues, the need for providing timely information, etc. Assuming that all transaction, security and counterparty data could be centralised, a number of "engines", ranging from risk engines to accounting and settlement applications, could then be applied onto the data warehouse. This would facilitate the true support of a trade life cycle, providing a paperless real-time trading and investment environment.

However, the diversity of transaction types and of the functions applied to these transactions makes it difficult, if not impossible, to develop a single database design, valid for all transactions and all functions. For example, spot foreign exchange trades and structured derivative transactions present very different characteristics in terms of data requirements. Spot trades are composed of a small, well-defined number of data elements. Spot trading operations are usually high volume operations, and, as a result, spot trades will require a product driven database, specialised by product type, which allows for high throughput. On the other hand, structured derivative trades are composed of multiple components, not always known in advance; trading volumes are usually very low. An efficient database for such products would need to be component driven, allowing for the easy definition of new transaction types. As this database would not be product driven, it would not usually offer any acceptable scalability for high volume trading environments.

More importantly, the very concept of data warehouses created a hub and spoke system, adding new unnecessary data exchanges. Going back to the airline analogy, the hub and spoke system has definitely been great for the airline industry, but it has been a disaster for the passengers. Data warehouses, which attempt to bring together heterogeneous data and analytical functions, are not a natural way to address the data flow and integrity issues faced by most investment management firms today. For the purposes of clarity, heterogeneous data designates data with different purposes – for example, back office for spot FX versus valuation for over-the-counter derivatives. Heterogeneous data does not mean data representing the same information – eg, a future earnings estimate for a company presented in different formats by various vendors.

Data can be categorised in four subsets, which are covered in the next four sub-sections.

1. Real-time prices and content, market-moving news such as changes in earnings estimates, issuance of research report, etc.
2. "Static" data, including securities terms and conditions, historical data, company information, counterparty data, client data, firm and client defined limits (eg, market, credit, settlement).
3. Trade and position information.
4. "Computed" data, including, for example, performance measurement, risk measures, valuations, payment amounts, etc.

Real-time data

Investment management firms rely essentially on data vendors for all of their real-time market data, which includes news and editorial content, economic data, prices and index values. Regarding prices, for a data vendor it may be as simple as receiving a feed from a given stock market, although the volume growth experienced by US markets in the late 1990s put serious strains on market vendors' ability to provide "tick by tick" price updates to their clients. This led to the development of technology that enabled vendors to provide real-time updates with a lower frequency. Another important aspect of real-time data for an investment management firm is the access to "transacted" prices, ie, prices at which transactions have been completed. Such transparency has existed in the equity markets for quite some time. The appearance of alternative trading venues, commonly referred to as ECNs in the equity markets, created additional opportunities and headaches for both vendors and investment management firms. On one hand, these ECNs made it easier and cheaper for the ultimate investor to get access to the order book, ie, all of the existing bids and offers behind the current market. On the other hand, due to the absence of an integrated order book, it created situations where a single security could have different prices at the very same instant. Although it has been changing rapidly since the beginning of 2000, the situation is slightly different in the fixed income market. Until the turn of the new millennium, the bond markets were essentially traded over-the-market, ie, with no central trading places. Hence, data vendors needed to secure the participation of either broker dealers, inter-dealer brokers agreeing to contribute price quotes on given securities, or end of day prices allowing index calculations. Initiatives announced in late 1999 and early 2000 regarding the launch of electronic trading market places for fixed income securities, in some cases sponsored by some of the largest bond dealers in the world, will create, if they succeed, significant transparency in the bond markets. They will also provide readily available actual transaction prices, based on executed trades. Such transparency may encourage more active participation by retail investors in the bond market. A similar trend can be observed in the foreign exchange markets. Price information is based on quotes contributed by bank participants. Although the inter-bank market has been run totally electronically in two market places since the early 1990s, it has not yet provided the pricing transparency, which characterises the equity markets. Price quotes are readily available, yet executed prices in the inter-bank market are not. The formation of foreign exchange consortia in early 2000, open to banks, corporations and institutional investors, is likely to bring to the foreign exchange market the pricing transparency it has lacked until now. Finally, less liquid or more esoteric markets (eg, over-the-counter derivatives) are less likely to experience such a rapid trend towards increased price transparency. Over-the-counter transactions are usually more complex, involving a larger number of attributes than fixed income or foreign exchange transactions. Attempts to create market places for these types of transactions are not likely to succeed in attracting the volumes necessary to create real-time pricing transparency. Clearly, most of these over-the-counter transactions can be valued using analytical libraries and more readily available market data. In any case, investment management firms are not always able to electronically source all of the market data they need, and therefore require manual processes to capture required data such as volatility, corporate spreads, etc.

In this context of such rapidly changing nature of real-time data and the growing availability of real-time "transacted" data, what are the main real-time data challenges for an investment management firm?

First and foremost, data cleanliness is of paramount importance, particularly in the context of trading decisions and end-of-day pricing for net asset value calculations. Although most market data vendors check the real-time data they provide to spot any excessive movement from one observation to the next, investment management firms may implement similar checks, at the very least in the context of end-of-day pricing.

Second, investment management firms need to implement application software and middleware technology able to leverage real-time data and events, and link them to the firm's existing orders, trades and positions. Without such ability, a firm cannot really leverage the information it receives in real-time. The widespread adoption of digital market data platform in during the 1980s and 1990s has facilitated the integration of real-time data and news into third-party and in-house software applications. Such integration must now be taken to a new level of intelligence. The need to link information to the firm's existing market activities is another illustration of the potential offered by an event-driven technology platform. A portfolio manager needs to see in real-time or near real-time which of his/her portfolios are potentially impacted by a given market event. Similarly, they need to be able to link market events to investment decisions. A simple example would be a change in a given market variable triggering a given transaction order. A more complex one would be a major news story about a given country activating the computation of a market risk exposure calculation, and then, if necessary, providing recommendations for lower such exposure. Moving into more futuristic territory, the application could then "learn" to relate given patterns of events to potential adverse market movements. In recent months, smart agents on the internet, which search for the best price on a book or a given auction, have become particularly popular. It is likely that such smart agents will take an important role in asset management firms, which are constantly struggling to cope with the floods of information they receive on a daily basis. On this last point, recent initiatives to form information "exchanges" – ie, a market place where an investment management firm subscribes to which Wall Street research it receives – will further clear analysts' and portfolio managers' desks.

Third, as mentioned earlier, not all data are captured electronically and therefore require the operation of manual processes and procedures. This will always remain the Achilles' heel of any financial institution, as manual processes are prone to error and fraud. A lot has already been written about the need for independent verification of the data, which we do not need to reiterate here. We argue for a more drastic approach: namely, all market data used by an investment management firm should be sourced externally and captured electronically. Such an approach will help investment management firms to systematically review their data need and force them to streamline the number of providers they use for market data.

Static data
We have also included in this category non-transaction data, which do not change with the same frequency as the real-time data we have previously covered.

Client and counterparty information
Once entered, this data should remain fairly static. However, it needs to be monitored as the situation of given clients or counterparties may change. This has a significant impact in terms of tax treatment, compliance rules

and suitability criteria in the case of clients, and limits in the case of trading counterparties. The biggest challenge investment management firms face in this area is the unification of the client and counterparty data. Too often, data are duplicated and triplicated, leading to clerical errors with potentially dramatic consequences.

Security terms and conditions
The universe of traded securities, when one includes both equities and fixed income, reaches into the millions of individual securities. Each of these securities may require more than 400 fields to fully define it. Investment management firms have long ago decided to outsource the provision of such data. Two major issues remain: the procurement of such data and the handling of corporate actions such as new issues, right issues, splits, calls, etc. Regarding procurement, a small number of large vendors is now capable of supplying complete securities terms and conditions, if not for the entire universe covered by a given investment management firm, then for large segments of it. In addition, several of these vendors now offer products combining security terms and conditions with historical time series, which can be deployed at a customer site, thereby facilitating local access to the data. In practice, an investment management firm can procure all the security terms and conditions it needs from, usually, no more than three data vendors. The challenge is then to make such information readily available to the firm's various stakeholders in need of it, including research analysts, portfolio managers, risk management and compliance people, and back-office staff. In our experience, whilst they spend significant money procuring the securities data they need, investment management firms too often do not invest adequately in making it easily available to their users, leading to duplicate efforts and inefficient procedures. Regarding corporate actions, investment management firms are dependent upon the automation efforts of a number of industry players, including custodians and agent banks. A number of initiatives, by both these industry players and technology providers, are taking aim at automating the corporate action process, which, because it follows a series of serial steps involving many players, is prone to errors and delays.

Historical data
Historical data play a central role in the risk management world. Most risk management theories depend heavily upon historical data, either directly in the case of historical simulations, or indirectly in the case of Monte Carlo simulations or the variance/covariance methodology. Whilst historical daily price data on US stocks going back 10 years can be found from at least 100 different reliable sources, the same cannot be said for data as apparently simple as corporate spreads, or fixed income security prices in emerging market countries. Part of the problem resides in the lack of

central marketplace for the trading of these securities, as discussed in the previous section. Additionally, in the case of some securities, prices may not be available simply because no trade took place on a given date. Some trades may have taken place but, due to poor liquidity, prices may not be representative of the market. An example the reader will easily relate to is the price behaviour of US equities in after-market trading. Due to poor liquidity, these prices do not always reflect actual market conditions and would taint the quality of a historical data series. Over the past five years, data vendors have significantly improved their offerings, which include cleaning the data and providing simulation algorithms which can "fill" a time series when no data has been observed. It is also likely that the development of transparent marketplaces for instruments ranging from foreign exchange to fixed income and derivatives will help create sources of readily available historical data series. Finally, as described in the "Computed Data" section below, any risk management model needs to select the market variables it will use wisely and carefully, and use these variables as a reference system against which all other transactions will be valued and analysed. The availability of clean, reliable historical data series should also play a role in the selection of these variables.

Company information
Regulatory decisions in the second half of 2000 suggest that public companies in the United States are now obliged to disclose any material information to all investors at once. Such a decision is likely to put an end to the cosy relationship that has existed until now between Wall Street firms and the public companies they cover. At the same time, pressure from investment management firms is likely to lead to the unbundling of the industry value chain, which until now has meant that research was implicitly paid for by commission dollars. These two complementary trends mean that company information, whether generated by company officials or by research analysts, will become more standardised and more accessible on a "pay per view" basis. Such standardisation and accessibility will facilitate the incorporation of company data (internal and external) into the investment management firm's internal information Web, valuation models, etc. It will facilitate the retrieval and indexing of company data as well as its linking to other data elements (eg, real-time prices, news, etc).

Order, trade and position data
Order, trade and position data represent the central nervous system of the investment management firm. This data affects all stakeholders in the enterprise and is intimately dependent upon client/counterparty information, as well as all the static data discussed in the previous section.

Throughout the day, a portfolio manager needs to possess the following information for each of the portfolio they are managing.

❑ Cash position and cash requirements, based trades which have yet to settle, fund redemptions and new cash invested in the fund. In most cases today, since firms do not operate in real-time, the portfolio manager will usually see a start of day cash position that reflects new cash invested one or two days earlier.

❑ Descriptive information for each position, including security name, symbol, company name, country of issuance, security industry code and number of shares held.

❑ The same descriptive information for each pending (not sent to traders yet), open (sent to traders, not filled yet) and filled order, as well as quantities remaining for be filled.

❑ Financial information for each position (possibly combining pending orders) including price, market value, risk indicators, performance indicators and weight in portfolio.

❑ Compliance indicators, if applicable.

Such information brings together transaction data, client data and static information, and usually presents a significant challenge for investment management firms. As importantly, drill-down and powerful selection capabilities must be made available so that portfolio managers can review the positions of various funds in a number of ways. For example, a portfolio manager may want to look at all pharmaceutical holdings across all growth funds they are currently managing. They may want to determine the total number of shares for a given security they are holding on behalf of tax exempt US clients, or understand the total foreign exchange position a given fund holds in euros, etc.

For most firms today, such position and order information is not available in real-time, meaning that portfolio managers need to wait for the next day to receive end-of-day information, based on the previous day market closing prices. It is likely that the winning firms will be the ones deploying real-time, event-driven infrastructure and application technology, providing their portfolio managers with up-to-the-minute position information, enabling them in term to make optimal investment and hedging decisions.

Computed data

The extent and the complexity of the data that an investment management firm needs to compute on a daily basis illustrates the massive challenge they face in providing the firm's stakeholders with the information they need. Rather than provide a summary listing of the different data sets which need to be computed across the transaction life cycle, including valuation, risk, performance, compliance, etc, we choose to look in more detail at the issue of performance measurement

The firm's stakeholders need to understand how a portfolio and its manager have performed relative to a benchmark and be able to identify where the portfolio and its manager strayed from objectives. Detailed calculations of geometrically chained daily returns of individual securities and mea-surements of portfolio performance allow an investment management firm to measure portfolio performance relative to its assumed risk, to the com-position of its asset class and investment style, or to other portfolios within a peer group. Once measured, performance may then be decomposed and attributed to a combination of manager skill as well as to specific risk expo-sures and factors.

Because performance attribution forms the cornerstone for change by determining the acceptability of past investment decisions, a performance measurement and attribution system must enable the firm's portfolio man-agers to measure and compare a portfolio against a broad market index, a style index, a custom benchmark or any other user-defined portfolio. Associated sources of return may then be quantified by allocating total return according to a portfolio's exposure to a number of risk factors. Such returns are usually measured within the context of a multi-factor index model. The manager may also customise performance analysis by link-ing/delinking certain accounts to model portfolios. Model portfolios may be created on multiple levels. For example, the investment management firm should be able to create a model country portfolio from all securities linked to a country-of-issue, create a regional portfolio from a list of coun-tries, or create a global portfolio from a list of regions.

Before a portfolio manager can attribute performance to manager skill or to specific factors, performance must obviously be measured. The first step in performance measurement is to calculate a portfolio's rate of return. Sur-prisingly, such calculation can depend on a very large number of variables. It should be possible to calculate returns on any of the following bases:

❑ pre-tax;
❑ post-tax ;
❑ per period;
❑ cumulatively;
❑ including absolute, time-weighted, or square-weighted cashflows and management fees
❑ excluding absolute, time-weighted, or square-weighted cashflows and management fees;
❑ including principal and accrued or realised income; or
❑ excluding principal and accrued or realised income.

Additionally, in order to comply with *AIMR Performance Presentation Standards*, performance measurement must provide the following return-calculation functionality. The list below may not be exhaustive, but it does illustrate the complexity of the task.

1. The ability to include realised and unrealised gains plus income in total return.

2. The ability to time-weight rates of return.

3. The use of accrual accounting method for securities that accrue income. Inclusion of accrued income in the market value calculation of the denominator and the numerator.

4. The use of beginning of period weightings for asset weighting of composites.

5. The inclusion of returns from cash and cash equivalents held in portfolios. Cash and cash equivalents included in portfolio amount (total assets) on which return is calculated.

6. The ability to value portfolios at least quarterly, with periodic returns geometrically linked.

7. The ability to value performance after the deduction of trading expenses (e.g. broker commissions and SEC fees), if any.

8. The ability to calculate return results on an actual basis and a restated "all cash" basis" for portfolios using leverage to purchase securities.

9. The ability to restate leveraged accounts to "all cash" when computing composite return for a composite that consists of externally leveraged and non-leveraged accounts (eg, securities on margin).

10. The ability to separate and subtract taxes on income and realised capital gains from results.

11. The maintenance of all documents that are necessary to form the basis for or demonstrate the calculation of the performance or rate of return of all managed accounts that the advisor includes in a composite (current and historical performance results).

12. The recognition of taxes on accrual basis.

13. The ability to calculate equal-weighted composites in addition to, but not instead of, asset-weighted composites.

14. The ability to use accrual accounting for dividends (as of the ex-dividend date).

15. The ability to include accrued interest in market value calculations in both the numerator and denominator for all periods (although inclusion is only required after the applicable implementation date).

16. The ability to value portfolios on a daily basis as well as at any other time when cashflows and market action combine to materially distort performance.

17. The ability to incorporate trade-date accounting.

18. The ability to incorporate cash basis accounting.

19. The ability to adjust calculations to reflect non-discretionary capital gains.

20. The ability to calculate benchmark returns using actual turnover in the benchmark index.

21. The ability to calculate a total rate of return for a composite without adjusting tax-exempt income to a pre-tax basis (for returns presented before taxes).

The list above is clearly not intended to discourage the reader from getting involved in this industry. Rather, its purpose is to show the nuances and the complexities which go with calculating data – in this case for the purpose of measuring and attributing performance, two essential ingredients to the risk budgeting process. Fortunately, accepted standards, such as the AIMR ones in the United States, have greatly simplified the basic performance calculations.

Risk measures present similar, albeit slightly different challenges. For a large money management firm, trading in multiple markets and holding positions in a large number of individual securities and currencies, the major challenge resides in the market representations of these positions. More precisely, it is not practical to measure jointly the risk of, for instance, 5,000 different securities, as it would require a 5,000 by 5,000 covariance matrix which would prove unmanageable and most likely meaningless. Instead, one needs to define a manageable number of market variables, against which the behaviour of each security and position will be represented. The problem is then greatly simplified, as the number of "factors" is reduced significantly. In the interest rate markets, this technique is known as principal component decomposition, whereby the likely movements of a given yield curve, eg, the US Treasury curve, is represented by its three variables, which happen to be close to a parallel, tilting and flexing of the yield curve. The approach can then be expanded to a multi-currency interest rate and debt portfolio. In the equity markets, a number of analytical software vendors provide these multi-factor models, including the "weights" of given equity securities against these market variables. The simplest form of such models is the well-known Capital Asset Pricing Model, where the equity Beta represents the weight of the securities. More complex multi-factor models are widely used by a majority of money management firms. The attribution of a portfolio's performance is also based on the same factors, providing the firm's stakeholders with a cohesive risk return analysis of the portfolio. If adequately chosen, these factors will provide insights into the portfolio's exposure to given sectors, currencies, countries, etc. Naturally, one needs to be aware that such reduction techniques clearly reduce the granularity of the analysis.

Such sophisticated multi-factor analysis does not eliminate the need for more traditional risk measures, such as positions generating the largest absolute and relative exposure, under various scenarios, including both VAR and user-defined scenario approaches.

THE FIRM OF THE FUTURE[2]

Background
Over the last two decades, hardware and software technology has progressed in leaps and bounds, affecting all facets of trading and investment

businesses, from front-office trading to back office application and operations. This rapid technological evolution has helped to transform trading and investment businesses, providing, for example, powerful analytical tools to traders and portfolio managers, improved position monitoring capabilities to risk managers, easier access and manipulation of data to back-office personnel, etc. Yet, despite massive technology investments over this same period, trading and investment businesses remain very paper intensive. Throughout the entire trading and investment process, from the origination of the order to the settlement of the trade, paper tickets, paper confirmations, faxes, etc, clog the desks of trading staff, portfolio managers and operations personnel. In the case of non-domestic investments, the complexity increases several fold, with some trades requiring more than 21 "touches" or manual interventions. "Reconciliations" between overlapping systems, multiple system interfaces laboriously developed between front-office trading tools, middle-office risk applications and back-office systems, double trade entries, correction of errors, etc, remain common-place in many firms, including the most sophisticated. In nearly all cases, these inefficiencies result from inadequate systems' infrastructure, itself typically the consequence of unfinished or failed systems projects. In fact, the marketplace is littered with half-completed software projects, which failed to achieve the original objectives, yet often cost twice the initial budget. In the worst case scenarios, institutions may have bought or developed a software application for some of its front, middle or back office activities, and eventually have given up implementing it, writing off the entire software cost.

Setting the stage

The general backdrop for the inadequacy of solution sets offered by technology does not lie in the technology itself, but rather in its execution through a consistent set of parameters combined with an overall business and technology vision. The major issue lies in the piecemeal approach adopted by most firms without the necessary architectural vision. Almost too often, the firm adopts a tactical approach, which limits the scope of possibilities available to it after rollout. Admittedly, a number of environmental and internal factors hinder the realisation of comprehensive solutions, including legacy infrastructure, urgent deadlines resulting from regulatory demands, etc. Ultimately, however, the sporadic, intermittent systems implementation effort is more a symptom of the disease rather than the disease itself. The disease is the absence of a structural foundation and framework.

The key to this impasse is not in the adoption of the latest and greatest technology, but rather in a comprehensive approach to rationalising workflow, tasks and processes, combined with a change in the firm's culture at all levels of the organisation. To this effect, the firm must first take stock of the limitations inherently existing in its current processes and technology. This signifies an ability to render a faithful representation of its operating procedures and guidelines, portraying the functional aspects of each of the components that provide the necessary set of business deliverables. In other words, the firm must be able to define and justify the use of specific software solution sets available to the firm's stakeholders. Additionally, the firm should be able to demonstrate the relevance, utility and timeliness of information for any business or operational decision. The second area of focus for the firm is the pursuit of an objective self-assessment against the backdrop of its industry and competitors. By generating a view of industry trends and developments alongside its own position, stature and market share, the firm is then, ideally, able to devise a strategic framework and vision for itself. These two steps, when taken in close conjunction, provide answers to the questions: "where are we now?" and "where do we want to be in the future?". The firm can then set the path that it must adopt to achieve its objectives.

Four key areas of need require thorough investigation in order to define the optimal functional and technological path to pursue.

1. *Data requirements*: real-time, snapshot and historical.
2. *Information requirements*: research, analytics, pricing histories, quantitative and qualitative assessments.
3. *Workflow requirements*: transaction processing, information flows, reporting.
4. *Enterprise component requirements*: business and functionality units within the enterprise, sequencing of tasks and processes.

The enterprise requirements may then be defined according to these requirements along the five key axes discussed in the first section, namely information, analytics, processing, transactions and events.

Proposed framework

Figure 2 represents a proposed functional and technology framework for an investment management firm. This iteration is not exhaustive as the particular aspects of each individual firm will be unique. All of the components depicted in the diagram are representations of effective usage of applications in an environment common to most financial services firms. The addition or deletion of components is a factor of the precise function of the enterprise, the markets it invests in, the instruments it trades, the customers it services, etc. The relative importance of each component, therefore, would be also a function of enterprise deliverables. The figure intimates the components necessary for a scaleable, event-driven and component-based solution set for the enterprise.

In Figure 2, we have assumed that task sequencing is not serial, as the process of information dissemination is initially de-coupled from the

Figure 2   Conceptualisation and framework

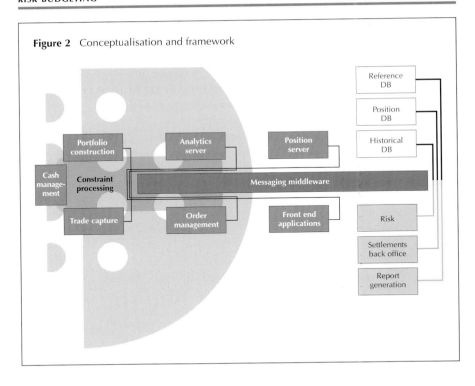

functional attributes of the components themselves. At later stages of the evolution of the solution set, sequencing becomes key in determining the appropriate attributes of the messaging infrastructure. The notes below summarise the attributes of various components for this proposed framework. They incorporate the ideals of a real-time event-driven framework, which is divorced from the specific attributes of the applications that exist on the structure.

The first group of applications provides all the analytical functions required to support the investment management decision process.

❑ *Portfolio construction*: This phase is essentially the nervous system of an investment management firm – its control module. A portfolio management system can be seen as a consolidation of smaller, more self contained components, including the following.

- *Viewing*: the display of information on funds and portfolios, as well as securities, must be at a portfolio manager's fingertips. The viewing component of a portfolio management system is responsible for providing this information in an intuitive, easy-to-use manner.
- *Ordering*: portfolio managers need to place orders for a single portfolio, as well as place orders to be allocated to several portfolios.

Orders should also be generated automatically when a portfolio is re-balanced against a model. Re-balancing is an overlapping function of the ordering and modelling components.

- *Modelling*: a portfolio management system should be capable of comparing two portfolios, or one portfolio against a model. These comparisons are not only critical in re-balancing a portfolio, but also provide the portfolio manager with vital information.
- *Complying*: this component of a portfolio management system deals with pre-trade compliance. Before orders are sent to the trading room, certain rules must be enforced to ensure that the prospective trades will comply with regulatory, departmental and fund level requirements.
- *Performance Analysis and Risk Reporting*: analysis and summary reports, including risk and performance reporting, are necessary features of any portfolio management system.

❑ *Trade capture*: the trade capture function within the enterprise needs to be integrated into the compliance and order functions. Additionally, there should be direct access to the security reference databases. Important points to include are adequate asset class coverage, pre-trade compliance interfaces, pre-trade limit monitoring and availability, real-time pricing, trade logs, and transaction messaging. Also, real-time analytics and pricing interfaces should be incorporated.

❑ *Order Management*: this function, along with constraint processing, provides the filtration and routing framework for enterprise transactions and messaging. Components include order routing and management, pre- and post-trade compliance checks and portfolio restrictions, blocking and allocation functions. The order routing component may be further subdivided into the two following attributes: downstream connectivity to the execution venues, and standard settlement and custody interfaces.

❑ *Analytics Server*: the conceptual underpinning of this component is to ensure a common analytic framework for the whole enterprise. Ideally, this should be the sole repository of all financial libraries, native and/or custom analytics for the whole firm. Scaleable and independent of applications, its use is extended to reports, pre- and post-trade analytics, compliance, and simulations/scenarios generation.

❑ *Position Server*: the role of the position server is to provide real-time or snapshot position updates to the rest of the application suite. This must be sufficiently granular for use in any application framework, but also scaleable to provide overall views for reporting and exception monitoring. The frequency of information dissemination would be determined by the final consumer of that information.

❑ *Front-end Applications*: the front-end applications have been defined here to represent any custom views that the enterprise may wish to generate.

These could include web portals, research toolkits, broker/wholesale service utilities, intranet resources and personalised delivery systems.

❏ *Back Office and Settlement*: back-office applications provide the processing capabilities required to account for, maintain, settle and clear all transactions. Back office and settlement applications also need connectivity to a number of external applications.

❏ *Cash Management*: the last decade has seen high market volatility, significant growth in assets under management, and more active participation on the part of investors. Therefore, the ability of an investment management firm to effectively manage cash inflows and outflows can have a meaningful impact on the firm's investment management performance, particularly if the performance of markets does not remain as stellar as it has been in the last decade.

The second set of applications, *Constraint Processing*, supports trade and operational constraints applied to the enterprise, based on the transactions and order generated through the firm's analytical applications. The compliance component could include exception reporting, pre- and post-trade compliance checks for institutional or retail clients, limit modelling and monitoring. The ability to resolve these constraints across a multi-asset, multi-currency environment is essential. Another important point to note for this depiction is that an internal constraint processing system for compliance, limit management and monitoring becomes a filtration entity that, to some extent, regulates and monitors the flow and processing of information within the enterprise.

This third component, *Middleware Messaging*, is the communications infrastructure within the enterprise. Event-driven messaging, using middleware technology, is rapidly becoming an essential ingredient to the technology infrastructure of more financial services firms. Middleware technology eliminates the need for costly point-to-point interfaces between various systems performing complementary tasks. Instead, each application interfaces to the middleware messaging platform, which then ensures the delivery of the data between any two systems. Let us take the example of an investment management firm, which needs to interface 10 different applications, thus in the worst case scenario requiring up to 45 different interfaces. The use of a middleware messaging platform would reduce the number of interfaces to a maximum of 10. The benefits of such a reduction are significant, as building and maintaining interfaces between applications represents one of the most significant technology challenges faced by an investment management firm. Furthermore, event-driven messaging allows for the intelligent transport of data in real time, whether it be transaction, market data, etc. Some of the tasks that it should perform are application-to-application integration, application and process monitoring.

The fourth component of this framework, *Databases*, represents the storage of all relevant data elements. These include reference data and historical and market data, as well as transaction data. Of particular importance are the reference databases, which are ubiquitous. Their usage and interfaces are essential backdrops for the functioning of all applications. They include all static data components, including security reference data. Possible extensions of reference databases include the storage of market data both for prices as well as economic data, enriched prices, which are either proprietary to the investment management firm or independently sourced. Additional extensions include position histories and audit trails, historical performance measurements, all constraint processing rules with audit trails and exception reports (both compliance and credit), all market conventions, holiday calendars, quote and pricing conventions. The critical importance of referential databases, real-time market data and qualitative and quantitative research as ultimate sources for this information needs to be underlined. The ability of the enterprise to incorporate external data or information sources within its own environment is paramount. Consequently, the enterprise would then succeed in internalising an external protocol, while conversely allowing for the extension of this internal protocol to external datasets.

The final component, *Reporting*, provides both real-time and on-demand reports to the firm's various stakeholders. In particular, the importance of risk reporting has grown significantly over the last few years, as both management and customers are demanding more detailed information regarding potential market and credit exposures of given portfolios, funds, etc. The major challenge of a reporting infrastructure remains the ability to provide customised reporting capabilities. This includes the ability for the user to easily "drill-down" in order to gain more insights beyond aggregated data, as well as being able to easily choose the criteria they want for aggregation and selection.

This proposed framework is not as daunting as it seems. The issue lies in the enterprise generating a rational functionality-driven view of its own processes and infrastructure. That is the first step towards realising a scaleable, event-driven architecture, which addresses both business and operational requirements rather than simply achieving a specific technological level. To summarise, to achieve such objectives, the investment management firm should:

1. perform a self assessment;
2. perform a business/functionality and process requirement analysis;
3. define the enterprise's position within the industry;
4. define a strategic vision for the enterprise; and
5. choose the technology that enables this vision without hijacking it.

The resulting cultural and operational challenges are the topic of the next section.

Cultural and operational challenges

Cultural and operational challenges have a significant impact on the outcome of large complex applications. In this brand new world of Application Services Providers (ASPs) and readily available bandwidth, we are told that the difficulties of implementing complex investment management software applications will be a painful memory of the past. While there is significant truth in such a statement, one ought to also remember that such projects involve not only software application implementations, but also changes in internal practices and procedures. The points below are not provided as a comprehensive checklist, but simply for illustration purposes.

❏ *Project Objectives: agree on them before starting the implementation.* All the constituencies affected and/or involved in the process should agree on the project's objectives, ie, what will the software provide, how it will modify/affect the firm's way of doing business, which operational and procedural issues will need to be tackled, etc. There ought to be a clear understanding and buy-in of the project deliverables by the ultimate users. More often than one could think, projects fail despite a successful implementation, simply because the ultimate users have not been properly involved in the definition of the project's objectives and educated on the system's capabilities.

❏ *Senior Management: keep them involved and escalate when needed.* As we all know, senior management does not "do", it "delegates". Keeping senior management involved in the process through, for example, a steering committee which meets on a regular basis will ensure that the entire organisation remains focused on the project's success. Senior management's involvement also allows for creating a sense of urgency, especially when internal resources do not focus on the project. Escalation procedures should be clearly defined to avoid any slippage in the project schedule, building up of tensions within the project team, etc.

❏ *Project Plan: define it and stick to it.* Successful implementation should not be a function of "odds", but should be derived from a collection of "certainties", ie, well-specified steps with clearly defined and enforced delivery dates. Of course, in all cases of a software implementation, a detailed project plan will be meticulously developed using a fancy project management software package, resources will be allocated, milestones defined, dates set, etc. Unfortunately, in many cases, this carefully developed plan will not be followed in terms of defined tasks, resources, dates and deliverables. A project plan must be enforced through regularly scheduled status meetings, an "enforcer" (ie, a project manager) must be appointed, be made accountable against the project plan and be compensated accordingly. The project manager is the "owner" of the project and will ensure that the institution remains focused on achieving a successful implementation within the specified deadlines.

❑ *Product Functionality: do not dream of the "all-in-one" system.* Software products usually offer a large range of existing functionality, some of which was intended when the product was designed, some of which was not really intended but was achievable through "work-arounds". For example, a front-office trading system designed to handle derivatives transactions is cashflow-driven, as opposed to being security or CUSIP driven. The whole system's philosophy is in complete contradiction to the notion of managing an inventory of individual securities. As a result, a derivative system might offer very attractive (or seductive) analytical capabilities, and yet be completely inadequate for managing a securities trading business. An institution should not expect to stretch the use of a software significantly beyond its functionality. In most cases, these and similar work-arounds will create additional manual processes and operational nightmares which will far exceed the benefits initially sought through extending the software's "natural" functionality.

❑ *Implementation Priorities: understand the key hurdles.* Too often in our experience, particularly when dealing with firm-wide risk management applications, institutions will spend an inordinate amount of time, usually with the help of consulting firms, determining which analytical approach, risk methodology, etc, is best suited to their business needs. We cannot help but think of the case of a large bank based in Latin America which has been pondering whether Garch techniques should be incorporated within the risk system they plan to purchase and implement. They focus on a very esoteric issue, while neglecting to understand that bigger and more basic issues, such as gathering transaction data, finding historical market data and building adequate interfaces to their legacy systems, must be tackled first. The implementation of such software applications is first and foremost a boring, yet complex, data gathering process. Contrary to the assertions of many consulting firms which strive on intellectual "debates", a successful implementation is highly dependent on data issues, such as where to get the position or market data, how to get the data from system A to system B, how to reconcile data sets, etc. Theoretical debates, regarding Garch, Arch or any other acronyms, are the "icing on the cake" once the more important data issues have been resolved.

❑ *Implementation Partners: choose the right one(s).* In nearly all cases, especially when it implements a third-party software, an institution will involve outside parties in the implementation process. The track record of the third-party, its knowledge of the application, its understanding of the institution and its culture are obviously important factors. In the case of third-party software applications, some vendors devote a significant proportion of their resources to support and technical staff as opposed to sales and marketing personnel. These vendors will place significant emphasis on successful implementation and will focus on putting a system into live production within the shortest timeframes. Furthermore, some third-party software products are more turn-key and better packaged than others and this typically shows in the vendor's track record on successful implementation. Firms should not neglect this key element. A fancy software package may be exciting during a sales presentation but the ability to putting it into live production effectively is far more important.

❏ *A Process, not an Event: look for a collection of singles, not for the grand slam.* Providing a set of tangible small successes throughout the project provides management with a visible progress report and further cements the buy-in process. These "singles", achieved before moving forward, may include valuation, risk measurement, trade processing, management report generation for a specific asset class, trader, desk, currency. The alternative, waiting many months (years) before seeing any tangible results, tends to create a sense of uneasiness and impatience ("Are we moving forward? Are we on schedule? When can I see reports?"). We have seen many projects crumble as a result of this latter approach. In fact, no system solution will be perfect and will always involve compromises. It is important that an institution and its management clearly understand this point.

1   FIX is a transaction protocol used by investment management firms and brokerage houses to send electronically indications of interest, orders, and executions of equity transactions.
2   Mohammad Ahmad, Director, Reuters America Holding, contributed to this section.

Part III

Practitioners' Thoughts: Case Studies in Risk Budgeting

Risk Budgeting in a Pension Fund

Leo de Bever, Wayne Kozun and Barbara Zvan

Ontario Teachers' Pension Plan Board*

*The Ontario Teachers' Pension Plan Board ("Ontario Teachers") imple-
mented value-at-risk (VAR) in 1995. Having a dynamic and comprehensive view of the changing risks of assets and liabilities immediately
improved operational efficiency. Gradually, it also shifted management
focus from returns above benchmark to optimisation of the Fund's true
objective function: financing pensions with the lowest expected cost to
members, constrained by a limited tolerance for short-term funding deficiencies. The VAR system has turned out to be a good workhorse for dealing with short-term market risk. It has also created the vocabulary and
intuitive understanding of risk for our Board and management, which is
very helpful in explaining our exploration of the deeper long-term issues
that take us beyond VAR.*

VAR and the "Risk capital budgeting" metaphor pour old wine into new
casks. The basic ideas are the same as in portfolio theory. In an uncertain
world, pursuing opportunity for investment gain on occasion brings out its
evil twin: the risk of a loss. Using historical returns on portfolio assets,
VAR estimates, over a specific time horizon, losses one rarely expects to
exceed. Whether "rarely" means 1% or 5% of the time and is measured
daily or annually affects the scaling of VAR, but is otherwise immaterial, if
everyone uses the same definitions.

A portfolio's VAR is referred to as its "risk capital" because, like capital
in a firm, VAR is the resource put at risk. The 1% worst outcome is typically a 2.5 to 3 times multiple of portfolio volatility or standard deviation.
But standard deviation has an image problem; "in our 1% worst case we
could lose C$15 billion" packs far more punch than "the standard devia-
tion is 8.5%".

* The views expressed here are those of the authors, and should not be attributed to the Ontario
Teachers' Pension Plan Board. Many thanks to Sandy Gemmill for her able technical assistance.

Using VAR in day-to-day management requires frequent estimation and reporting of portfolio positions and portfolio risk. Faster computers and better risk software have only recently made this realistic for complex portfolios. Portfolio risk capital usage, set by management as a measure of how much capital it is willing to put at risk, can now be compared with a risk budget. The portfolio's estimated "risk capital usage" must fall within its "risk budget".

At Ontario Teachers, we adapted VAR to our long term focus. A defined benefit plan invests contributions to build up the assets needed to fund pensions, while limiting the risk that assets will fall below liabilities. So, our goal is building surplus (assets-liabilities) and managing risk of surplus loss. We express our "surplus risk" budget as the surplus loss we are prepared to absorb as the worst one in 100 annual outcome. One in 100 years may seem remote, but the same number also captures the one in 10 worst 4-year outcome, which ties in better with the regulatory requirements to test the adequacy of contribution rates every three years. Our surplus risk budget is currently 22% of assets or C$16 billion.

Surplus risk arises mostly because the risk-return characteristics of the policy asset mix do not match those of the liabilities. Active risk, created when managers hold portfolios different from the policy asset mix, turns out to be a trivial, incremental component of surplus risk. However, it occupies centre stage in the minds of most boards and determines manager rewards. In 1995, Teachers first attacked the active piece of the risk puzzle: setting an "active risk budget" and ensuring that managers were motivated to generate a return on their active risk allocation. Active risk budgeting appealed to managers because it eliminated a lot of detailed risk controls based on cumbersome and ineffective position limits. People work best when "Thou Shalt" and "Thou Shalt Not" is spelled out concisely. That's why Moses gave us Ten Commandments and not two hundred.

As we gained experience with the risk system, we realised that even marginal improvements to the risk-reward trade-off for surplus growth would be far more rewarding for the Fund than improving the return on active management risk. It would appear that actual and prospective surplus growth has improved because of a better risk management process. However, measuring this is difficult. Short-term surplus performance reflects not only management skill, but also market returns, risk fluctuations in policy asset benchmarks, changes in the structure of our liabilities, and even the policy around disposition of surplus. We have not found an answer to this serious agency problem.

Activating our VAR system immediately raised standards for operational efficiency. Accurate risk estimates depend on correct prices and positions. Execution or recording errors show up as "risk spikes". VAR also highlighted some internal inconsistencies between fund objectives and the sum of asset class objectives.

Frequent risk reporting caused a noticeable change in the role of risk in management discussions. Risk-return trade-offs were at the heart of periodic asset/liability (A/L) policy mix studies, but without "live" risk estimates to connect all asset and liability risks, each asset class manager focused mostly on his own risks and returns. Having access to current risk numbers facilitates a disciplined discussion of the trade-off between risks and return. Asset managers now routinely describe the expected outcome of various strategies in terms of active management risk. The debate is not about basis points on assets, but about return on risk. This is also reflected in the more pronounced split into "beta" portfolios implementing policy mix, and "alpha" factories aiming for return on risk.

Creating comfort with the ideas of risk correlation and diversification is the hardest part of implementing VAR risk budgeting. Before 1995, standard deviation was rarely used in polite boardroom conversation. When VAR became our risk definition, management and our Board had to share at least an intuitive understanding of the nature and arithmetic of risk. Risk is not to be exterminated like a noxious weed, yet should be treated as a scarce resource required to earn returns. Risk estimates will always be flawed and they will never add up. Risk diversification makes pension management a team sport: opportunity for risk-taking in one portfolio depends on the risk in all other asset portfolios, and on the liabilities.

One can debate whether VAR risk estimates include all relevant risks, or whether we have enough information to calculate reliable 1% estimates. Nevertheless, VAR has standardised and simplified the measurement and comparison of risk across asset classes. Emphasising its faults is like discovering iron in the Stone Age and getting complaints about rust. Yet rust and all, VAR-based risk budgeting has probably moved us from a 20% solution to a 60% risk solution. That has less to do with precise risk estimates than with frequent risk reporting and the discipline it brings to risk-return discussions. Risk budgeting is a tool, not a miracle.

VAR is not our only risk measure. For example, we use various stress tests to gauge our ability to settle mark-to-market losses on a large portfolio of equity swaps during a market crisis. In addition, we use a detailed A/L model to capture multi-period effects like mean reversion in equities, and trends in interest rates and inflation.

Viewed from the cutting edge of academic risk research, this description of how we made VAR and risk budgeting part of our organisational culture may seem like a quaint tale. However, our job was not to break new ground in risk modelling: we needed a robust risk management framework for a large pension fund. The object was not to make risk complicated (although on occasion some people thought we did that pretty well), but to make it understandable, comparable, and reliable for decision-making by professionals with varying degrees of affinity for mathematics.

ONTARIO TEACHERS

Ontario Teachers was privatised in 1990, and is a 50-50 partnership between the Ontario Teachers' Federation and the Government of Ontario. The partners have joint legal responsibility for deficiencies in funding pensions for 250,000 teachers. These pensions are indexed to inflation. Our liabilities resemble zero-coupon real return cash flows, due between now and 2080. In structure and duration, they behave like CPI-linked Real Return Bonds (RRBs in Canada, TIPS in the US, Indexed Linked Bonds elsewhere).

We value both assets and liabilities at market prices. On a financial statement basis, our assets are about C$77 billion (US$52 billion); accrued pension obligations are approximately C$63 billion (US$42 billion). Surplus is therefore C$14 billion (US$10 billion).

We expect our policy asset mix to yield long-term surplus growth (asset growth minus liability growth) of 1.3% per year, with a 1% worst-case annual "surplus risk budget" of 22% of assets. We aim to add 0.8% to surplus growth with an "active risk budget" of 3.2%. The incremental risk of active management is small.

Prior to 1990, the Fund held only illiquid, non-marketable Ontario debentures. Today, the policy mix has 60% equities, 20% fixed income, and 20% real return assets (mostly RRBs and real estate). Exposure to major currencies is hedged at 50% and, excluding 10% allocated to external non-North American equity mandates, most assets are managed internally. The Fund also has a 35% exposure to non-Canadian equity returns and it made extensive use of interest rate swaps and equity swaps to convert returns on the illiquid Ontario debentures into foreign equity returns. Derivatives also help us stay within the 25% Canadian government limit on cash investment in foreign securities.

DEFINING RISK

At Ontario Teachers we define "risk" as the loss we expect to exceed only in the 1% "worst-case" outcome. We measure daily risk from 14 years worth of historical daily return data, but quote it over an annual horizon, ie, as the one in 100 worst annual loss. Scaling of risk is not terribly important. Our choice reflects the view that only rare and persistent losses are important to a fund with an 80-year stream of obligations. In theory, pension funds should probably have a risk horizon much longer than a year. In practice, however, short-term losses get enormous attention. Besides, solvency and funding rules dictate an increase in pension contribution rates when assets fall short of liabilities on their valuation date – usually once in every three years.

Talking about risk as a one in 100 year event works well for active management risk. In discussions of surplus risk, it invites quips about being long gone when year 100 rolls around. The equity market decline in 1998 came close to creating a one in 100 running 12-month surplus loss. By year-end, surplus had completely recovered. Still, we found that some people were more inclined to question the risk system than their mistaken belief that rare events are distant events.

If the one in 100 annual loss seems too remote, think of it instead as the one in 10 loss over four years. Absolute risk increases approximately with the square root of time, so it doubles every four years. We also like to show that the one in 10 worst annual surplus loss is half the one in 100 estimate.

MOTIVATING THE ARITHMETIC OF RISK

When risk was primarily discussed during reviews of asset mix, it remained the speciality of the quants tending A/L models, so the details of correlation and diversification could be kept safely in the background. As VAR-based risk management became central to monthly strategy reviews, and was connected to incentive compensation, it had to be reasonably well understood by the Board, managers, compliance officers, auditors, legal staff, and the Human Resources department.

Initially, we made the mistake of turning the volume up a little too high on the technical parts of our risk jingle. It all worked out in the end, but if we had to do it again, we would try the "easy listening" approach outlined below. Be prepared to repeat the message. Managers and board members change, and the retention rate of new ideas fades with time. Success is near when you hear people tell you with amazement that "this stuff is starting to make sense to me".

One metaphor that seemed to help in getting the idea of portfolio diversification across was a comparison of paintings by Mondrian and van Gogh. Unlike the coloured squares in a painting by Mondrian, risk is not precisely measurable, additive and separable. Rather, risk estimates will always be imprecise, fuzzy and intertwined like the trees in van Gogh's Orchard. Therefore, we can all agree that its pattern depicts an orchard, even though we may disagree on the number of trees and branches that exist. Most arguments over risk, however, still boil down to trying to turn a van Gogh into a Mondrian.

There is a tendency to ignore portfolio risk interdependence. Yet, a portfolio that is risky by itself may be quite safe when combined with other active and passive portfolios and with the liabilities. Long real bond duration is risky by itself, but not when judged together with long duration liabilities. Having a venture capital group with a large passive asset pool within a fund is less risky than it would be on its own. Mortgages increase risk in a real estate portfolio, but that risk nets out in a fund for which nominal bonds are risky relative to its real return liabilities. Control of specific risks is of limited value unless it can be shown that it reduces surplus risk.

When it comes to the arithmetic of risk, we discovered that many smart people suffer from "financial agoraphobia", the fear of entering a risk market place bustling with numbers that only make sense if you understand squares and square roots. Some of us will do almost anything to avoid both. As one colleague put it: "I have not taken a square root in 30 years, and I am not about to start now".

Our historical full valuation method of VAR shows risk diversification at work without resorting to a great deal of maths. We simply calculate how much the Fund and any of its component portfolios would have lost on the 1% worst day, had we held it over the last 14 years. It is easy to show that the 1% worst event occurs at different times for each portfolio. The sum of the 1% worst portfolio outcome is a much larger number than the 1% worst case for the Fund, demonstrating the effect of diversification.

Formulas can be conversation stoppers. However, softened with words and examples, we have had some success (see Figure 1) in explaining how the combined risk of two individual risks of losing C$100 depends on correlation, ie, on the tendency of gains and losses to move together.

Identical risks are "perfectly correlated" and will add up in the usual way – ie, if a portfolio invested in a company's shares could lose C$100, doubling the portfolio will double the risk. Toronto Stock Exchange (TSE) stocks and Goldman Sachs Commodity Index (GSCI) commodities show no pattern of gain and loss by period. They have "zero correlation", and if one combines a TSE and a GSCI portfolio that could each lose C$100, their combined risk is less than the sum of the individual risks. Finally, if a portfolio of real return bonds with a risk of C$100 is paired with a pension obligation of the same size and duration, the gain in one will always be mirrored by a loss in the other, ie, their correlation is "perfectly negative", and their combined risk will be zero.

Ultimately, people need to be reminded that any job requires the right tools. At one time, multiplication was hard, because we used Roman

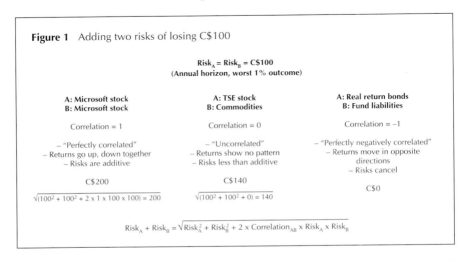

Figure 1 Adding two risks of losing C$100

$$Risk_A = Risk_B = C\$100$$
(Annual horizon, worst 1% outcome)

A: Microsoft stock	A: TSE stock	A: Real return bonds
B: Microsoft stock	B: Commodities	B: Fund liabilities
Correlation = 1	Correlation = 0	Correlation = –1
– "Perfectly correlated"	– "Uncorrelated"	– "Perfectly negatively correlated"
– Returns go up, down together	– Returns show no pattern	– Returns move in opposite directions
– Risks are additive	– Risks less than additive	– Risks cancel
C$200	C$140	C$0

$$\sqrt{(100^2 + 100^2 + 2 \times 1 \times 100 \times 100)} = 200 \qquad \sqrt{(100^2 + 100^2 + 0)} = 140$$

$$Risk_A + Risk_B = \sqrt{Risk_A^2 + Risk_B^2 + 2 \times Correlation_{AB} \times Risk_A \times Risk_B}$$

numerals. Now a child can do it, because of Arabic positional notation and its concept of zero. So, if risk requires squares and square roots, buy a simple calculator, push a few buttons and learn how it all works.

CALCULATION OF HISTORICAL VAR

VAR comes in three basic variants that differ in terms of how they combine historical information with assumptions about the future. We opted for the "historical full valuation" variant. The "historical" part of this assumption reflects reliance on historically observed outcomes, rather than on views on how the future may differ from the past. "Full valuation" refers to the fact that we take our current portfolio and calculate the change in value for all assets and for every day. We do not have to make any assumptions about distributions or correlations: whatever happened in history will be mirrored in our estimates. Our risk calculation recipe for a specific investment or portfolio is simple.

❏ Using a historical database with 14 years of daily returns, find out how much would have been gained or lost on any day over that period.
❏ Rank results from worst to best. The 1% worst day is our estimate of daily risk.
❏ To derive annual risk estimates, assume that today's return does not affect tomorrow's return. Adding two uncorrelated daily risks (which have the same size) only increases risk by a factor of 1.4, ie, absolute risk goes up with the square root of the number of time periods. There are about 256 trading days in a year. So, annual risk is $\sqrt{256} = 16 \times$ daily risk.

If an asset does not have enough daily history, we use the nearest proxy. For illiquid assets, we use liquid proxies or synthetic prices that have the right long-run volatility and correlation with other assets. This process will always remain a bit of an art. For active management risk, the risk estimation problem often arises from weaknesses in the benchmark.

Full valuation historical VAR will capture variations in return volatilities and correlations over the 14-year history. One can argue that the future could be different, but that is as arbitrary as relying on the historical estimates. With some interpretation, history is still the most indicative. Too much history can underestimate the effect of structural change in financial markets. One also finds cases where the reverse is true: the present is a close echo of the distant past.

Using a lot of history also avoids a potential conflict between risk control and investment strategy after big market moves. In 1998, a typical 250-day VAR model would have signalled a huge rise in risk. After the market fell as much as 30% in a few days, those observations became the 1% worst-case tail. To stay within risk budget, positions had to be cut. However, investment theory would argue that risk was lower after the correction.

History is not contained in 250 days of data. Our 14-year history was minimally affected by the new observations, in part because this episode had historical precedent.

SURPLUS RISK AND ACTIVE MANAGEMENT RISK

In theory, we could perfectly match the risks in our real return liabilities by investing 100% of our assets in real return bonds. However, this would make the plan expensive, because real return bonds do not typically have the 4–4.5% real return required to maintain current contribution levels.

To reduce long-term pension funding costs, we aim for "surplus growth" (asset growth in excess of liability growth) by accepting "surplus risk", or Surplus-at-Risk (SAR). Actual SAR has two components:

❑ "policy surplus risk" or "policy SAR", the risk from selecting a policy asset mix that does not match the characteristics of the liabilities; and

❑ "active management risk" or Management Effect at Risk (MEAR), ie, the risk from deviating from the assets in the policy asset mix benchmarks (see Figure 2).

Policy surplus growth objectives are set through the approval of the policy asset mix. By using conservative long-run return expectations in our policy asset mix, expected long-run policy surplus growth is 1.3%. In return, we accept a policy SAR of 22%.

Return from active management can shift the distribution of long-term surplus growth to the right, with an above average management team. Our goal is to increase surplus growth by 0.8% per annum. The MEAR active risk budget is 3.2%. These targets may seem low, but they reflect the passive bias to asset

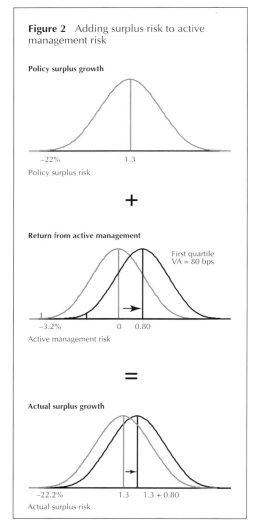

Figure 2 Adding surplus risk to active management risk

Policy surplus growth

−22%   1.3
Policy surplus risk

+

Return from active management

First quartile
VA = 80 bps

−3.2%   0   0.80
Active management risk

=

Actual surplus growth

−22.2%   1.3   1.3 + 0.80
Actual surplus risk

mix from foreign content restrictions, and perhaps the lingering perception that active risk is incremental.

Actual surplus growth is the sum of policy surplus growth and active returns (see Figure 2). These risks diversify. Assuming no correlation (which is empirically reasonable most of the time) between policy and active returns, actual surplus risk is $\sqrt{(22 \times 22 + 3.2 \times 3.2)} = 22.2\%$, which is not materially different from 22%. This conforms to the common observation that asset mix largely shapes a fund's risk profile. Active management may or may not add much surplus growth, but incremental risk is minimal.

THE LINK BETWEEN ACTIVE RISK AND RETURN TARGETS

At Ontario Teachers, our annual active management objective of 80bp includes recovery of all active and passive fund expenses of 30bp, for a net value-added target of 50bp.[1]

Surveys of active returns above benchmark for any asset class tend to show roughly a normal distributed set of outcomes, with a zero mean, before expenses. Any non-normality may simply reflect different risk constraints across managers. So, we may assume that a large sample of active managers subject to the same risk constraints will show a fat-tailed normal distribution of outcomes.

To allow for fat tails (the fact that investment outcomes tend to have more than "normal" bad occurrences), we place the 1% worst percentile at 2.6σ (2.6 standard deviations) instead of 2.33σ from the mean. We round off the top quartile to 0.65σ, and top decile at 1.3σ. Return on risk then becomes a pure number: top quartile performance equals (0.65σ/2.6σ) = 25% return on risk. Top decile represents (1.3σ/2.6σ) = 50% return on risk.

It then follows that if 80bp is a top quartile target (ie, 25% return on risk), the appropriate annual risk budget is 80/25% = 320bp. The circles in Figure 3 denote annual active management outcomes since 1992. They suggest that average active performance has been between median and first quartile over this period.

Managers and the board tend to overestimate the degree to which skill can reduce the year-to-year volatility of excess returns. Specifically, most people have trouble with the notion that first quartile managers will have losses in one in four years, a tautology if the assumptions above are more or less correct.

Figure 3 Active management risk and return

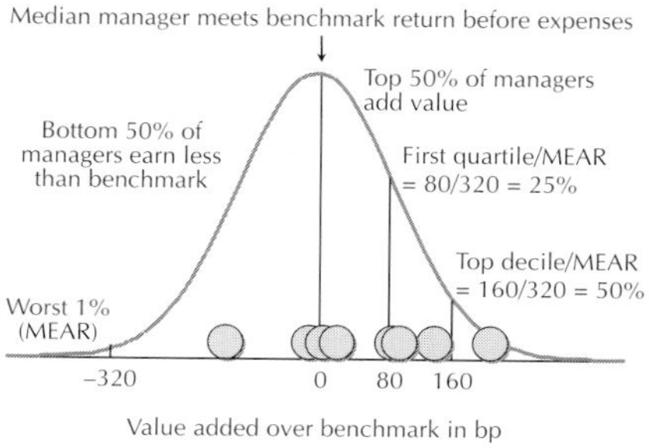

Median manager meets benchmark return before expenses

Bottom 50% of managers earn less than benchmark

Top 50% of managers add value

First quartile/MEAR = 80/320 = 25%

Top decile/MEAR = 160/320 = 50%

Worst 1% (MEAR)

−320   0   80   160

Value added over benchmark in bp

Points on normal distribution with fat tails 1% = −2.6σ, 75% = 0.65σ, 90% = 1.3σ

We also encountered initial scepticism about internal studies (since replicated by others) showing that a first quartile manager will earn less than his benchmark on 45 out of 100 decisions. Making many decisions and letting that small margin over randomness accumulate eventually builds a consistent long-term track record. However, that does not preclude long random stretches of drought, or seemingly awesome skill.

CREATING THE ACTIVE RISK BUDGET

Theory and empirical observation suggest that the risk between active programmes is largely uncorrelated.[2] There is no reason why aiming to add value with non-North American stock picks will be systematically related to attempts to beat a Canadian bond benchmark. Uncorrelated risks facilitate the construction of an *ex ante* risk budget. Nine uncorrelated programmes with risks R1 to R9 have total risk R defined as:

$$R = \sqrt{(R_1^2 + R_2^2 + R_3^2 + R_4^2 + R_5^2 + R_6^2 + R_7^2 + R_8^2 + R_9^2)}$$

Equal distribution of risk across nine active programmes would diversify at 3:1. Unequal programme size has caused us to target risk diversification of 2.5:1. If all active programmes consistently deliver a 10% return on risk at their programme level, the Fund will produce $10\% \times 2.5 = 25\%$ on its diversified active management risk budget.

Table 1 shows risk budgets for the nine programmes when the total fund had C\$60 billion in assets. Total fund risk R was set at 320bp x C\$60 billion or C\$1920 million. With a target diversification of 2.5:1, the sum of the asset class risks will be 2.5 x C\$1920 million or C\$4800 million.

Table 1 Risk budgets for nine active risk programmes

	Assets (C\$ million)	Risk/ assets (%)	Risk (C\$ million)	1st Q gross VAT (C\$ million)	Tracking + costs (C\$ million)	1st Q net VA (C\$ million)
Fixed income	8000	3	250	25.0	10	15.0
Active equities	11000	11	1225	122.5	25	97.5
Indexed equities – CDN	13000	3	325	32.5	12	20.5
Indexed international equities	12000	1	140	14.0	43	−29.0
Private capital	2500	30	750	75.0	6	69.0
Real estate	2000	28	550	55.0	7	48.0
Swap warehouse	6000		0	0.0	0	0.0
Research and economics	4500	9	425	42.5	8	34.5
Foreign exchange			175	17.5	17	0.5
Rebalancing – overlay	1000	96	960	96.0	52	44.0
Sum of assets			4800	480.0	180	300.0
Total fund	60000	3.2	1920	0.80% of assets	0.30% of assets	0.50% of assets

The sum of the gross value-added targets has to be 80bp x C$60 billion or C$480 million, and net value-added 50bp x C$60 billion or C$300 million. The net value-added target for each programme equals gross value-added minus a cost allowance.

Note that the distribution of risk and the distribution of assets need not be related. One can use a lot of risk capital (eg, in fund re-balancing) without managing a lot of assets. Few programmes can get by without any risk: "passive" and "active" are not binary choices. Programmes like Private Capital are intrinsically risky. Allocating some risk to index portfolios for "enhanced indexation" is low-level active management by another name.

RISK BUDGET STRATEGY AND APPROVAL

Once a year, the Ontario Teachers' Board and management agree on an active strategy to deliver the value-added target. The Executive Vice-President of Investments can re-allocate risk between programmes during the year. The annual allocation of active risk by asset class is revised by negotiation, in view of changes in perceived opportunity and available external or internal resources. We are aware of quantitative methods for optimisation of risk capital, but we have so far found that the quality of the inputs (manager skill, expected return) are typically not known with enough accuracy to make the exercise meaningful.

Our long-term strategy calls for more emphasis on activities that cater to our strengths (ie, cash and patience) and non-emphasis of our weaknesses (ie, visibility, large size relative to the domestic market). This means more emphasis on private capital, quantitative techniques that attempt to pick up small gains on a large base, with greater effort to gain from supplying liquidity to the market.

We avoid allocating active risk to markets like the US equity where we have no comparative advantage. A large part of our Canadian equity programme is devoted to enhanced indexation. We account for about 4–5% of TSE trading, making it difficult to look very different from the market.

More active risk is going into activities with no logical nominal capital base. This means that more active portfolios are taking on the characteristics of absolute return funds. Not all activities have a return on assets, but all activities have a return on risk. In one case, we moved assets from an active equity portfolio to an index portfolio in the same asset class. That left the active portfolio manager with a zero notional base, free to focus on investing in stocks he strongly prefers, and shorting stocks he profoundly dislikes (by borrowing from the index portfolio).

MONITORING ACTIVE RISK

The annual plan assumes that all portfolios contribute a 10% return on allocated risk to the aggregate value-added target. Managers must therefore generate a return on their risk budget, whether they use it or not. The

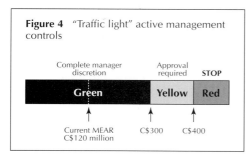

Figure 4 "Traffic light" active management controls

objective is return. The risk budget is both the resource and the constraint.

Risk is generally reported with a lag of about one day. A simple green, yellow, red zone control system has been in place from the beginning to measure compliance. Figure 4 assumes a manager with a risk budget of C$300 million. His "green zone", running from C$0 to C$300 million is where the manager is free to take positions, as long as the estimated 1% worst annual loss on the portfolio is less than C$300 million. Current risk usage in the example is C$120 million, well within the green zone.

The "yellow zone" stretches 33% above the upper green risk limit to C$400 million. Operating in this range requires concurrence of the next level of management. Managers are expected to operate near the yellow zone most of the time, indicating full utilisation of allotted risk. Hitting the "red zone" requires a pullback, and results in an exception report to the CEO and the board of directors.

SURPLUS MANAGEMENT ISSUES

Our ongoing research focuses on the following four factors, which could lead to a better decision process around the surplus risk-return trade-off:

1. improving on asset mix as a way to set the size of the surplus risk budget;
2. incorporating prospective rates of return in optimising return on surplus risk;
3. finding better benchmarks; and
4. surplus disposition policies.

Policy asset mix does not define a constant risk budget. The surplus risk budget is set through the choice of asset mix, ie, the assumption is that the policy portfolio is made up of asset classes with benchmark returns that have a constant standard deviation. Recently, technology stocks have become a more pronounced component of many country indexes, including Canada's TSE300. These stocks are volatile, so some market indexes have become more volatile. Our 30% allocation to Canadian equities is so large that a more volatile TSE300 has increased surplus risk without a change in asset mix. This suggests that fixing policy asset mix is not sufficient to fix surplus risk.

The pay-off from taking surplus risk changes with expected returns. Our policy asset mix and its 22% estimated surplus risk budget were derived using a vector of long-term historical returns with a conservative equity premium.

This implies that the starting point does not matter, although A/L models do make allowances for equity mean reversion and interest rate trending. However, we have just experienced 10 years of incredible surplus performance, and there is evidence that 10-year prospective equity returns are negatively correlated with the starting P/E ratio. This suggests that the starting point does matter. The 10-year expected return on equity risk may not be as high in 2000 as it was in 1992, so 65% equities and 22% surplus risk may not be optimal.

Poor benchmarks can induce the wrong behaviour. The quality of the split between surplus and active management risk depends on appropriate benchmarks. A good benchmark matches the key risk and return characteristics of the assets being judged. Some assets do not have natural benchmarks. If a unique asset reduces surplus risk, but is measured against a poor market benchmark, estimated active management risk would be high. If the manager then tries to reduce his active risk, he may end up increasing his surplus risk. Illiquid assets (private capital, real estate) will have volatile short-term performance against almost any benchmark. This is less a risk issue than a matter of making sure those good strategies are given enough time to work.

Surplus disposition policies have a larger impact on surplus risk than policy asset mix. Asset-liability modelling typically assumes that surplus gains in good years are used to reduce contributions or build up surpluses to buffer bad years. In practice, most North American funds have used surpluses to improve benefits or take contribution holidays. Benefit improvements increase the future rate of return required to create the benefits for future members that were funded with surplus for existing members. Combined with the ageing of most funds, this has dramatically raised the risk that surplus losses will trigger contribution increases over the next ten years.

SYSTEMS IMPLEMENTATION

Selecting a good risk engine is important, but about 70% of implementation consists of building links to other systems to extract the required inputs: investment positions and prices, and derivative contract details. It helps that 90% of our assets are managed internally, and that we receive daily feeds from external managers on their activity.

These are not turn-key risk systems: some customisation will typically be required. Vendor flexibility and support should therefore be given prominence in system selection. Most risk systems run on dedicated Sun hardware under Unix. New PC-based systems may better fit organisations with no other Unix applications. The emerging service bureau approach (ie, "give me your positions and I will calculate your risk") could make VAR faster and easier to implement.

At Ontario Teachers, system design and implementation was a joint effort between the Research and Economics group within Investments,

MIS, and our Finance department, which independently reports the risk numbers. To foster acceptance of VAR as a management tool, we carefully avoided the "risk police" syndrome. Risk management needs support from senior management, but it lives by acceptance from the entire organisation.

Since this was one of the first applications of VAR to pension management, it took us about a year to work out the conceptual kinks and to optimise for the large amount of historical data we are using. We then operated the system for a year on a *pro forma* basis. One could accomplish all of this today in less than a year.

SO... DOES IT WORK?

The risk system has been in use for about four years at Ontario Teachers and is generally working well. Unexpected changes in active management risk often flag operational errors, or a structural change that requires attention. Measuring risk initially seemed to make managers risk adverse. But this effect fades over time.

No risk system is immune to gaming (eg, using high intra-day risk, but returning to the green zone by the close of business), but this has not been a major problem. There is a lot of healthy debate on proper ways of defining risks for illiquid assets or instruments without a good historical record. A lot of work remains to be done in areas like credit risk, and better representation of equity risk factors.

A risk system usually starts with a focus on numbers, systems, controls and reporting. It should instead be mostly about strategy, alternative structures and finding better risk-return trade-offs. Using risk management to control "those cowboys in investment" is a waste of potential.

Risk management should encourage a discussion on the big issues: surplus, surplus risk and surplus return. You are likely to find that some of the traditional ways of thinking about asset mix, benchmarks and active management need updating. Pension funds say that they manage surplus return (a very tricky problem), constrained by surplus risk (very large). But instead they worry most about beating active management benchmarks (which is conceptually easy) and active management risk (very small).

Measuring risk initially shocks people because of the size of the numbers involved. Yet, the measuring of risk does not create it, and recent market volatility attests to the reality of risk. We hope that, over time, risk measurement reduces the emphasis on short-term outcomes. Pension strategies should be about what happens in the long run: anything less than four years is meaningless. For surplus, that period is likely to be longer.

VAR-based risk management and the discipline of the risk budgeting process is a good tool, not a panacea. It has turned portfolio theory into a useful investment management tool. It is old wine in new casks, packaged to sell well in a broader market.

1   About half of the 10bp of direct costs relate to the 10% of assets that are externally managed. Another 10bp is the cost of obtaining foreign indexed equity exposure through derivatives. The remainder covers internally managed assets, re-balancing, custody and governance.

2   The major empirically important exception is tactical asset allocation shifts in the weight between equities and fixed income.

12

Risk Budgeting with Conditional Risk Tolerance

Michael de Marco and Todd E. Petzel

Putnam Investments and Commonfund Group

Too many of the most critical assumptions made by plan sponsors are so deeply imbedded in the organisation's investment philosophy that trustees and investment staffs no longer consider questioning them. This is potentially a very costly oversight. "Risk budgeting" is a management tool for planning and controlling investment fund decision making. The immediate benefit is a clarification of the assumptions that drive an investment's thinking. The process activates a re-examination of each and every key assumption underlying the fundamental policy decisions and strategy for the investment fund. By explicitly accounting for the need and appetite for risk, portfolios may be optimised for long-term performance.

There are many dimensions to this challenge. The right definition (and therefore measurement) of the fund's objective, the validity of benchmarks, and the dichotomy of skill versus luck in the assessment of asset managers' performance are just some of the topics touched on in this chapter. There are lessons from behavioural finance and the trading in derivatives that may shed light on each of these areas. The principal focus of this chapter, however, is an exploration of the hidden assumptions surrounding risk-taking and risk tolerance.

A conceptual model is developed that brings together considerations of opportunity, skill and conviction for conditionally setting suitable levels of risk for an investment fund. Change in risk-taking philosophy will ultimately come from two sources: the importance of the investment fund to a sponsor's achievement of its overall organisational objectives and the way in which policy makers and strategic decision makers are rewarded for their successes and their failures. This is where consideration of investment horizons becomes critical.

The chapter concludes with a brief introduction to the core principles of risk budgeting, with an eye towards developing a risk budgeting menu and an appropriate tool kit for executing decisions consistent with this process. The chapter closes with a discussion of how risk budgeting may be used to augment conventional asset allocation.

PLANNING AND CONTROL TOOLS

Well-managed investment funds are structured around a three-part framework: an investment policy and philosophy, a strategic plan with a liability analysis and a tactical or operating plan. Generally, the investment policy is revised infrequently, the strategic outlook is generated in three to five-year cycles with annual tune-ups, and the tactical plan is prepared annually with a one-year horizon. Investments are made with expectations for returns and risk over a specified time horizon. Yet the compensation of key decision makers and the evaluation of investments are usually made explicitly in terms of current-year returns, and only implicitly, if at all, in terms of risk.

This loose and often faulty linkage of return, risk and time horizon can result in illogical decisions during episodes of high market stress. What seems like an obvious course of action from a three-day perspective, looks irrational with the hindsight gained from a three-year perspective. Short-term risk events trigger high-cost portfolio shifts with very long-term consequences, as market conditions reverse course. Steps should be taken to minimise this short-term focus and potentially destructive behaviour.

Virtually all business and non-profit organisations have adopted a similar three-part framework (of policy, strategy and tactics) for managing their primary (ie, non-investment) operations. However, "the budget" is their single most important planning and control tool for managing capital spending projects (like construction) and for business operations. Yet, budgets for managing investment funds, ie, risk budgets, are only just emerging among the industry's "thought leaders".

Let us examine the analogy between the capital budgeting exercise and risk budgeting. Capital budgeting addresses an allocation problem directly. The cashflow discounting model determines whether alternatives are acceptable or not and then ranks them. But what about the size of the capital budget? The model also implicitly captures this problem. Changes in conditions of the capital markets are reflected in the duration-blended risk free rate. Changes in the condition of the borrower are reflected in the risk premium. A firm may then create its slate of acceptable projects by employing all of the capital necessary to fund projects that satisfy the valuation model. Note that the capital budget will not remain static. The hypothetical capital budget will be "sized" by both of the variables noted above and by the menu of projects identified as suitable and feasible (ie, a "skill" dimension for the organisation). Thus, the capital/credit environment in

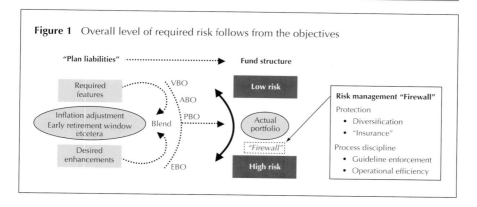

Figure 1 Overall level of required risk follows from the objectives

conjunction with the ability to find attractive investments helps to establish "size".

Risk budgets, like their traditional counterparts, must address two problems: first, establishing the right size and then, second, determining the *allocations*. The size of a risk budget represents a trade-off between the amount of risk the investor needs to achieve its strategic objectives and the amount of risk it can tolerate. Figure 1 illustrates that the risk budget's size flows from the objectives of the investment fund. Macroeconomic factors like inflation adjustments are frequently incorporated into plan needs either by law or because they produce desirable business outcomes such as higher workforce satisfaction and retention in increasingly competitive labour markets. Adding early retirement features or converting to a cash balance plan without reducing benefits for long-service, middle-aged employees materially increases a plan's obligations. Plans that are dominated by high requirements and low tolerance for risk are forced into low risk portfolios that will be limited in their expected returns. Minimising the volatility of pension fund surplus is a common form of low risk policy. Even minimising the present value of expected contributions implies a value to pension fund asset growth limited to accommodating the current definition of the liability to designated plan beneficiaries. If a plan seeks enhancements, there must be a commensurate willingness to take on risk.

Risk management should provide a firewall that increases the likelihood of achieving plan objectives. It should ensure that the benefits of diversification and appropriate hedging are in place to maximise risk-adjusted returns. Well-crafted risk management programmes allow higher levels of risk in the fund design (see Stux and de Marco, 1997). Risk management should also look to minimise the chance of loss through guideline violations or operational errors.

Risk for an investment fund must be judged in terms of the ability to fulfill obligations over different time horizons. What is meant by risk? Risk

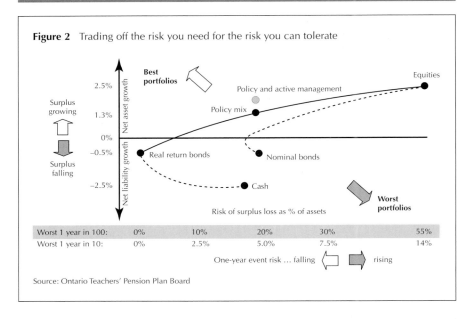

Figure 2 Trading off the risk you need for the risk you can tolerate

| Worst 1 year in 100: | 0% | 10% | 20% | 30% | 55% |
| Worst 1 year in 10: | 0% | 2.5% | 5.0% | 7.5% | 14% |

One-year event risk ... falling ⇦ ⇨ rising

Source: Ontario Teachers' Pension Plan Board

might be characterised as a willingness to take on more uncertain exposures. For instance, more equities in the policy mix. More active management in the implementation programme, such as broader charters for investment managers or narrowly focused strategies. More credit exposure. More illiquid exposures. Finally, investment programmes that are more difficult to measure in terms of valuation or performance, such as financing of entrepreneurs versus short-term advances to finance known cashflows or, more generally, holding private-market assets versus capital-market assets.

Both near-term solvency and long-term capital growth must be accommodated. There is a trade-off that must be balanced between sensitivity to event risk (ie, the short-run risk of insolvency) and the strategic risk of wealth erosion – ie, when the plan's cumulative asset growth lags cumulative liability growth. Figure 2 provides a planning tool to visualise the trade-off. It demonstrates that reducing the amount of risk that must be managed in the short-run can increase the risk of failing to achieve long-run objectives. Cash and real return bonds carry less event risk but considerably more long-term "strategic" risk than equities.

The chart defines risk in terms of net surplus – eg, withstanding a loss of pension surplus of no more than 5% for the worst year in any 10-year period would be the short-run risk goal. A strategic risk target might be maintaining a long-term growth rate for pension fund net surplus of 2% per annum. This would presumably eliminate the need for contributions to the pension fund. The chart shows the expected long-term return from various combinations of traditional assets: stocks, nominal bonds, real return bonds and cash. Each portfolio on the chart represents a 100% exposure to the indicated asset class. It illustrates that investment portfolios with vastly different levels of asset-only risk may be quite similar in terms of surplus event risk. Only a portfolio entirely composed of real return (ie, inflation indexed) bonds carries a negligible event risk, and that is because of the assumed inflation sensitivity of pension fund liabilities. Interestingly, an investment fund consisting entirely of conventional bonds has the same surplus event risk as a diversified mix of equity and fixed-income securities, and an all-cash portfolio is only modestly lower.

For one year in every 10 (ie, the 90% confidence level) a diversified investment fund should anticipate a mark-to-market loss of surplus equivalent to 5% of fund assets. This is the type of shock for which every investment organisation should be highly confident it is prepared for, since the key decision makers are likely to experience such events "on their watch". Once in every 100 years (ie, the 99% confidence level), a 20% loss should occur. While the occurence is highly remote, this is the risk threshold that can bankrupt the unmindful investment organisation. The thoughtful organisation will realise that it must be prepared to check "steering and brakes" regularly in actual market situations and that its "airbag" should be tested in a simulator (see "Plan B" in Conviction section, below).

The portfolios in Figure 2 are also differentiated in the dimension of their ability to achieve a long-run surplus (ie, the vertical axis). Pure fixed income portfolios (ie, cash, conventional bonds or real return bonds) are unable to generate the returns necessary to match the growth in obligations of the investment fund (ie, the liabilities). The addition of equities can increase exposure to event risk, but also increases the likelihood of increasing the surplus. The black dot labelled "Policy Mix" consists of 65% equities, 20% nominal fixed income securities and 15% real liability hedges such as real estate, real return bonds and commodity futures contracts. The shaded-dot portfolio in Figure 2 suggests a portfolio structured with a combination of assets and active management that could produce a projected surplus growth of 2% per annum. If successful, such a strategy would offset the need for annual contributions.

In this fashion, the objectives of plan sponsors can be translated into target return and risk levels for the investment fund. Allocating risk (ie, absolute risk) among investment asset classes is clearly integral to this process. The allocation of active risk (ie, relative risk or tracking error) is addressed later in this chapter.

THE RISK-TAKING MODEL

In the conventions of investment theory risk tolerance is essentially taken as a constant, albeit a unique constant, for any particular individual or organisation. Modelling this factor explicitly has received little attention

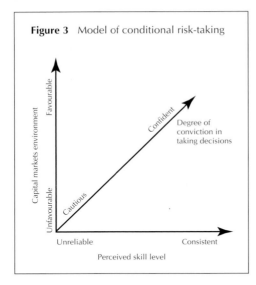

Figure 3 Model of conditional risk-taking

(see Bernstein, 1996). A starting point would be expected utility theory. This traditional approach is based on two assumptions. First, that investor satisfaction increases with wealth at a rate with "diminishing returns" to higher levels of wealth. And second, that investors have an aversion to risk. Satisfaction, or expected utility, is taken as a "certainty equivalent" equal to an expected return less a risk premium. Behavioural finance introduces human factors and utility theory is being replaced by prospect theory. This encompasses the prospect of gains, the prospect of bearing losses and horizon effects.

Typically, even the effort of targeting an absolute risk level in the construction of policy portfolios is made implicitly. Organisations commonly use a very long history of actual investment fund holdings to estimate policy-level absolute volatility. Sensitivity to risk (ie, risk tolerance) as well as the most appropriate level of risk to be taken in portfolio construction should be treated dynamically. Figure 3 illustrates a schematic for thinking about modelling risk-taking. The three dimensions that influence an investor's willingness to take risk are as follows.

1. The reaction to expected, risk-adjusted payoff derives from the shifting tides of perceived opportunity in the capital markets environment.
2. A cognitive element relates to the growth and attenuation of skill as the learning process and staff turnover change the level of intellectual capital in an organisation.
3. The degree of conviction in decision-making, which changes episodically with one's fortunes and with changes in the roster of key decision-makers.

THE ENVIRONMENT

How much risk is worth taking? What are the chances of adding substantial value to the portfolio? How big is the expected payoff, for the amount of risk that must be taken? The changing environment in which investors operate is the first aspect of the risk targeting exercise. Occasionally dismissed by traders as well as by economists as "sentiment", this factor has received a broader acceptance with the increase in recognition of behavioural finance research findings (see Thaler, 1999). Like most factors that are less than perfectly understood, this one is ignored at some peril. For

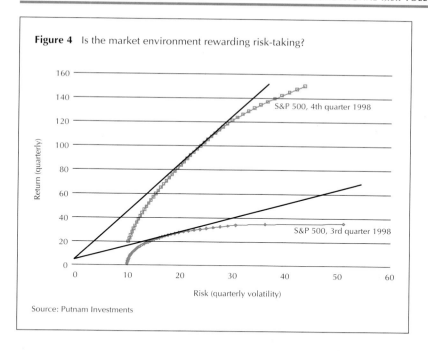

Figure 4 Is the market environment rewarding risk-taking?

Source: Putnam Investments

example, traders at Long Term Capital Management were reported to have dismissed this factor as irrelevant to their model prior to their 1998 experience (see Zuckerman, 2000).

The slope of the capital market line and cross-sectional volatility are two ways of gauging the environment. Figure 4 contrasts two consecutive quarters during 1998 in the United States equity market to illustrate how the market environment can reward risk-taking. The efficient frontiers portfolios are constructed from the stocks in the S&P 500 index, using trailing volatility and covariance information from the Barra optimiser (see www.barra.com) and a "perfect information forecast" of the next quarter's returns – ie, the actual return, since forecasting skill is treated as a separate factor in this model. Not only is the risk level of the "optimal portfolio" quite different in the two periods (about 17% in the third quarter of 1998 versus about 23% in the fourth quarter) but the implied risk tolerance for holding the unleveraged "optimal portfolio" is dramatically different as well.

In the absence of a well-articulated utility function, the investor is left with only intuition and inference to select the "best" portfolio. In the third quarter of 1998, an investor certainly could have made better use of marginal risk in a different market or asset class, whereas in the fourth quarter, risk should have been added to the "normal" exposure to US equity. Thus, an investor's implied risk tolerance clearly would change as the interpretation of a "best portfolio for the circumstances" changes. Using a static

Figure 5 Cross-sectional performance – spreads reveal opportunity

Composite portfolio returns by sector

Estimated Russell 1000 sample,
1st quarter 1987–1st quarter 1998

Compustat economic sector	Mean returns (%)	Tracking error (%)	Sharpe ratio	Percent of positive quarters (%)
Transportation	3.1	13.00	0.24	55.1
Communication services	2.7	11.84	0.23	55.0
Technology	11.7	10.07	1.16	72.3
Health care	7.4	10.01	0.74	64.4
Energy	2.8	8.62	0.33	56.3
Basic materials	4.9	5.98	0.82	66.2
Capital goods	6.2	5.96	1.05	69.9
Consumer staples	4.7	5.59	0.84	66.5
Consumer cyclicals	7.2	5.53	1.30	74.4
Financials	3.4	3.75	0.91	67.6
Utilities	1.6	3.41	0.46	59.1
Cap-weight sector Long-short quintiles	5.4	1.88	2.88	91.0

Source: Goldman Sachs Research

approach to target risk (eg, 20%) would certainly cause investors to take too much risk in some environments and not enough risk in others. A simplified approach to using the same information may be employed with the comparison of risk premiums. This could be carried out across asset classes, country markets, economic sectors, times or regimes, etc.

Cross-sectional volatility of returns can be employed to judge over-valued or under-valued environments using style segments, industries, sectors, or all stocks in a market. The patterns of volatility using realised returns can be assessed in terms of rising or falling volatility trends, as well as high or low volatility levels. Whether performance patterns are smooth and broadly dispersed, or clumped and concentrated, is a factor representing important differences in "accessible" opportunity. Estimates of cross-sectional volatility based on expected returns also provide useful pictures of opportunity in the environment. The forecast error of each alternative segment-return and the reliability of forecasts, using standard error or information coefficient, are useful measures. Figure 5 illustrates the wide divergence of sector-level opportunity for taking risk in the large cap segment of the US equity market. The column labelled Tracking error represents the volatility of quarterly-rebalanced portfolios holding long and short positions in the best and worst stock quintiles, respectively, in each sector. Clearly, the rewards for taking risk were not constant from sector to sector during these 12 years. Nor should willingness to have taken risk have been constant across sectors. This economic-sector gradient of

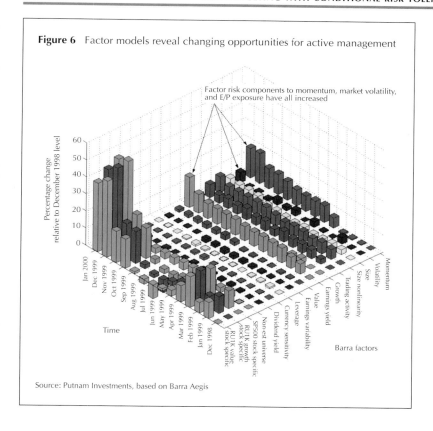

Figure 6 Factor models reveal changing opportunities for active management

Source: Putnam Investments, based on Barra Aegis

opportunity also illustrates that investment organisations should focus on the allocation of risk in the long-term management of intellectual capital as well as financial capital.

In the autumn of 1998, most financial markets showed significant declines in value and increases in volatility. The confident, informed investor understood that a significant portion of that distress was due to liquidity problems, which should be expected to ease over time. If the investors' horizons were long term, the market events of that period represented a genuine opportunity to add value. Similar opportunities may arise at different times across sectors, as suggested in Figure 5.

Factor models provide yet another perspective on changing opportunities in a capital market taken from a risk viewpoint. The monthly time series in Figure 6 illustrates how momentum, market volatility and valuation factors drove overall risk in the 1999 large-cap US equity market, and in growth style stocks in particular. Since these factors tend to move in cycles and not completely randomly, they may be used to adjust risk exposures by sector through time.

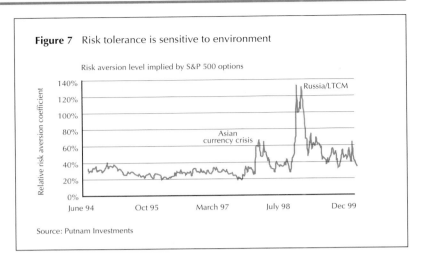

Figure 7 Risk tolerance is sensitive to environment

Risk aversion level implied by S&P 500 options

Source: Putnam Investments

Constructing an optimal investment organisation is like constructing an optimal investment portfolio. Like securities in a portfolio, each member of the decision-making team provides expected return with periodic variability and correlation properties. Executive management's tolerance for performance variability will determine the ultimate wealth formation of the team. Indeed, a weighted blend of their individual risk tolerance "vectors" will be the key factor in this outcome. Policy makers who are not satisfied with long-term performance may simply not have gauged this factor correctly for their organisations. An example of this kind of failure would be the firm that dumps a long-term asset class, like emerging markets or real estate, at the time of a negative market shock in the name of risk avoidance. Risky assets always will disappoint at times. What is critically important is to recognise that risk is most often symmetric and leaving an asset class after a large drop clearly eliminates any opportunity for a recovery. Furthermore, concentration on individual asset performance ignores the correlation effects across the assets, which should be net positive.

Derivatives provide a lens for examining risk tolerance that was not available to the mathematicians and economists who developed the foundations of investment analysis. Figure 7 provides an insight into the willingness of market participants to adjust their level of risk aversion to the risk/reward environment of the capital markets. The period from mid-1994 through 1996 represented a relatively dull period for global equity investors in the developed markets. The time series plotted in Figure 7 represents the relationship of out-of-the-money (so-called 25 delta) options contracts on the S&P 500 index versus contracts struck at-the-money. This is sometimes called the volatility skew. Options theory specifies that implied volatility is a function of the volatility of the underlying asset.

Investors are assumed not to have a preference for protection with out-of-the-money options, ie, "risk-neutral" behaviour is taken to be the norm. So, for any particular expiration, implied volatility should be the same for all "strikes", in which case the risk aversion coefficient in Figure 7 would be uniform, with the actual level determined by the theoretical model, eg, zero for Black–Scholes or somewhat positive for more recent models.

This theory is never observed in practice. Due to "fat-tailed" distributions of price changes, one usually sees a higher implied volatility for the out-of-the-money option. Figure 7 demonstrates how this relative value can change dramatically through time when shocks hit the market. The time series' slight skew is relatively stable with a modestly declining trend until episodes such as the Asian currency crisis in 1997, or the Russian bond default and collapse of Long Term Capital Management in 1998. During such episodes, the implied volatility of out-of-the-money contracts soars. The heightened sensitivity to risk can be measured by the willingness to pay what is effectively a substantial insurance premium for "downside" protection with a large "deductible", ie, according to how far away from the money a strike is selected.

While the US equity market was relatively quiet during 1994 and 1995, the Mexican peso devaluation and subsequent "contagion" of emerging market debt provided us with another interesting example of shifts in risk tolerance. In early 1995, Polish debt began to trade at the same deep discount as Latin American debt, even though there was no coincident shift in Poland's macroeconomic fundamentals. Yet because of the situation in Latin America, the market increased its expectation of Poland's default risk. This was an interesting display of "cross-market ownership correlation" risk; a consequence of global-investor behaviour.

The equity index futures contract is another derivative that reveals contrasts in the risk/reward profile of capital markets. According to efficient market theory, assets trade to quickly achieve their fair market value. Were this always the case, there would be no material spread between the trading price and their economic value (estimated by prevailing dividend schedules for the underlying index equities and holding-period interest rates for the term to expiration of these contracts). In that case, Figure 8, which plots the September 1999 DAX and FTSE index futures contracts' fair value spreads, would be single lines at the zero point, ignoring the effect of taxes. Participants in these two markets are clearly indicating a lower tolerance for FTSE risk, shown by the lower efficiency (ie, larger standard deviation) and negative mean of the fair-value-spread distribution. One may infer higher expectations of reward per unit of risk in the German market during this period. Clearly using a constant risk target across international equity markets or an allocation of absolute risk to markets based on measures like market capitalization (inherent in an index like MSCI-EAFE) can be sub-optimal (see also Figure 15 later in the chapter).

Figure 8   Futures fair-value-spreads show preferences

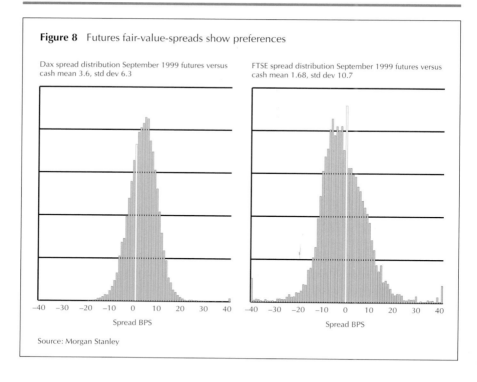

Dax spread distribution September 1999 futures versus cash mean 3.6, std dev 6.3

FTSE spread distribution September 1999 futures versus cash mean 1.68, std dev 10.7

Spread BPS

Spread BPS

Source: Morgan Stanley

Skill

An exceptionally skilled person will be comfortable doing things that the amateur only takes on with much higher levels of stress. Skill, the second dimension of the conceptual model for risk taking, is sometimes thought of as investment IQ. While there is certainly a large component of native talent to investment skill, it remains that skill is inherently acquired through effective learning. This is just as true for an investment organisation as it is for an individual. Moreover, because of staff turnover, skill is clearly a dynamic factor for an institutional investor. Genuinely effective investment organisations are using total quality management, knowledge management and the development of true teams to institutionalise their skill (see Katzenbach and Smith, 1993).

Skill involves making the right selection and weighting choices for a pyramid of decisions including the choice of asset classes, benchmarks and the indexes which proxy them, asset managers, securities, etc. An investment organisation can take a reality check of its current skill level by evaluating the drivers of perceived skill. This is a three-step exercise.

1. *People*: measure the depth of talent and experience and evaluate how

effectively the people work as a team – ie, is there more reliability and consistency in process or results because of effective collaboration?

2. *Process*: how robust is the process design, how accurately is it mapped, and how disciplined is the implementation?

3. *Performance*: estimating the likelihood that performance will be repeated is largely an exercise of determining how well the investment team understood the bets they took and the reasons for those bets paying off as they did.

It is moot to say definitively whether a successful outcome was skill or luck. It is worth remembering what Napoleon said, "Give me generals who know something about tactics and strategy, but best of all give me generals who are lucky" (see Merida and Milbank, 2000). Good performance is a combination of both. Clearly, an element of skill is knowing when circumstances are promising. Still, there are things to look at to increase one's confidence in "ability", ie, the likelihood that good results will be repeated. Have implied views from portfolio over- and under-weightings matched their expressed views on capital market performance expectations? Have unintended bets in the portfolio or unconscious biases in the investment process been revealed in the performance analysis? These, then, are the "Three Ps" of skill assessment – people, process and performance.

Choosing an index to proxy a benchmark represents the outsourcing of a skill area to the intuition and/or algorithm of the index provider. An analysis of the S&P 500 index committee's work is provided in Figure 9.

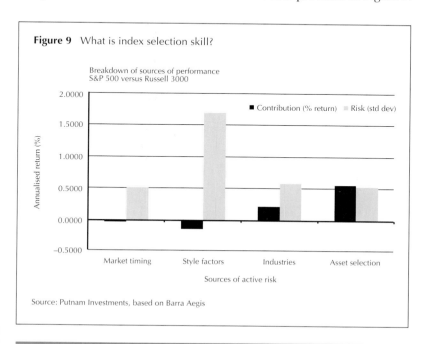

Figure 9 What is index selection skill?

Breakdown of sources of performance
S&P 500 versus Russell 3000

Source: Putnam Investments, based on Barra Aegis

Comparing that index with the broader Russell 3000 index over the past 23 years reveals significant style bets and a modest beta bet, which provided no value-added. That is, these variations in the S&P index from the Russell index led to lower returns than would have been achieved from merely holding the benchmark. The modest industries bet and asset selection bet have been a source of positive value for the S&P 500. Indexes are an important source of risk for institutional investors, since they are used in asset allocation decisions as well as in the evaluation of active managers' performance. Assuming that such indexes are unbiased profoundly compromises investors' efforts to budget risk properly.

Each investment decision-maker, from trustee to trader, attempts to add value within a particular decision horizon. Each layer of decision making comes with a unique horizon-sensitive risk tolerance and set of assumptions. Policy portfolios assume that markets are at equilibrium, while strategic and tactical portfolios assume that cyclical and technical biases exhibited by markets can be captured through skilful, active bets. But is the investor acting on information or "noise", ie, patterns that your model does not explain reliably? Of course, this is exactly how skilful investors actually differentiate themselves: all market movements that are not understood are by definition noise. The assumption that we understand equilibrium prices implies that we understand the forces at work changing technology, demographics, preferences, and every other market factor for the strategic holding period. This kind of assumption is clearly not equivalent to the

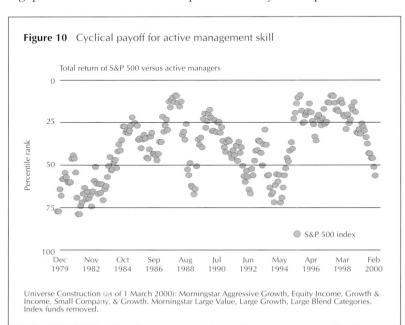

Figure 10 Cyclical payoff for active management skill

Total return of S&P 500 versus active managers

Percentile rank

S&P 500 index

Universe Construction (as of 1 March 2000): Morningstar Aggressive Growth, Equity Income, Growth & Income, Small Company, & Growth. Morningstar Large Value, Large Growth, Large Blend Categories. Index funds removed.

routinely applied estimating procedure of extrapolating past price patterns. Thus the assessment of decision making skill must consider the effect of horizon, risk tolerance and the explicit and implicit assumptions.

The differences in equity and fixed income total returns for very long periods within various non-US capital markets may cast doubt on the investment committee that is highly confident of having solved this problem. Path-dependent analysis of long-term returns need to recognise that the equity markets of many countries, like Germany, have gone to zero. Some have done so more than once. Consider that the conventional 60:40 equity fixed income policy mix in the US has looked more like 45:55 in Canada and 80:20 in the UK. Experience in creating "optimal" portfolios cannot rely on too narrow a range of investment experience or risk tolerance.

Numerous studies of the attempt to measure persistence of value-added by active managers have been published (see Grinblatt and Titman, 1989; Lakonishok, Shleifer and Vishny, 1992; Goetzmann and Ibbotson, 1994; Kahn and Rudd, 1995; Gruber, 1996 and Daniel, Grinblatt, Titman and Wermers, 1997). The 20-year time series illustrated in Figure 10 demonstrates a cyclical nature to the relationship between the market index and the performance of active managers. In the chart, each observation gives the percentage of active managers outperforming the benchmark, eg, a value of 10 means 10% added value and 90% underperformed. There is no attempt to adjust for the riskiness of the portfolios held by the indexes or the managers.

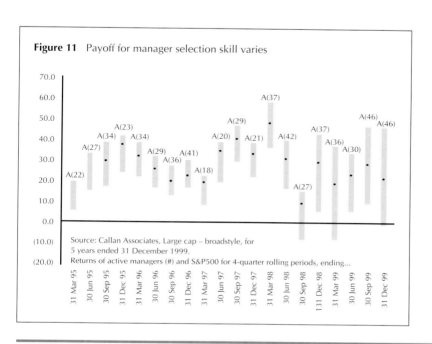

Figure 11 Payoff for manager selection skill varies

Figure 12 Manager selection skill improves reliability

Median manager tracking error:

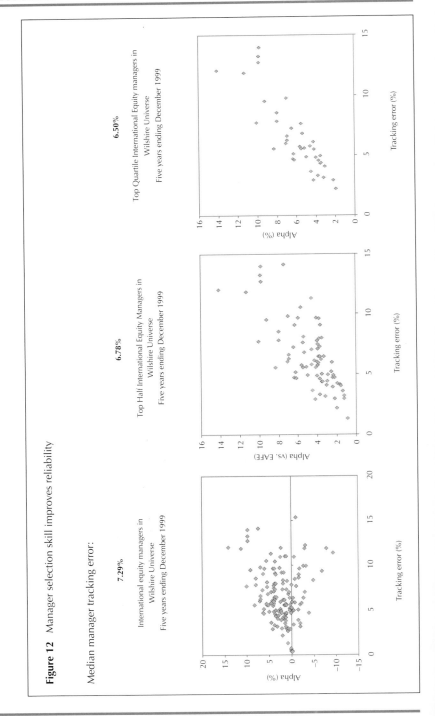

7.29%

International equity managers in
Wilshire Universe
Five years ending December 1999

6.78%

Top Half International Equity Managers in
Wilshire Universe
Five years ending December 1999

6.50%

Top Quartile International Equity managers in
Wilshire Universe
Five years ending December 1999

Although indexes are episodically difficult to beat (ie, in high momentum markets), the ability to select and retain above-median and top-quartile managers adds substantial value over the long term to the performance of an investment fund. Looking at the data from a somewhat different perspective, Figure 11 reveals that the payoff for manager selection skill varies significantly from time to time. During the mid-1990s the range of performance between more and less successful US equity managers was relatively compressed. More recently, the payoff from differentiating between large-cap equity managers has been substantial. Style factors help to explain this (see Figure 6), yet few investment fund sponsors position themselves to capture this, particularly for international equity.

Manager selection skill improves the reliability of a portfolio as well as providing excess return. The three panels in Figure 12 provide separate scatter-plots of the five-year performance of all, of top-half, and of top-quartile international equity managers. Not only does alpha (excess return properly adjusted for portfolio beta, ie, without tactical beta variation) improve, but active risk (ie, relative VAR or tracking error) improves as well. Thus, for a specified risk budget, the skilful selection of investment managers provides greater expected excess return. The challenge through time is to identify the likely population of skill-based managers. This is certainly the case where past performance is no guarantee of future results, but by accurately analysing the "Three Ps" discussed above, one increases the likelihood of success.

Large cap stocks inherently dominate the performance of any equity market. From time to time, however, this phenomenon becomes exaggerated. In such environments, stock selection skill provides enormous added value and justifies higher levels of risk taking. As Figure 13 illustrates, during the late 1980s, the largest 25 stocks in the Russell 1000 index represented about a quarter of the return of the entire index. Ten years later, the 25 largest stocks were producing about *half* the contribution to total index return. In such environments, allocating higher portions of an equity risk budget to managers with a high level of stock selection skill would improve the payoff to these risk decisions. So, as the last series of figures show, in some market environments more skillful managers produce substantially better returns than average managers and indexes. The performance pattern appears to be almost cyclical. Market concentration may be a factor. Underlying style may also be a factor.

Because of difficulties in dealing with non-linear and non-normal relationships, analysis with traditional hypothesis testing requires vast amounts of data for assessments of skill, with reasonably high degrees of confidence. Performance attribution analysis of the patterns of manager decisions can provide more insight into a portfolio manager's decision-making process and the consequential impact on performance. Figure 14 provides a historical sketch of one element of portfolio decision making to

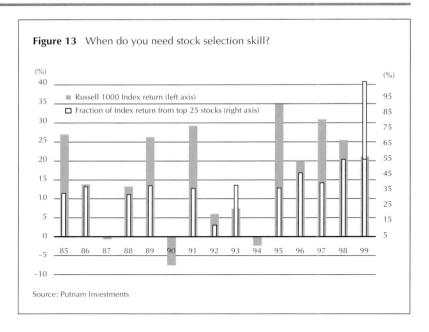

Figure 13 When do you need stock selection skill?

Source: Putnam Investments

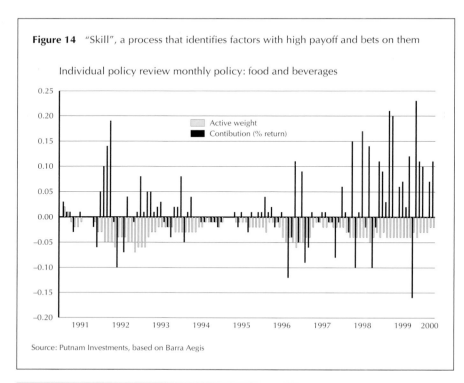

Figure 14 "Skill", a process that identifies factors with high payoff and bets on them

Individual policy review monthly policy: food and beverages

Source: Putnam Investments, based on Barra Aegis

illustrate this approach. The use of benchmarks to gauge the performance of active managers represents the concept of opportunity cost in decision making. That is, one should simultaneously measure the cost of the path not taken and the consequences of the choice selected.

In Figure 14, the decision to underweight portfolio exposure to food and beverages on average during the 1990s is examined using the Barra Aegis system. By definition, the underweight in one sector produces an average overweight in all others. Focusing only on food and beverages, the analysis demonstrates that although there were a number of months when these decisions caused underperformance relative to the S&P 500 benchmark, in the long run it proved a highly reliable source of value-added. Food and beverages were great in the 1970s and 1980s, but the US economy changed in the 1990s. McDonald's no longer helped your portfolio. Putting together many such vignettes would complete a picture of manager skill.

According to intuition and the most commonly used methodology in portfolio construction, the Capital Asset Pricing Model, more risky assets should, in the long-term, provide higher expected return. Five years is a somewhat limited slice of capital markets history; realistically, however, it is the long run for an investment management staff. Figure 15 illustrates the relationship between risk and return among developed international equity markets, ie, the US and those included in the MSCI-EAFE index, for the five years ending 1998. If the usual metric of return volatility could be strictly relied upon, this rank correlation scatter plot essentially would be a linear series following the dotted line from lower left to upper right: more risky exposures producing higher realised returns. At times, the relationship is obviously a very weak one. Such periods represent profitable opportunities for more aggressive risk taking, where reliable country selection skill could provide value-added over country weightings based on the conventional long-term risk/return metrics.

Figure 15 reflects the volatility and return effects of the stimulus accompanying the launch of the euro, the Asian currency shock and the long economic recovery in the United States. Shifting allocations away from Asia and into Europe (as an index or a conventional optimiser would) and assuming that the US would continue to be a low-volatility equity market, could produce unattractive performance surprises for the investor. The "skilful" manager would be able to recognise the opportunities provided when the expected risk/return relationships are aberrations, which could then be exploited.

Conviction

The third dimension for this conceptual model of risk taking is "conviction". Conviction, the capacity to take risky decisions, is related to the financial fitness of the investor as well as to human factors. Financial fitness, like physical fitness, consists of three elements: flexibility, strength

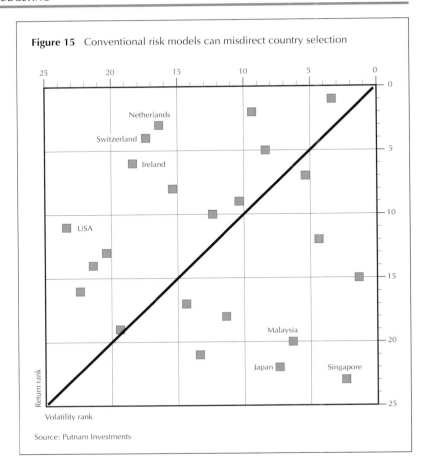

Figure 15 Conventional risk models can misdirect country selection

Source: Putnam Investments

and endurance. Collectively, they form the ability to make up for adverse surprises in a financial plan. Financial endurance is the long-term earnings power and earnings stability of the investor – ie, the ability to sustain a higher level of contributions over time. Financial strength is represented by the investor's wealth. Deep financial resources can be converted to borrowing power, when necessary, or converted to liquid assets, over time. Liquidity, indeed, is the source of financial flexibility – ie, the ability to respond immediately to an unscheduled claim for resources.

Risk tolerance is a feature of corporate culture. And corporate culture, in turn, can be thought of as a sort of correlation matrix of the personal values and instincts of the organisation's key decision-makers. Personal experience shapes personal values. And personal values shape risk taking decisions. The rational model assumed in economic theory does not, therefore, provide a reliable description of actual risk taking behaviour. Several relevant examples of such personal values have received public attention recently. Gene Krantz was popularised in the film *Apollo 13* as the charismatic mission commander in the white vest who appeared to single-handedly take charge of the death-defying return to earth by a NASA lunar mission crew. The inspirational quotation of Margaret Thatcher chosen as the title for his memoirs – "Failure is Not an Option", makes a very clear statement about the link between personal values and risk tolerance. In Spring this year, the *Boston Globe* carried a front-page photograph of Christopher Reeves addressing the Biotech-2000 conference from his wheelchair. Unlike many severely handicapped individuals, Reeves was defiantly unwilling to accept his condition and said that he would walk in four years. Moreover, he insisted that it was the people in his audience who would make it possible. He said that while they were entrepreneurs driven by a profit motive, their research would allow him to finally recover from his back injury. He summed up this connection between personal values and risk tolerance with his statement, "The American mantra is 'Nothing is impossible'".

This theme of "taking on the impossible" also shows up in "Curing the Incurable", the *New Yorker* (7 February 2000) article about two brothers, Stephen and Jamie Heywood, who are challenging the medical establishment to attempt gene therapy for ALS (Lou Gehrig's disease) before the infected brother dies. Referencing the ham and eggs breakfast joke where the chicken is "interested" but the pig is "committed", they address the alignment of interests problem in medical R&D today, where only the patient can assume the risk/reward of an unproven treatment. The analogue of an investor's decision to take on uncertainty (rather than risk) seems clear (see Knight, 1921).

In investment management, everything has been geared to a return world, not a risk world. However, if peoples' compensation is tied to risk management, they will focus on it. Perhaps all roads lead back to considerations of economic wealth. Success is often a matter of how well prepared you are to manage the inevitable episodes of failure. An organisation's cultural flexibility to provide the resilience for bouncing back from adversity is an essential feature of high conviction. Evidence of this can be found in the soundness of an organisation's "Plan B". How much time was spent in developing it? When was it tested? The effort invested in contingency planning and quality of "preparedness" may provide a measure of the non-financial side of conviction, ie, the ability to absorb shocks, either from the market or originating from internal sources.

This "conviction" dimension can be seen implicitly by examining profiles of investment portfolios. Figure 16 summarises the holdings of all corporate defined benefit plan investment portfolios of about a year ago. The investments have been arranged in a category labelled "Certainty", along with "Risk" and "Uncertainty", two categories suggested by Frank Knight (1921) in his explanation of why entrepreneurs appear to earn

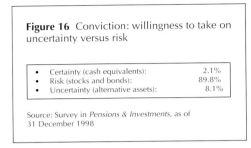

Figure 16 Conviction: willingness to take on uncertainty versus risk

• Certainty (cash equivalents):	2.1%
• Risk (stocks and bonds):	89.8%
• Uncertainty (alternative assets):	8.1%

Source: Survey in *Pensions & Investments*, as of 31 December 1998

exceptionally high returns. While risky decisions are bets with uncertain outcomes, they can be based on extensive histories of similar actions, ie, we can rely on statistical interpretation of data over the long term. Investments in stocks and bonds represent such exposures to risk.

"Uncertainty" describes those actions or events that are unique or rare to the degree that there is no experiential basis for the decision to undertake them. Therefore, Figure 16 takes liberty with this notion and places cash equivalents into the basket labelled Certainty, stocks and bonds are assigned to Risk, and alternative assets to Uncertainty. The modest albeit significant allocation to uncertain exposures by ERISA investors in the United States (under the 1974 Employee Retirement Investment Security Act) is partially a matter of the accounting recognition of their current value. (Year end 1999 figures suggested a modest shift from uncertain to risky exposures, presumably due to this accounting convention of deferred recognition of private market asset values versus mark-to-market recognition of the momentum-driven public equity markets.) In contrast, university endowments frequently have two to three times this allocation to alternative investments. Perhaps the absence of the Internal Revenue Service and Department of Labor framework for controlling contributions and limiting benefits to the entire set of stakeholders provides the incentive for endowments to hold a very different mix of uncertain and risky exposures. Presumably, these endowments expect to be able to have greater flexibility in the use of the upside potential of entrepreneurial returns. For example, universities are able to use their endowments as competitive weapons by being able to attract faculty and students who might otherwise be unavailable. Whether the potential for achieving a "quality of life" shift or because of taxes and regulation, different categories of investors exhibit different degrees of sensitivity to uncertain versus risky exposures. So the expression for wealth, at the bottom of Figure 16, adds a separate term for tolerance of uncertainty to tolerance of risk, thus better describing an investor's objective function.

THE RISK BUDGET

Like a financial budget for managing the organisation, a risk budget can be *the* planning and control tool for the investment fund. Fiduciaries first determine how much overall risk should be taken in the investment programme. The next step in risk budgeting is to determine how that risk should be allocated. As with financial budgeting, the two steps in risk budgeting of setting size and *then* setting allocations are linked together in a continuous feedback loop.

Sources of absolute risk

Total fund risk is expressed through the determination of a policy benchmark. Potential pitfalls in this process arise from the specification of which liabilities are modelled for establishing investment objectives – ie, the Vested Benefit Obligation (VBO), the Accumulated Benefit Obligation (ABO), the Projected Benefit Obligation (PBO), or the true or economic benefit obligation (which we will term the EBO). An ABO or VBO essentially assumes the plan sponsor will be liquidated and pension benefits are frozen in the present state. (VBOs exclude obligation to current employees not yet vested in the retirement plan.) The PBO is a first approximation of a going-concern view of the plan sponsor. It assigns future salary increases to service, to estimate "final salary" for the present work force. An EBO is a stochastic approach to estimating the pension liability modelling workforce and related retirement benefit consequences of each possible "path" of the plan sponsor's business development strategy with appropriate path probabilities and valuations (see Stux and de Marco, 1997).

A specification of the selection and weighting of asset classes in the policy mix can be made with high precision using the wrong objectives. Failing to use an EBO for determining the appropriate level of total plan risk implies that the sponsor organisation is not a going concern or that the investment fund need not provide for the strategic change anticipated in its own long-term plans. US organisations attempting to convert to cash balance retirement plans have experienced another aspect of this potential tripwire. Many of their middle-aged career employees learned that their retirement benefit would be reduced through such a plan change. In one case, this led to complaints to US Congressional representatives and subsequent Internal Revenue Service probes regarding "fairness". Consequently, other corporate management entities have elected to shelve otherwise attractive cash benefit plans indefinitely.

Investing means you are buying into a set of models, either explicitly or implicitly: a valuation methodology and a risk model, at the security as well as the portfolio and total fund levels. The bets taken, which create absolute or relative risk, are a consequence of these models. The most fundamental bets are inherent in the investor's assumptions. The indexer's model is Efficient Market Theory, with its principle bet that assets quickly trade to fair market value. Investors in actively managed portfolios buy a process including explicit models as well as intuition.

If the policy mix is constructed with the correct liability assumptions, the next potential pitfall is in the selection of proxies for each asset class. The normal working assumption is that asset class benchmarks represent the full theoretical opportunity set. After all, this will be the basis for allocating the organisation's capital in the investment fund and for judging the performance of active managers who are delegated responsibility for portions of the fund. Typically, however, policy makers and investment staffs select one of the popular indexes for each benchmark. Because of biases in their construction and distortions from their reconstitution methodologies, these indexes introduce considerable problems. Trustees and investment committees, not the investment staff, must deal with implementation issues of these indexes, such as whether the index provider maintains a timely and robust reconstitution process, and how relevant the index is to active managers selected for outsourced portfolio management.

The use and extent of active management is another important factor in total investment fund risk and the expectation of achieving the plan's objectives. Figure 2 illustrates the assumption that a blend of above-median and top-quartile managers would add 80 basis points to total fund performance over the long run. (These measures depend on the analysis horizon; consistent one and three-year above-median managers are typically five and 10-year top-quartile managers.)

As Charlie Ellis observed in his book, *Investment Policy* (1985), the biggest obstacle to achieving long-run objectives is taking too little risk. A common policy objective for institutional plan sponsors is minimising surplus volatility. This parsimonious approach to "sizing" the risk budget minimises risk for the investment staff. It is not designed for long-run surplus maximisation. Many plans will attempt to defease (ie, render void) a portion of the plan liabilities through annuity contracts or fixed-income portfolios, particularly when a significant proportion of retirement fund beneficiaries are already retired. This "breakeven portfolio" approach effectively hedges a specified liability stream. Although highly efficient, in this context, it does not make effective use of the investment sponsor's capital. Referring to the risk-taking model presented earlier, a breakeven structure is a suitable target under two possible conditions. The investor has no perceived *skill* at making key investment decisions which would be inherent in introducing strategic or tactical risk with regard to the specified liabilities. Or, the investor's level of *conviction* is too low to introduce investment risk for these liabilities. If an investor believes its levels of *skill* and/or *conviction* are not minimal, then some investment risk is appropriate and the breakeven portfolio should be restructured.

Benchmarks and indexes

Benchmark selection contributes to the level of absolute risk in an investment fund. The expected level of risk from asset allocation policy changes as the index committee or the index-rebalancing algorithm periodically restructures the index. For instance, the S&P 500 index represented a relatively cyclical basket of stocks in 1989 due to the high representation of traditional industrial companies. During the 1990s, the index committee gradually repositioned the index to produce higher expected returns by adopting more of a growth style with a particularly high exposure to technology and telecommunication companies. During the same period, momentum factors in the market also caused this capitalisation weighted index to become considerably more concentrated. Thus, a combination of style decisions, index methodology and market developments increased the absolute level of risk for those investment funds that had adopted this index. The Frank Russell Company change of growth/value style methodology in June 1996 caused an even more abrupt exposure-profile shift.

Benchmarks contain several kinds of embedded risks. The most fundamental is what might be called opportunity-set selection. Each index provider differentiates itself by a "unique" characterisation of what best represents the asset class. Construction biases have many sources. For international indexes, they begin with country selection. A secondary effect is the change in weightings of countries that *are* selected by the absence in the index of countries that *are not* selected from the full "universe". The effect is amplified by the selection and omission of companies that represent the country. At the country level, indexes differ according to the treatment of such things as "available" float, foreign stocks, real estate companies and commodity vehicles (eg, real estate or oil trusts) as well as the weighting of segments of the equity universe such as sector, style or size (ie, capitalisation). As with country weightings in international indexes, what each index provider chooses to omit is an important contributor to weightings in the index. Changes in the level of absolute risk attributable to industry level and security level concentration change episodically. As noted above, this has been a much more pronounced source of risk in recent years.

Finally, the methodology of the index provider itself is a unique source of risk. A gap in the absolute risk level occurs each time an index reconstitution is completed. Index providers have moved from quarterly to semi-annual to annual cycles. High IPO volumes and massive sector rotations in recent years are bringing renewed scrutiny to this source of risk. Thus, design changes such as frequency of reconstitution or segment definition, such as growth and value, further alter the level of absolute risk due to the index provider's methodology.

Risk allocation

The objectives of asset allocation and risk allocation are quite similar, even though the means of arriving there differ materially. Asset allocation is moving *funds* from one portfolio or asset class to another. Figures 17 and 18 describe the categories and measures of risk that would be used in the allocation process. Figures 19 and 20 provide a simple example of risk reallocations. Risk allocation is moving the *flexibility to take risk* from one asset class or portfolio to another. Risk allocation uses the same decision framework as traditional asset allocation. An investment policy committee sets an overall, absolute target level of risk for the investment fund. This is equivalent to the policy mix specification with its assumption of the achievement of

Figure 17 Alternatives for the risk budgeting menu

Type of outcome	Type of asset	Type of market
Certain	Cash	Money markets
Risky	Stocks and bonds	Capital markets
Uncertain	Alternative investments	Private markets

Figure 18 Tool kit for the risk budgeting decision process

Absolute risk
- Funded ratio
- Probability of surplus shortfall
- Downside risk measures (eg, VAR and draw-down)
- Beta range
- Credit and liquidity

Relative risk
- Tracking error or relative VAR
- Capitalisation outside of benchmark
- Concentration targets and collars
- Liquidity profile
- Quality profile (earnings and credit or default)

equilibrium asset prices, benchmark selection and determination of the extent of active management. Similarly, a chief investment officer or portfolio strategist determines the risk structure at the fund and asset class levels for the strategic horizon. Finally, portfolio managers establish the tactical risk framework, at the portfolio level, through their cash-level and beta policies, their style biases (credit or earnings quality, growth, valuation, etc), sector and industry tilts, as well as company and security selection risk policies and preferences

The investment policy committee must determine the right balance of investment risk exposures, as illustrated in Figures 1 and 2. This fundamental decision is driven by investors' sensitivity to the range of outcomes inherent in the principal categories of assets and their related markets. Figure 17 provides a summary profile of these relationships from which a risk budget is drawn. This framework can be thought of as a menu for risk budgeting. The adage that 80% of what you accomplish comes from 20% of what you do (Pareto's Law) applies fully to the risk-taking activities of investment fund managers and trustees. Initiatives to better understand the composition of risk in the liabilities as they relate to the organisation's structure and mission, and to recognise how different they might be in five years' time, receive a relatively modest degree of attention, even in quarterly or annual board level investment fund reviews. Similarly, the appropriate mix of "risky" versus "uncertain" exposures is rarely addressed either robustly or frequently. On the other hand, a great deal of discussion is directed at capital markets gyrations, recent surprises of one sort or another and, especially, recent performance. Comparisons of performance with peers and with the fund's investment benchmarks are often prominent subjects of discussion, rather than probing discussions about the nature of the investment benchmarks or about the liabilities and objectives of peers. A peer's performance will be significantly determined by the overall structure of its fund which, if well-designed, reflects its policy and liability structure, both of which may be only superficially relevant to the institutional investor comparing its performance to that organisation).

Establishing a risk budget involves the two-level framework of absolute risk and relative risk. Investment fund policy makers and managers have an array of choices that may be selected individually or in combination, as illustrated in Figure 18, in building their risk budgeting decision process. Overall risk, whether absolute or relative, is of course governed by how big the bets are in the investment fund – ie, how concentrated, how volatile, and how highly correlated with other holdings or exposures. Such bets must be judged both in asset-risk "space" as well as surplus-risk "space". Absolute risk is important in the long run, because of the efficiency with which objectives might be achieved. However, it is perhaps even more important in the short run, because of the propensity of decision-makers to initiate "course changes" in response to short-run benchmark-relative risk or market

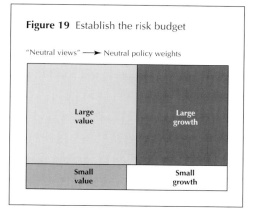

Figure 19 Establish the risk budget

"Neutral views" ⟶ Neutral policy weights

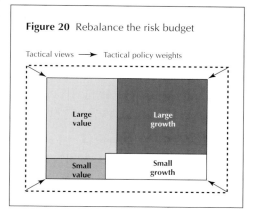

Figure 20 Rebalance the risk budget

Tactical views ⟶ Tactical policy weights

shocks. These risk measures must, therefore, anticipate and capture the sudden impact of potentially adverse exposures.

The risk budget must address the severity of these infrequent events using sensitivity analysis, stress tests and scenario analysis. An implied target level for VAR can be taken from the investment fund's policy mix. Since this VAR will change with prevailing capital markets conditions, it is useful to compare this implied value with the actual views of policy makers for the investment fund in terms of surplus-risk tolerance as well as in terms of asset-risk tolerance. There can be a material mismatch between the implied value and the intended value.

For example, any change in interest rates will affect the value of a bond portfolio. But it will also affect the discounting of the liability stream. The net effect on the riskiness of reaching one's targets must incorporate both impacts and could be greater or less than the risk of the bonds taken in isolation.

Implementing a risk budget

The risk budgeting decision process is carried out through a combination of asset allocation and risk allocation. Asset allocation is implemented by *moving funds* among asset classes and portfolios, whereas risk allocation is *moving flexibility to take risk* from one portfolio or asset class to another (see Figure 18).

Tracking error targets will reflect the volatility of the underlying asset category. For instance, if large-cap US equities are targeted at 300 basis points (for *ex ante* tracking error), small-cap equities might be targeted at 500 basis points. Capitalisation targets for exposure to non-benchmark assets will also depend upon the asset category. Large-cap US equities might be limited to 10 to 15%, while small-cap equities would be 15 to 20%.

Concentration targets and collars in the risk budgeting decision process (see Figure 18) apply to a number of aspects of the portfolio. Security-level concentration limits are typically set according to market capitalisation for equities. A large-cap ceiling might be 1.5 times the benchmark weight, whereas a small-cap ceiling would be 3.0 times the benchmark weight. Industry or economic sector limits might be an absolute level, such as five percentage points, or a relative level, such as 1.2 to 0.8 times the benchmark sector-weighting. Holdings may be targeted in relative terms such as a percentage of assets in the benchmark index or as a minimum number, eg, 90 securities for a large-cap equity portfolio or 125 securities for a mid-cap portfolio. Size bets can be targeted by style or by sector as well as by an overall portfolio target. Fundamental valuation ratios such as price to book, price/earnings, cashflow to price, debt to equity, or return on equity can also be included in the targeting scheme. Finally, the Barra Common Factors (see www.barra.com) can be used in this risk budgeting control system. Notwithstanding this daunting array of possible exposure controls, unless a quantitative strategy is being implemented, a simple two-factor scheme (eg, size and sector) may provide the most effective risk allocation framework.

Managing the risk budget involves a combination of asset allocation and risk allocation. A normal starting point would be the policy mix or, more likely, an allocation reflecting the strategic outlook. If there were no strategic outlook or if markets were expected to trade at equilibrium prices from the outset of the planning period, these "neutral views" would be reflected in the implementation of the "policy weights" for the fund. For instance, in the US equity segment, a large-cap:small-cap allocation of 85%:15% would be used with a slight value-style bias (ie, 55% value and 45% growth) in the large-cap segment but style neutrality (ie, a 50:50 value:growth split) would be the starting point for small-cap equities. This is illustrated schematically in Figure 19. The neutral views are depicted as a "heat map" with an equal "particle density" in all four zones.

Risk budgeting or asset allocation planning use a horizon-segmented process and organisation structure. Tactical decision making horizons are typically three to twelve months. This situational or opportunistic planning is the responsibility of the portfolio management teams. Chief investment officers normally oversee the capital markets assumptions for the three to five-year horizons of the strategic allocation decisions. Policy horizons, usually 10 years or longer, require the specification of equilibrium or fair-value prices, returns, or risk premiums, and are the domain of investment committees and trustees. Rigid horizon boundaries are not necessary. They simply indicate an intention to maintain macro- and micro-level forecasts with increasing degrees of precision for trend detection as much as for setting expectations for the probable level of performance. The three horizons linking philosophy to strategy to tactics address the three key issues for an investment fund: "Where are we heading? How will we get there? What do we do now?" Each is addressed most effectively in terms of the associated risk considerations.

Once the initial portfolio has been established, conditional risk allocation can be used to respond to changes in the risk-taking model. While maintaining the initial asset allocation, absolute risk (or VAR) can be reallocated with derivatives or by allowing the portfolio beta to shift, reflecting more or less favourable expectations for the performance of an asset class or segment. Similarly, tracking error (or relative VAR) may be reallocated to reflect the changing expectations for value-added in each segment of the portfolio. Conditional risk allocation can be carried out at more granular levels by actively changing limits for out-of-benchmark assets – ie, by allowing or disallowing them, by following predefined rules for determining limits, or by using a variable to control the range. Finally, reallocating limits for exposures and concentrations provides additional capability for conditional risk allocation.

Combining risk reallocation with conventional portfolio or fund level rebalancing has a number of advantages. It can help avoid over-responding to temporary fluctuations in investment conditions. Reallocating risk can be used to test the desirability of an asset reallocation before the costs and delays of implementation in the cash market are born. Compared to cash market trading, with the associated costs of implementation, it is relatively easy to rebalance the risk budget and therefore must be undertaken with care. As conditions are perceived to change, isolating the sources of apparent changes in the risk dimensions is essential. This is diagnosis before treatment, so to speak. If *ex ante* tracking error is the indicator being monitored, the investor must determine whether perceived risk is coming from the managed portfolio or the benchmark. (Figure 6 illustrated the development of these risk shifts in a benchmark.) Separate time series of Sharpe ratios for the active portfolio and for the benchmark provide an important diagnostic. As tracking error shifts, it is essential to determine how the portfolio alpha (active return adjusted for long-term portfolio beta) is shifting. By monitoring a time series of the information ratio for the portfolio, the investor can determine whether or not it is stationary and whether there is a broad or narrow "inflection point" in the function. Developing this picture of risk-elasticity of skill would allow the investor to understand how aggressive or passive the risk level should be for a particular strategy.

A new schematic can be developed to reflect changing views. One could hypothesise that at the beginning of the period the investor had no particular views on the US equity market that were different from the policy perspective (ie, Figure 19). One could further assume an environment like that experienced during 1999 when growth stocks, particularly the emerging technology and telecommunications companies, began to dominate performance. Simultaneously the "old economy" industries sagged in performance. A view that these conditions would prevail throughout the tactical horizon (eg, for three months) could be reflected in another "heat map". As illustrated in Figure 20, risk is being reallocated to the equity segments expected to perform strongly and taken from segments proportional to the expectation of their underperformance. The "particle density" represents a contrast of the hot zones (large-cap and small-cap growth) versus the cooling zones (on the value side). The decision to make an overall reduction in the absolute risk allocated to US equity is illustrated as a downsizing of the map.

If the shift in tactical views and the direction of market price momentum are congruent, a reallocation of budgeted risk reduces or eliminates some degree of cash-market rebalancing trades. Winners would be held longer and trading would be focused on cleaning up pockets of underperformance. Risk budget adjustments notwithstanding, of course, long-run performance is dictated by the accuracy of trend detections that drive reallocations in the risk budget. Rebalancing the risk budget produces higher expected alpha and information ratios by allowing more aggressive risk-taking where the expectations for higher payoff have increased. This approach also should allow for lower trading costs, further contributing to superior performance in the less liquid market environments of restricted dealer-capital commitments.

CONCLUSION

We began this chapter by examining how portfolio construction starts with a philosophy and proceeds to strategies and tactics to carry out that vision. The strategy must incorporate considerations of risk in order to meet plan objectives and be consistent with risk tolerances. It is not an easy task to reconcile long-term attitudes toward risk and short-term market events, but with discipline and preparation it can be done.

By using "risk budgets" one can stay on top of the investment process, add value where opportunity arises, and maintain appropriate risk exposures. While there are a number of analytical tools available to achieve these goals, in the end it is a combination of data quality and skill in interpreting market events that determines the degree of consistency and success. Portfolio construction methods that do not incorporate this type of risk analysis are doomed to substandard performance. Such portfolios either will take on unanticipated risks and suffer negative shocks, or will not take on enough risk and achieve low average returns.

BIBLIOGRAPHY

Bernstein, P., 1996, *Against the Odds* (John Wiley & Sons).

Daniel, K., M. Grinblatt, S. Titman and R. Wermers, 1997, "Measuring Mutual Fund Performance with Characteristic-Based Benchmarks", *Journal of Finance* 52(3), pp. 1035–58.

Ellis, C.D., 1985, *Investment Policy* (Dow Jones – Irwin).

Gruber, M.J., E.J. Elton and C.R. Blake, 1996, "The Persistence of Risk-Adjusted Mutual Fund Performance", *Journal of Business* 69(2), pp. 133–57.

Goetzmann, W.N., and R.G. Ibbotson, 1994, "Do Winners Repeat?", *Journal of Portfolio Management*, Winter, pp. 14–23.

Grinblatt, M., and S. Titman, 1989, "Mutual Fund Performance: An Analysis of Quarterly Portfolio Holdings", *Journal of Business* 62(31), pp. 393–416.

Kahn, R.N., and A. Rudd, 1995, "Does Historical Performance Predict Future Performance?", *Financial Analysts Journal*, November–December, pp. 43–52.

Katzenbach, J., and D. Smith, 1993, *The Wisdom of Teams* (Harvard Business School Press).

Knight, F., 1921, *Risk, Uncertainty and Profit* (Houghton Mifflin & Co.).

Lakonishok, J., A. Shleifer and R.W. Vishny, 1992, "The Structure and Performance of the Money Management Industry", *Brookings Papers on Economic Activity*, pp. 339–91.

Merida, K., and D. Milbank, 2000, "Luck Be a First Lady", *The Washington Post*, Final Edition; pp. C–01; May 20.

Stux, I., and M. de Marco, 1997, "A Framework for Managing Pension Surplus Shortfall Risk", *Journal of Pension Plan Investing* 2(1), pp. 43–61.

Thaler, R., et al., 1999, Special Issue on Behavioural Finance. *Financial Analysts Journal* 55(6), pp. 12–127.

Zuckerman, G., 2000, "Meriwether Admits Mistakes In Long-Term Capital Debacle" (Heard on the Street), *The Wall Street Journal*, August 21.

13

VAR for Fund Managers*

Stephen Rees

Baring Asset Management

The buy-side is waking up to risk management and techniques originally developed for trading desks are finding a new audience. Stephen Rees argues that the traditional buy-side risk management tool, tracking error, should be put to the sword and replaced by value-at-risk.

Value-at-risk (VAR) has long been the primary risk measure in the banking and securities businesses. However, it has not generally been adopted by fund managers. This chapter considers the applicability of VAR to investment management and considers some of the differences in methodology that need to be applied when transplanting this technique from the trading to the investment arena. In particular, the applicability of the four different ways of modelling VAR are considered in an investment context and the issue of long time horizons is raised. Tentative moves towards establishing a methodology for the long-term case are developed.

Fund managers commonly use tracking error (or standard deviation if risk is measured in an absolute sense) as their primary risk measure and then misinterpret this statistic as a range for likely outperformance or underperformance. This chapter aims to show that, if appropriately defined, VAR can give a far more realistic estimation of performance bounds and, in particular, a far better answer to the question: "How much can I lose or underperform?".

VAR VERSUS TRACKING ERROR

Currently, most fund managers use the standard deviation – or volatility – of returns to define risk. As many fund managers' performance is measured with respect to a benchmark, this standard deviation is often

*This chapter was first published in *Risk* 13(6), (2000), pp. 67–70.

calculated on benchmark-relative, or "active", returns. This is known as the "tracking error".

In a portfolio context, the risk of one stock relative to another is charac-terised by the covariance of the two stocks. Risks do not add up, but the squares of the risk (ie, the variances and covariances) do. Consequently, covariance matrix (each weighted by the product of the portfolio weights) and then taking the square root. Henceforth, the job of modelling risk effec-tively becomes one of modelling the covariance matrix.

Now consider the negative comments concerning tracking error and per-formance mentioned in the introduction. To verify these observations, some "paper portfolios" have been constructed (with the benefit of hind-sight) and their past performance measured (see Figure 1).

These are active performances – that is, relative to the market – and the top portfolio in Figure 1 continually outperforms over a two-year period. It outperforms by almost 10% a year, in spite of having only a 3% tracking error. If this was your portfolio, you probably would not be too concerned. However, what would be of greater concern is the portfolio on the bottom of Figure 1, which also has a 3% tracking error, but which underperforms consistently by 11% a year. Incidentally, the *ex ante* tracking error predicted by a leading risk model and the actual, measured *ex post* tracking error were both about 3%. The dichotomy is that the tracking error considers the standard deviation of active returns – not any systematic trend in them. In both these portfolios, there is a systematic trend, or drift, that the tracking error does not pick up. The standard deviation of X is the same as the stan-dard deviation of X plus a constant.

It is at this point that the utility of VAR for asset managers becomes apparent. First, consider the familiar expression for VAR:

$$VAR = (\sigma \times (\text{\#standard deviations for P}) \times \sqrt{n/255} - n \times \langle R \rangle /255) \times 1 \tag{1}$$

Thus there are two principal terms or ingredients. The first is still basi-cally the volatility or tracking error, σ. This is acted upon in two essentially cosmetic ways: namely, it is multiplied by the square root of $n/255$ to scale it back to the n day period that is of interest – based on 255 trading days in a year. One also multiplies by the required confidence level P.[1] VAR is con-ventionally quoted as a monetary amount rather than a percentage, so the whole thing is multiplied by 1, the value of the portfolio in the currency of interest.

The component of VAR that provides new added value for the invest-ment manager is the second term, the so called "drift" term. If this is ignored, there is tracking error or volatility. Securities traders and the like, who are interested in short time scales, do indeed ignore it. However, over longer time scales, which are of interest to fund managers, this term can be

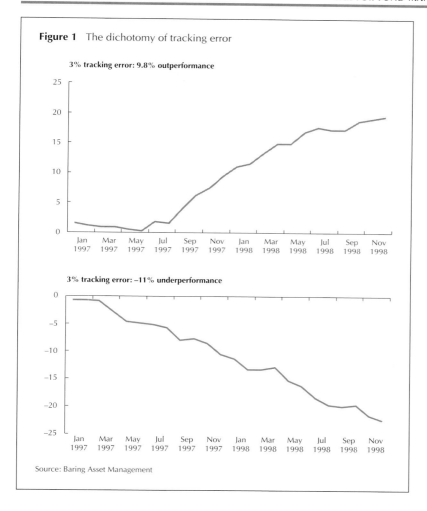

Figure 1   The dichotomy of tracking error

Source: Baring Asset Management

very significant indeed. It is the mean or expected return of the portfolio ⟨R⟩, or, in the case of a benchmark-relative fund, the expected active return of any "tilts" that exist in a portfolio. The correct modelling of this term explains the performance charts in Figure 1.

MODELLING VAR

In the securities field, there are four different methods used to model VAR (Simons, 1996):

❑ The parametric method uses the historic mean and standard deviation of asset returns to parameterise risks (as well as correlation numbers to combine them), which is essentially a direct implementation of

Equation (1). This approach facilitates combining risks of many different asset classes together to produce a combined VAR estimate for large multi-asset class portfolios. It does, however, have various implicit assumptions that are most likely not to be true. It assumes volatilities and correlations are constant through time; that returns are serially independent of each other (which they are not); and that return distributions are normal. In investment management, this approach is most likely to be used as a quick way of estimating VAR for asset or market allocation where the number of assets is small.

❏ The historical method, as its name implies, uses the historical distribution of past asset returns to infer future risks. Quite simply, a long history of price movements is assumed to define adequately the shape of an asset's return distribution – eliminating the need to parameterise it by mean or standard deviation. Given that we have a history of period-by-period returns, one can calculate VAR to n% confidence by simply measuring the return of the (100 – n)th percentile. No attempt needs to be made to analytically model the shape of the distribution and no assumptions need to be made about the stabilities of correlations and volatilities. A flip side of this, however, is that new simulations are required for each new scenario, ie, when the asset mix is changed or when we are interested in different periodicities of return, etc. Thus, if the smallest of 100 daily returns is –5% we can infer from this that the daily VAR is 5% with a 99% confidence level.

Investment managers are unlikely to use historical VAR. Those involved in currencies and, particularly, derivatives, however, might use its sister technique, the stochastic or Monte Carlo method. This technique uses computers to generate thousands and thousands of simulated histories of asset or portfolio returns that conform to the same distribution as that of the real asset return histories. A random number generator is used to generate these simulated returns – thereby introducing period-by-period uncertainty. The modeller can then infer VAR from the simulated returns in exactly the same way as for the historical method, ie, observing the return at the nth percentile for n% confidence – which can, in principle, be arbitrarily high. But, because they have so much more simulated history than real history, they may be more confident that the VAR estimated by this method is more accurate than that from the historical approach. This technique is particularly useful when return distributions are extremely non-normal or where there are non-linearities involved, such as with options.

❏ The modelling approach that the majority of fund managers are most likely to use for VAR is the one they use already for tracking errors, the factor approach or the arbitrage pricing theory (APT) approach. The main feature of this approach is that it models the systematic risk of a portfolio, which might contain many thousands of assets with a relatively small number (typically between four and 20) of risk factors. In effect it greatly reduces the dimensionality of the risk problem. The crucial point is that while the majority of an individual asset's risk may be specific to that asset, on a portfolio level the specific risks cancel each other out and it is the systematic risk that becomes dominant. Once we have identified these systematic risk factors – which are hopefully (but not necessarily) both comprehensible and tangible – we can use them to estimate portfolio volatilities using the returns to these factors.

So the first difference we see in applying VAR to investment as opposed to trading is in the type of modelling methodology used. Factor models are used rather than simple parametric or stochastic models. The reasons for this are:

❑ Securities houses' holdings are less diverse than those of investment portfolios. Hence, there is more specific risk, and factor modelling (which models systematic risk) therefore becomes less accurate.

❑ Traders' positions are turned over more frequently, so the underlying "factor portfolio" changes much more rapidly (ie, there is a stability issue). This is related to the fact that factor returns are generally modelled over quite long time horizons (monthly is typical), reflecting long-term holding periods, while the trader's timescale is measured in days.

❑ Traders are more concerned with absolute rather than relative risk whereas the opposite is often true for fund managers. Market risk is thus more important to traders. As for the market factor's contribution to variance way outstrips the other principal components, these become less relevant. Thus, the secondary APT factor structure becomes less important.

❑ Monte Carlo methods cope better with instruments with asymmetric payouts, eg, options, of which securities houses might hold more.

ADAPTING VAR FOR LONG-TIME HORIZONS

As we have said, the "drift" term in VAR is usually ignored by securities dealers and the like, whose time horizons are typically days or weeks. Therefore, VAR, as we have said, would reduce to tracking error or volatility. On fund management timescales, however, which may be months or years, and where expected mean returns are very different from zero, this term can have quite an impact on the bottom-line VAR numbers.

When VAR is calculated in an absolute sense, this drift term reduces to something close to the expected return of the market. Attempts have been made to model this. Of particular interest to the fund manager, however, is the relative case, when the drift term relates to returns over the benchmark – or active returns.

To examine why there should be non-zero expected active returns in the first place, it is necessary to delve into modern portfolio theory. Factor risk models are all variants of APT (Ross, 1976):

$$R_i = r_f + \beta_i^1 R_1 + \beta_i^2 R_2 + \beta_i^3 + \ldots + \alpha_i \qquad (2)$$

This separates out excess returns (rf is the risk-free rate) into systematic components (β_i^1, R_1, etc) due to common factors and specific components, or alphas (α_i). The fund manager's job, of course, is to maximise alpha. But for alphas genuinely to be "alphas" – ie, stock specific – this model requires that they are all uncorrelated with each other, or have no systematic component. It is this property of the independence of alphas that is the acid test of APT. The capital asset pricing model (Sharpe, 1964), the precursor of APT, had just one systematic return factor, the "market", with each stock having a different sensitivity or beta to the market and all the rest of the stock returns absorbed in the "alpha". It became apparent, however, that these capital asset pricing model alphas were not at all independent – hence the need for APT (Grinold, 1993).

The systematic factors in APT can be modelled in various ways (Roll & Ross, 1979): statistically, using macroeconomic parameters and using stock accounting/valuation ratios are some options. This is why we usually try to fit the APT factors to something tangible. Whether we try to fit them to macroeconomic parameters or stock characteristics, the approach is the same and starts by estimating the "factor returns" of the parameters. The interpretation of a factor return is that it is the active return – or outperformance – of a notional stock with a factor exposure one standard deviation above the market. It is obtained from cross-sectional regressions of the parameter, normalised to a zero mean and unity standard deviation, against *ex post* returns. Cutting through the jargon, this would be similar to the return we would get from a long/short portfolio formed by buying all the stocks with a high book/price, for example, and shorting all the stocks with a low book/price. To build our risk model, we estimate these factor returns for a large number of factors that we believe drive all the systematic returns in the market. We can then do our principal components analysis on these to try to isolate orthogonal or independent factors. Thus, in the spirit of APT, we replace a large number of stocks with a much smaller number of factors. The APT factors, though, are now described not in terms of portfolios of stocks but in terms of portfolios of factors – which should be much easier to interpret as to their meaning.

For many equity markets, including the UK, Europe and Japan, a four-factor APT model based on stock parameters works very well. The factors are value (based on aggregates of dividend yield, earnings yield, etc), growth (return on equity and sustainable growth), size (market capitalisation) and momentum. Examples of some of the returns associated with these factors are shown in Figure 2.

Figure 2 Risk factor returns

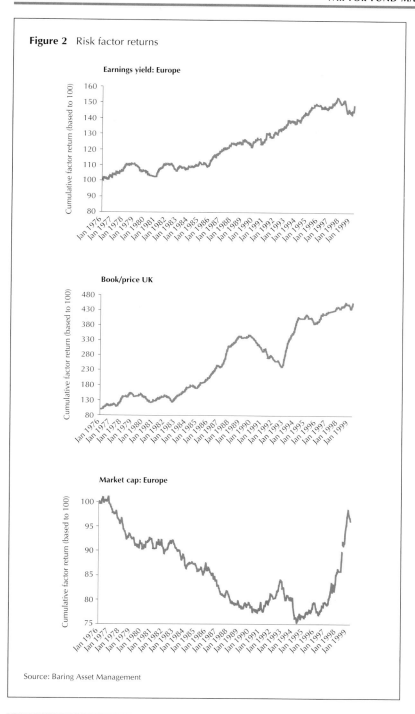

Source: Baring Asset Management

The overriding impression from these is that they trend for long periods of time – and this is in fact typical of factor returns (Fama & French, 1992). In Europe, stocks with high earnings yields have, apart from a few years, systematically outperformed stocks with low earnings yield (upward slope). Also, in Europe from 1976 to 1991, small stocks outperformed large – as shown by the downward slope of the market capitalisation factor returns. From 1991 to 1993 and 1995 to 1999, large capitalisation stocks consistently outperformed – as shown by the upward slope. Similarly, the UK has seen long trending periods of outperformance and underperformance by "value" and "growth" stocks, as shown by the upward and downward slopes in the book/price factor return.

Many contemporary investors are so-called style investors. They typically buy only value stocks, growth stocks or small capitalisation stocks, for example. What they are doing is trying to capture the trends in these factor returns. But even traditional investors introduce these style "tilts" when they take into account a stock's valuation, earnings growth and capitalisation. As we have seen, these styles are representations of systematic risk factors. So, far from picking securities based purely on alphas, that is, genuine stock specific reasons – fund managers of all kinds tilt their portfolios toward systematic risks. That is why active returns have a non-zero expected mean and why it is necessary to estimate a drift term in VAR calculations.

There is no "correct" way of modelling the drift term, but the use of factor or "style" analysis, as above, provides several possibilities. Some practitioners have considered absorbing these style effects into the VAR variance term by calculating the distribution around a conditional mean (Di Bartolomeo, 2000). However, one can also build on the analysis above. A suitable method might be:

❏ Identify a set of style factors, denoted by subscript i (eg, value, growth, size, momentum).
❏ Work out the standard deviation exposure of the portfolio to these factors β_i, bottom up, by cap weighting the security exposures β_i^j (the security exposures are obtained simply by subtracting off the mean price/ earnings, for example, and dividing by its cross-sectional standard deviation).
❏ Work out the "factor return forecast" for each of the risk factors. This can be done using cross-sectional regression on the factor exposures of the stocks in the universe versus *ex post* stock returns to obtain the factor return, F_i. Repeat this regression for each time interval (eg, one month) and use a suitable weighted average (eg, exponentially weighted over a medium-term look-back period) to get the forecast $E(F_i)$.
❏ The drift term, D, can then be estimated by multiplying the portfolio exposure by the magnitude of the factor return forecast $|E(F_i)|$ for each factor, i, and adding the four contributions together. Strictly speaking, correlations between the factor returns should be used when doing this,

although the four factors considered here are reasonably orthogonal:

$$D = \sum_{i=1,4} \beta_i \mid E(F_i) \mid$$

It is necessary to consider the magnitudes of the factor return forecast because some of the factor returns will be negative (which would decrease it, if applied without adjustment). It is nonsensical to say that an active tilt to a style factor can ever reduce VAR – it must increase it. We need to allow for the worst and consider that our factor tilts might be against us. If this was the case, the magnitude of the factor return would stay similar under a style reversal, so focusing on these magnitudes and always subtracting this term from the variance portion will increase the calculated VAR, as we would expect.

From Equation (1), the long-term VAR can then be estimated by:

$$VAR = (\sigma \times (\#\text{standard deviations for P})$$
$$\times \sqrt{n/255} + D \times \langle R \rangle / 255) \times 1 \qquad (3)$$

This approach has not been extensively back-tested. To do so would require Monte Carlo-type simulations of a wide range of portfolios with different style exposures over long time periods. However, it will clearly provide a VAR considerably greater than the tracking error when the timescale is long and the style exposure large. Intuitively, one can see that this will be a better downside risk measure given that style factor returns can be large.

CONCLUSION

Most fund managers use the volatility or tracking error to parameterise risk. However, this can sometimes be misleading as many portfolios have active tilts to risk factors, which have non-zero means that the tracking error simply does not pick up. VAR theory provides a way to take account of these effects, which can be significant over long periods, via the drift term. The factor returns to styles can be estimated using a cross-sectional technique and, based on the portfolio's exposure to these styles, the drift term can be calculated.

VAR, appropriately calculated in this way, probably better answers the question: "How much can I lose?" or underperform, which is what most fund managers really mean by risk.

---

1 This formula is only strictly true when return distributions are normal. So, for example, tracking error or volatility is by definition one standard deviation of a return distribution and, if that distribution is normal, 67% of returns will lie within that range about the mean. Therefore, 33% must lie outside it. But normal distributions are symmetric so only half of these observations, ie, 16.5%, will be below the range. So the tracking error or volatility is the variance portion of VAR to an 83.5% (= 100 − 16.5%) confidence. The number of standard deviations for different confidence levels for normal distribuitons are published in tables, eg, 2.33 for 95% confidence.

BIBLIOGRAPHY

Di Bartolomeo, D., 2000, "Getting an Early Jump on Market Anomalies: Lessons from the Internet Stock Phenomenon", forthcoming, *Indexes: The Journal of Index Issues in Investment.*

Fama, E., and K. French, 1992, "The Cross Section of Expected Stock Returns", *Journal of Finance* 47(2).

Grinold, R., 1993, "Is Beta Dead Again?", *Financial Analysts Journal* 49(4).

Roll, R., and S. Ross, 1979, "An Empirical Investigation of the Arbitrage Pricing Theory", *Journal of Finance* 35.

Ross, S., 1976, "The Arbitrage Theory of Capital Asset Pricing", *Journal of Economic Theory* 13.

Sharpe, W., 1964, "Capital Asset Prices: A Theory of Market Equilibrium under Conditions of Risk", *Journal of Finance* 19(3).

Simons, K., 1996, "Value-at-risk – New Approaches to Risk Management", *New England Economic Review*, September/October.

Index

Other Titles by Risk Books

Managing Hedge Fund Risk: From the Seat of the Practitioner – Views from Investors, Hedge Funds and Consultants

Edited by Virginia Reynolds Parker, Parker Global Strategies
ISBN 1 899 332 782

Pension Fund Management within the EU

Published in association with the European Economics and Financial Centre
By H.M Scobie, S. Persaud and G. Cagliesi
ISBN 1 899 332 421

Extremes and Integrated Risk Management

Published in association with UBS Warburg
Edited by Professor Paul Embrechts, Federal Institute of Technology, Zurich
ISBN 1 899 332 74X

Options – Classic Approaches to Pricing and Modelling

Edited by Professor Lane Hughston, King's College, London
ISBN 1 899 332 669

Rubinstein on Derivatives

By Mark Rubinstein, Haas School of Business, University of California
ISBN 1 899 332 537

Classic Futures – Lessons from the Past for the Electronic Age

Edited by Lester G. Telser, University of Chicago
ISBN 1 899 332 928

The New Interest Rate Models – Recent Developments in the Theory and Application of Yield Curve Dynamics

Edited by Professor Lane Hughston, King's College, London
ISBN 1 899 332 979

Model Risk – Concepts, Calibration and Pricing

Edited by Professor Rajna Gibson, University de Lausanne
ISBN 1 899 332 898

For more information on these as well as the full range of titles published by Risk Books, please visit the on-line bookstore at **www.riskbooks.com**. Alternatively, phone +44 (0)20 7484 9757 or fax +44 (0)20 7484 9758 and request the latest book catalogue.